S0-BSQ-945

Civil Litigation in Connecticut
Anatomy of a Lawsuit

Kimberly A. Peterson, J.D.
Attorney at Law

PRENTICE HALL PARALEGAL SERIES

Prentice Hall
Upper Saddle River, New Jersey 07458

Library of Congress Cataloging-in-Publication Data
Peterson, Kimberly A

    Civil Litigation in Connecticut: Anatomy of a Lawsuit / Kimberly A. Peterson
    p   cm
    Includes index.
    ISBN 0-13-757840-7
    1 Civil procedure--Connecticut. 2. Trial practice--Connecticut.
3. Actions and Defenses--Connecticut. Title. I
KFC4130.Z9P48 1998
347.746 ' 05--dc21   97-1783
                                          CIP

"This publication is designed to provide accurate and authoritative information in regard to the subject matter covered. It is sold with the understanding that the publisher is not engaged in rendering legal, accounting, or other professional service. If legal advice or other expert assistance is required, the services of a competent professional person should be sought. "—*From the Declaration of Principles jointly adopted by a Committee of the American Bar Association and a Committee of Publishers and Associations.*

Permission to reprint:
The Judicial Branch forms in the Instructor's Manual and the contents of Appendix B and C in this text are reprinted with permission from the Connecticut Judicial Branch.

The names, addresses, and other information contained in the pleadings in this text are fictitious.

Acquisitions Editor Elizabeth Sugg
Director of Production and Manufacturing Bruce Johnson
Managing Editor Mary Carnis
Editorial Production Supervision. Inkwell Publishing Services
Manufacturing Buyer Edward O'Dougherty

©1998 by Prentice-Hall, Inc.
A Pearson Education Company
Upper Saddle River, NJ 07458

All rights reserved. No part of this book may be
reproduced, in any form or by any means,
without permission in writing from the publisher.

Printed in the United States of America

10 9 8 7 6 5 4 3 2 1

ISBN 0-13-757840-7

PRENTICE-HALL INTERNATIONAL (UK) LIMITED, *London*
PRENTICE-HALL OF AUSTRALIA PTY. LIMITED, *Sydney*
PRENTICE-HALL CANADA, INC., *Toronto*
PRENTICE-HALL HISPANOAMERICANA, S.A., *Mexico*
PRENTICE-HALL OF INDIA PRIVATE LIMITED, *New Delhi*
PRENTICE-HALL OF JAPAN, INC., *Tokyo*
PRENTICE-HALL OF SOUTHEAST ASIA PTE. LTD., *Singapore*
EDITORA PRENTICE-HALL DO BRASIL, LTDA., *Rio de Janeiro*

Contents

14
Pleadings: Motions Against Defendant Who Do Not File an Appearance   139

15
Pleadings: Motions Against Defendants Who Do Not File Pleadings   153

16
Pleadings: Motions Against Plaintiffs Who Do Not File Comply with Rules of Court   158

17
Prejudgment Remedies   166

23
Discovery: Depositions of Parties   *218*

24
Depositions of Persons Who Are Not Parties   *227*

25
Discovery: Disclosure of Experts   *238*

26
Discovery: Motions for Order of Compliance   *244*

27

Motions for Summary Judgment 249

28

Closing the Pleadings and Pretrial 261

29

The Trial Stage: Preparations for Trial 272

30

The Trial 280

31

Motions Made During and After Trial 293

Preface

Nothing in life can prepare us for practicing civil litigation. Sure, we can watch the fictional legal programs on television, but actually litigating a case is an entirely different matter. In real life, we deal with real people, on opposite sides, who have their own ideas of black and white, right and wrong. These differing ideas lead to a dispute. If people can't resolve the dispute themselves, they will then hire attorneys to "prove" the "truth" as they see it.

To illustrate this point, I often use an example involving a dispute over a simple shade of blue. When you think about it, blue can be labeled sapphire, cobalt, navy, royal, dark or even sky blue, depending on one's perception and the direction of the lighting.

If this issue were to go to trial to be decided by a jury, you can only imagine how many different opinions the jurors would express before finally determining, based on the evidence presented, the "real" shade of blue. Therefore, always remember that no matter how simple or trivial a matter may seem, no matter how right or wrong, black or white it may appear, in law, there are absolutely no absolutes.

With all this ambiguity in mind, I set out to write this text to provide students, paralegals and new attorneys with a practical guide to civil litigation in Connecticut. While we can't control people's perceptions and opinions, we can control, to a certain extent, the litigation process. The first step is figuring out what the first step is. To accomplish that task, I created a Litigation Checklist Summary and a Serving and Filing Summary, found at the beginning of the text. The first summary spells out each stage of the litigation process from beginning to end. The second explains how to serve specific documents and which documents must be filed in court. Following the summaries, each stage of the litigation process is explained throughout the text by referencing applicable Connecticut Practice Book Sections, Connecticut General Statutes and terminology, along with explanations of court forms and realistic pleadings.

Examples of pleadings begin in Chapter 4. The end of that chapter contains three sample complaints, each depicting a common civil litigation case: a personal injury action resulting from an automobile accident; a personal injury action resulting from a fall down; and a contract action to collect a debt. These cases are revisited over and over again to demonstrate various pleadings commonly filed in each stage of the litigation process. Two of the three cases end pursuant to settlements at different stages. The remaining case is decided by a jury verdict and then appealed to the Connecticut Appellate Court. Therefore, students have the opportunity to witness the progression of each case from the beginning to its conclusion.

In addition to a glossary and index at the end of the text, three appendixes provide easy access to practical information. Appendix A contains a more detailed litigation checklist, intended to be photocopied and placed at the beginning of each litigation file. Its purposes are to assist paralegals and attorneys in keeping track of the case and to provide a thorough summary and status report at a quick glance. Appendix B and Appendix C provide information necessary to select the proper court location to file a lawsuit, including the addresses and telephone numbers that are current as of the date this text was printed.

Keep in mind that this text is to be used as a *guide* to maneuver through a maze of uncertainty. Rules and statutes constantly change and must be thoroughly researched before they can be relied on. In addition, individual courthouse procedures may differ. As a result, there are no guarantees or expectations that the reader will be an expert litigator after reviewing this text or that all the information is 100% accurate. Instead, I embarked on this project to provide a foundation and understanding of Connecticut's litigation process that will enable readers to confidently enter a law firm and know what to do with the litigation files handed to them.

Civil litigation never ceases to amaze me. It's exciting and invigorating. It can also be nerve racking and even torturous at times. *Civil Litigation in Connecticut*, when used in conjunction with the Connecticut Practice Book, Connecticut General Statutes and case law, dispels a lot of the mystery regarding procedure, allowing time to address the various shades of blue.

Kimberly A. Peterson
Attorney at Law

ACKNOWLEDGMENTS

This book is dedicated to my family, students, friends and clients. In addition, there are numerous people I wish to thank for helping me make this text a reality: Dana Meltzer and Elizabeth Sugg at Prentice Hall, for their encouragement and enthusiasm; my husband Alan, for the time to pursue this goal; the following attorneys who provided their expertise and examples of pleadings: Janet Spaulding, Heidi Zultowski, Ken Friedman, Ceil Gersten, Carl Lombard, Robyn Johnson, Paul Cramer and the attorneys at the Law Office of James Picket; my paralegals, Edwina Martin and Candy Woodward for their research and editing; the Connecticut Judicial Branch for permission to reprint court forms and portions of the Judicial Directory; my sister-in-law, Barbara Clifford, Fred Dahl and the editors at Inkwell Publishing Services for their great assistance in producing this text.

LITIGATION CHECKLIST SUMMARY

I. The Prelitigation Stage (P: Plaintiff, D: Defendant)

P and D:	Identify all possible parties
P and D:	Determine cause(s) of action
P and D:	Determine statute of limitations
P and D:	Investigation
P and D:	Settlement discussions
P:	Draft Summons and Complaint
P	Contact proper officer to serve copy of Summons and Complaint to all Defendants
P:	File original Summons and Complaint, Return of Service, and entry fee in proper Superior Court

II. The Pretrial Stage: Pleadings and Discovery Occur Simultaneously

A. Pleadings

D: file Appearance in Court
D: file one or more of the following three *optional* pleadings:

Motion to Dismiss	P: Objection to Motion to Dismiss
Request to Revise	P: Comply or file Objection
Motion to Strike	P: Comply or file Objection

D: file Answer (presume there are no Special Defenses or a Counterclaim)
Either or both parties: file Motion for Summary Judgment and Objection
Either party: file Certificate of Closed Pleadings to place case on Trial List
Either party: file Jury Claim if necessary
Pretrial Conferences: scheduled by the court and attended by both parties

B. Discovery

P and D:	Interrogatories, Objections and Compliance
P and D:.	Requests for Production, Objections and Compliance
P and D:	Request for Inspection, Objection and Compliance
P and D:	Requests for Admission, Objection and Compliance
P and D:	Disclosure of Expert Witnesses
P and D:	Depositions of parties
P and D:	Depositions of nonparties

III. The Trial Stage

Preparation
Jury selection

P:	Opening argument and Case-in-Chief: witnesses and exhibits	
P:	Direct examination	D: Cross examination
P:	Re-direct examination	D: Re-cross examination

D: Motion for Directed Verdict P: Objection to Directed Verdict

D: Opening argument and Case: witnesses and exhibits

D: Direct examination   P: Cross examination

D: Re-direct examination   P: Re-cross examination

D: Rebuttal

P and D: Closing Arguments

P: Rebuttal Closing Argument

Bench Trial: Judge's decision; or

Jury Trial: Requests to Charge, Charge Conference and Jury Instructions

Jury deliberations, Jury verdict, Judge accepts verdict

P or D or both: Motion to Set Aside Verdict and Objection

P: Motion for Additur   D: Objection

D: Motion for Remittitur   P: Objection

D: Motion to Reduce Verdict due to Collateral Source Payments

P: Obj. to Mot. to Reduce Verdict due to Collateral Source Payments

IV. The Appeal Stage   (AP: Appellant, AE: Appellee)

A. Appellate Court:

AP: File Appeal form and pay filing fee at Superior Court Clerk's Office. Afterward, file the following at the Appellate Clerk's Office:

AP: Endorsed Appeal form and Docket Sheet (from Superior Court)

AP: Transcripts Order Form

AP: Preliminary Statement of Issues   AE: Counter Issues

AP: Preliminary Design. of Contents of Record   AE: Additional Records

AP: Preargument Conference Statement

AP: Judgment File   AE: Response

AP: Docketing Statement   AE: Additional Information

AP   Brief

AE: Brief

AP: Reply Brief

Preargument Conference

Oral Argument

Appellate Court's Decision

B. Supreme Court   (P: Petitioner, OP: Opposing Party)

P:.   Petition for Certification   OP: Objection

P: Brief

OP: Brief

P: Reply Brief

Preargument Conference

Oral Argument

Supreme Court's Decision

SERVING AND FILING SUMMARY

1. Summons and Complaint: A copy must be served upon the Defendant by a proper officer: a sheriff, deputy sheriff, constable, borough bailiff, and in some situations, an indifferent person. Service must be made in hand or abode, unless an applicable statute allows otherwise. Then file the original Summons and Complaint in the proper court.

2. After being served, the Defendant files an **Appearance** in court:

3. Pleadings: Motions and Objections: file original in court and mail or hand deliver a copy to all appearing counsel and pro se parties, pursuant to Pbs 120 et seq.

4. Discovery:

    A. *Notice of Deposition:* Do not file in court. Serve opposing party by certified mail, registered mail or hand delivery. (Regular mail is not sufficient.)

    B. *Interrogatories and Requests for Production:* Do not file in court. Serve opposing party by regular mail or hand delivery. File *cover sheet with objections* (to nonstandard requests) in court and serve opposing party as described in **3.** above.

    C. *Request to Inspect:* Do not file in court. Serve opposing party by mail or hand delivery. File *objection* in court and serve opposing party as described in **3.** above.

    D. *Request for Mental or Physical Exam:* File in court and serve opposing party as described in **3.** above. File *objections* in court and serve opposing party the same way.

    E. *Requests for Admission:* File *Notice of Serving Requests for Admissions* in court. Do not file the actual requests. Serve the notice and the requests to the opposing party as described in 3. above. File *Cover sheet with responses* and *objections* in court and serve opposing party the same way.

    F. *Subpoenas* including a *subpoena duces tecum:* A proper officer, including an indifferent person, must make in hand service. Remember, a sheriff, deputy sheriff, constable or borough bailiff may make service outside of his or her precinct as an indifferent person.

    G. *Mechanic's Liens* and *Notice of Lis Pendens:* a proper officer, including an indifferent person, must record the original on the applicable land records and serve (in hand or abode) a copy upon the owners of the real estate at issue.

CASE HISTORIES: Sample Pleadings and Forms

SARAH A. DONAHUE vs. RICHARD P. ANDREW: Motor Vehicle Accident, DOA: 9/13/96

Summons and Complaint: Date: 5/1/98; Return Date: 5/26/98

Letter to Sheriff	Cover Sheet: Discovery Responses
Appearance	Motion for Summary Judgment
Motion to Dismiss and Obj.	Obj. to Motion for Sum. Judg.
Notice of Intent to Argue	*Pretrial Memo*
Answer and Special Defenses	Motion for Additur
Reply to Special Defenses	Obj. to Motion for Additur
Certificate of Closed Pleadings	*Appeal to Appellate Court*
Notice of Serv. Interr. and Req. for Prod.	*Not. of Appeal, Trans. Order*
Motion for Extension of Time (2)	*State. for Preargum. Conf.*
Motion for Order of Compl. and Nonsuit	*Court Rep. Trans. Deliv. Cert.*

SHEILA WILKENSON vs. RYAN KEEGAN: Fall Down, DOA: 5/20/96

Summons and Complaint: Date: 3/2/98; Return Date: 3/31/98

Return of Service: Abode	Answer
Motion for Default for Failure to Appear	Reply to Special Defenses
Appearance	Notice of Serv. Interr. and Prod.
Request to Revise Complaint	*Notice of Application for*
Cover Sheet with Obj. Request to Revise	*PJR/Claim for Hearing*
Court Notice	Def. Offer of Judgment.
Notice of Filing Revised Complaint	Plaintiff. Accept. Offer of Judg.
Motion for Default for Failure to Plead	

GEORGE SKILLMAN, ET AL. vs. AUTO SERVICE CENTER, INC.:

Breach of Contract; Date of Breach: 1/16/98

Summons and Complaint: 2/2/98; Return Date: 2/24/98

Notice of Ex Parte PJR/Claim for Hearing	Req. to File Amended Complaint
Return of Service: in hand	Requests for Admission
Motion for Def. Fail. to Appear and Judg.	Motion for Summary Judge.
Motion to Open Judgment, Affidavit and	*Short Calendar Claim/Recl.*
Appearance	Stipulation Re: Judgment
Motion for Disclosure of Assets	

MISCELLANEOUS PLEADINGS AND DOCUMENTS

Motion to Strike	Mechanic's Lien
Objection to Motion to Strike	Notice of Lis Pendens

xvi

1 *The Legal Profession and Practice*

Terminology

Litigation	Suit	Civil Litigation
Connecticut Practice Book	Parties	Litigants
Connecticut General Statutes	Statute of Limitations	Plaintiff
Case	Defendant	Malpractice
File	Pro Se	Damages
Action	Criminal Litigation	Lawsuit
Diarying	Case Law	Precedent
Clerk	Intern	Pro Hac Vice
Pbs	C.G.S.	Et seq.

Pbs: 6, 7, 7CC, 24, 216
C.G.S. sections: 51-88, 52-584

I. LITIGATION: THE ART OF PERSUASION

Welcome to the legal profession and to **litigation,** specifically. As you can see from the Table of Contents and Litigation Checklist Summary found at the beginning of this book, you will have plenty of work to do, challenging work with results that will never cease to astound you.

From now on, when you hear the word litigation, immediately picture a courtroom in your mind. Ultimately, that's where litigation takes place. It begins when two or more people disagree about something and one decides to bring the other to court to have a judge or jury settle their dispute.

I believe the easiest way to describe the litigation process is to think of it as a game. The game is entitled, "The Art of Persuasion." The object is for each side to persuade the judge or jury that his or her version of the facts best describes the truth. Sounds simple, doesn't it? After all, the truth is the truth, right? Just wait. It's amazing how many versions of the truth you will encounter.

As you delve into this game, you will discover litigation is a unique animal. Nothing in life can compare or prepare you to play. Almost immediately, you will realize that the rules change as you go along, and 20/20 hindsight constantly causes you to second-guess yourself. To sum it all up, what's right today can be wrong tomorrow, but may be quite acceptable the next day. And just like any game, no matter how talented the attorneys and staff on each side are, when it's finished, one side must lose.

Anatomy of a Lawsuit is designed to provide you with a clear and concise guide to the game of civil litigation in Connecticut.

Civil litigation typically involves disputes in which one side is seeking **damages** from the other. These damages are usually money. **Criminal litigation**, on the other hand, involves the government which charges individuals with committing crimes and seeks to punish them with criminal penalties such as prison sentences, fines, etc.

I have divided the litigation process into four stages: the ***Prelitigation Stage***; the ***Pretrial Stage***, which encompasses both *pleadings* and *discovery;* the ***Trial Stage***; and the ***Appeal Stage***. These stages are detailed throughout the remaining 33 chapters of this text. If at anytime you become confused, simply refer to the Litigation Checklist Summary on page xiii to determine what stage you are working in. In addition, you will find specific instructions for court-issued forms and other checklists to help you keep track of every stage of your case. These will save you time in answering questions about a file and keeping it organized.

Recently, I took a poll among a group of my attorney friends. Each agreed that successful paralegals and law clerks must demonstrate the same characteristics as successful lawyers: Each must be extremely conscientious and persistent, detail oriented, dependable and creative. A good sense of humor never hurts either. Remember, you're dealing with human beings, each of whom has quirks and agendas in most cases, clients find themselves in law offices because they have problems. They want to be able to rely upon the people in that office to help solve those problems. That's a huge responsibility to undertake.

It's important that you do your absolute best to remain flexible and go with the flow. When you practice litigation, your life will revolve around deadlines you can't control. That means no matter how far in advance you prepare, there will always be "one last thing" to do. And nothing ever takes "just five minutes." Remember that sense of humor? It will definitely come in handy.

Anybody who works in this profession can tell you that photocopiers break down just when you need to make that final copy of a twenty-page brief due at court within the next half hour. Or your computer will freeze you out of the one file you absolutely must access, now! Then there's the laser printer that simply refuses to print a document you desperately need. And finally, don't forget the stapler that runs out of staples at the most inopportune moment, making you want to fling it and yourself right out the nearest window.

We won't get into lapses of electricity, traffic jams, flat tires, dead batteries and blizzards. Trust me. The author of Murphy's Law knew what he was talking about. If it can happen, it will. So don't start questioning your intelligence or wondering if you chose the wrong profession. You didn't. At times like these, the best you can do is take a deep breath, smile and plunge forward. So let's do it!

II. ADMISSION TO THE BAR: STATE AND FEDERAL COURTS

Keep in mind that *Anatomy of a Lawsuit* addresses civil litigation practice in the state of Connecticut. Every state in the United States operates its own unique court system, according to its laws and court procedures. In addition, there is a federal court system which operates under its own set of laws and court procedures. Each person in this country is required to follow all applicable state and federal laws.

Attorneys who practice law must first be granted a license or permission by the specific state or federal court they choose to work in. This license, or permission, is referred to as an "admission to the bar" of that state or federal court. Such admission is obtained once the attorney passes the applicable state's "bar exam." The bar exam is a written exam which is held around the country every July and February. In addition, each person taking the bar is subject to a personal background investigation regarding specific educational requirements and moral character.

Understandably, the bar exam is cause for much concern. It's made worse by the fact that the results are usually not released until three or more months after the exam is given. Paralegals and other law office staff are not subject to such admission requirements.

Law students and graduates who have not yet passed the bar may work for licensed attorneys as **clerks** or **interns**. They may also obtain permission to appear before a specific court, under the guidance and direction of their employers. (See Connecticut Practice Book Section 7CC, et seq.)

It is possible for attorneys to work in more than one state or federal court at the same time, as long as they are admitted in those state or federal courts. At times, a court will permit an out-of-state attorney who is not admitted to its bar to appear in court to handle a specific case. This is called being admitted **Pro Hac Vice**: temporarily, under the guidance of an in-state attorney. (See Connecticut Practice Book Section 24, et seq.)

Most law firms practice in the state court where they are located. Others prefer the federal court system, or practice in both systems. This, of course, requires the attorneys, paralegals, law clerks and other office staff to juggle both sets of complicated laws and rules at the same time.

III. THE PARTIES TO A LAWSUIT

As you will learn, the terms **case, file, action** and **suit** are often used interchangeably with **lawsuit.** Attorneys are never named in a lawsuit in which they represent a client. Instead, they file such suits and defend them in the names of their clients.

Just as there are at least two sides to every argument, there are at least two sides to every lawsuit. The individuals or groups on each side are known as the **parties.** Parties named in a lawsuit include individuals, corporations, partnerships, associations, governmental agencies, etc. (See Connecticut Practice Book Section 216.)

Once a lawsuit is filed in court, these parties become the **Plaintiff** and the **Defendant.** Together, they are also known as **litigants**. (After a lawsuit is filed in court, the terms **parties** and **litigants** are often used interchangeably.)

A **Plaintiff** is the party who brings a lawsuit against someone. Plaintiffs are often identified by the pi symbol.

A **Defendant** is the party being sued and is often identified by a triangle. In addition, Connecticut General Statutes Section 51-88(d) allow *individuals* to represent themselves in court, instead of hiring an attorney. These individuals are called **pro se** parties and are still known as Plaintiffs and Defendants. (Please note that in most circumstances, corporations, partnerships and associations may not represent themselves in court as pro se parties. Instead, these entities must hire an attorney.)

IV. CONNECTICUT GENERAL STATUTES

Laws in Connecticut are created and enacted by the legislature. These laws are known as **statutes**. Each statute is assigned a number, called a **section**, and published in a series of volumes entitled the **Connecticut General Statutes**. Connecticut's courts interpret the statutes through deciding cases brought before them. Such decisions are published and are referred to as **case law**. Attorneys and courts rely upon such case law as **precedent**: examples and authority for deciding future cases that are similar in nature. Hereinafter, Connecticut General Statutes and it's sections will be abbreviated as **C.G.S. sec.**

V. CONNECTICUT PRACTICE BOOK

While statutes address some litigation procedures, the majority of these procedures are found in the **Connecticut Practice Book**. These procedures are referred to as **Practice Book Rules,** or **rules**, and will soon become your best friends.

Practice Book rules are established by a Rules Committee and are intended to "facilitate business and advance justice." See Practice Book Sections 6 and 7.) Like statutes, each rule is assigned a number, called a **section**. Hereinafter, the Practice Book Rules will be abbreviated as **Pbs**.

At times you will see a section of the Connecticut Practice Book or Connecticut General Statutes followed by the term, **et seq.** Et seq. refers to that section and those sections that immediately follow. For example: Connecticut Practice Book Section 120 et seq. Section 120 addresses service of pleadings and other papers, along with sections 121, 122, 123, 124, 125 and 126.

Anatomy of a Lawsuit is intended to be used in conjunction with the Connecticut Practice Book and the Connecticut General Statutes, not as a replacement. In addition, some practice book rules will cite a statute at the end. These statutes may contain language that is identical to the rule, or slightly different. Therefore, be sure to have access to both sets of materials.

VI. THE STATUTE OF LIMITATIONS

I can't stress enough the importance of the **statute of limitations** in civil litigation. The statute of limitations is a specific time limit any potential Plaintiff has to bring a lawsuit against someone. If the time limit expires, the Plaintiff will not be able to recover damages from the Defendant. These time limits are found in the Connecticut General Statutes.

For example, C.G.S. sec. 52-584 requires that most personal injury lawsuits be brought within two years of the date of the incident that caused the Plaintiff's alleged injuries. If a lawsuit is brought after that two-year time period, the Defendant will claim the statute of limitations has expired and ask the court to grant judgment in his or her favor. In other words, throw the case out of court. If the court agrees, and the Plaintiff's attorney is at fault, there is a strong likelihood that the Plaintiff will then turn around and sue his or her attorney for **legal malpractice** because of the missed deadline.

The term legal malpractice makes everyone in an office uncomfortable. Essentially, the phrase means that an attorney made a mistake in handling a client's case. As a result of that mistake, the client was prevented from recovering damages from the Defendant. In a suit for legal malpractice, the client sues his or her former attorney, hoping to recover such damages from him or her. Being sued for legal malpractice is one of the worst things that can happen to an attorney, and it seems to occur much more frequently now than ever before.

Future chapters will address the statute of limitations in conjunction with preventing malpractice by **diarying** (also known as calendaring) such important dates and other court-imposed deadlines that arise once a lawsuit is filed in court. For now, suffice it to say that there are no exceptions to the statute of limitations -- none. Paralegals, interns and other office staff are expected to play a large role in making sure all deadlines are met. This role includes realizing their importance and cooperating to the fullest extent possible.

Always make certain someone else in your office will handle your files in your absence. Prepare ahead of time to address issues that may arise while you're on vacation or out due to illness. Inform others of potential problems and any impending deadlines. Being prepared might mean staying late at the office a few nights before you're scheduled to be away. You won't be alone. This same conscientious conduct is expected of everyone, including attorneys. To do otherwise could result in your being out of a job when you return and compromising an attorney's professional career. It's an awful situation, one which is best avoided at all costs.

VII. CONCLUSION

You've been exposed to a lot of terminology in this chapter. Don't fret. There is a glossary at the end of the text and the terms will be used over and over again throughout the following chapters. Soon, they will become part of your everyday vocabulary. With all of this in mind, review the material listed below. Then move on to Chapter 2 and explore Connecticut's court system.

A. *Key Issues in This Chapter Include:*

1. There are four stages in the litigation process: *Prelitigation, Pretrial* (which includes *Pleadings* and *Discovery), Trial* and *Appeal.*
2. The *Plaintiff* brings the lawsuit against the *Defendant.*
3. Plaintiffs and Defendants are called *parties.*
4. *Pro se* parties can be individual Plaintiffs or Defendants. These parties do not have attorneys. Instead, they represent themselves. Note that corporations and most businesses must hire attorneys to represent them.
5. *Civil litigation* typically involves disputes about money damages. They are not criminal cases and do not usually involve jail or prison terms, etc., as punishment.
6. *Statutes of limitations* are found in the *Connecticut General Statutes* and are established time limits to file specific civil actions.
7. Be sure to *diary* deadlines. (See Chapter 3, Section VIII, B.)
8. *Legal malpractice* occurs when an attorney negligently handles a client's case.

B. *Relevant Connecticut Practice Book Sections Include:*

Pbs 6:	Rules to Be Liberally Interpreted
Pbs 7:	Publication of Rules; Effective Date
Pbs 7CC:	Legal Interns
Pbs 24:	Attorneys of Other Jurisdictions--Appearing Pro Hac Vice
Pbs 216:	Definitions

C. *Relevant Connecticut General Statutes Include:*

C.G.S. sec. 51-88.: Practice of law by persons not attorneys.
C.G.S. sec. 52-584.: Limitation of action for injury to person or property.

2 *The Connecticut Court System*

Terminology

Supreme Court	Appellate Court	Superior Court
Probate	Administrative Actions	Trial Court
Trier of Fact	Judicial District	Geographical Area
Small Claims	Housing Session	Juvenile Matters
En Banc	Trial	Hearing
Connecticut Reports	First Impression	Transcript
Superior Court Reporter	Jury	Brief
Record	Appeal	Court Reporter
Connecticut Appellate Reports		

C.G.S. sections: 4-183, 51-197a, 51-197b, 51-197c, 51-197f, 51-198, 51-199, 52-216
C.G.S. Title 45a

Introduction

Before you begin practicing litigation in Connecticut, you will need a clear understanding of the state's court system. The easiest way to start is to introduce you to its three tiers, which are described below.

I. A THREE-TIERED SYSTEM

A. The Courts

In general terms, Connecticut's court system consists of the Supreme Court, the Appellate Court and the Superior Court. Most lawsuits, except those involving **probate** and **administrative actions**, start in the **Superior Court**. The Superior Court is also known as the **trial court**. Of the three courts, it is the only court that actually conducts a **trial**. A trial gives both parties their only opportunity to explain their side of the story, call witnesses, and provide evidence directly to a **judge** or **jury**. The Superior Court is also the only court to allow juries to decide cases.

The **Appellate Court** and the **Supreme Court** do not conduct trials. Instead, they review specific cases that were decided in the trial court and determine if the trial court judge made an error that should be corrected.

B. The Trier of Fact

At trial, the judge or jury who listens and decides the case is referred to as the **trier of fact**: They have the only opportunity, firsthand, to observe and determine the credibility of each witness, including the parties, and to weigh the evidence presented. Therefore, they are in the best position to determine the facts of a case, i.e., the truth, and make a decision based upon those facts and the law.

Chapter 28 discusses reasons to choose a trial to a judge versus a trial to a jury. For now, suffice it to say that some cases are more appropriate for a judge to decide, while in others, your client may obtain a better result with a jury. In any event, this choice must be made. Only one or the other will hear and decide a case, not both.

Assume the parties want a jury to decide their dispute. Does this mean a judge isn't needed? No. In those situations, a judge must still be present to preside over the case. He or she will keep order in the courtroom and decide issues based upon the law, as these issues 'arise during the trial. The jury, on the other hand, is solely responsible for determining the facts and applying the law, *as the law is explained to it by the judge.* (See C.G.S. sec. 52-216.)

By contrast, judges who decide a case without a jury are responsible for both tasks: determining the facts and applying the law.

Don't be confused if you read a case or hear an attorney referring to a judge as "the Court," or "Your Honor." The three labels are often used interchangeably.

II. THE SUPERIOR COURT

A. The Superior Court Contains Four Divisions: Family, Civil, Criminal and Housing

1. The *Family Division* handles divorces, child support, paternity actions, etc.
2. The *Civil Division* handles non-criminal lawsuits, decided by judges and juries.
3. The *Housing Division* handles cases involving landlord and tenant matters.
4. The *Criminal Division* handles cases in which individuals are accused of committing crimes.

B.   Superior Court Locations: Judicial Districts, Geographical Areas, Housing Sessions and Juvenile Matters

Connecticut's numerous Superior Courts are located throughout the state's twelve **judicial districts,** also referred to as **JDs.** (In 1998, Hartford and New Britain are expected to split into two separate JDs.) As you can see from the list below, each JD is named after one of the cities, towns or counties in that district:

Ansonia-Milford	New Haven
Danbury	New London
Fairfield	Stamford-Norwalk
Hartford-New Britain	Tolland
Litchfield	Waterbury
Middlesex	Windham

Each JD contains at least one JD courthouse that usually handles all major civil and family litigation, as well as major criminal cases. In addition, each JD contains one or more **geographical area** courthouses. These **GA** courthouses tend to be smaller than the JD courthouses and handle less significant criminal cases, housing cases and **small claims** cases.

> **1.** *Small claims* cases are civil disputes involving $2,500 or less, not including interest. The process is quicker, easier and less expensive than in the JD court. Most often, these cases involve claims for unpaid bills.
>
> **2.** All *criminal* cases start out in the GA. Very serious cases involving crimes such as murder and other A and B felonies are eventually transferred to the JD.
>
> **3.** *Housing matters*, also known as landlord and tenant matters, can be decided in the GA or the **Housing Session**. Five (six if you include New Britain as a JD) of the JDs have their own Housing Session to address housing matters by a specific judge who is authorized to preside over housing matters exclusively. The Housing Session may take place in the JD or the GA courthouse, or in a separate facility. The remaining JDs often send their housing matters to their GAs.

In total, there are presently 16 JD courthouses and 22 GA courthouses throughout Connecticut. In addition, there are 13 facilities that handle **Juvenile Matters**. Juvenile Matters involve children under the age of seventeen who are in crises or legal trouble. Last, the state's one tax court is located in Hartford and addresses Connecticut state tax issues. A list of all the courts appears in Appendix C.

C.   Superior Court Decisions

Superior Court judges are required to follow the law found in cases decided by the Connecticut Supreme Court, as well as the Connecticut General Statutes and the

Connecticut Practice Book. If an issue arises that the Supreme Court has not yet addressed, the Superior Court should follow the law found in cases decided by the Connecticut Appellate Court. If neither the Supreme Court nor the Appellate Court has addressed an issue, the issue becomes one of **first impression**. The Superior Court will then look for guidance from other state and federal decisions and determine the issue on its own.

The Superior Court makes decisions that arise at trial, as well as decisions on motions, applications and objections prior to trial, as explained in future chapters. Many Superior Court decisions are printed in the *Connecticut Superior Court Reporter*.

A party who believes the Superior Court made a mistake by misinterpreting the law already determined by the Supreme Court or Appellate Court, or in ruling on an issue of first impression may **appeal** to the Appellate Court. In some cases, the party may appeal directly to the Supreme Court.

III. THE APPELLATE COURT

Unlike the Superior Court, there is only one Appellate Court in this state. It is located on the fourth floor at 95 Washington Street in Hartford and hears all types of cases that are appealed from the Superior Court.

The Appellate Court consists of nine judges. According to C.G.S. sec. 51-197c (a), in most situations, three judges will sit as a panel to hear and decide each case. There are, however, situations in which all nine judges will hear and decide a case. This is called sitting **en banc.**

C.G.S. sec. 51-197a states that the Appellate Court may decide **appeals** of final judgments or actions that occurred in the Superior Court. An appeal is brought to the Appellate Court by a party who is aggrieved by that final judgment or action. In the appeal, the party asks the Appellate Court to rule that an error was made in the Superior Court. As a result of that error, the party is entitled to a new trial, or to judgment in his or her favor.

The Appellate Court reviews the Superior Court **record** in order to make its decision. This record includes all the documents and exhibits that were filed in the Superior Court relating to the case and a **transcript** of the court proceedings. This transcript is a typewritten or computer-printed booklet created by a **court reporter** or court monitor who attended the trial or other court proceeding and recorded every word that was said. Transcripts may consist of one or two pages, or as much as several hundred pages, depending upon the length of the trial.

In addition to filed documents and transcripts, the Appellate Court reviews the **briefs** provided by the attorneys for both sides of each case. A brief contains a written summary of the trial, and points to specific examples and legal arguments regarding whether or not the Superior Court made a mistake during the trial.

The Appellate Court permits each side to present oral argument. Keep in mind, however, that this oral argument does not include testimony from witnesses or new evidence. That already occurred back in the Superior Court. Instead, this argument is simply a short presentation which enables the Appellate Court judges to listen to each side and, if necessary, ask questions.

Like the Superior Court, the Appellate Court decides issues based upon Connecticut Supreme Court cases. If the Supreme Court has not addressed an issue, the Appellate Court may rely upon previous Appellate Court decisions on the issue, or look to other states and decide the issue based upon first impression.

If the Appellate Court determines that the Superior Court made a mistake, it could order the case to be sent back to the Superior Court for a new trial or completely reverse the Superior Court decision and enter judgment in favor of the appealing party.

All Appellate Court decisions are printed in a series of gray volumes known as the *Connecticut Appellate Reports*. In addition, these decisions are published in a hard-bound series called the *Atlantic Reporter*.

IV. THE SUPREME COURT

The Connecticut Supreme Court is the highest court in the state. In dramatic terms, this court decides the law of the land. As a result, all lower courts, including all probate and administrative courts, all the Superior Courts and the Appellate Court, are obligated to follow the law set forth by the Supreme Court.

There is only one Connecticut Supreme Court. It is located at 231 Capitol Avenue in Hartford. Like the Appellate Court, the Supreme Court hears various types of cases. In addition, it's decisions are based upon the court record, transcripts, briefs and oral argument, as well as its previous decisions regarding the issue on appeal.

Pursuant to C.G.S. sec. 51-198, the Supreme Court consists of a total of seven justices, including one Chief Justice. Any combination of five of these justices sit together to hear and decide an appeal, or if the situation warrants, they sit **en banc**.

In most instances, there is no right to appeal a Superior Court decision directly to the Supreme Court. Instead, appeals usually begin in the Appellate Court. If a party wishes to appeal an Appellate Court decision to the Supreme Court, they must first ask permission by filing a Petition for Certification, which is sent to the Supreme Court. (See C.G.S. sec. 51-197f.) If the Petition for Certification is granted, the parties will then file the appropriate appeal documents. If the certification is denied, there is no further appeal and the Appellate Court's decision stands as law. (See C.G.S. sec. 51-199 for Superior Court decisions that may be appealed directly to the Supreme Court.)

All Supreme Court decisions are printed in a series of gold volumes known as the *Connecticut Reports*. Like Appellate Court decisions, Supreme Court decisions are also published in a hard-bound series called the *Atlantic Reporter*.

V. PROBATE

Years ago, the legislature created the Probate Court to preside over issues such as administering estates, wills and trusts, including collecting and distributing deceased persons' assets to their heirs, paying applicable taxes, etc. Adoptions, guardianships, conservatorships and some termination of parental rights cases were also included. Most cities and towns throughout Connecticut have their own Probate Courts and elect their own Probate judges.

A party who disagrees with a Probate Court's decision may appeal to the Superior Court, and if necessary to the Appellate Court and, if permitted, to the Supreme Court. See Title 45a of the Connecticut General Statutes, Probate Courts and Procedure, for more information.

VI. ADMINISTRATIVE ACTIONS

Administrative actions pertain to disputes involving any Connecticut state agency. Before a lawsuit can be brought against a state agency in Superior Court, the individual or entity who disagrees with an agency's actions must attempt to resolve his or her dispute by using the applicable agency's administrative remedies. These remedies are set forth in the Connecticut General Statutes and each agency's regulations.

As with the Probate Court, if a party disagrees with the agency's decision, he or she may appeal to the Superior Court. Whichever party disagrees with the Superior Court's decision may then appeal to the Appellate Court and, if permitted, to the Supreme Court. (See C.G.S. sec. 4-183 and 51-197b for more information.)

VII. CONCLUSION

A. Key Issues in This Chapter Include:

1. There is only one Connecticut Supreme Court. Its decisions are the law of the land in Connecticut. Every other court in this state must follow the law set forth by the Supreme Court.

2. *Trials* take place in the Superior Court, not the Appellate Court or the Supreme Court.

3. An *appeal* to the Appellate Court is a claim that the Superior Court made an error during the trial or other specific court proceeding.

4. Very few cases may be appealed directly to the Supreme Court from the Superior Court. (See C.G.S. sec. 51-199.)

5. A party who wishes to appeal an Appellate Court decision must first file a Petition for Certification with the Supreme Court, asking the Supreme Court for permission to file the appeal. If the petition is denied, there is no further appeal and the Appellate Court's decision stands as law. If the petition is granted, the party may file his or her appeal.

6. *Issues of first impression* arise when an issue has not yet been decided by the Connecticut Appellate Court or the Connecticut Supreme Court. (It is easy to see why issues of first impression are appealed. Either party has a fifty-fifty chance of winning.)

B. Relevant Connecticut General Statutes Include:

C.G.S. sec. 4-183.:	Appeals to Superior Court.
C.G.S. sec. 51-197a.:	Appeals to the Appellate Court. Writs, Transfer of jurisdiction from appellate session.
C.G.S. sec. 51-197b.:	Administrative appeals.
C.G.S. sec. 51-197c.:	Appellate Court; judges, appointment, terms, Chief Judge.
C.G.S. sec. 51-197f.:	Further review by certification only.
C.G.S. sec. 51-198.:	Constitution of the Supreme Court; retired judges, terms, participation in meetings.
C.G.S. sec. 51-99.:	Jurisdiction.
C.G.S.: Title 45a:	Probate Courts and Procedure

Now turn to Chapter 3 where we will address different causes of action and prelitigation.

3 *Prelitigation and Determining Causes of Action*

Terminology

Tort	Tortfeaser	Negligence
Claims Adjuster	Judgment Proof	Clients' Funds
Intake Sheet	Prelitigation Stage	Certificate of Good Faith
Intentional Tort	Personal Injury	Claims Commissioner
Retainer Letter	Notice Requirement	Sovereign Immunity
Contingency Fee	Cause of Action	Contract
Retainer	Breach	

C.G.S. sections: 4-141 et seq., 4-146, 4-147, 13a-144, 13a-149, 52-556, 52-190a, 52-251c, 52-576, 52-577, 52-581, 52-584, chapters: 925 and 926

Introduction

Welcome to the Prelitigation Stage. In this chapter, we will address various causes of action, the statute of limitations, investigating a case, and settlement discussions. Chapters 4, 5, and 6 will complete the Prelitigation Stage by discussing how to draft a Complaint, serve a Defendant, and file a lawsuit in court.

As you enter the legal profession and begin meeting clients, keep the following in mind: People go to lawyers because they need help. It's only the degree of help that varies.

On one end of the spectrum, a client may seek help buying or selling a home. In most situations, residential real estate closings are quick and involve little if any argument. Everybody leaves the law office relatively happy. On the other end, you may have a client who needs assistance convincing a jury he or she is not guilty of the crimes charged against him or her (criminal law). Obviously, the stakes are much higher in these types of cases and emotions run high.

14

Most civil litigation involves torts and contract disputes, which Xare described below. These disputes are known as **causes of action**. While family law and housing law cases are considered civil disputes, each has its own set of unique rules and procedures and they are not addressed in this text.

Chapters 925 and 926 of the Connecticut General Statutes contain lists of several causes of actions and the applicable statutes of limitations.

I. TORTS GENERALLY

Torts are injuries or wrongs suffered by a Plaintiff's person, property, rights or economic relationships with others. Individuals who commit torts are called **tortfeasers**.

Tort cases are based on the principle of fairness: Individuals harmed by torts should be compensated for their injuries or damages by the tortfeaser. In addition, tort cases hopefully act as a deterrent by causing people to act more carefully in order to reduce their chances of being sued.

II. TYPES OF TORTS

Generally speaking, there are two types of torts: unintentional torts and intentional torts.

A. *Unintentional Torts: Negligence*

1. *Unintended Harm*

Negligence cases presume the Defendant did not intend to harm the Plaintiff. Instead, the harmful act was accidental. Oftentimes negligence is described as the failure to use such care as a reasonable, prudent and careful person would use under similar circumstances.

Negligence cases are the most common type of civil cases found in a courthouse. Most often they involve situations in which a person was physically injured, for instance during an automobile accident, or from falling on a patch of ice on a sidewalk or down a cluttered stairway.

For example: John Doe drove his car through a red light at an intersection and smashed into a car driven by Jane Smith. During the collision, Jane broke her leg in two places and a piece of glass from the windshield cut her cheek, causing a three-inch scar. Jane sued John for her injuries suffered during the accident. At trial, she needs to prove the following:

> **a.** that John owed a duty to Jane and everyone else on the road to operate his car in a safe and reasonable manner;
>
> **b.** that John negligently operated his car (i.e., he operated his car in an unsafe and unreasonable manner);

c. that John breached his duty, and as a result of that breach, Jane was harmed.

Therefore, John must compensate Jane for her injuries.

2. *Generally: The Statute of Limitations*

C.G.S. sec. 52-584 requires that the following actions be brought *within two years*:

        a. injuries to persons, (personal injuries) *or* injuries to real property (real estate);

        b. caused by negligence or reckless or wanton misconduct; or

        c. caused by malpractice by a physician, surgeon, dentist, podiatrist, chiropractor, hospital or sanitarium.

The two years begins:

        a. on the date the injury is first sustained; or

        b. discovered; or

        c. in the exercise of reasonable care should have been discovered.

If the injury was not discovered within the two years, the case may be brought "no more than three years from the date of the act or omission complained of, except that a Counterclaim may be brought in any such action before the pleadings are closed."

Caution: C.G.S. sec. 52-584 is being cited above as a general example to demonstrate the statute of limitations in some negligence cases. Be sure to double-check all the statutes to be certain your negligence cause of action does not fall under another category. In addition, C.G.S. sec. 52-584 applies to reckless or wanton misconduct and malpractice committed by members of the medical profession.

B. *Intentional Torts*

1. *Intended Harm*

Many intentional torts are difficult to prove. In essence, the Plaintiff is accusing the Defendant of purposely causing the Plaintiff harm. Some examples include:

        a. assault;

        b. battery;

        c. intentional infliction of emotional distress;

        d. tortious interference with business relations;

        e. libel;

        f. slander;

        g. defamation of character.

2. *Generally: The Statute of Limitations*

C.G.S. sec. 52-577 provides that an action based on a tort must be brought *within three years* from the date the act or omission occurred.

III. BREACH OF CONTRACT CASES

A. An Agreement

Breach of contract cases often involve some type of business deal. In general terms, a contract is an agreement between two or more parties. It can be in writing or oral. Under the terms of this agreement, both parties should benefit in some way.

A breach of contract occurs when one party does not follow through with his or her part of the agreement and the other party is harmed. This harm is usually financial.

Like tort cases, breach of contract actions are based on fairness and compensation for injuries. In our society, it is imperative that parties be able to rely upon each other's promises. Otherwise, we would be in a state of chaos.

B. Generally: The Statute of Limitations

1. *Oral Contracts*
C.G.S. sec. 52-581 provides that a suit for breach of an oral contract must be brought *within three years* after the breach occurs.

2. *Written Contracts*
C.G.S. sec. 52-576 provides that a suit for breach of a written contract must be brought *within six years* after the breach occurs.

IV. SOVEREIGN IMMUNITY

The State of Connecticut, its agencies and employees, as well as cities, towns and boroughs are protected from being sued by **sovereign immunity**. This means they may not be sued by any Plaintiff unless they consent to a lawsuit, pursuant to a specific statute, or, if the case is against the State of Connecticut, the **Claims Commissioner** authorizes such a suit.

A. Statutes that Waive Sovereign Immunity: Notice Requirements

The State of Connecticut has consented, by statute, to be sued in certain circumstances, a few of which I have listed below. Note that **2. 3.** and **4.** have **notice requirements** which, in most instances, must be met. Otherwise, the Plaintiff's lawsuit may be dismissed.
   1. C.G.S. sec. 52-556 permits a suit if the Plaintiff alleges to have suffered personal injuries or damage due to a state employee's negligent operation of a state-owned and insured motor vehicle;
   2. C.G.S. sec. 13a-144 permits a suit if the Plaintiff alleges to have suffered personal injuries or damage due to a state-owned defective sidewalk or highway.

Caution: In addition, the statute requires the Plaintiff to give *written notice* of the potential claim against the State of Connecticut to the Commissioner of Transportation within *90 days* of the incident at issue. Otherwise, if the Plaintiff files a lawsuit, it could be dismissed for lack of notice. See C.G.S. sec. 13a-144 for specific details.

3. C.G.S. sec. 13a-149 permits a suit if the Plaintiff alleges to have suffered personal injuries or damages due to a defective road or bridge.

Caution: In addition, the statute requires the Plaintiff to give written notice to a "selectman, or the clerk of such town or to the clerk of such city or borough, or to the secretary or treasurer of such corporation" within *90 days* of the date of the incident at issue. See C.G.S. sec. 13a-149 for specific details.

4. C.G.S. sec. 4-146 permits a suit if the Plaintiff alleges to have suffered personal injures or damage due to a "defective condition of a building, park or ground owned or leased by the state... ."

This statute's written notice requirement appears less stringent than C.G.S. sec. 13a-144 and 13a-149. Instead of a specific deadline, the statute allows the written notice to be given "*within a reasonable time*" to the "official having control of or the agency using such building..." If no notice is given, a lawsuit is still permitted, "except upon a showing by the state that it was substantially prejudiced thereby." See C.G.S. sec. 4-146 for specific details.

Be sure to consult the Connecticut General Statutes for other causes of action against governments. If there is no statute, the Plaintiff is out of luck, unless it's a case against the State of Connecticut and the Claims Commissioner grants permission to bring suit.

B. The Claims Commissioner

If the Plaintiff cannot find an applicable statute that indicates the State of Connecticut has waived its right to sovereign immunity, he or she must file a claim with the Claims Commissioner within *one year* of the date the cause of action arose, regardless of the length of the statute of limitations. If this one-year time limit is missed, the Plaintiff has lost his or her right to file the claim and a suit, if brought, will probably be dismissed. Once the claim is timely filed, the Claims Commissioner will determine if the Plaintiff should be permitted to bring suit against the State of Connecticut. If the Claims Commissioner grants permission, the suit must be filed within *one year* of the date permission was granted. See C.G.S. sec. 4-141 et seq., and specifically sections 4-147 and 4-160.

V. MEDICAL MALPRACTICE CLAIMS: GOOD FAITH CERTIFICATE

When bringing a medical malpractice action, in tort or contract, against a health care provider, C.G.S. sec. 52-190a requires the Plaintiff to file a "certificate of good faith." The purpose of this certificate of good faith is to require the Plaintiff to "make a reasonable inquiry" to determine if there are grounds for a good faith belief that doctor or other health care provider had been negligence in caring or treating the Plaintiff. No medical malpractice action can be filed without the certificate.

A Plaintiff who obtains a written opinion from an appropriate heath care provider that evidence of medical malpractice exists has probably met the good faith test. If necessary, the Plaintiff may petition the court for an automatic **90-day** extension of the statute of limitations to meet this requirement. See C.G.S. sec. 52-190a for specific details.

VI. DIFFERENT TYPES OF LAW FIRMS

Parties involved in civil disputes often attempt to settle their matters without hiring an attorney. This makes sense. After all, attorneys cost money and it could take years before the court assigned the case for trial. If the parties' efforts fail, the Plaintiff may have no choice but to sue.

Many firms specialize in the types of cases they handle. For instance, some firms practice only Plaintiff's personal injury law. They do not represent insurance companies, nor do they handle breach of contract cases, real estate, criminal or family cases.

Other firms devote themselves to personal injury defense. In fact, it is quite common for insurance companies to hire specific attorneys or firms to represent them exclusively. Finally, there are firms that bring and defend personal injury cases, as well as practice other areas of the law.

Many potential clients prefer to shop around for an attorney before hiring anyone in particular. Some firms provide free consultations. Others charge a fee for this time, regardless of whether the client hires the firm. Remember, practicing law is a business as well as a service. Time is valuable.

It is not uncommon to find complete strangers calling your firm expecting free legal advice over the telephone. Don't give it. You don't know the entire story and you don't want to be blamed later for providing someone with faulty advice. Nor do you have time to listen to their entire situation. Don't worry, you're not being mean. Depending upon your location in the telephone book, you can bet that the caller has already called, or will call, at least half a dozen other firms seeking the same advice.

VII. REASONS ATTORNEYS DECLINE CASES

A law firm may have many reasons to decline a case. For instance:
1. The potential client may not have sufficient financial resources to hire the firm and properly pursue the case.
2. The cost of litigating the case may outweigh the results. For instance, the Defendant may be **judgment proof**: He or she may not have insurance to cover the incident or may have filed bankruptcy or may not have sufficient assets to

pay a judgment. Therefore, even if the Plaintiff wins the case, there won't be any damages to collect.

3. The case may be too time consuming for the firm.

4. The firm may lack expertise in the area and prefer to do other types of cases.

5. There may be personality clashes with the client. Some clients can be extremely difficult to deal with and unreasonable in their expectations. In those situations, it's often better not to accept the case.

6. The attorney may decide not to risk a legal malpractice suit because the statute of limitations will expire before the attorney can realistically and properly prepare the case for suit.

7. There is a conflict of interest or a potential conflict of interest because the attorney or the law firm currently represents or previously represented the opposing party.

VIII. AGREEMENTS FOR REPRESENTATION

A. Retainer Letter

Once a party decides to hire a law firm and the attorney agrees to take the case, the party will become a client and will need to sign an agreement with the firm. This agreement is often called a **retainer letter** or **agreement for representation.** In most situations, this agreement should be obtained prior to the attorney beginning work on the case. Most firms already have a standard agreement form. It states the name of the client, the type of case at issue, and the applicable legal fee arrangements.

B. Plaintiffs and Contingency Fee Cases

Attorneys who handle Plaintiff's personal injury claims and debt collection cases do not usually require any payment from their clients until the case ends. Instead, the attorneys work on a **contingency** basis.

Under a contingency agreement, in many cases, the Plaintiff's attorney's fees will be no more than one-third of the entire amount of damages paid by the Defendant. In addition, the Plaintiff will have to pay all the costs incurred during the lawsuit, such as the court entry fee, sheriff's or constable's fees, witness fees, report fees, etc. If there is no settlement and the Defendant wins at trial, the Plaintiff will not owe his or her attorney any legal fees. Note, however, that these Plaintiffs are still responsible for the above-mentioned expenses. See C.G.S. sec. 52-251c.

C. Defendants: Insurance Company Attorneys

Most Defendants in negligence cases are covered by auto or homeowners' insurance. As a result, any payments for damages are usually paid by their insurance companies who hire attorneys to represent them.

Insurance companies have claim departments to address potential and actual lawsuits against the people they insure. Individuals who work in these departments are often called **claims adjusters**. Their responsibilities include determining how much a case is worth and negotiating a settlement on behalf of the insurance company and their insureds.

Presume for a moment that a case falls within the two-year statute of limitations for negligence cases, and the Plaintiff retains an attorney a week after the accident. That attorney and the insurance company's claims adjuster will probably spend the next year attempting to settle the case. I call this time period the **Prelitigation Stage**. It begins when the cause of action occurs and continues until a lawsuit is brought.

If settlement attempts fail, the Plaintiff's attorney will then file suit before the statute of limitations expires. Once the lawsuit starts, the insurance company must hire its own attorney to represent its interests, including its insured, in court.

D. Other Types of Cases

If the attorney does not take the case on a contingency basis and does not typically represent an insurance company, he or she will usually require the client (either a Plaintiff or a Defendant) to pay a **retainer** before he or she begins work on the case.

A retainer is an advance payment for legal fees. It may range anywhere from a few hundred dollars to several thousand dollars. It is placed in the attorney's **clients' funds** bank account and is drawn on when work is performed on the file.

Retainers ensure the attorney will be paid for work and expenses, regardless of the outcome of a case. In addition, they demonstrate how much clients are committed to proving their claims or defending themselves in court. People have no trouble fighting for their rights or defending themselves, as long as little or no money is involved. Once money is required, they tend to reevaluate and reprioritize.

IX. OBTAINING INFORMATION AND DIARYING

When reviewing new files or meeting clients to discuss their cases, determine the following information:

1. Identify the parties: Who is the Plaintiff and who is the Defendant?

2. Determine the cause of action: tort, contract, etc.

3. Has legal action started, and if not, what is the applicable statute of limitations?

4. If the client is the Plaintiff, what are his or her damages? If the client is the Defendant, what is the maximum exposure he or she faces? In other words, what is the worst-case scenario?

A. *The Intake Sheet*

Most firms have an **intake sheet** they use to list the above-stated information. This intake sheet is usually kept in the client's file and the information is often entered into the firm's computer system.

An intake sheet for a personal injury case will probably request the following information:

1. The client's complete name, address and telephone numbers where he or she can be reached;
2. Whether the client is the Plaintiff or the Defendant;
3. The date of the accident;
4. Next of kin;
5. Emergency contact numbers;
6. Social security number;
7. Client's version of how accident occurred:
   a. description of accident;
   b. whether client was driver or passenger;
   c. location of accident;
   d. name and address of opposing party, if known;
   e. what the client remembers happened immediately prior to the accident and during the accident.
8. Other people involved in accident: driver or passengers in Plaintiff's car and in Defendant's car;
9. Witnesses to the accident;
10. Health issues prior to accident;
11. Injuries sustained from the accident: scars, broken bones, sprains, strains, etc.
12. List of all hospitals, clinics, doctors, chiropractors, and therapists involved in treating the client before the accident for any reason;
13. List of all hospitals, clinics, doctors, chiropractors and therapists involved in treating the client's injuries caused by the accident;
14. Amount of wages, if any, the client lost as a result of the accident;
15. Any impairment to the client's earning capacity as a result of the accident;
16. Amount and type of property damage to the car the Plaintiff was in;
17. Amount and type of property damage to the car the Defendant was in;
18. Amount and type of other property damage caused during accident, such as trees, guard rails, other cars, etc. and who caused the damage;
19. The make, model and year of each car involved and who owned them;
20. Plaintiff's auto insurance company's name and policy numbers;
21. Defendant's auto insurance company's name and policy numbers, if known;
22. Was either insurance company notified yet?
23. Client's motor vehicle driving history;
24. Client's history of any previous litigation;

25. Any other information the client has about the case.

B. Diarying

Every law firm should have a diary system. It usually consists of *at least two or more calendars* in the office that list important deadlines. These calendars are the regular type you can buy in any store. To diary, simply state the name of the case and the purpose of the date on the appropriate date on the calendar.

1. Calendars should be located in the following areas:
a. the attorney's desk calendar; and
b. the paralegal/legal assistant's desk calendar; and
c. a large master calendar that hangs in a visible place for everyone in the office to see; and
d. more recently, if a computer programs for diarying is available, on everyone's computers in the office.

2. Diarying the Statute of Limitations
a. Diary the actual deadline for the statute of limitations; and
b. Diary the one-year anniversary of the date of the accident or date the cause of action occurred.
In addition, Plaintiffs and some Defendants add the following:
c. Diary the date that falls six months before the statute of limitations expires; and
d. Diary the date that falls three months before the statute of limitations expires; and
e. Diary the date that falls one month before the statute of limitations expires.

This may seem excessive, but it's one of the best ways to avoid malpractice. As we move forward in this text, you will discover the other important dates to diary. Fortunately, they won't be as complicated and are usually limited to the attorney and office staff working on a particular file.

C. Who May Be a Defendant

1. Individuals and Entities

Individuals over the age of eighteen can be Defendants. In addition, Defendants can be corporations, partnerships, voluntary associations, municipalities, the State of Connecticut, etc. This information is important to determine in order to contact the appropriate individual who has authority to discuss settlement and, if necessary, to sue.

2. Owners and Operators or Managers

In many personal injury cases involving a motor vehicle accident, the individual Defendant who drove the vehicle at the time of the accident may not own the motor vehicle involved in the accident. Note, however, that both the owner's and the operator's insurance will usually cover the operator's acts. Therefore, you must identify the owner and well as the operator and contact both insurance companies to make a claim, and sue, if necessary.

The same holds true when a Plaintiff is injured falling on a piece of property. The manager of the property may differ from the owner, yet both insurance policies may cover the claim. So be sure to identify and bring a claim against the owner, as well as any party who may lease, manage or use the property.

X. INVESTIGATION AND ANALYSIS

A. The Police Report

Once you have the preliminary information, take all necessary steps to obtain as much additional information about the opposing party and the cause of action as possible. If the police were called to the scene of the incident at issue, the police report will often provide useful information.

A motor vehicle accident report will often contain the following:
1. the parties' names, including the owners of the vehicles, if known;
2. addresses;
3. dates of birth;
4. operators' license numbers;
5. make, model and year of each vehicle;
6. names of insurance companies, policy numbers;
7. if possible, a diagram of the accident.

The police accident report should also list the names and addresses of any witnesses and other people involved in the accident.

A copy of the police accident report or any other type of police report may be obtained by simply calling the records department of the police station that responded to the incident. Someone there will make a copy for you to pick up or to mail to you. It usually doesn't cost more than a few dollars per report. It's even faster if you pick up the report in person.

In most situations, once the Plaintiff's attorney has confirmed the Defendant was insured at the time of the accident, he or she will want to contact the Defendant's insurance company and apprise them of the claim. The case will be assigned to a claims adjuster, if it hadn't been already, who has authority to discuss the matter.

If the Defendant was not insured, the Plaintiff may make a claim under the Uninsured Motorist Coverage portion of the Plaintiff's insurance policy. This portion enables Plaintiffs to collect damages under their policies and sue their insurance companies if their claim cannot be settled.

B. When There Is No Police Report

The parties will need the above-stated information in any personal injury case, with or without a police report. If no such report exists, a thorough investigation will definitely be needed.

C. Obtaining Other Information: The Plaintiff

During the Prelitigation Stage, the following action should be taking place:

1. The Plaintiff should be sending the attorney all bills relating to the accident.

2. The attorney's office should prepare forms entitled "Authorization to Release Information" for the Plaintiff to sign. These forms permit the office to obtain the Plaintiff's medical and employment information.

3. The attorney's office should be contacting the Plaintiff's physicians to obtain an opinion regarding the extent of the Plaintiff's injuries, the need for future treatment, permanent disability, if any, etc. Much of this information is sent to the claims adjuster in an effort to encourage settlement.

4. The attorney's office should be contacting the Plaintiff's employers to obtain information regarding the Plaintiff's lost wages, etc., incurred due to the accident.

5. The opposing party and the accident must be investigated.

    a. What do the witnesses say about the accident?

    b. What does the opposing party say about the accident?

    c. Was either party under the influence of alcohol or drugs at the time of the accident?

    d. Did one of them fall asleep at the wheel?

    e. Do either of them fail to wear prescription eyeglasses?

    f. Was either one of them talking on a cellular phone?

    g. Did either car's brakes give out?

    h. What were the weather conditions at the time of the accident?

    i. What were the driving conditions at the time of the accident?

    j. Was the sun in either of the parties' eyes?

    k. Obtain all of this information and identify any discrepancies.

XI. THE PRELITIGATION FILE

Every firm has its own method of maintaining client files. To stay organized, many offices label various manila folders and place them all in a larger file.

A. Personal Injury Cases

In personal injury cases, these file labels often include but are not limited to:

1. Correspondence: all written communications regarding the file, including the retainer letter if it is not in a separate file;
2. Authorizations: signed by the client to obtain necessary information that is relevant to the case from third parties such as medical providers, employers, etc.
3. Medical reports and list of injuries client suffered and/or will continue to suffer;
4. Medical bills: with a summary sheet on top listing all of the bills and whether they have been paid;
5. Proof of lost wages and/or reduced earning capacity;
6. Police accident reports and any other reports regarding the incident such as accident reconstruction, etc.;
7. Legal billing and/or expenses incurred;
8. Witness information and other statements by client, opposing party, etc.;
9. Plaintiff's insurance information;
10. Defendant's insurance information;
11. Settlement negotiations, with notes describing conversations, offers, demands, etc.;
12. Attorney's notes;
13. Evidence;
14. If representing the Plaintiff, drafts of the potential Complaint.

B. Contract Cases and Others

Select all of the above that are applicable and add others including a documents file containing *copies* of the contract, etc. In most circumstances the *original* documents are kept elsewhere for safekeeping. In the event of litigation, the original documents will be needed to obtain a judgment against the Defendant. **Do not lose the originals or give them to anyone!**

XII. SETTLEMENT DISCUSSIONS

A. Analyzing the Information

Remember, there are always two or more sides to every story. Proper analysis requires the parties to determine their own strengths and weaknesses as well as those of their opponents. Don't overlook anything. Even the smallest detail could come back to haunt you when you least expect or want it to.

B. Settlement Discussions

The purpose of obtaining information and analyzing it is to enter into effective settlement negotiations. The more you know about the case, the more prepared you are to use your own persuasion tactics.

Do not rely on anyone when discussing settlement. If you represent the Plaintiff and you are down to six months before the statute of limitations will expire, I suggest starting litigation proceedings as described in the next chapter. Remember, Defendants have everything to gain by convincing Plaintiffs to delay. They have their own diary system to remind them when the statute will expire. Statements like "I'll see what I can do." or "We won't need to go to court on this one." will not stop the statute from running. Unless you receive a check for the Plaintiff from the Defendant and that check has cleared the bank, there is no settlement. Don't wait until the last minute and risk a legal malpractice suit. Start litigation no later than at the six-month mark. Sooner is even better.

XIII. PREPARING TO BRING SUIT

A. Steps to Take

If your office represents the Plaintiff and you have been instructed to bring a lawsuit, I suggest you take the following steps:
1. Draft the Complaint, as described in the next chapter;
2. Take steps to verify the Defendant's current home and business addresses;
3. Diary the deadline for the Complaint and all other necessary documents to be completed, as explained in future chapters;
4. Add the following individual files to the client's file:
    a. Complaint and officer's Return of Service;
    b. Defendant's Appearance;
    c. Defendant's pleadings;
    d. Plaintiff's pleadings;
    e. Plaintiff's discovery;
    f. Defendant's discovery;
    g. court calendars;
    h. Defendant's Answer and, if applicable, Special Defenses, Counterclaim;
    i. Plaintiff's response to Defendant's Answer, Special Defenses, Counterclaim.

Each of these items will be discussed later in this text.

B. The Statute of Limitations

For purposes of meeting the statute of limitations, the term "action must be brought" means that the Defendant must be **served** a copy of the Summons and Complaint before the expiration date. We will discuss serving the Defendant in Chapter 6. For now, keep in mind the following example:

If the statute of limitations expires May 16, 1999, the Defendant must be served no later than 11:59 p.m. on May 16, 1999. There is one exception to this rule that is discussed in Chapter 6. Of course, it's really better practice to bring the suit months before the statute of limitations expires.

XIV. CONCLUSION

The lists in this chapter are not exhaustive. Instead, they should be used as guidelines and adapted to fit the circumstances of each case.

As we move into litigation itself, you will note that I refer to the Plaintiff and the Defendant, instead of directing my comments to the reader. These titles are directed to the role of Plaintiffs' attorneys and their staff, and the role of Defendants' attorneys and their staff. They do not apply to pro ses or individual clients unless otherwise specified.

A. Key Issues in This Chapter Include:

1. The Plaintiff must promptly identify all possible causes of action at issue in each case.

2. Both parties should determine the *statute of limitations* for each cause of action in each case and *diary* these dates.

3. Both parties should obtain an *Agreement for Representation* from their clients prior to working on a case. Obtain an *retainer*, if appropriate.

4. Prior to suit, if time permits, both parties should obtain as much information about the case as possible in order to conduct appropriate settlement discussions.

5. Create a *prelitigation file* to keep information organized and expand the file if litigation is necessary.

B. Relevant Connecticut General Statutes Include:

C.G.S. sec. 4-141 et seq.: Definitions (Claims Against the State).

C.G.S. sec. 4-146.: Notice of injury by claimant.

C.G.S. sec. 4-147.: Notice of claim. Filing fees.

C.G.S. sec. 4-160.: Authorization of actions against the state.

C.G.S. sec. 13a-144.: Damages for injuries sustained on state highways or sidewalks.

C.G.S. sec. 13a-149.: Damages for injuries by means of defective roads and bridges.

C.G.S. sec. 52-190a.:	Prior reasonable inquiry and certificate of good faith required in negligence action against health care provider.
C.G.S. sec. 52-251c.:	Limitation on attorney contingency fee in personal injury, wrongful death and property damages actions.
C.G.S. sec. 52-556.:	Actions for injuries caused by motor vehicles owned by the state.
C.G.S. sec. 52-576.:	Actions for account or on simple or implied contracts.
C.G.S. sec. 52- 577.:	Action founded upon a tort.
C.G.S. sec. 52- 581.:	Action on oral contract to be brought within three years.
C.G.S. sec. 52-584.:	Limitation of action for injury to person or property.
C.G.S. Chapter 925:	Statutory rights of action and defenses.
C.G.S. Chapter 926:	Statute of limitations.

4 Commencing a Lawsuit: The Plaintiff's Complaint

Terminology

Complaint	Case Caption	Counts	Pleading
Venue	Juris Number	Return Date	Et Al.
Statement of Amount in Demand			

Introduction

Once a Plaintiff decides to sue a Defendant, he or she must draft a **Complaint**. A Complaint is a typewritten or printed document that is divided into numbered paragraphs and contains the facts that support the Plaintiff's cause of action against the Defendant.

A Complaint serves two purposes:

1. It notifies the Defendant that he or she is being sued by the Plaintiff; and

2. It is (usually) the first **pleading** to be filed in court in each lawsuit.

When the Plaintiff finishes drafting the final version of the Complaint, he or she must then make arrangements to serve a copy of the Complaint, along with other necessary documents, to the Defendant. After this is accomplished, the Plaintiff must *file* the original Complaint, the necessary documents, and an entry fee, at the proper courthouse. Once filed, the Plaintiff's case officially becomes a lawsuit.

The process of serving the Defendant and filing the Complaint in court will be addressed in Chapter 6. For now, we will concentrate on the Complaint itself.

I. FORMAT OF THE COMPLAINT AND PLEADINGS IN GENERAL

Pbs 7KK requires that all pleadings:
1. be typed or printed on 8.5" x 11" paper;
2. have top and bottom margins of 2" each;
3. have 2 holes punched at the top, 2 and 12/16" apart, centered;
4. have a 1.5" margin on the left and at least a .5 inch margin on the right;
5. be double spaced; and
6. are printed on only one side of the paper.

Note that most law firms have *pleading paper* and computer systems that are already designed to address these requirements.

II. THE THREE PARTS OF A COMPLAINT

I've divided the Complaint into three parts:
1. the case caption;
2. the body of the Complaint;
3. the Demand for Relief (The Statement of Amount in Demand).

As you explore each part, be sure to compare it to the sample Complaints found at the end of this chapter.

III. THE CASE CAPTION

According to Pbs 7KK, a case caption (also known as a heading) must be present at the top of the first page of every pleading filed in court. Although it appears that Complaints are not included in this rule, the majority of Complaints I've seen over the years contain a case caption.

To complete a case caption, the Plaintiff will need to determine the following:

RETURN DATE: _____	:	SUPERIOR COURT
(The Plaintiff's name)	:	JUDICIAL DISTRICT OF _____
VS.	:	AT _____
(The Defendant's name)	:	(Date)

IV. THE RETURN DATE

A. *Return Dates Must Fall on a Tuesday in the Future*

Pursuant to C.G.S. sec. 52-48(a), **return dates** must fall on a Tuesday. (The only exception involves summary process cases. Summary process cases address landlord and tenant matters and are not discussed in this text.) In addition, the return date selected must be in the future. At minimum, this date can be approximately two weeks after the Complaint is ready to be served, but no more than two months into the future. (See C.G.S. sec. 52-48(b).)

The purpose of the return date is to act as an anchor: It determines the following three extremely important deadlines:

1. The Plaintiff must make certain the Defendant is served a copy of the Complaint *at least 12 days before the return date.* (See C.G.S. sec. 52-46.)
2. The Plaintiff must make certain the original Complaint is filed in court *at least six days before the return date.* (See C.G.S. sec. 52-46a.)
3. A Defendant who has been served a copy of the Complaint must file an Appearance in court *on or before the second day following the return date.* (See Pbs 7Q(a).)

B. How to Select a Return Date

Take a look at the calendar below.

FEBRUARY

S	M	T	W	TH	F	S
					1	2
3	4	5	6	7	8	9
10	11	12	13	14	15	16
17	18	19	20	21	22	23
24	25	26	27	28		

As a Plaintiff, presume your Complaint is completely ready to be served on Monday, February 3 and the statute of limitations will not expire for another six months. Which Tuesday date in February will allow you to meet the 12 day-deadline and the 6-day deadline stated above?

The earliest Tuesday you may select is February 19. Using this date requires the following:

a. the Defendant to be served by Thursday, February 7; and
b. the Complaint to be filed in court by 5:00 p.m. on Wednesday, February 13.

Try another example: The Complaint is ready on February 11.

What is the earliest return date?	February 26
When must the Defendant be served?	February 14
When must the Complaint be filed in court?	February 20

Must a Plaintiff always select the earliest return date? No In fact many Plaintiffs give themselves at least one extra week or even a month in order to provide enough time to address any last-minute problems that may arise.

V. THE PARTIES' NAMES, COURT AND DATE

The Superior Court title, the Plaintiff's name and the Defendant's name are self-explanatory. Note, however, that if a case involves more than one Plaintiff or Defendant, it is customary to state one name, followed by the abbreviation: Et Al. For example:
GEORGE SKILLMAN, ET AL.
The "date" is the date the Complaint is finished and ready to be served.

VI. VENUE: THE CORRECT JUDICIAL DISTRICT AND SUPERIOR COURT

Next, the Plaintiff must select the proper **venue** to file the lawsuit. In Connecticut, venue involves selecting a Judicial District or Geographical Area and Superior Court location.

A. *The Proper Judicial District*

C.G.S. sec. 51-345 addresses how to select the proper venue, based upon the parties involved and the type of action being brought. For our purposes, we will use the following scenario to demonstrate how to select the proper venue:
1. A personal injury case that resulted from a motor vehicle accident in Connecticut.
> **a.** If one or both of the parties (Plaintiff and Defendant) are residents of Connecticut, select the JD where either of them resides. It's the Plaintiff's choice.
> **b.** If neither of the parties are Connecticut residents and suit is to be brought in Connecticut, select the JD in which the accident occurred.
2. For cases that involve corporations as parties, or land, consumer transactions, etc., consult C.G.S. sec. 51-345.

B. *The Proper JD Courthouse Location*

Once the Plaintiff selects the proper JD, he or she may turn to C.G.S. sec. 51-346 to find the proper courthouse location in that JD.
Nine of the twelve JDs have only one courthouse location (not including the GA, housing sessions or juvenile matters) where lawsuits may be filed. Therefore, all a Plaintiff needs to do is consult the JD list to find the name of the town or city where its courthouse is located.

Judicial Districts with One Courthouse for Civil Cases:

1. All civil cases in Middlesex are filed at the courthouse in Middletown.
Therefore, the case caption would read: Judicial District of Middlesex
at Middletown.

2. All civil cases in Tolland are filed at the courthouse in Rockville.
Therefore, the case caption would read: Judicial District of Tolland
at Rockville

3. All civil cases in Ansonia-Milford are filed at the courthouse in Milford.
Therefore, the case caption would read: Judicial District of Ansonia-Milford
at Milford

4. All civil cases in Danbury are filed at the courthouse in Danbury.
Therefore, the case caption would read: Judicial District of Danbury
at Danbury

5. All civil cases in Fairfield are filed at the courthouse in Bridgeport.
Therefore, the case caption would read: Judicial District of Fairfield
at Bridgeport

6. All civil cases in Litchfield are filed at the courthouse in Litchfield.
Therefore, the case caption would read: Judicial District of Litchfield
at Litchfield

7. All civil cases in Waterbury are filed at the courthouse in Waterbury.
Therefore, the case caption would read: Judicial District of Waterbury
at Waterbury

8. All civil cases in Stamford-Norwalk are filed at the courthouse in Stamford.
Therefore, the case caption would read: Judicial District of Stamford
at Stamford

9. All civil cases in Windham are filed at the courthouse in Putnam.
Therefore, the case caption would read: Judicial District of Windham.
at Putnam

Judicial Districts with More Than One Courthouse for Civil Cases:

1. Case captions for the Judicial District of Hartford-New Britain may read:
Judicial District of Hartford-New Britain at Hartford
or
Judicial District of Hartford-New Britain at New Britain

(It is anticipated that by 1998, Hartford and New Britain will each have separate JDs. Thereafter, all Hartford JD cases will be held at Hartford. All New Britain JD cases will be at New Britain or possibly Bristol. See C.G.S. sec. 51-344a, 51-345, 51-346)

2. Case captions for the Judicial District of New Haven may read:

Judicial District of New Haven   or   Judicial District of New Haven
at Meriden   at New Haven

3. Case captions for the Judicial District of New London may read:

Judicial District of New London   or   Judicial District of New London
at New London   at Norwich

Plaintiffs who later discover they selected the wrong venue may ask the court to transfer the case to the proper location. (See Chapter 10.)

C. Geographical Area Cases

For cases filed in GAs, consult C.G.S. sec. 348 and C.G.S. sec. 349. These cases typically involve small claims, criminal matters and possibly summary process if the JD at issue does not have its own Housing Session court.

VII. THE BODY OF THE COMPLAINT

A. The Content

Drafting the body of a Complaint is no easy task. One may take an hour, while another could take as long as a week or more. It depends upon the complexity of each case.

Always keep in mind that the purpose of the Complaint, as stated in Pbs 131, is to set forth the facts that lead up to the cause of action. Like all pleadings, Pbs 108 requires the Complaint to be a "plain and concise statement of the material facts...divided into paragraphs, numbered consecutively...." If possible, each paragraph should contain a separate allegation.

My first offer of advice here is not to reinvent the wheel. Your time is precious. If your firm handles a lot of litigation, there's a good chance a Complaint reciting the cause of action you are working on already exists in another case. Many firms have a forms file in their computer systems. Usually, the Complaint forms are categorized according to their causes of action. All you'll have to do is change the case caption and facts to conform the sample to your facts and cut and paste where needed.

In addition, check the numerous forms books that are available in law libraries. In most instances, you will find at least one example of the type of dispute you are working on. I personally try to find as many different versions as possible and compare them, borrowing certain parts from one, and combining and deleting from others. In law, perfecting the art of persuasion means you can never have too much information.

If you still can't find what you're looking for, don't just sit there wracking your brain and feeling incompetent. Take a deep breath and give it your best shot. Remember what I said earlier: Nothing in life prepares you to excel in the legal profession. It's a matter of trial and error and patience and experience.

B. *Counts of a Complaint: Pbs 138*

1. *Cases That Involve More Than One Cause of Action*

If the Plaintiff's case involves more than one cause of action against the Defendant, these causes of action should be separated into **counts**.

Turn to the *Skillman* Complaint found at the end of this chapter (Example 3). Notice that the Complaint contains two counts. The first count alleges Breach of Contract: The Defendant promised to pay the Plaintiff a certain sum and failed to meet this obligation. The second count alleges the Defendant was unjustly. enriched because it (a corporation) received a benefit, yet failed to comply with its part of the bargain, to the Plaintiff's detriment. The Plaintiff may prevail on either or both counts at trial.

2. *Multiple Parties*

Another reason to have more than one count in a Complaint is that some cases involve more than one Plaintiff and/or more than one Defendant.

The easiest example that comes to mind involves a two-car accident. The Plaintiff's car contained a driver and a passenger. Both were seriously injured in the crash, caused by the Defendant. Each Plaintiff had a different role in the accident: driver and passenger. In addition, each Plaintiff suffered different injuries. Therefore, one count should focus on the Plaintiff driver's actions and injuries. The other count should focus on the Plaintiff passenger's actions and injuries.

C. *The WHEREFORE Page*

It is customary to list separately, on the last page of the Complaint, what relief the Plaintiff wants from the Defendant. Typically, as you see from the examples provided, the WHEREFORE page consists of the following, depending upon the facts in each case:

WHEREFORE, the Plaintiff prays for the following relief:
1. Money damages;
2. Attorney's fees;
3. Interest and costs; (though not necessary to state, according to Pbs 139)
4. Such other and further relief as the Court may deem equitable and just.
(See Pbs 140.)

Pursuant to Pbs 7LL (b), the attorney's signature and additional information are mandatory for all pleadings filed in court. (See page 40) The signature certifies that the attorney has read the Complaint and confirms that it is true to the best of his or her "knowledge, information and belief...."

All the information except the **Juris Number** is self-explanatory. The Juris Number is each attorney's Connecticut registration or license number that he or she received from the State of Connecticut after passing the bar exam and being sworn in as an attorney for this state. In addition, each law firm is assigned its own juris number. If an attorney works for a law firm, that firm's Juris Number should be used on pleadings. An individual attorney's Juris Number is used if he or she works as a solo practitioner.

Many firms have preprinted pleading paper that states the firm's address, telephone, fax and Juris Number. Therefore, this information does not need to be added after each signature. Check your firm's policy.

VIII. STATEMENT OF AMOUNT IN DEMAND

According to Pbs 131 and C.G.S. sec. 52-91, a Complaint which seeks only money damages must include a separate sheet of paper entitled **Statement of Amount in Demand.**

C.G.S. sec. 52-91 requires the Statement of Amount in Demand to contain one of the following:

1. The amount, legal interest or property in demand is fifteen thousand dollars or more, exclusive of interest and costs; or

2. The amount, legal interest or property in demand is two thousand five hundred dollars or more but is less than fifteen thousand dollars, exclusive of interest and costs; or

3. The amount, legal interest or property in demand is less than two thousand-five hundred dollars, exclusive of interest and costs.

In addition, in contract cases in which the Plaintiff only seeks money damages that are less than fifteen thousand dollars, exclusive of interest and costs, the Statement of Amount in Demand should state whether or not "the remedy sought is based upon an express or implied promise to pay a definite sum."

Last, the Statement of Amount in Demand should contain a case caption at the top of the page. The attorney's signature and other information should again be stated at the bottom.

IX. CONCLUSION

A. Key Issues in This Chapter Include:

1. The *Complaint* is the first pleading to be filed in court in each lawsuit.
2. The Complaint has three parts:
a. The *case caption*: the *return date*, the parties' names, the proper judicial district, the proper court location and date of the Complaint. In almost all cases, except summary process cases, the return date *must* be a Tuesday.
b. The body, including the counts in the Complaint, followed by the attorney's signature and other identifying information;

c. The Statement of Amount in Demand, which begins with a case caption and ends with the same attorney's signature and identifying information.

B. Relevant Connecticut Practice Book Rules Include:

Pbs 7KK: Form of Pleading
Pbs 7LL: Signing of Pleading
Pbs 7Q: Time to File Appearance
Pbs 108:   General Rules of Pleading-Fact Pleading
Pbs 131:   The Complaint--Contents of Complaint
Pbs 138:   The Complaint--Separate Counts
Pbs 139:   The Complaint--Claim for Equitable Relief
Pbs 140:   The Complaint--Interest and Costs Need Not Be Claimed

C. Relevant Connecticut General Statutes Include:

C.G.S. sec. 51-344a.:   Term "judicial district of Hartford-New Britain" deemed to refer to "judicial district of Hartford" on and after September 1, 1998.
C.G.S. sec. 51-345.:   Venue in civil actions. Return of civil process.
C.G.S. sec. 51-346.:   Location in judicial district where civil process may be made returnable. Trial locations.
C.G.S. sec. 51-348.:   Geographical areas. Venue, courthouse use. Housing docket.
C.G.S. sec. 51-349.:   Where actions commenced in geographical areas.
C.G.S. sec. 51-351.:   Return to improper locations.
C.G.S. sec. 52-46.:   Time for service.
C.G.S. sec. 52-46a.:   Return of process.
C.G.S. sec. 52-48.:   Return day of process.
C.G.S. sec. 52-91.:   Pleadings; contents of Complaint.

D. Examples of Complaints

On the following pages you will find examples of three types of Complaints which will be referred to throughout the text. They involve a:
   1. personal injury auto accident;
   2. personal injury fall down, with Special Defenses; and a
   3. breach of contract/unjust enrichment, two counts.
   (This is also considered a debt collection action.)
The remaining chapters will demonstrate each step Plaintiffs and Defendants take in the litigation process. Although all pleadings should be double spaced, they are single spaced in this text and the margin are larger than permitted.

Example 1, Personal Injury: Motor Vehicle

RETURN DATE: MAY 26, 1998	:	SUPERIOR COURT*
SARAH A. DONAHUE	:	JUDICIAL DISTRICT
	:	OF TOLLAND
VS.	:	AT ROCKVILLE
RICHARD P. ANDREW	:	MAY 1, 1998

<u>**COMPLAINT**</u>

1. On September 13, 1996, at approximately 8:15 a.m., the Plaintiff, Sarah A. Donahue, was traveling in a westerly direction along Manor Avenue, a public highway in Vernon, Connecticut, near its intersection with Wolcott Street, and stopped in preparation for making a right-hand turn onto said Wolcott Street.

2. At said time and place, an automobile owned and operated by the Defendant, Richard P. Andrew, was traveling in a westerly direction along said Manor Avenue when suddenly and without warning, it collided with the rear of the Plaintiff's vehicle, causing her to suffer serious injuries and losses that are set forth below.

3. The Defendant was negligent and careless in one or more of the following ways:

a) In that he failed to keep a reasonable and proper lookout and pay attention to where he was going;

b) In that he operated said automobile at a greater rate of speed than the circumstances warranted;

c) In that he failed to sound his horn to give timely warning, or any warning whatsoever, of the impending collision;

d) In that he operated said automobile with defective or inadequate brakes or failed to apply his brakes in time to avoid said collision;

e) In that he failed to keep and operate said automobile under proper control;

f) In that he failed to turn said automobile to the left or to the right to avoid said collision;

g) In that he violated Connecticut General Statutes Sections 14-219 and 14-222 by operating said automobile without regard to the width, traffic and use of the highway, the intersection of streets and the weather conditions;

h) In that he violated Connecticut General Statutes Section 14-218a.by operating said automobile at a rate of speed greater than was reasonable, having regard to the width, traffic and use of the highway, the intersection of streets and the weather conditions;

i) In that he violated Connecticut General Statutes Section 14-240 by following the Plaintiff's automobile too closely.

4. As a direct and proximate result of the aforesaid negligence and carelessness of the Defendant, the Plaintiff suffered a cervical strain and damage to her lower back, spine, neck, chest, shoulders, right leg, right knee, right ankle and both feet, together with

aggravation of preexisting fibromyalgia. In addition, the Plaintiff suffered headaches and a severe shock to her entire nervous system. From all of the aforesaid injuries, or effects thereof, the Plaintiff has suffered and will continue to suffer pain, mental anguish, and nervousness, some of which injuries or effects thereof are, or are likely to be, permanent.

5. As a further result of the Defendant's negligence and carelessness, as aforesaid, the Plaintiff has lost wages and her earning capacity has been impaired.

6. As a further result of the Defendant's negligence and carelessness, as aforesaid, the Plaintiff has incurred expenses for ambulance, hospital care, medical care, x-rays and physical therapy, and it will be necessary for her to incur additional expense for such items in the future.

7. As a further result of the Defendant's negligence and carelessness, as aforesaid, the Plaintiff's ability to enjoy life's offering has been impaired, and will continue to be impaired.

(Separate Sheet)

WHEREFORE, the Plaintiff claims:
1. Money damages,
2. Such other relief as the Court deems fair, just and equitable.

THE PLAINTIFF
SARAH A. DONAHUE

BY _____

Christine Kulas, Esq.,
Law Offices of Christine Kulas,
her attorney
P.O. Box 2005
Ellington, CT 06066
Tele. #(860) 222-2222
Juris #989898

RETURN DATE: MAY 26, 1998   :   SUPERIOR COURT

SARAH A. DONAHUE   :   JUDICIAL DISTRICT

     :   OF TOLLAND

VS.   :   AT ROCKVILLE

RICHARD P. ANDREW   :   MAY 1, 1998

STATEMENT OF AMOUNT IN DEMAND

The amount, legal interest or property in demand is FIFTEEN THOUSAND DOLLARS or more, exclusive of interest and costs.

THE PLAINTIFF
SARAH A. DONAHUE

BY_____

Christine Kulas, Esq.,
Law Offices of Christine Kulas,
Her attorney
P.O. Box 2005
Ellington, CT 06066
Tele. #(860) 222-2222
Juris #989898

Example 2, Personal Injury: Fall Down

RETURN DATE: MARCH 31, 1998	:	SUPERIOR COURT
SHEILA WILKENSON	:	JUDICIAL DISTRICT
	:	OF FAIRFIELD
VS.	:	AT BRIDGEPORT
RYAN KEEGAN	:	MARCH 2, 1998

COMPLAINT

1. At all times relevant to this Complaint, the Defendant, Ryan Keegan, owned, occupied and controlled the premises known as 43 Camelot Court, Bridgeport, Connecticut.

2. The Defendant bought said premises during September of 1995 and personally made several renovations to the house located on the premises. These renovations included adding a second story upstairs, complete with two bedrooms and a bathroom on that second story.

3. The Plaintiff was born in Dublin, Ireland, and has lived the majority of her life there.

4. In May 1996, the Plaintiff arrived from Ireland to Connecticut for the first time in her life with her husband and two children to visit the Defendant for one week at his home at 43 Camelot Court, Bridgeport, Connecticut.

5. The Plaintiff and her family arrived at the Defendant's home on May 20, 1996. That night, the Plaintiff and her family were directed to sleep in the two upstairs bedrooms in the Defendant's residence. The Defendant slept in his bedroom downstairs.

6. During that first night, the Plaintiff left the bedroom in an attempt to utilize the bathroom facilities.

7. The Plaintiff was unable to find and turn on the hall lights due to the switch being placed at an unusual position at the bottom of the stairwell.

8. The Plaintiff attempted to open the bathroom door, which opened out into the hallway.

9. In order to open the bathroom door, the Plaintiff was compelled to step backward and fell down the stairway which was opposite the bathroom door.

10. As a result of this fall, the Plaintiff suffered serious injuries and was transported by ambulance to the hospital.

11. The Defendant acted negligently and carelessly and is responsible for the Plaintiff's injuries in one or more of the following ways in that he:

a) knew or should have known that the door to the bathroom was not constructed in accordance with building codes and created a hazard to those attempting to open it.

b) knew or should have known that the light switches were not constructed and located according to the building codes and created a hazard to those upstairs who seek to use the light for the hallway.

c) knew or should have known that the light switch in the hallway adjacent to the bathroom connected to a light found on the porch outside of the house and did not illuminate the upstairs.

d) failed to make and keep his property safe for persons, such as the Plaintiff, who he invited onto the property.

e) failed to warn the Plaintiff of the hazardous conditions then and there existing.

12. As a result of the Defendant's negligence and carelessness, the Plaintiff suffered an epidermal hematoma, multiple skull fractures involving the left skull base, the right temporal bone, nerve deafness, a traumatic brain injury and numerous other injuries involving muscles, ligaments, nerves, torn tissues, bones, joints, and discs. All of the aforesaid injuries and the affects thereof are, or are likely to be, permanent in nature.

13. As a further result of the Defendant's negligence and carelessness, as aforesaid, the Plaintiff incurred and will continue to incur expenses for medical care and attention, hospitalization, medication, x-rays, physical therapy, etc., all to her further financial loss.

14. As a further result of the negligence and carelessness of the Defendant as aforesaid, the Plaintiff has lost time and wages from her employment and her earning capacity has been greatly impaired, all to her further financial loss.

15. As a further result of the Defendant's negligence and carelessness as aforesaid, the Plaintiff has suffered great physical and mental pain and suffering.

(Separate Sheet)

WHEREFORE, the Plaintiff claims:

1. Money damages;
2. Such other relief as this Court deems fair, just and equitable.

THE PLAINTIFF
SHEILA WILKENSON

BY_____

Ann Lambert, Esq.,
Lambert and Smith, P.C.,
Her attorneys
529 Corporate Place
Fairfield, CT 04540
Tele. #(203) 777-7777
Juris # 545454

RETURN DATE: MARCH 31, 1998   :   SUPERIOR COURT
SHEILA WILKENSON   :   JUDICIAL DISTRICT
                                 :   OF FAIRFIELD
VS.   :   AT BRIDGEPORT
RYAN KEEGAN   :   MARCH 2, 1998

STATEMENT OF AMOUNT IN DEMAND

The amount, legal interest or property in demand is FIFTEEN THOUSAND DOLLARS or more, exclusive of interest and costs.

THE PLAINTIFF
SHEILA WILKENSON

BY_____

Ann Lambert, Esq.,
Lambert and Smith, P.C.,
Her attorneys
529 Corporate Place
Fairfield, CT 04540
Tele. #(203) 777-7777
Juris #545454

Example 3, Breach of Contract/Unjust Enrichment, 2 counts

RETURN DATE: FEBRUARY 24, 1998   :   SUPERIOR COURT
GEORGE SKILLMAN, ET AL.   :   JUDICIAL DISTRICT OF
    :   HARTFORD/NEW BRITAIN
VS.   :   AT HARTFORD
AUTO SERVICE CENTER, INC.   :   FEBRUARY 2, 1998

COMPLAINT

COUNT ONE

1.   The Defendant, Auto Service Center, Inc., is a Connecticut corporation with its principal place of business at 126 Maple Street, Hartford, CT.

2.   On or about September 1, 1997, the Defendant, through its duly authorized President, Joseph Kelly, executed a Promissory Note promising to pay the Plaintiffs the sum of ONE HUNDRED THOUSAND DOLLARS ($100,000.00), plus interest, pursuant to the terms of said promissory note, a copy of which is attached hereto and incorporated herein.

3.   Pursuant to the terms of said promissory note, the Defendant promised to pay the Plaintiffs in the following manner: $10,000.00 on January 15, 1998, and $10,000.00 per month, every month thereafter through and including October 15, 1998.

4.   The Defendant failed, refused, and/or neglected to pay the Plaintiffs the first payment when due and in fact has failed to make any payments due to the Plaintiffs as of the date of this Complaint.

5.   Pursuant to the terms of said promissory note, the Defendant is in Default of such terms and the entire amount of said note is now due and payable, without notice or demand, and the Defendant is liable for costs of collection, including reasonable attorney's fees.

6.   Pursuant to the terms of said promissory note, the Defendant waived presentment for payment, notice of dishonor, protest and notice of protest hereof, as well as any and all defenses on the ground of any extensions or partial payments which may be accepted by the Plaintiffs before or after Default.

7.   Pursuant to Paragraph 11 of said promissory note, the Defendant as Maker acknowledges that the loan evidenced by this note is a Commercial Transaction and waives its rights to notice and hearing under Chapter 903a of the Connecticut General Statutes, with respect to any Prejudgment Remedy which the Plaintiff Lender may desire to use.

8.   The Defendant is indebted to the Plaintiffs in the amount of $100,000.00, exclusive of interest, attorney's fees and costs of collection.

9.   The Plaintiffs have suffered damages as a result of the Defendant's actions as described herein.

COUNT TWO

1. Paragraphs One through Nine inclusive of Count One are hereby incorporated as Paragraphs One through Nine inclusive of this Count Two, and made part hereof as if more fully set forth herein.

10. The Defendant has been unjustly enriched by failing to pay the Plaintiffs the amount(s) as mentioned herein.

(Separate Sheet)

WHEREFORE, the Plaintiffs pray for the following relief:

1. Money damages, pursuant to the terms of said promissory note;
2. Attorney's fees, pursuant to the terms of said promissory note;
3. Interest and costs, pursuant to the terms of said promissory note;
4. Legal interest,
5. Costs;
6. Such other and further relief as the Court may deem equitable and just.

THE PLAINTIFFS,
GEORGE SKILLMAN AND
BARBARA SKILLMAN

BY_____

Kenneth I. Marcus, Esq.,
Friedman & Marcus, P.C.,
Their attorneys
27 Main Street
Bristol, CT 00000
Tele. #(860) 955-9595
Juris #424242

RETURN DATE: FEBRUARY 24, 1998   :   SUPERIOR COURT
GEORGE SKILLMAN, ET AL.   :   JUDICIAL DISTRICT OF
                              :   HARTFORD/NEW BRITAIN
VS.   :   AT HARTFORD
AUTO SERVICE CENTER, INC.   :   FEBRUARY 2, 1998

STATEMENT OF AMOUNT IN DEMAND

The amount, legal interest or property in demand is FIFTEEN THOUSAND DOLLARS or more, exclusive of interest and cost.

THE PLAINTIFFS,
GEORGE SKILLMAN AND
BARBARA SKILLMAN

BY_____
                Kenneth I. Marcus, Esq.,
                Friedman & Marcus, P.C.,
                Their attorneys
                27 Main Street
                Bristol, CT 00000
                Tele. #(860) 955-9595
                Juris #424242

*A copy of the promissory note would be attached if this were a real Complaint.

5 *Preparing to Serve the Complaint*

Terminology

Summons   Writ of Summons
Recognizance   Writ

Pbs: 49, 52

Introduction

Once the Complaint is finished, the Plaintiff must complete a Writ of Summons. A **Writ of Summons**, or more commonly called a **Writ** or a **Summons,** is mentioned in Pbs 49. This is a court-issued form and must accompany every Complaint. Hereinafter, it will be referred to as a Summons.

There are three types of Summons forms: one for civil actions, one for family actions and one for housing actions. Each type of form is designated in the left-hand corner of the document and they all request similar information. They can be picked up, free of charge, at the appropriate courts.

I. COMPLETING THE SUMMONS

I have divided the civil Summons into 26 parts. All the information should be typewritten, except the signatures. Find each number and examine it closely. It is extremely important to complete this form properly. Accordingly:

1. Mark the box that corresponds with your Statement of Amount in Demand.
2. Mark the JD box for civil lawsuits (not including Small Claims).
3. Type the name of the town where the courthouse is located and the telephone number.
4. Type the return date selected.

5. Type the address of the court where you will file this case.

6. Type the telephone number of the court.

7. and 8. Major and Minor: This information deals with the case type codes used by each courthouse. Turn over the Summons to find an accurate description and code for your case. A motor vehicle tort involving two drivers is V for Major and 01 for Minor.

9. Form JD-CV2 is a form used when there are more than two Plaintiffs or four Defendants. It simply gives additional space to type in their names and addresses. f needed, attach it to the Summons.

10. and 11. Type the name and address of each Plaintiff.

12. and 13. Type the name and address of each Defendant.

Note: If the Defendant is a corporation, be sure to use the proper name and address of the corporation as well as the name and address of the officer or *Agent for Service* to be served. See Chapter 6. (Only the proper corporate name is needed on the Complaint.) Furthermore, if the Defendant is an out-of-state insurance company, or otherwise involved in the insurance industry, the Connecticut Insurance Commissioner should probably be listed on the Summons as the Agent for Service. See C.G.S. sec. 38a-25 et seq. for specific details and Chapter 6.

14. Type the date of the Complaint.

15. and 16. The signature of the Plaintiff's attorney. Also, mark the Commissioner of Superior Court box. (We are not addressing pro ses in this chapter.)

17. Type the name of the attorney who signed the Summons.

18. Type the name of the Plaintiff attorney's law firm. (This is the Plaintiff's *Appearance*. See Chapter 7.)

19. Type the law firm's telephone number.

20. Type the law firm's Juris Number.

21. Pursuant to Pbs 52, this item requests information known as the recognizance or certification of financial responsibility. Its purpose is to designate a third person who will take financial responsibility for the Plaintiff, up to $250, to cover any costs that may later be taxed to the Plaintiff if he or she loses at trial and cannot pay. The Plaintiff's attorney cannot be this person. Usually, a paralegal or secretary will insert his or her name and address here. The Plaintiff's attorney will then sign at item 25. Note: Instead of the recognizance, the attorney who signs at item 14 can certify that he or she has personal knowledge as to the Plaintiff's financial responsibility and deems it sufficient.

22. State the number of Plaintiffs.

23. State the number of Defendants.

24. State the number of counts in the Complaint.

25. and 26. The attorney's signature for the recognizance. Also, mark the Commissioner of Superior Court box.

As we are not dealing with pro ses, we do not need to address the information under "If this Summons is signed by a clerk" or the box entitled "Signature of Plaintiff if pro se."

II. THE ORIGINAL AND COPIES: PREPARING THE DOCUMENTS TO BE SERVED

Note that the Summons contains an original and three copies. The instructions at the top of the sheet and at the bottom indicate that each Defendant in a lawsuit receives a copy of the Summons and the Complaint. If you need more copies of the Summons, simply photocopy the original. In addition, be sure to make a least one copy of both the Summons and the Complaint for your litigation file.

Once the copies are made, staple the *original* Summons (the top sheet) to the *original* Complaint. (They will eventually be filed in court.) The copies should be stapled in the same manner. Now it's time to serve the Defendant.

III. CONCLUSION

A. *Key Issues in This Chapter Include:*

1. At this point, the Plaintiff should be diarying important dates on his or her litigation calendar. For instance,

> **a.** the return date;
> **b.** the deadline to serve the Defendant;
> **c.** the deadline to file the original Summons and Complaint in court;
> **d.** the deadline for the Defendant to file his or her Appearance in court.

Simply write the name of the case and the purpose of the date on the calendar. Like the statute of limitation deadlines, the law firm may use more than one calendar, and may also place the deadline dates on a computer system. It doesn't matter what system is used, as long as it works.

2. Fill out the Summons completely and correctly. If the Defendant is a corporation, be sure to state the name and address of the Agent for Service or the officer of the corporation to be served, in addition to the name and address of the corporation. (See Chapter 6.)

3. Be sure to make one copy of the Summons and Complaint for each Defendant listed on the Summons.

B. *Relevant Connecticut Practice Book Sections Include:*

Pbs 49: Mesne Process
Pbs 52: Certification of Financial Responsibility

6 *Serving the Complaint and Filing the Lawsuit in Court*

Terminology

Proper Officer	High Sheriff	Deputy Sheriff
Constable	Service of Process	In Hand Service
Abode Service	Return of Service	Entry Fees
Return to Court	Affidavit	Borough Bailiff
Domestic Corporation	Agent for Service	Indifferent Person
Foreign Corporation		

Pbs: 7MM, 7SSS, 199
C.G.S. sections: 6-31 et seq., 33-660, 33-663, 33-920, 33-926, 33-929, 38a-25, 51-59,
51-347, 51-347c, 51-350, 52-46, 52-46a, 52-50, 52-56, 52-57, 52-59b,
52-62, 52-63, 52-64, 52-68, 52-69, 52-70, 52-76, 52-259, 52-259b,
52-261, 52-261a, 52-593a

Introduction

Now that the Plaintiff has completed the Summons and Complaint and made sufficient copies of both, he or she must contact the **proper officer** to properly **serve** the Defendant with a *copy* of these documents. After the Defendant is served, the Plaintiff must timely file the *original*s, along with a **Return of Service** and **entry fee**, at the appropriate Superior Court.

I. SERVICE OF PROCESS: GENERALLY

Service of process is the term used to address delivering a copy of the Summons and Complaint to a Defendant. It is also called "serving the Defendant." The purpose of

51

serving a Defendant is to ensure that he or she receives adequate notice of the lawsuit and the opportunity to present a defense.

A. Deadline to Serve Defendants

Pursuant to C.G.S. sec. 52-46, all Defendants listed on the Summons must be served no later than **12 days** before the return date.

B. Types of Service

According to C.G.S. sec. 52-57(a), a Defendant who is an *individual* and who is a *resident* of Connecticut should be served **in hand**, or at his or her usual place of **abode** in this state. Corporations, partnerships, associations and nonresidents are discussed later in this chapter.

In hand service is exactly what it sounds like: The officer personally meets the Defendant and hands him or her a copy of the Summons and Complaint.

Abode service is made when a copy of the Summons and Complaint is left inside the Defendant's home or other place where he or she is most likely to have knowledge of a service. Abode service can be accomplished by handing the documents to someone other than the Defendant who opens the door to the Defendant's abode, or by slipping the copies under the Defendant's door. Abode service cannot be made by leaving the copies in a mailbox or by nailing them to the Defendant's door, unless the court orders otherwise.

Plaintiffs prefer in hand service. That way, Defendants can't claim they didn't live at the address where abode service was made, or that they never received the documents. Remember, no one is happy to be sued. If Defendants can find a way to delay the process until after the statute of limitations has expired, they will.

II. STEPS INVOLVED IN SERVICE OF PROCESS

Each of the following steps is discussed below:
1. Selecting and contacting a proper officer;
2. Properly and timely serving the Defendant;
3. Receiving a Return of Service from the officer to prove that the Defendant was properly served a copy of the required documents.

A. Different Kinds of Proper Officers

Pursuant to C.G.S. sec. 52-50, **service of process**, or serving the Defendant, must be made by a **proper officer**. A proper officer can be a **sheriff**, a **deputy sheriff**, **constable, borough bailiff**, and in some instances, an **indifferent person**. It's the Plaintiff's choice. Please note, however, that service is usually performed by sheriffs, their deputies or constables. See the applicable parts of C.G.S. sec. 52-50 if you are interested in service made by an indifferent person (see also page 223) or borough bailiff.

1. The Sheriff's Department

Sheriffs and their deputy sheriffs have authority to serve legal documents to Defendants who are located anywhere within a specific county. There are eight counties in Connecticut. Each county has its own sheriff who is elected every four years. In many counties, this person is referred to as the High Sheriff. His or her responsibilities are listed in C.G.S. sec. 6-31 et seq. and include maintaining courthouse security, prisoner transportation and serving legal documents in the county that elected them. To assist with these responsibilities, High Sheriffs appoint several deputy sheriffs to work throughout the county. In order to simplify the terminology in this text, we will use the term sheriff to include High Sheriffs and deputy sheriffs.

2. Constables

Constables are elected every two years by the city or town in which they run. Once elected, constables are authorized to serve legal documents only in the town or city that elected them.

B. Selecting a Proper Sheriff to Make Service

In most cases, Defendants are served where they live or where they work. Therefore:

1. If a Defendant lives and works in Hartford county, the Plaintiff should contact a sheriff in Hartford County to serve the Defendant at either location.

2. If the Defendant lives in Hartford County, but works in New Haven County, the Plaintiff should select a sheriff from either Hartford County or a New Haven County to make service. The decision depends upon which county the Defendant will be served in. Oftentimes, it is easier finding a Defendant at work rather than at his or her abode. It depends upon the circumstances in each case.

C. Selecting the Proper Constable to Make Service

If a Plaintiff believes a Defendant can be served in a particular city or town, he or she may contact a constable elected to make service in that city or town.

D. Exceptions

C.G.S. sec. 52-56 permits a sheriff or constable to make service outside his or her precinct in the following situations:

1. In cases involving more than one Defendant, if the officer can properly begin service in his or her precinct, then he or she can serve the remaining Defendants in any other precinct. For example: Presume a case involved three Defendants.

One Defendant lives and works in New Britain which is part of Hartford County, another lives and works in Litchfield County and the other lives and works in Middlesex County. The Plaintiff may select a sheriff from any of the three counties as follows:

    a. If a sheriff from Hartford County is used, the sheriff must first make service upon the Defendant in Hartford County. Then, he or she may serve the remaining Defendants anywhere.

    b. If a constable is used, the Plaintiff may select a constable who has jurisdiction in one of the cities or towns where one of the Defendants would be served, for instance, New Britain. Once service is made in New Britain (by a New Britain constable), the constable may leave his or her city and serve the remaining two Defendants elsewhere.

2. Any sheriff or constable from any precinct may make service upon the Connecticut Secretary of the State or the Commissioner of Motor Vehicles, if service is being made pursuant to C.G.S. sec. 52-57, 52-59b, 52-62 or 52-63.

As always, be sure to review the applicable statutes before service is made. Some technicalities come into play when attachments or garnishees are involved.

E. How to Contact the Proper Sheriff or Constable

As stated earlier, service of process is an extremely important part of the litigation process. Therefore, the Plaintiff must select a sheriff or constable who is competent and capable of properly performing this function. Otherwise, the Plaintiff's case may be dismissed. (See Chapter 10.)

Each courthouse usually has a list of sheriffs and their deputies authorized to make service in the county where the courthouse is located. A list of constables can be found at the applicable town or city hall. In addition, the Plaintiff may:

    1. Call the sheriff's department in the appropriate county. Someone there will provide a list of available sheriffs to contact. For constables, call the applicable city or town hall.

    2. Mail or hand deliver the copies to the Sheriff's Department. Someone there will then forward them to the sheriff in that county.

    3. Obtain a copy of a *current* State of Connecticut Register and find the names and addresses of the High Sheriff and the deputies listed in the appropriate county, or the constables listed in the appropriate city or town.

    4. Contact an acquaintance in the legal profession and ask them the names of reliable and competent sheriffs and constables they work with.

After selecting an appropriate sheriff or constable, the Plaintiff should contact him or her by telephone as soon as possible to determine if he or she is available to serve the Defendant at least 12 days before the return date. If not, the Plaintiff should quickly contact someone else.

F. Providing Instructions to a Sheriff or Constable

Once the sheriff or constable is contacted, the Plaintiff should do the following:
1. Make arrangements for the officer to receive the original documents and necessary copies.
2. Specify what type of service the Plaintiff wants, in hand or abode.
3. Be sure the officer is aware of the return date.
4. Determine who will file the original documents in court: the Plaintiff or the officer, as described in Section III below.

Many law offices put the information listed above in a letter to the sheriff or constable. Those officers who frequently work for a Plaintiff's office will usually come to the office to pick up the documents. Out-of-county sheriffs or out-of-town constables may ask the Plaintiff to mail them the documents or hand deliver them. This decision depends on how quickly service must be made. If I'm working with an officer for the first time, I may hand deliver the documents and meet him or her personally to discuss how service should be made and who will be filing the documents in court. That way, there is less chance for error.

Provide the officer with as much information about the Defendant as possible. For instance, his or her age, sex, physical description, where he or she works and the hours, what kind of car he or she drives, date of birth, social security number, etc. If the case involves a police report, the Plaintiff should give the officer a copy. It provides a lot of this information, and possibly more.

If the officer is having difficulty serving the Defendant, the officer can use the information mentioned above to request the Department of Motor Vehicles to verify the Defendant's address and type of vehicle that is registered to him or her. The officer can then drive by the home or place of employment and keep an eye out for the Defendant's car.

G. Officer's Return of Service

After the Defendant is served, the officer must complete a **Return of Service**. (It is also called an affidavit of service, or a Sheriff's Return, a Constable's Return, etc.)

The purpose of the Return of Service is to prove that a Defendant was properly served. As a result, the Defendant has received proper notice of the lawsuit and is aware of his or her responsibilities as stated on the Summons.

The contents of a Return of Service should include:
> **1.** the name of each Defendant served and the address where each Defendant was served;
> **2.** the type of service made: in hand or abode;
> **3.** a list of the type of documents served on each Defendant;
> **4.** a statement that the documents served were "verified true and attested" copies of the original documents;

5. the officer's signature.

Caution: It is extremely important that Plaintiffs review the Return of Service before filing the documents in court. Sheriffs and constables are human, just like everybody else. If there is an error in the Return itself, or in the way service was made, it's best to correct the error as soon as possible. Otherwise, the case may be subject to a Motion to Dismiss.

H. Fees for Service

Consult C.G.S. sec. 52-70, 52-261 and 52-261a for allowable fees and expenses officers may charge to make service. In addition, C.G.S. sec. 52-259b addresses obtaining a waiver of fees and costs for indigent clients.

III. FILING A LAWSUIT IN COURT

A. Deadline to File Lawsuits in Court: Six Days Before the Return Date

Pursuant to C.G.S. sec. 52-46a, the original Summons, Complaint, Return of Service and **entry fee** must be filed in court, at least *six days* before the return date. This means the documents should be filed in the proper court no later than 4:59 p.m., on the Wednesday before the Tuesday return date. (See Appendix B and C and C.G.S. sec. 51-347 for JD court locations and C.G.S. sec. 51-350 for GA court locations.)

B. The Clerk's Office

According to Pbs 7SSS, the clerk's office in each courthouse is open to file documents from 9:00 a.m. to 5:00 p.m., Monday through Friday, except for legal holidays. If the clerk's office is not open on the last day a document must be filed, that document may be filed on the next day the clerk's office is open for business. See also C.G.S. sec. 51-59 and 51-347c.

Note that many clerk's offices throughout the state are closed to the public from 1:00 p.m. until 2:30 p.m. and then again from 4:00 p.m. to 5:00 p.m. for most services other than filing documents.

Pbs 7MM states that when a document is **filed** in court, the clerk will enter the time and date on the document. No document is officially filed without this endorsement, also called a court stamp.

C. Filing Documents

Anyone may file documents in court. Many law offices that have established relationships with sheriffs and constables have no difficulty entrusting those officers with this task. In that situation, the law firm will give the officer a check for the **entry fee** when he or she receives the Summons and Complaint to be served. Pursuant to a new bill, this fee is $185 for cases seeking more than $2,500 in damages. (This new bill amends the language found in C.G.S. sec. 52-259 regarding court fees.) After making service, many officers will fax or deliver the Return of Service to the law office. Once the Return is approved, they file everything in court by the deadline.

On the other hand, to reduce the risk of error, some offices insist that their staff file all their cases in court themselves. Attorneys and staff at busy litigation firms frequently find themselves in court on a regular basis anyway. Therefore, it is no trouble to simply stop by and file the documents at the clerk's office on or before the deadline.

Last, a case may also be filed by sending all the documents to the court by mail. In these situations, it is common for the law firm to send a copy of the Summons and Complaint, along with a self-addressed stamped envelope and letter, asking the clerk to stamp the copy and send it back to the law firm. This is known as a *court stamped copy* and provides proof that the clerk's office received the original documents and filed them, if the issue ever arises.

Regardless of how a lawsuit is filed, be sure all the documents and the entry fee are ***filed in court at least six days before the return date.*** Once the lawsuit is filed, the Prelitigation Stage ends and the Pretrial Stage begins. Before going further, however, let's address the specific types of Defendants described below.

IV. SERVING THE STATE OF CONNECTICUT

Pursuant to C.G.S. sec. 52-64, if the State of Connecticut is the Defendant, service should be made at the Office of the Connecticut Attorney General which is located in Hartford. This includes any case in which any state institution, board, commission, department or administrative tribunal or agency officer, servant, agent or employer of the above is a Defendant.

V. SERVING CONNECTICUT MUNICIPALITIES AND CORPORATIONS

A. Connecticut Municipalities

Connecticut municipalities include towns, cities and boroughs, school districts and municipal corporations.

1. Towns: C.G.S. sec. 52-57(b)(1) states that service should be made upon the following:
> **a.** the town clerk; or
> **b.** assistant clerk; or
> **c.** its manager; or
> **d.** one of its selectmen.

2. Cities: C.G.S. sec. 52-57(b)(2) states that service should be made upon the following:
> **a.** the clerk; or
> **b.** assistant clerk; or

    c. the mayor; or
    d. the manager.

3. Boroughs: C.G.S. sec. 52-57(b)(3) states that service should be made upon the following:
    a. the manager; or
    b. the clerk; or
    c. the assistant clerk; or
    d. the warden or one of its burgesses.

4. School Districts: C.G.S. sec. 52-57(b)(4) states that service should be made upon the following:
    a. the clerk; or
    b. one of its committee.

5. Other municipal and quasi-municipal corporations:
C.G.S. sec. 52-57(b)(5) states that service should be made upon:
    a. the clerk; or
    b. the chief presiding officer; or
    c. the managing agent.

B. Private Connecticut Corporations

A private Connecticut corporation is formed under the laws of Connecticut. These corporations are also called domestic corporations.

The Connecticut Secretary of the State's Office, located at 30 Trinity Street in Hartford, Connecticut, contains a wealth of information about businesses incorporated in this state. This information includes the names and addresses of all the corporation's officers and directors, its **Agent for Service**, etc.

A Connecticut corporation may be served in one of two ways: by serving its Agent for Service, or by serving specific officers, directors or employees.

1. Agents for Service: C.G.S. sec. 33-660

Pursuant to C.G.S. sec. 33-660, each corporation should appoint an Agent for Service. An Agent for Service is a person or corporation who agrees to be served on behalf of a specific corporation. He or she may be:
    a. a natural person who is a resident of Connecticut; or
    b. a domestic corporation; or
    c. a corporation not organized under the laws of Connecticut, but that has a Certificate of Authority to transact business or conduct its affairs in Connecticut.

It is common for a corporation's attorney to be appointed as an Agent for Service. Once served, the Agent for Service will notify the corporation of the lawsuit.

According to C.G.S. sec. 33-633(a), Agents for Service may be served in the following ways:

> **a.** if the Agent for Service is a natural person, he or she may be served in hand or at his or her abode;
>
> **b.** if the Agent for Service is a corporation, service can be made by leaving the process as described below pursuant to C.G.S. sec. 52-57(c).

Note that if there is no Agent for Service, or if for some reason the Agent cannot be served, C.G.S. sec. 33-633(b) permits service by sending a copy of the process to the corporation's secretary at its principal office, by registered or certified mail, return receipt requested. Check the statute for more specifics. As an alternative, however, service may be made upon the corporation's officers or employees as described below.

2. Serving Specific Officers or Employees: C.G.S. sec. 52-57

C.G.S. sec. 52-57(c) permits service of a Connecticut corporation by serving the following corporate officers, directors or employees (in hand or abode):

> **a.** president, vice president, or assistant vice president; or
> **b.** secretary or assistant secretary; or
> **c.** treasurer or assistant treasurer; or
> **d.** cashier or assistant cashier; or
> **e.** teller or assistant teller; or
> **f.** general or managing agent or manager; or
> **g.** any director who is a Connecticut resident; or
> **h.** any person in charge of the business of the corporation; or
> **i.** any person who is at the time of service in charge of the office of the corporation in the town in which its principal office or place of business is located.

VI. SERVING CONNECTICUT PARTNERSHIPS AND ASSOCIATIONS

A. Connecticut Partnerships

C.G.S. sec. 52-57(d) states that service in Connecticut should be made in hand or abode, upon any one of the partners.

If none of the partners are Connecticut residents, the officer should:

1. make service, at least 12 days before the return date, upon the Connecticut Secretary of the State by leaving a copy of the Summons and Complaint, along with the fee; and

2. send by registered or certified mail, postage prepaid, return receipt requested, to the last known address of every partner named in the Summons who was not personally served; and

3. include a statement of this mailing and receipt in his or her Return of Service.

B. Connecticut Voluntary Associations

C.G.S. sec. 52-57(e) states that service in Connecticut should be made upon:

1. the presiding officer; or

2. the secretary; or

3. the treasurer.

If all the above are not residents of Connecticut, and the association does business in Connecticut or carries out its operations or functions in Connecticut, the officer should make service in the following manner:

a. at least 12 days before the return date, leave a copy of the Summons and Complaint, along with a $25 fee, at the Secretary of the State's Office; and

b. at least 12 days before the return date, mail a copy of the above to one of the above-named persons, by registered or certified mail, postage prepaid, return receipt requested.

Note: Consult C.G.S. sec. 52-76, Actions by and against Voluntary Associations, before commencing suit.

VII. SERVING FOREIGN CORPORATIONS

A. Authority to Transact Business in Connecticut

Foreign corporations are corporations formed in another state, under the laws of another state. Pursuant to C.G.S. sec. 33-920 et seq., in order to legally transact business in Connecticut, these corporations must file all the appropriate documents and pay a fee required by the Connecticut Secretary of the State's Office.

Like Connecticut corporations, each foreign corporation should provide the Connecticut Secretary of State's office with the following information:

1. the name and address of its principal place of business; and

2. the names and addresses of its directors and officers; and

3. pursuant to C.G.S. sec. 33-926, the name and address of the Agent for Service appointed in Connecticut to accept service on its behalf.

B. Suing Foreign Corporations

C.G.S. sec. 33-929(e) permits a resident of Connecticut or a person having a usual place of business in Connecticut to sue a foreign corporation under the following circumstances:

1. whether or not the foreign corporation currently transacts business in Connecticut or has transacted business in Connecticut; or

2. whether or not the foreign corporation is exclusively engaged in interstate or foreign commerce and if the cause of action arises out of the following:

> **a.** a contract made in Connecticut or to be performed in Connecticut;
>
> **b.** "business solicited in Connecticut by mail or otherwise, if the corporation has repeatedly so solicited business, whether the orders or offers relating thereto were accepted within or without the state";
>
> **c.** if the corporation distributed, produced or manufactured goods that are to be used or consumed in Connecticut and are so used or consumed, "regardless of how or where the goods were produced, manufactured, marketed or sold or whether or not through the medium of independent contractors or dealers";
>
> **d.** from tortious conduct in Connecticut, "whether arising out of repeated activity or single acts, and whether arising out of misfeasance or nonfeasance."

C. The Agent for Service of a Foreign Corporation

An Agent for Service of a foreign corporation may be one of the following:

1. An individual who resides in Connecticut and whose business office is identical with the registered office; or

2. A domestic corporation or not-for-profit domestic corporation; or

3. A foreign not-for-profit corporation authorized to transact business in Connecticut whose business office is identical to the registered office; or

4. Pursuant to C.G.S. sec. 33-660, the foreign corporation may appoint the Connecticut Secretary of the State's Office as its Agent for Service.

D. Serving a Foreign Corporation

1. C.G.S. sec. 52-57(c) states that service can be made upon a foreign corporation's officers, etc., as stated above; or

2. C.G.S. sec. 33-929(b) permits service in the same manner as described above upon the corporation's Agent for Service, unless the Agent for Service is the Connecticut Secretary of the State's Office.

If the Agent for Service is the Connecticut Secretary of the State's Office, C.G.S. sec. 33-929(b) directs the officer to leave two copies of the Summons and

Complaint at the Secretary of the State's Office, with the required fee, or mail the copies to that office, by registered or certified mail, return receipt requested.

VIII. SERVING THE INSURANCE COMMISSIONER

See C.G.S. sec. 38a-25 et seq. regarding when the Connecticut Insurance Commissioner is an Agent for Service, or should otherwise be served a copy of the Summons and Complaint, and how to make service.

IX. WHEN A DEFENDANT CANNOT BE LOCATED: MOTOR VEHICLE ACCIDENTS

What can an officer do if he or she cannot locate an individual Defendant? If the cause of action involves a motor vehicle accident, C.G.S. sec. 52-63 permits service to be made in the following manner:

1. At least 12 days before the return date, leave a copy of the Summons and Complaint, along with a $25 fee, at the office of the Commissioner of Motor Vehicles; and

2. At least 12 days before the return date, send by registered or certified mail, postage prepaid and return receipt requested, a copy of the Summons and Complaint to the Defendant at his or her last address on file at DMV; and

3. Include in the Return of Service that he or she made a "diligent effort to obtain service at the address of the owner and/or operator on file in the motor vehicle department and has been unable to make such service."

The same provisions of C.G.S. sec. 52-63 apply if the Defendant owner or operator moved out of Connecticut after the accident, but before the Plaintiff began the action. In addition, see Pbs 199 and Chapter 14 for Applications of Orders of Notice.

X. SERVING NONRESIDENT DEFENDANTS

A. *When a Motor Vehicle Accident Is Not Involved*

If a nonresident individual or partnership is a Defendant and falls under the list in C.G.S. sec. 52-59b, as stated above, (but the case does not involve a motor vehicle accident) the officer should make service according to C.G.S. sec. 52-59b(c):

1. within 12 days before the return date, by leaving a copy of the Summons and Complaint, along with a $25 filing fee, at the Connecticut Secretary of the State's Office; *unless* the cause of action involves a motor vehicle accident; and

2. within 12 days before the return date, by sending, by registered or certified mail, return receipt requested, a copy of the Summons and Complaint to the Defendant at his or her last known address.

B. *When a Motor Vehicle Accident Is Involved:*

If the Defendant is not a Connecticut resident, service should be made upon the Commissioner of Motor Vehicles, as described in C.G.S. sec. 52-63 and confirmed in C.G.S. sec. 52-62.

XI. SERVING DECEASED DEFENDANTS

If the Defendant dies before the Plaintiff commences suit, the Plaintiff must serve the Defendant's executor, administrator or other legal representative. This information can usually be found at the probate court in the town or city where the Defendant resided before his or her death. See C.G.S. sec. 52-69.

XII. SERVICE AND THE STATUTE OF LIMITATIONS

A Defendant must be served before the statute of limitations expires. The only exception to this requirement can be found in C.G.S. sec. 52-593a. This statute allows the Defendant to be served after the statute of limitations expires if:

1. the Summons and Complaint are delivered to the officer or his or her office **before** the expiration of the statute of limitations; and
2. service is made upon the Defendant **within 15 days of such delivery**; and
3. in the Return of Service, the officer states the date he or she received the documents to make service.

This requirement is usually accomplished by an **affidavit**. An affidavit is a written statement an individual swears to or affirms, under oath. (Note that this section does not apply to an appeal from an administrative agency governed by C.G.S. sec. 4-183.)

XIII. UNKNOWN INTERESTED PARTIES

C.G.S. sec. 52-68 addresses the steps a Plaintiff should take if he or she believes there are other potential parties to an action who are unknown. This statute, along with Pbs 199, Applications for Order of Notice, is addressed in Chapter 14.

XIV. CONCLUSION

A. *Key Issues in This Chapter Include:*

1. *Deadlines to Remember*

> **a.** the Defendant must be served *a verified, true and attested copy* of the original Summons and Complaint at least *12 days* before the return date. (C.G.S. sec. 52-46.)

b. the Defendant must be served prior to the expiration of the statute of limitations, with one exception: If the officer receives all the documents to be served prior to the expiration of the statute of limitations, he or she may serve the Defendant within *15 days* of such receipt. (C.G.S. sec. 52-593a.)

c. the Plaintiff must file the *original* Summons and Complaint, along with the Return of Service and the entry fee, at the proper Superior Court at least *6 days* before the return date. This means no later than Wednesday before the Tuesday return date. (C.G.S. sec. 52-46a.) Once the case is filed in court, the Prelitigation Stage ends and we enter the Pretrial Stage.

2. Who May Serve a Summons and Complaint

a. the *High Sheriff, deputy sheriffs, constables, borough bailiffs* and, in some cases, an *indifferent person*, may serve a Defendant with a Summons and Complaint.

b a High Sheriff's authority to make service is limited to the county that elected him or her. A deputy sheriff's authority is limited to the same county as the High Sheriff who appointed him or her.

c. a constable's authority to make service is limited to the city or town that elected him or her.

d. exceptions:

i. When there is more than one Defendant in a case, a sheriff or constable who serves one of the Defendants in his or her own precinct may then serve the remaining Defendants anywhere in the state. (Check C.G.S. sec. 52-56 to determine what constitutes service.)

ii. Any sheriff or constable may serve the Commissioner of Motor Vehicles and the Connecticut Secretary of the State's Office.

3. Assisting the Officer

Remember, always take all steps necessary to assist the sheriff or constable in making service upon a Defendant. In addition, if the officer is having trouble locating the Defendant, the Plaintiff may change the return date on all of the documents to give the officer more time to make service. Just be careful the statute of limitations does not expire.

4. Making Service Pursuant to C.G.S. sec. 52-593a

If the statute of limitations may expire before the officer can serve the Defendant, follow the requirements in C.G.S. sec. 52-593a.

B. Relevant Connecticut Practice Book Sections Include:

Pbs 7MM: Filing and Endorsing Pleadings
Pbs 7SSS: Clerks' Officers
Pbs 199:   Applications for Orders of Notice

C. Relevant Connecticut General Statutes Include:

C.G.S. sec. 6-31 et seq.:	Authority (Sheriffs).
C.G.S. sec. 33-660.:	Registered office and registered agent.
C.G.S. sec. 33-663.:	Service of process on corporation.
C.G.S. sec. 33-920.:	Authority to transact business required.
C.G.S. sec. 33-926.:	Registered office and registered agent of foreign corporation.
C.G.S. sec. 33-929.:	Service of process on foreign corporation.
C.G.S. sec. 38a-25 et seq.:	Insurance Commissioner as agent for service of process.
C.G.S. sec. 51-59.:	Clerk's office, when open.
C.G.S. sec. 51-347.:	Where writs may be filed.
C.G.S. sec. 51-347c.:	Last day for filing next business day if clerk's office is closed.
C.G.S. sec. 51-350:	Filing in a geographical area.
C.G.S. sec. 52-46.:	Time for service.
C.G.S. sec. 52-46a.:	Return of process.
C.G.S. sec. 52-50.:	Persons to whom process shall be directed.
C.G.S. sec. 52-56.:	Service of process out of officer's precinct.
C.G.S. sec. 52-57.:	Manner of service upon individuals, municipalities, corporations, partnerships and voluntary associations.
C.G.S. sec. 52-59b.:	Jurisdiction of courts over nonresidents and foreign partnerships. Service of process.
C.G.S. sec. 52-62.:	Service upon nonresident in action for negligent operation of motor vehicle.
C.G.S. sec. 52-63.:	Service upon motor vehicle operator or owner not found at his recorded address.
C.G.S. sec. 52-64.:	Service in action against state.
C.G.S. sec. 52-68.:	Notice to nonresident adverse or interested parties and interested parties unknown to plaintiff.
C.G.S. sec. 52-69.:	Notice to "representatives and creditors," "widow" or "widower" and "heirs".
C.G.S. sec. 52-70.:	Endorsement on process for fees. Penalty for exacting illegal fees.
C.G.S. sec. 52-76.:	Actions by and against associations.
C.G.S. sec. 52-259.:	Court fees.
C.G.S. sec. 52-259b.: for	Waiver of fees and payment of the cost of service of process indigent party.
C.G.S. sec. 52-261.:	Fees and expenses of sheriffs, deputies and constables.
C.G.S. sec. 52-261a.:	Fees and expenses of sheriffs, deputies and constables serving

	process for the Judicial Department or Division of Criminal Justice.
C.G.S. sec. 52-593a.:	Right of action not lost where process served after statutory period.

At the end of this chapter, you will find a sample letter to an officer and three examples of Returns of Service.

Finally, don't forget to check the current Connecticut General Statutes regarding service to verify that all the information in this chapter is accurate.

Example 1, Letter to Deputy Sheriff

CHRISTINE KULAS
ATTORNEY AT LAW
P.O. BOX 2005
ELLINGTON, CT 06066
(860) 222-2222

May 1, 1998
Deputy Sheriff Alex J. Zaniewski
Tolland County
P.O. 545
Vernon, CT 06340

RE: SARAH A. DONAHUE VS. RICHARD P. ANDREW
          (Defendant's operator #111111111)

Dear Deputy Sheriff Zaniewski:

Enclosed please find the original Summons and Complaint, along with a copy of each to be served upon the Defendant, Richard P. Andrew, in the above-captioned case.

As stated on the Summons, Mr. Andrew lives at 329 Lakeside Blvd., Rockville, CT. Please try to make in hand service. Service should be made by Thursday, May 14, 1998.This case involves an automobile accident between the Plaintiff and the Defendant. I have attached a copy of the Police Accident Report which will provide you with additional information about Mr. Andrew.

After serving the Defendant, please return the original Summons and Complaint, along with your Return of Service, by Monday, May 18, 1998.

Thank you for your assistance with this matter. Do not hesitate to contact me should you have any questions or concerns.

Sincerely,

Christine Kulas
encl.

Example 2, Return of Service, abode

STATE OF CONNECTICUT   )

)   ss: Bridgeport   March 3, 1998

COUNTY OF FAIRFIELD   )

Then and there by virtue hereof, on March 3, 1998, in the city of Bridgeport, County of Fairfield, I left at the usual place of abode of Ryan Keegan, the within named Defendant, 43 Camelot Court, Bridgeport, CT, a true and attested verified copy of the original Writ,* Summons and Complaint, with my endorsement thereon.

The within and foregoing is the original Writ, Summons and Complaint, with my doings thereon endorsed.

ATTEST

Barry Smith
Deputy Sheriff
Fairfield County

Fees:
Pages:	6.00
Ends.:	2.00
Service:	20.00
Travel:	2.00
Total	$30.00

*Please note that while the terms Writ and Summons are often used interchangeably, it is common for a Return of Service to state, "Writ, Summons and Complaint."

Example 3, Return of Service, in hand

STATE OF CONNECTICUT   )
)   ss: Hartford   February 4, 1998
COUNTY OF HARTFORD   )

Then and there by virtue hereof, on February 4, 1998, in the city of Hartford, County of Hartford, I left within and in the hands of Joseph Kelly, President, Auto Services Center, Inc., the within named Defendant, 126 Maple Street, Hartford, CT, a true and attested, verified copy of the original Writ, Summons and Complaint with my endorsement thereon.

The within and foregoing is the original Writ, Summons and Complaint, with my doings thereon endorsed.

ATTEST

Robert Matthew
Deputy Sheriff
Hartford County

Fees:
Pages: 5.00
Ends.:   2.00
Service: 20.00
Travel: 2.00
Total $29.00

Example 4, Service made pursuant to C.G.S. sec. 52-593a

In addition to a Return of Service, the following affidavit must be included if the documents were delivered to the officer before the expiration of the statute of limitations expired, and service was made within 15 days of delivery, but after the statute of limitations expired.

Case Caption

AFFIDAVIT OF SERVICE

STATE OF CONNECTICUT   )
)   ss: HARTFORD

COUNTY OF HARTFORD   )

The undersigned, being duly sworn, deposes and says:

1. I am over the age of 18 years and understand the obligation of an oath.

2. I am a Deputy Sheriff for the County of Hartford.

3. On _____, the original Writ, Summons and Complaint and copies in the above-entitled action were personally delivered to me for service.

4. In accordance with Connecticut General Statute Sec. 52-593a, I made service upon the Defendant within 15 days of said receipt of said Writ, Summons and Complaint, on _____.

                               _____
                                 Name
                                 Deputy Sheriff
                                 County

Subscribed and sworn to before me on _____, 1998.

                               _____
                                 Notary Public (or)
                                 Commissioner of the Superior Court

7 *The Pretrial Stage: The Appearance*

Terminology

Appearance	In Addition To...	In Lieu Of...

Pbs: 7P, 7Q, 7R, 7S, 7W

Introduction

Up until this point, we have been addressing the Prelitigation Stage, where the litigation burdens have been placed almost exclusively upon the Plaintiff. Now we are entering the Pretrial Stage which encompasses specific *pleadings* and *discovery*. At this juncture, the litigation burdens shift to the Defendant. A Defendant who intends to present a defense to the lawsuit must begin to file various documents in court in a timely manner.

I. THE APPEARANCE

In spite of its title, an Appearance is actually a court-issued form. No one needs to physically show up in court. The purpose of an Appearance is to identify the names of the attorneys and pro ses involved in a case.

Defense attorneys (and pro se Defendants) can obtain a blank Appearance form from any courthouse. The forms are usually pink and are free of charge. Most law firms keep extras on file and may include them in the forms section on their computer systems.

Pbs 7Q and 7S require Defendants to file an Appearance in the proper court *within two days after the return date*. The court and its address is listed on their copy of the Summons, which also informs them of this filing requirement. Hence, Defendants have approximately two weeks from being served to find an attorney to represent them.

Pursuant to Pbs 7P, the Plaintiff's Appearance is incorporated into the Summons. (Note that Pbs 7P uses the term "Writ" instead of Summons.) There, the Plaintiff discloses the attorney's individual name, the name and mailing address of the law firm, the telephone number and the Juris Number (items 18, 19, 20 and 21 of the Summons).

II. THE DEFENDANT'S APPEARANCE

The Appearance is fairly basic and seeks the information stated below, as required by Pbs 7P. Using a typewriter, all Defendants (whether represented by an attorney or pro se) at this stage of the lawsuit must to complete the majority of the 22 items described below.

1. Docket Number or Return Date: At this point, Defendants usually do not know the docket number because they have not been receiving court correspondence. They can call the court for the docket number or simply fill in the return date found on the Summons and Complaint;

2. Name of Case: See the Summons and the case caption on the Complaint. (You only need the first-named Plaintiff and the first-named Defendant. Use et al., if applicable.);

3. Mark the appropriate box: JD, housing session or GA and number from the Summons;

4. The full address of the court listed on the Summons;

5. The name of the law firm representing the Defendant or the Defendant's name, if pro se;

6. The law firm's street or P.O. box address;

7. The law firm's Juris Number;

8. The law firm's city or town;

9. The law firm's state;

10. The law firm's zip code;

11. The law firm's telephone number;

12. Mark the box for "The Defendant" (for cases that have one Defendant). The remaining selections will be discussed further below;

13. & 14. Skip for now;

15. The signature of an attorney at the law firm. This attorney signs on behalf of the law firm in item 5 above;

16. The typed name of the individual attorney who signed item 15.

17. The date the Appearance is signed;

18-22. Skip for now;

Once the court receives an Appearance, the information contained therein is entered into the computer system. From that point on, all court correspondence will be mailed to the attorneys and pro ses listed on the Appearances.

In addition, within approximately three weeks after an Appearance is filed, the court will send a notice to all appearing attorneys and pro ses, listing all of their names and addresses. Parties who did not yet appear are listed as such. The court will send a new notice to all attorneys and pro ses of record whenever a new Appearance is filed. (See Section III below.)

In addition to providing necessary information, a Defendant who files an Appearance in court is telling the court that he or she is aware of the lawsuit. This does not, however, prevent the Defendant from later filing a Motion to Dismiss pursuant to Pbs 142. (See Chapter 10)

III. OTHER REASONS TO FILE AN APPEARANCE

A. *Multiple Plaintiffs and Defendants*

Note that item 12 of the Appearance refers to Plaintiffs as well as Defendants. Each individual client is entitled to have an attorney. On the other hand, one attorney can represent a group of Plaintiffs or a group of Defendants, providing there is no conflict of interest. It depends upon the nature of the case.

Accordingly, when more than one Plaintiff or Defendant is involved in a case, the attorneys filing their Appearances must designate which party they represent by marking the appropriate box found in item 12 and filling in the name of their client. If one attorney represents all the Defendants or all the Plaintiffs, then he or she would mark the box for "All Defendants" or "All Plaintiffs."

B. *New Attorneys: "In lieu of"*

Item 13 addresses the fact that parties sometimes change attorneys. The reasons vary: personality conflicts, inability to pay high fees, more confidence in another attorney, an attorney requests the client to find a replacement, etc. In addition, pro ses can decide to hire an attorney, rather than continue to represent themselves. Or, clients can fire their attorney and decide to represent themselves pro se.

Pursuant to Pbs 7W, if, during the course of a lawsuit, any party obtains a new attorney to replace the one currently on file in court, that new attorney must file his or her own Appearance. (Note that a new attorney at the same law firm does not need a new Appearance.) In this situation, the new attorney must complete the Appearance and:

1. mark the applicable box in item 12 (who the attorney or pro se represents); and

2. mark item 13, "In lieu of appearance of attorney or firm;" and

3. fill in the name of original attorney or firm already on file; and

4. complete items 18-22:

> **18.** Mark the "in lieu of" box;
>
> **19.** The signature of the new attorney;
>
> **20.** The date copies of the Appearance were mailed to the attorney being replaced;
>
> **21.** The name of the party the copy of the Appearance was mailed or delivered to;
>
> **22.** The address where the copy was mailed or delivered.

5. Mail or hand deliver a copy of the Appearance to the attorney or firm being replaced.

Under Pbs 7W, the attorney being replaced has ten days from the time the new Appearance is filed to file an objection. If no objection is filed, the new Appearance replaces the former one. Two to three weeks later, each party of record should receive a court notice acknowledging the new Appearance.

C. New Attorneys: "In Addition to"

Sometimes a party will hire more than one attorney or law firm. In this situation, the new attorney or firm must complete an Appearance and mark the appropriate box in item 12, as well as mark item 14, "In addition to Appearance already on file." No copy needs to be sent to anyone, although copies could be sent to the other attorneys as a courtesy. Usually within two to three weeks after the additional Appearance is filed, each attorney and pro se who has already appeared in the case will receive a court notice acknowledging the addition.

D. Summary Process and Criminal Actions

When filing an Appearance in a summary process case or a criminal action, the party who files an Appearance must send a copy to all other parties of record because the clerk's offices who handles these types of cases do not send notice of the Appearance to the parties. As a result, be sure to mark item 18 if it is applicable to your case and complete items 21 and 22.

IV. CONCLUSION

A. Key Issues in This Chapter Include:

Appearances are quite basic, compared to the rest of litigation practice. For the Plaintiff, he or she must remember to check the calendar to determine when the Defendant's Appearance is due and whether or not it has been filed.

Though not required, some attorneys will send a copy of the Appearance to the Plaintiff. Others will not. In either situation, the court will eventually send all appearing parties notice of all Defendants' Appearances, usually within two to three weeks of being filed. If, on the other hand, a law firm is appearing "in lieu of" another law firm, it must send a copy of the Appearance to the law firm being replaced.

B. Relevant Connecticut Practice Book Sections Include:

Pbs 7P: Appearance for Plaintiff on Writ or Complaint in Civil and Family Cases
Pbs 7Q: Time to File Appearance
Pbs 7R: Form and Signing of Appearance
Pbs 7S: Filing Appearance with the clerk--copies
Pbs 7W: Appearance for Represented Party

8 *Pleadings: An Overview*

Terminology

Pleadings	Discovery	Trial List	Motion
Request	Objection	Testimony	Continuance
Arguable	Short Calendar	Claim Slip	Motion to Reargue
Marking	Oral Argument	Nonarguable	Closed Pleadings
Notice of Intent to Argue		Memorandum of Law	

Pbs: 7KK, 7MM, 98, 112, 113, 114, 117, 120, 131, 142, 147, 151, 197, 204, 204B, 206, 211, 211A, 326, 363, 379

Introduction

Drafting pleadings and conducting discovery occur simultaneously. As a result, their requirements and deadlines will keep both sides of any lawsuit extremely busy. To help you stay organized, you may find it helpful to photocopy the checklist found on page xiii and in Appendix A and include them in each litigation file you handle.

At this point, I suggest that you simply read this chapter and become familiar with the numerous terms. Do not try to memorize anything. The majority of the information will be explained in detail in future chapters.

I. PLEADINGS VS. DISCOVERY

Once a lawsuit is brought, each side usually drafts and files various documents, such as motions, requests and objections. These documents, along with the Complaint, are called **pleadings**. Pleadings address legal issues that are part of the lawsuit and litigation procedures. They may assist in narrowing the issues to be presented at the trial or ask the court to penalize a party for not complying with practice book rules.

Shortly after filing an Appearance, the Defendant will begin to contemplate which pleadings listed in Pbs 112 he or she should file. The Pretrial Stage ends when the Defendant files an *Answer*. An Answer *closes the pleadings* and permits either party to place the case on a waiting list, known as the **Trial List**, to be scheduled for trial. (See Chapter 28.)

Discovery provides each side with the opportunity to formally investigate his or her case. Our practice book rules provide specific discovery guidelines and parameters. In addition, the practice book rules permit each side to file certain discovery-related pleadings in court that are separate from those filed pursuant to Pbs 112. Discovery will be addressed in depth beginning in Chapter 18. For now, we will focus on the pleadings listed in Pbs 112.

II. DIFFERENT TYPES OF PLEADINGS

In this section, we will concentrate on basic pleading terminology. Afterward, we will address the common elements found in most pleadings, including specific motions, objections, and requests.

A. Motions and Objections

In simplistic terms, **motions** are pleadings that ask the court to decide an issue, based upon the facts of the case and the law. (See Pbs 196 and 197.) When a party receives a motion from the opposing party, he or she has two basic options:
    1. object to the motion; or
    2. do nothing, and wait for the court's ruling on the motion.

An **objection** is the most common type of response. Essentially, it is a pleading that challenges the claims, arguments and case law contained in the motion and asks the court to disregard them. On the other hand, if a party fails to respond to a motion, some judges treat this as an acknowledgment that the motion is correct and should be granted. Others will still review the motion, and deny it if it is contrary to the law.

B. Requests, Compliance and Objections

Requests are pleadings that are automatically granted by the court, unless the opposing party files a timely objection. If no objection is filed, it means that the party who received the request agrees to simply comply with what is being asked. (Again, see Pbs 196 and 197.)

III. PLEADINGS LISTED IN PBS 112

After filing an Appearance, the Defendant has the option of filing two specific motions and one specific request, in an effort to convince the court to end the lawsuit at this stage of the proceedings. If the Defendant is successful, the lawsuit is over. If he or she is not successful, the lawsuit continues and the Defendant will be required to file an Answer.

A. *Specific Pleadings Filed by the Defendant*

Pbs 112 provides a list of pleadings an appearing Defendant may file:
1. *Motion to Dismiss* (Pbs 142 et seq.);
2. *Request to Revise* (Pbs 147 et seq.);
3. *Motion to Strike* (Pbs 151 et seq.);
4. *Answer.*
5. Along with the Answer, the Defendant has the option of filing *Special Defenses.*
6. With or without Special Defenses, the Defendant also has the option of filing a *Counterclaim.*

B. *The Plaintiff's Response to the Defendant's Pleadings*

1. As stated earlier, the Plaintiff may file an *objection* to a Motion to Dismiss, Request to Revise, and a Motion to Strike. If the case survives these pleadings, the Defendant must file an Answer, with or without Special Defense or a Counterclaim.
2. If the Plaintiff finds the Defendant's Answer satisfactory and no Special Defense or Counterclaim is filed, the Plaintiff (or the Defendant) may file a *Certificate of Closed Pleadings*, informing the court that the pleadings are closed and that the case may be placed on the *Trial List.*
3. Instead of closing the pleadings, the Plaintiff may decide to challenge the Defendant's Answer and file a *Request to Revise Defendant's Answer* or a *Motion to Strike Defendant's Answer.* The Defendant may then file an objection.
4. If the Plaintiff decides to challenge the Defendant's Special Defenses, he or she may file a *Request to Revise Defendant's Special Defenses Answer* or a *Motion to Strike Defendant's Special Defenses.* The Defendant may then file an objection.
5. If the Plaintiff decides to challenge the Defendant's Counterclaim, he or she may file a *Request to Revise Defendant's Counterclaim* or a *Motion to Strike Defendant's Counterclaim.* The Defendant may then file an objection.

6. If the Defendant's Special Defenses survive the Plaintiff's challenge, the Plaintiff ***must*** file a *Reply to Special Defenses*. If there is no Counterclaim, the pleadings are closed.

7. If the Defendant's Counterclaim survives the Plaintiff's challenge, the Plaintiff ***must*** file an *Answer to Counterclaim*. In addition, the Plaintiff may file *Special Defenses to Counterclaim*.

8. If the Plaintiff files an Answer to Counterclaim and no Special Defenses, either party may claim the case to the Trial List. If Special Defenses are filed, refer to 2 and 4 above. The pleadings may be closed after the Defendant files a *Reply to Special Defenses to Counterclaim*.

C. *The Sequence of Pleadings*

Pursuant to Pbs 113, if the Defendant intends to file one or more of the motions or the request, he or she must *follow the order* specified in Pbs 112. For example:

1. if the Defendant's first pleading is a Request to Revise, he or she has waived the right to file a Motion to Dismiss; or

2. if the Defendant's first pleading is a Motion to Strike, he or she has waived the right to file a Motion to Dismiss or a Request to Revise;

3. if the Defendant's first pleading is an Answer, he or she has waived filing any of the above.

If the Defendant filed Special Defenses alone, or with a Counterclaim, the Plaintiff must follow the order stated in Pbs 112 and above.

IV. TIME LIMITS TO FILE PLEADINGS LISTED IN PBS 112

Pursuant to Pbs 114, the Defendant's first pleading is due ***thirty days*** from the return date. Each pleading is filed one at a time. No further pleadings should be filed until a motion or objection is ruled on by the court. If the case survives the Defendant's first motion or request, the Defendant's remaining pleadings are due in ***15-day*** increments as follows:

1. If the Defendant's first pleading is a Request to Revise, and the Plaintiff complies by filing a Revised Complaint, no court action is needed and the Defendant has 15 days from the filing of that Revised Complaint to file the next pleading.

2. On the other hand, what happens if the Defendant's first pleading is a Motion to Dismiss and the Plaintiff files an objection? If the motion is granted, the case is over and no other pleadings are necessary. If, however, the motion is denied, the Defendant has 15 days from the court's decision to file another pleading.

Don't be surprised if, in some situations, several months pass before you obtain a court's decision on a motion or objection. A judge's time constraints, as well as the complexity of the pleading at issue, often play a large role.

V. MEMORANDUMS OF LAW

Some motions are quite short in length. Others require you to attach a **memorandum of law**. A memorandum of law is a document in which a party presents the facts of the case, the applicable statutes, rules and case law, and his or her supporting legal arguments.

In accordance with Pbs 204, the following motions must be accompanied by a memorandum of law. You will find examples of some of these pleadings throughout this text.

1. Pbs 98:   Motions to Add or Substitute Parties;
2. Pbs 117:   Motions to Implead a Third-Party Defendant;
3. Pbs 142:   Motions to Dismiss, except those filed pursuant to Pbs 251;
4. Pbs 151:   Motions to Strike;
5. Pbs 326:   Motions to Set Aside Judgment;
6. Pbs 378:   Motions for Summary Judgment.

VI. HOW PLEADINGS ARE DECIDED: SHORT CALENDAR

Short Calendar is a computer-generated list of all motions and objections that are filed in a courthouse to be decided by a judge. If you are filing a pleading for a case that has been assigned a date for trial, you must type "assigned for trial" on the bottom of the first page. (See Pbs 206.)

The term, Short Calendar, is also used to describe the court appearance that is necessary if the parties wish to present oral arguments and possible testimony. For instance, you may hear the following phrases: "I've got Short Calendar next week," or "That motion was decided last week at Short Calendar."

In most courthouses throughout the state, Short Calendar takes place each Monday. The parties usually receive a copy of the Short Calendar by mail on the Tuesday before the scheduled court date.

Motions and objections appearing on the Short Calendar can be decided by a judge in three different ways:

1. In an open courtroom, after both sides have explained why the judge should or should not rule a certain way on the pleading. This is called **oral argument.** In some situations, one or both sides will call witnesses to court to answer questions under oath regarding the pleading. This is called **testimony**. When both sides are finished, the judge will inform the parties of the decision orally from the bench.

2. After oral argument, the judge may decide to *take the papers* and inform the parties of the decision in writing, instead of ruling orally from the bench.

3. If there is no oral argument, the judge will rule on the pleading by relying solely upon the parties' written pleadings and the law. This method is called deciding or ruling *on the papers*.

A. Contents of a Short Calendar

You will find an example of a Short Calendar at the end of this chapter. As you can see, it contains a lot of very important information.

In the top left-hand corner, you will find:

1. The name and address of the court where the pleading will be heard;

2. The date of the Short Calendar: this means the date the pleading will be assigned to a judge to hear oral argument or consider the pleading without oral argument;

3. The time court opens to address the pleadings listed on the Short Calendar;

4. Special instructions pertaining to that courthouse;

5. It will often state the name of the judge and the courtroom; if not, you can obtain this information in court the day of Short Calendar.

For each case listed on the Short Calendar, you will find:

1. The docket number;

2. The name of the case: Plaintiff's name at the top and the Defendant's name below;

3. The name of the pleading, underneath the case name;

4. The number directly before the pleading is the number assigned to the pleading when it is filed in court, pursuant to Pbs 7MM;

5. The Plaintiff's attorney's law firm is on the left and the Defendant's attorney's firm is on the right;

6. The **position number** is in parentheses; this number assists in locating a case on the Short Calendar;

7. The **column number** appears at the bottom of each column; this number also assists in locating a case on the Short Calendar;

8. In the bottom left corner, either N/A for **nonarguable** (taken on the papers) or Arg for **Arguable** (oral argument and possible testimony) appears.

B. To Find Your Pleading

The position number of your case(s) can be found on the envelope the Short Calendar was mailed in. Usually, it is directly above the law firm's address. Find your case by simply following the list of position numbers.

C. Oral Argument As a Right

Pursuant to Pbs 211, the parties are *entitled* to oral argument and, if necessary, to present witnesses to testify in the following situations:

1. A Motion to Dismiss, with or without an objection;
2. A Motion to Strike, with or without an objection;
3. A Motion for Summary Judgment, with or without an objection;
4. A Motion for Judgment of Foreclosure, with or without an objection.

Pursuant to 7KK, the party who drafted any of the above and wants oral argument must take two steps to notify the court:

1. Type: ORAL ARGUMENT REQUESTED
TESTIMONY (NOT) REQUIRED
on the bottom left-hand corner of the first page of the pleading; and

2. Inform the court by "marking the pleading ready" according to the directions found on the applicable Short Calendar. (See Section G below.)

D. When Oral Argument Is Not Requested

If the party who drafted any of the above-listed pleadings does not want oral argument, he or she should state the following on the bottom left-hand corner of the first page of the pleading:

ORAL ARGUMENT NOT REQUESTED
TESTIMONY NOT REQUIRED

E. When an Opposing Party Wants Oral Argument

The opposing party who files an objection to any of the above-listed motions will still have the opportunity to argue or present testimony by filing a **Notice of Intent to Argue,** pursuant to Pbs 211(A)(3).

1. Deadline to File Notice of Intent to Argue

This notice must be filed no later than the third day before the date the motion is scheduled to be decided. In addition, some courts request the party filing the notice to also inform the court clerk by telephone. Once the clerk (or the judge assigned to the case) is aware of the Notice of Intent to Argue, the case will be scheduled for argument. (Some courthouses permit oral argument that same day. Others will reschedule the case to be heard on another day.)

2. *Contents of a Notice of Intent to Argue*

> **a.** Case caption;
> **b.** Name of the party filing the notice;
> **c.** Name of the pleading at issue;
> **d.** That the party intends to appear and argue the pleading (and if necessary, present testimony);
> **e.** The date of the Short Calendar;
> **f.** certification of service, pursuant to Pbs 120 (see Chapter 9).

It is helpful to include the position number and column number where the pleading is listed.

F. *Oral Argument for Other Pleadings*

Each court has specific instructions that are stated on the Short Calendar for parties to follow if they want oral argument on a pleading not listed above. The decision rests solely within the court's discretion.

G. *Marking Cases*

1. *Ready and Off Markings*

The party who files a pleading that appears on a Short Calendar has the option of **marking** it "ready" or "off." It doesn't matter if the pleading is Arguable or Not Arguable. **Marking** simply means to inform the court, pursuant to the instructions on the Short Calendar, whether or not the party wants the pleading assigned to a judge on the Short Calendar date. A *ready* marking means yes. An *off* marking means no. The opposing party cannot contact the court and mark a pleading ready or off without the consent of the party who filed it.

2. *Reasons for an Off Marking*

The party who filed the pleading may mark it off for any reason: conflicting court appearances elsewhere in the state, illness, vacation, he or she wants more time to research the issues, etc. In addition, the opposing party may ask the party for a **continuance**, in other words, a postponement. The decision to grant or deny a continuance is a matter of professional courtesy and should be decided on an individual basis. If a continuance is unreasonably refused, the issue can be addressed in court the day of the Short Calendar or at a later time through a Motion to Reargue pursuant to Pbs 204B (see Section VII, C below).

3. Short Calendar List Claim/Reclaim Slip

A **Short Calendar List Claim/Reclaim** is a yellow, court-issued form that serves two purposes:

> **a.** to **reclaim** a pleading to the Short Calendar, if it has been previously marked off; or
>
> **b.** to **claim** a pleading to the Short Calendar.

Most pleadings automatically appear on the Short Calendar two to three weeks after they are filed in court. If the pleading is marked off, it must be reclaimed in order for it to appear on the Short Calendar again. A few pleadings do not appear until the party who drafted them claims them, for instance, a Motion for Nonsuit and Motion for Default pursuant to Pbs 363.

Pleadings are typically claimed or reclaimed by the party who drafted them. Note, however, that recent revisions to Pbs 206 permit the following:

1. If a motion is marked off the Short Calendar, any party may reclaim it.
2. If an objection to a request is marked off, the party who drafted the request may reclaim the objection.
3. If the case is on the Dormancy Calendar (see Chapter 16), any party may reclaim the motion or objection if it must be ruled upon in order to close the pleadings.

A pleading should appear on a new Short Calendar approximately two to three weeks after it is claimed or reclaimed.

A Short Calendar List Claim/Reclaim slip requires the following information:
1. type of court;
2. address of court;
3. docket number and return date;
4. name of case;
5. indicate whether the Plaintiff or the Defendant is filing this slip;
6. indicate whether the pleading is being claimed or reclaimed;
7. date of pleading being claimed or reclaimed;
8. number of pleading, if known; this is stated in the court file;
9. indicate if oral argument and testimony are desired;
10. name of pleading;
11. date of form;
12. name of each party that was served a copy of the form;
13. addresses where the copies were served;
14. signature of the attorney filing the form;
15. name and address of the person filing the form;
16. telephone number of the person filing the form.

In addition, if the case has been assigned for trial, add: "assigned for trial" on the bottom of the form.

VII. THE JUDGE'S DECISION

A. 120-Day Time Limit

Pursuant to Pbs 211A, Short Calendar matters "taken on the papers" should be decided no later than *120 days* after they are assigned to a judge. If the judge requires additional information such as a hearing or briefs, the 120-day time limit does not start running until all these procedures are completed.

B. Motion for Reassignment

Many pleadings are decided the day of Short Calendar, or within a week or two. Others take longer. If, after the 120-day limit, a decision is still not made, either party may file a Motion for Reassignment. This motion must be filed within *14 days* of the expiration of the 120 days. Otherwise, the 120-day deadline is waived.

In a Motion for Reassignment, the party should ask the pleading to be reassigned to another judge and should state:
  1. the date the pleading was submitted to the judge;
  2. the name of the judge it was submitted to;
  3. that a timely decision has not been made;
  4. whether oral argument and testimony on the pleading are necessary.

C. Motion to Reargue

Pbs 204B permits a party who disagrees with a judge's ruling to ask that judge to reconsider the ruling.

1. Time Limit

A Motion to Reargue must be filed within *20 days* after notice of a judge's ruling was issued. If more time is needed, the party may file a Motion for Extension of Time, within that same 20-day period.

2. Contents of the Motion to Reargue

The motion must specify the decision or order challenged and the party's grounds for making the challenge. It can include new or additional cases or arguments not previously addressed and may request a new hearing to present oral argument and testimony, if appropriate.

VIII. CONCLUSION

Again, you're facing a lot of new terminology. Don't worry. The following chapters address how to draft several different motions, requests and objections and their purposes.

A. Key Issues in This Chapter Include:

1. Pleadings under Pbs 112 and discovery take place simultaneously.

2. The Plaintiff's goal is to *close the pleadings* and place the case on the *trial list*.

3. Pleadings under Pbs 112 may be filed once the Defendant files an Appearance.

4. Pleadings under Pbs 112 are complete when the pleadings are closed.

5. Pleadings filed pursuant to Pbs 112 appear on *Short Calendar* to be decided by judges. Other pleadings filed after the pleadings are closed will also appear on Short Calendar, unless they should be decided by the judge who is assigned to conduct the trial.

6. Mondays are typically "Short Calendar days" in most courthouses throughout the state. (Meriden holds Short Calendar on Thursdays.)

7. If a case has been assigned for trial, the party filing a pleading should indicate this on the bottom of first page of the pleading or on the *reclaim slip*.

8. The party who filed a pleading that appears on Short Calendar must *mark* it ready or off.

9. If a pleading is *marked off*, it must be reclaimed in order to appear on a new Short Calendar.

10. Remember to state either of the following on the bottom left-hand corner of the first page of pleadings:

ORAL ARGUMENT NOT REQUESTED,
TESTIMONY NOT REQUIRED
or
ORAL ARGUMENT REQUESTED,
TESTIMONY NOT REQUESTED
or
ORAL ARGUMENT REQUESTED,
TESTIMONY REQUIRED

11. If a pleading is *arguable*, the attorneys or pro se parties must appear in court on the date of the Short Calendar to orally argue the merits of the pleading. If the pleading is *nonarguable*, no one needs to appear in court. Instead, the judge will make a decision based *on the papers*.

12. A party who wishes to appear in court and argue a pleading that is nonarguable may file a *Notice of Intent to Argue* and follow the court's instructions.

13. Pbs 204 provides a list of pleadings which must be accompanied by a *memorandum of law.*

14. Pbs 211 provides a list of pleadings which are entitled to oral argument.

15. A Superior Court judge has *120 days* to decide pleadings that appear on Short Calendar and are marked ready.

16. A party who disagrees with a judge's decision on a pleading may file a *Motion to Reargue.*

B. Notice of Intent to Argue

An example of a Notice of Intent to Argue is on page 86. (The actual motion and objection can be found in Chapter 10.) After reviewing it, turn to Chapter 9, which discusses what motions, requests and objections should look like.

C. Relevant Connecticut Practice Book Sections Include:

Pbs 7KK:	Form of Pleading
Pbs 7MM:	Filing and Endorsing Pleadings
Pbs 98:	Addition or Substitution of Parties
Pbs 112:	General Rules of Pleading--Pleadings Allowed and Their Order
Pbs 113:	General Rules of Pleading--Waiving Right to Plead
Pbs 114:	General Rules of Pleading--Time to Plead
Pbs 117:	General Rules of Pleading--Impleading of Third Party by Defendant
Pbs 120:	General Rules of Pleading--Service of Pleadings and Other Papers
Pbs 131:	The Complaint-Contents of the Complaint
Pbs 142:	Motion to Dismiss
Pbs 147:	Request to Revise
Pbs 151:	Motion to Strike
Pbs 197:	Definition of Motion and Request
Pbs 204:	Memorandum of Law Required
Pbs 204B:	Motion to Reargue
Pbs 206:	Short Calendar--Short Calendar List
Pbs 211:	Short Calendar--Oral Argument of Motions in Civil Matters
Pbs 211A:	Short Calendar--Time Limit for Deciding Short Calendar Matters
Pbs 326:	Setting Aside or Opening Judgments
Pbs 363:	Procedure Where Party Is in Default
Pbs 379:	Summary Judgment

Example 1, Notice of Intent to Argue

DOCKET NO. CV 98-0333333 S	:	SUPERIOR COURT
SARAH A. DONAHUE	:	JUDICIAL DISTRICT
	:	OF TOLLAND
VS.	:	AT ROCKVILLE
RICHARD P. ANDREW	:	JULY 8, 1998

NOTICE OF INTENT TO ARGUE

The Plaintiff hereby gives notice that she intends to appear at the Short Calendar to argue against the Defendant's Motion to Dismiss, dated June 19, 1998.

Said Motion to Dismiss appears on the July 13, 1998 Short Calendar #6, position number 5, column 1.

THE PLAINTIFF

BY_____

Christine Kulas, Esq.,
her attorney
Law Officers of Christine Kulas
P.O. Box 2005
Ellington, CT 06000
Tele. #(860) 222-2222
Juris #989898

CERTIFICATION

I hereby certify that a copy of the foregoing was mailed on July 8, 1998 to all counsel and pro se parties of record, namely: Neil Clifford, Esq., of Michaels, Sabrina and Alexander, P.C., 259 Sage Road, Suite 200, West Hartford, CT 08080.

_____
Commissioner of the Superior Court

Example 2, Short Calendar Envelope

NAME AND ADDRESS OF COURT

FST/SC01/## 144
KIMBERLY A. PETERSON
P.O. BOX 5101
ROCKY HILL, CT 06067

(The pleading that appears on the Short Calendar inside the envelope will be found at position number 144.)

9 *The Pleadings Format*

Terminology

Order	Overrule	With Prejudice	Certification of Service
Grant	Sustain	Ex Parte	Without Prejudice

Pbs: 7KK, 7LL, 7HHH, 120, 121, 123, 196

Introduction

The examples found on the next few pages demonstrate that motions, requests and objections resemble a Complaint. The paper is the same size, the margins and hole punches are the same and both contain a case caption, pursuant to Pbs 7KK. Furthermore, a pleading must be signed by the person who drafted it, pursuant to Pbs 7LL. Note that Pbs 7HHH reiterates these filing requirements.

I. DIFFERENCES BETWEEN THE COMPLAINT AND OTHER PLEADINGS

Once a case is assigned a docket number, that docket number replaces the return date in the case caption. In addition, there are three other differences between the Complaint and subsequent pleadings:
1. The **order**, as mentioned below;
2. The **certification of service**;
3. Whether or not oral argument and testimony are requested.

A. The Order

Pursuant to Pbs 196, the order appears on all motions and objections, after the signature line. A request, on the other hand, does not need an order, because the judge need not make a decision unless someone files an objection.

An order on a *motion* asks the judge to **grant** or **deny** the motion.

An order on an *objection* asks the court to **sustain** or **overrule** the objection. You may be familiar with these terms but I'll explain them, nevertheless. To **sustain** means the judge agrees with the objection and denies the motion or request. To **overrule** means that the judge disagrees with the objection and will grant the motion or request.

In addition, the court could grant or deny a motion **with prejudice**. This means that the court has made its final decision on the issue and the issue should not be raised again. Or, the court could grant or deny a motion **without prejudice**. This permits a party to raise the issue at a later time and ask the court to reconsider its previous decision.

B. The Certification of Service

The certification of service verifies that a copy of the document has been served on the opposing party. In Chapter 6, we addressed service of process: when a proper officer, such as a sheriff or constable, serves a Defendant with a copy of a Summons and Complaint. The most common types of such service are in hand and abode.

In this section, we will address another type of service. Pursuant to Pbs 120 et seq., once the Summons and Complaint are filed in court and the Defendant has appeared, each party who files a document in court must serve a copy of that document to every other party in the lawsuit. This type of service, however, does not require a proper officer. Instead, regular mail or hand delivery is sufficient.

The certification of service is also referred to as the *certification.* It is signed by an attorney as Commissioner of the Superior Court. See the example on page 86.

1. The Types of Documents Included under Pbs 120, et seq.

Pbs 121 provides that a copy of every document filed in court must be served to all parties of record in an case. In addition, copies of any letters written to a judge or clerk about a case should also be served on the other parties.

2. The Purpose of Service under Pbs 120 et seq.

Like serving a Complaint, the purpose of serving opposing parties with copies of documents filed in court is to ensure that everyone in the lawsuit has notice of what the other hopes to accomplish. As a result, they have the opportunity to take appropriate action, such as object, etc.

There are, however, rare situations in which a party will ask the court to make a ruling without first providing notice to the opposing party. These are known as **ex parte** proceedings and are sometimes needed in extreme circumstances like those addressed in Chapter 17. In these matters, a certification of service is not necessary. Any document which is intended to be decided ex parte must state the words "ex parte" on it.

3. *Who Is Served under Pbs 120 et seq.*

Attorneys or their staff are not permitted to communicate directly with a party who is represented by an attorney. A Defendant's Appearance, or any subsequent Appearances filed by any party, clearly discloses such representation, or whether the party is a pro se. If an attorney appeared on behalf of a party, all communication, **including service**, must be made to that attorney. If the party appeared pro se, all communication, including service, must be made to the pro se directly.

4. *How to Make Service Pursuant to Pbs 120: U.S. Mail vs. Hand Delivery*

According to Pbs122, service by mail is complete upon mailing. In addition, service by hand delivery is complete upon:
   a. handing it to the attorney or pro se,
   b. leaving it at the attorney's office or pro se's office with the person in charge;
   c. leaving it in a conspicuous place in that office; or
   d. if the office is closed or if there is no office, leaving it at that attorney's or
   pro se's dwelling, house or usual place of abode.

The circumstances surrounding each document you file will determine whether mail or hand delivery is appropriate. It's usually a matter of how fast you must communicate something. In addition, the use of fax machines has decreased the necessity of hand delivery in rushed or emergency situations. Even though copies are faxed, however, it's common to serve a copy by mail as well.
   Courier services and proper officers are available to make hand delivered service. In addition, law offices may hire messengers or clerks to make such deliveries.

5. *Proof of Service: Content of the Certification of Service*

Pbs 123 requires all documents listed above to contain a certification of service at the end of a document which should state either of the following:

a. *Service by Mail*

I hereby certify that a copy of the above was mailed on (date) to all counsel and pro se parties of record, namely: (list the name of each party served and the address the document was mailed to.)

_____
signature of serving attorney

b. *Service by Hand Delivery*

I hereby certify that a copy of the above was hand delivered on (date) to all counsel and pro se parties of record, namely: (List the name of each party and the address the document was delivered to.)

_____

signature of serving attorney

C. *Oral Argument or No Oral Argument*

As we discussed in Chapter 8, pleadings that are to be decided on the papers should include the following information in the bottom left-hand corner of the first page:

ORAL ARGUMENT NOT REQUESTED
TESTIMONY NOT REQUIRED

Pleadings that are entitled to oral argument before a judge should state:

ORAL ARGUMENT REQUESTED
TESTIMONY REQUIRED
or
ORAL ARGUMENT REQUESTED
TESTIMONY NOT REQUIRED

II. CONCLUSION

See? Wasn't that easy? There are several sample pleadings throughout the text. Compare them to the rules set forth in this chapter.

A. *Key Issues in This Chapter Include:*

1. All pleadings require a case caption. The docket number replaces the return date in the case caption.
2. All pleadings must be signed by the attorney who drafted them.
3. In addition, be sure to include an *order*, a *certification of service* and an indication of whether *oral argument and testimony are requested*, on all motions and objections.
4. Requests and notices do not need an *order*.
5. Motions are *granted* or *denied.*
6. Objections are *overruled* or *sustained.*
7. Copies of all documents filed in court (except those marked *ex parte*) must be *served* upon the opposing party. In most cases, once the parties have filed their

Appearances, a proper officer is not needed. Instead, service is usually sufficient when a party sends a pleading by regular mail or hand delivery.

B. *Relevant Connecticut Practice Book Sections Include:*

Pbs 7KK:	Form of Pleading
Pbs 7LL:	Signing of Pleading
Pbs 7HHH:	Filing of Papers
Pbs 120:	General Rules of Pleadings--Service of Pleadings and Other Papers
Pbs 121:	General Rules of Pleadings--Responsibility of Counsel or Pro Se Parties: Documents and Persons to Be Served
Pbs 123:	General Rules of Pleadings--Proof of Service
Pbs 196:	Form of Motion and Request

10 *Pleadings: Defendant's Motion to Dismiss and Plaintiff's Response*

Terminology

> Subject Matter Jurisdiction   Personal Jurisdiction   Venue
> Insufficiency of Process   Insufficiency of Service of Process

Pbs: 7Q, 112, 113, 114, 142, 143, 144, 145, 146, 204, 205, 212, 213
C.G.S. sections: 51-347b, 51-351, 52-57, 52-59b, 52-72, 52-592

Introduction

Pursuant to Pbs 112, a Motion to Dismiss is the first pleading a Defendant may file after the Appearance. Interestingly enough, the time limit to file this motion varies from the time specified in Pbs 114. In addition, many cases that are dismissed under this section may be brought again, even if the statute of limitations has expired. But that's a different matter and is discussed later.

I. GROUNDS FOR A MOTION TO DISMISS

Pbs 143 lists five grounds for a Motion to Dismiss:
1. the court's lack of jurisdiction over the subject matter;
2. the court's lack of jurisdiction over the person, i.e., the Defendant;
3. improper venue (Chapter 4);
4. insufficiency of process (Chapter 6);
5. insufficiency of service of process (Chapter 6).

A. Subject Matter Jurisdiction

A court that lacks subject matter jurisdiction does not have authority to hear, decide and enforce its decision regarding a specific case. Typically, it lacks this authority because the Complaint was filed in the wrong court or because there is a problem involving the return date.

1. Time Limit to File Motion to Dismiss for Lack of Subject Matter Jurisdiction

Contrary to Pbs 114, Pbs 145 permits a Motion to Dismiss based on lack of subject matter jurisdiction to be filed *at any time*. Therefore, the 30-day rule in Pbs 114 does not apply. In addition, a judge may notice the error itself and dismiss the case at any time during a proceeding.

2. Cases Filed in the Wrong Court, Examples

a. If a Plaintiff filed a landlord-tenant case in the regular Superior Court, rather than in the appropriate housing session or the GA, the case may be dismissed for lack of subject matter jurisdiction.
b. If the return date on the Complaint is not a Tuesday, the case may be dismissed for lack of subject matter jurisdiction.
c. If the Summons and Complaint were returned to court less than six days before the return date, or after the return date, the case should be dismissed for lack of jurisdiction.

3. The Plaintiff's Remedies if A Case Is Filed in the Wrong Court

Fortunately for Plaintiffs, many subject matter issues are correctable. In many cases, the clerk will recognize the mistake at the time the Summons and Complaint are filed, and send the documents back to the Plaintiff. If the error is undetected and the Summons and Complaint are filed, a clerk who later notices the error will bring it to the attention of the court. The court will then order the Plaintiff to file a **Motion to Transfer** (which will be granted) within a certain period of time, and notify the Defendant. If, however, the Plaintiff fails to file the motion within the time ordered by the court, the court may dismiss the case.

Pursuant to Pbs 212 and 213 and C.G.S. sec. 51-347b(a) and 51-351, a Motion to Transfer is appropriate to transfer a case from:
    a. one JD to another;
    b. one GA to another;
    c. one JD to any GA;
    d. one GA to any JD.

If the error is undetected by the clerk and the Plaintiff receives a Motion to Dismiss from the Defendant, he or she should immediately file a Motion to Transfer, as mentioned above. A Motion to Transfer may also be granted by written agreement of the parties. If this is the case, the agreement should be stated in the motion.

5. *Motion to Dismiss Regarding the Return Date*

C.G.S. sec. 52-72 now permits a Plaintiff to correct many mistakes involving the return date. In the past, if the Plaintiff selected the wrong return date, or if a case was filed after the return date, the case would be dismissed for lack of subject matter jurisdiction. Now, as long as the Defendant was properly served, C.G.S. sec. 52-72 appears to permit the Plaintiff to amend the civil process (the Summons and Complaint) to correct the jurisdictional defect.

The amended process will have to be served again and shall have the same effect, from the date of the original service, as if no amendment was necessary.

B. *Personal Jurisdiction*

A Motion to Dismiss claiming lack of personal jurisdiction challenges the court's authority to render and enforce a judgment against a specific Defendant. Under most circumstances, each state has personal jurisdiction over its residents. Questions, however, tend to arise when a case involves a nonresident.

C.G.S. sec. 52-59b states that Connecticut courts have personal jurisdiction over nonresidents and foreign partnerships, their executors or administrators who, in person or through an agent:

1. transact any business in this state; or

2. commit a tortious act within the state, except a cause of action for defamation of character arising from the act;

3. commit a tortious act outside the State of Connecticut, which causes injury to persons or property within the State of Connecticut (except a cause of action for defamation of character arising from the act), if the Defendants regularly do or solicit business, or engage in any other persistent course of conduct, or derive substantial revenue from goods used or consumed or services rendered in Connecticut; or expect or should reasonably expect the act to have consequences in Connecticut and derive substantial revenue from interstate or international commerce; or

4. own, use, or possess any real property situated in Connecticut.

A Defendant who challenges the court's jurisdiction is claiming that he or she does not fall within any of the provisions listed in sec. 52-59b. Therefore, the case must be dismissed for lack of personal jurisdiction.

C. Motion to Dismiss for Improper Venue

Venue is discussed in Chapter 4. If a Motion to Dismiss claiming Improper Venue is filed, the Plaintiff may file a Motion to Transfer to correct the mistake.

D. Insufficiency of Process

Insufficiency of process may arise when a Defendant is not served all the appropriate paperwork required, such as a properly completed Summons and Complaint, and any other documents that may be required in a particular action.

E. Insufficiency of Service of Process

In most cases, insufficient service of process means the Defendant was not served in the required manner, according to an applicable statute or rule.

1. Examples of Improper Service of Process

a. The Defendant was not served because he or she did not live at the abode address that was served; or

b. The officer is mistaken and never left the paperwork at the address stated in the return of service; or

c. The officer made service by certified mail, but only abode or in hand service was appropriate; or

d. Defendants who live out of state may claim that the Plaintiff or officer failed to take the required steps necessary to perform proper out-of-state service.

2. To Avoid Improper Service of Process

a. Instruct the officer to serve the Defendant in hand.

b. If abode process is necessary, double check the Defendant's address.

Note: A person can have more than one abode. This issue becomes a matter of fact for the court to decide. At a hearing on a Defendant's Motion to Dismiss, the Plaintiff will have the burden of proving that service was left at a location where the Defendant was most likely to find or learn about it. (Parties who fail to pick up their mail cannot claim they were not properly served.)

c. If the officer is unable to locate the Defendant and resorts to certified mail as described in Chapter 6, be sure the return of service states that he or she made a diligent search.

II. DEADLINE TO FILE MOTION AND OBJECTION

A. Waiver

Pursuant to Pbs 144, a Defendant will waive any claim of "lack of jurisdiction over the person, or improper venue or insufficiency of process" unless:

1. a Motion to Dismiss is filed within 30 days of filing the Appearance; *and*

2. no other pleadings listed in Pbs 112 have been filed.

Note that this deadline may fall on a different date than the 30-day deadline (from the return date) stated in Pbs 114. Defendants who miss the deadline or who have filed any of the other pleadings listed in Pbs 112 have submitted themselves to the court's jurisdiction.

B. Receiving a Motion to Dismiss for Lack of Personal Jurisdiction, Insufficiency of Service or Insufficiency of Service of Process

A Plaintiff who receives a Motion to Dismiss on these grounds should:

1. Be sure the motion was filed timely and the Defendant has not filed any other Pbs 112 pleadings. Include the existence of either situation in the objection.

2. Contact the officer who served the Summons and Complaint. Verify how service was made. Perhaps the return of service contains an error, or is missing some relevant information. In that case, amend the return of service and attach it to the objection.

3. Pursuant to Pbs 143, file an objection and memorandum of law no later than *five days* before the date the motion appears on the Short Calendar to be decided.

III. SHORT CALENDAR

Pursuant to Pbs 211, a Motion to Dismiss and an objection may be orally argued at Short Calendar, if requested by one or both of the parties.

IV. IF A CASE IS DISMISSED

If the statute of limitations has not expired, the Plaintiff may bring the action again by re-serving the Defendant and filing a new case in court.

If the statute of limitations has expired, C.G.S. sec. 52-592 *may* give a Plaintiff one year from the date of dismissal to serve and file the case again. This statute is called, "Accidental Failure of Suit; allowance of new action." See the statute itself for specific details.

V. CONCLUSION

A. Key Issues in This Chapter Include:

1. A memorandum of law must be filed with a Motion to Dismiss and an Objection to Motion to Dismiss.
2. A Defendant who wants to file a Motion to Dismiss for any reason listed in this chapter other than *subject matter jurisdiction* must do so within 30 days of filing the Appearance. Otherwise the defect is *waived.*
3. A Motion to Dismiss claiming lack of subject matter jurisdiction may be filed at any time and cannot be waived. Instead of a dismissal, a *Motion to Transfer* or a *Motion to Amend Process* may correct the defect.
4. A Plaintiff's objection to a Motion to Dismiss and memorandum of law must be filed at least five days before the matter will be presented to a judge at Short Calendar. If the motion appears as N/A (nonarguable) on the Short Calendar and the Defendant wishes to appear in court and argue the objection, file a *Notice of Intent to Argue*, as described in Chapter 8.

B. Sample Motion and Objection

A sample Motion to Dismiss, memorandum of law and affidavit and a sample Objection to Motion to Dismiss, memorandum of law and Return of Service for the *Donahue v. Andrew* case are found on the following pages. Note that these pleadings are based upon the facts of the case and the applicable law. Also note that Pbs 143 does not appear to require an objection to a Motion to Dismiss to contain an actual Objection to Motion to Dismiss page. Instead, it appears a Memorandum of Law in Support of Objection is sufficient. I've seen both methods used without a problem. Pbs 196, however, seems to indicate that an objection page, with an order, is proper. Don't forget the certification of service. Last, the spacing in these examples and all others in this text is incorrect. Be sure to double space and use the proper margins as discussed in Chapter 4.

C. Relevant Connecticut Practice Book Sections Include:

Pbs 7Q: Time to File Appearance
Pbs 112: Pleadings Allowed and Their Order
Pbs 113: General Rules of Pleading--Waiving Right to Plead
Pbs 114: General Rules of Pleading--Time to Plead
Pbs 142: Motion to Dismiss
Pbs 143: Motion to Dismiss-Grounds
Pbs 144: Motion to Dismiss-Waiver Based on Certain Grounds
Pbs 145: Motion to Dismiss-Waiver and Subject Matter Jurisdiction
Pbs 146: Motion to Dismiss-Further Pleading by Defendant

Pbs 196: Form of Motion and Request
Pbs 204: Memorandum of Law Required
Pbs 205: Short Calendar
Pbs 212: Procedure for Transfer
Pbs 213: Transfer of Action Filed in Wrong Location of Correct Court

D. Relevant Connecticut General Statutes Include:

C.G.S. sec. 51-347b.:	Transfer of causes by court, motion or agreement. Transfer by Chief Court Administrator.
C.G.S. sec. 51-351.:	Return to improper locations.
C.G.S. sec. 52-57.:	Manner of service upon individuals, municipalities, corporations, partnerships and voluntary associations.
C.G.S. sec. 52-59b.:	Jurisdiction of courts over nonresidents and foreign partnerships. Service of Process.
C.G.S. sec. 52-72.:	Amendment of process.
C.G.S. sec. 52-592.:	Accidental failure of suit; allowance of new action.

Example 1, Motion to Dismiss

DOCKET NO. CV 98-0333333 S	:	SUPERIOR COURT
SARAH A. DONAHUE	:	JUDICIAL DISTRICT
	:	OF TOLLAND
VS.	:	AT ROCKVILLE
RICHARD P. ANDREW	:	JUNE 19, 1998

MOTION TO DISMISS

Pursuant to Connecticut Practice Book Section 142 et seq., the Defendant, Richard P. Andrew, hereby moves the court to dismiss the Plaintiff's Complaint due to insufficiency of service of process.

A memorandum of law and an affidavit are attached hereto in support of this motion.

THE DEFENDANT

BY_____

Neil E. Clifford, Esq.,
Michaels, Sabrina and Alexander, P.C.,
his attorneys
259 Sage Road, Suite 200
West Hartford, CT 08080
Tele. # (860) 111-1111
Juris #626262

ORAL ARGUMENT NOT REQUESTED
TESTIMONY NOT REQUIRED

ORDER

The foregoing Motion having been heard and considered by the Court, is hereby ORDERED: GRANTED/DENIED.

_____

BY THE COURT

CERTIFICATION

I hereby certify that a copy of the foregoing Motion and the attached memorandum of law and affidavit were mailed on June 19, 1998 to all counsel and pro se parties of record, namely: Christine Kulas, Esq., P.O. Box 2005, Ellington, CT 06066.

_____

Commissioner of the Superior Court

DOCKET NO. CV 98-0333333 S	:	SUPERIOR COURT
SARAH A. DONAHUE	:	JUDICIAL DISTRICT
	:	OF TOLLAND
VS.	:	AT ROCKVILLE
RICHARD P. ANDREW	:	JUNE 19, 1998

MEMORANDUM OF LAW
IN SUPPORT OF MOTION TO DISMISS

FACTS

The Plaintiff brought this action against the Defendant, claiming that she was seriously injured in an automobile accident which he negligently caused. The Defendant was not served a copy of the Summons and Complaint in accordance with Connecticut General Statutes Section 52-57. Therefore, pursuant to Connecticut Practice Book Section 142 et seq. this case must be dismissed due to insufficiency of service of process.

ARGUMENT

The Plaintiff's Complaint should be dismissed due to insufficiency of service of process, pursuant to Connecticut Practice Book Section 142 et seq.

C.G.S. Sec. 52-57 of the Connecticut General Statutes provides:

Except as otherwise provided, process in any civil action shall be
served by leaving a true and attested copy of it, including the
declaration or Complaint, with the Defendant, or at his usual place
of abode in this state.

The Defendant is a Connecticut resident in this civil action. Consequently, the Plaintiff was required to serve the Defendant by leaving a true and attested copy of the Summons and Complaint in his hands, or at his usual place of abode.

In this case, however, the officer merely sent a copy of the Summons and Complaint to the Defendant by certified mail. This does not amount to sufficient service of process as required by C.G.S. Sec. 52-57.

Where a particular method of serving a Defendant with a Summons and Complaint is identified by statute, that method must be followed. Westhelle v. Turner Liedertafel Singing Society, Inc., 18 Conn. Sup. 107, 109 (1952). See also Balkun v. DeAnzona, 5 Conn. Cir. 580 (1969) where the case was dismissed because the officer left the Summons and Complaint in a mailbox in a hallway outside the Defendant's apartment, rather than in the abode.

CONCLUSION

Accordingly, the Defendant was not properly served pursuant to C.G.S. Sec. 52-57. Therefore, this action should be dismissed.   THE DEFENDANT

BY_____

Neil E. Clifford, Esq.,
Michaels, Sabrina and Alexander, P.C.,
his attorneys
259 Sage Road, Suite 200
West Hartford, CT 08080
Tele. # (860) 111-1111
Juris #626262

DOCKET NO. CV 98-0333333 S	:	SUPERIOR COURT
SARAH A. DONAHUE	:	JUDICIAL DISTRICT
	:	OF TOLLAND
VS.	:	AT ROCKVILLE
RICHARD P. ANDREW	:	JUNE 18, 1998

AFFIDAVIT OF RICHARD P. ANDREW

The undersigned, being duly sworn, sayeth:

1. I am over the age of 18 years and I believe in the obligation of an oath.

2. I, Richard P. Andrew, am a Defendant in the above-captioned case.

3. I am a resident of Connecticut.

4. The Writ, Summons and Complaint were sent to me by certified mail.

5. A sheriff did not serve me a copy of the Writ, Summons and Complaint, in hand.

6. A sheriff did not leave a copy of the Writ, Summons and Complaint at my usual place of abode.

7. I have reviewed the above statements and they are true and accurate to the best of my knowledge and belief.

_____

Richard P. Andrew

Subscribed and sworn to before me this 18th day of June, 1998.

_____

Commissioner of the Superior Court

Example 2, Objection to Motion to Dismiss

DOCKET NO. CV 98-0333333 S	:	SUPERIOR COURT
SARAH A. DONAHUE	:	JUDICIAL DISTRICT
	:	OF TOLLAND
VS.	:	AT ROCKVILLE
RICHARD P. ANDREW	:	JUNE 29, 1998

OBJECTION TO MOTION TO DISMISS

In accordance with Sections 142, 143 and 144 of the Connecticut Practice Book, the Plaintiff hereby objects to the Defendant's Motion to Dismiss, dated June 19, 1998, for the following reasons:

1. Service of process was sufficient, pursuant to Connecticut General Statutes Section 52-63; and

2. The Defendant's Motion to Dismiss was untimely filed. Therefore, he has waived any defects in the service of process.

A memorandum of law and the Sheriff's Return of Service are attached hereto in support of this objection.

THE PLAINTIFF
BY_____
Christine Kulas, Esq.,
Law Offices of Christine Kulas,
her attorney
P.O. Box 2005
Ellington, CT 06066
Tele. #(860) 222-2222
Juris #989898

ORAL ARGUMENT REQUESTED
TESTIMONY NOT REQUIRED

ORDER

The foregoing Objection having been considered by the Court, it is hereby ORDERED: SUSTAINED/OVERRULED.

_____
BY THE COURT

CERTIFICATION

I hereby certify that a copy of the foregoing Objection and the attached memorandum of law and Return of Service were mailed on June 29, 1998 to all counsel and pro se parties of record, namely: Neil Clifford, Esq., of Michaels, Sabrina and Alexander, P.C., 259 Sage Road, Suite 200, West Hartford, CT 08080.

_____
Commissioner of the Superior Court

DOCKET NO. CV 98-0333333 S   :   SUPERIOR COURT
SARAH A. DONAHUE   :   JUDICIAL DISTRICT
     :   OF TOLLAND
VS.   :   AT ROCKVILLE
RICHARD P. ANDREW   :   JUNE 29, 1998

MEMORANDUM OF LAW IN SUPPORT
OF
OBJECTION TO MOTION TO DISMISS

FACTS

The Plaintiff brought this action for personal injuries she suffered in an automobile accident allegedly caused by the Defendant's negligence.

The Sheriff's Return of Service, attached hereto, states that after a diligent attempt, he could not make service on the Defendant at his address on file with the Department of Motor Vehicles, or anywhere else in his precincts. As a result, pursuant to C.G.S. Section 52-63, the Sheriff made service upon the Defendant through the Department of Motor Vehicles (hereinafter DMV), and sent copies of said service to the Defendant, by certified mail, postage pre paid, to his last address on file at DMV, at least 12 days before the return date.

The Defendant filed his Appearance on May 21, 1998. Although his Motion to Dismiss is dated June 19, 1998, it was not filed and time stamped in court until June 23, 1998.

ARGUMENT

A. The Defendant's Claim

The Defendant claims this action must be dismissed because the sheriff's service of process was insufficient, pursuant to C.G.S. Sec. 52-57. He fails to realize, however, that C.G.S. Sec. 52-57 does not provide the only method of service of process in cases involving motor vehicles.

B. The Defendant Was Properly Served Under C.G.S. Sec. 52-63

The Sheriff's Return of Service clearly states that after diligent attempts, he was unable to make service upon the Defendant at its last address on file with DMV or anywhere else in his precinct. Therefore, he could not make in hand or abode service as stated in C.G.S. Sec. 52-57. Instead, he invoked the provisions found in C.G.S. Sec. 52-63. This statute provides for service upon the Commissioner of the Department of Motor Vehicles and by certified mail to the Defendant when it is alleged that the Defendant caused injuries through the negligent operation of a motor vehicle, and the Defendant cannot be located at its last address on file with DMV. Therefore, the Defendant was properly serviced and its claim of insufficient service of process is without merit.

C. The Defendant Waived All Claims for Insufficient Service of Process

Even if service upon the Defendant was defective, he waived such claim pursuant to Connecticut Practice Sec. 142 et seq.

Connecticut Practice Book Sec. 142 requires a Defendant's Motion to Dismiss to challenge the court's jurisdiction to be filed within thirty days of filing its Appearance. In addition, Connecticut Practice Book Sec. 144 states that:

> Any claim of lack of jurisdiction over the person or improper venue or insufficiency of process or insufficiency of service of process is waived if not raised by a Motion to Dismiss filed in the sequence provided in Sections 112 and 113, and within the time provided by Section 142.

In the instant case, the Defendant filed this Motion to Dismiss more than thirty days after he filed his Appearance. Hence, he has waived his defective process claim and submitted himself to the court's jurisdiction.

CONCLUSION

Based on the foregoing, this instant case should not be dismissed, and the Plaintiff's Objection to the Defendant's Motion to Dismiss should be sustained.

THE PLAINTIFF

BY_____

Christine Kulas, Esq.,
Law Offices of Christine Kulas,
her attorney
P.O. Box 2005
Ellington, CT 06066
Tele. #(860) 222-2222
Juris #989898

STATE OF CONNECTICUT   )

) SS: WETHERSFIELD, May 11, 1998

COUNTY OF HARTFORD   )

       Then and by virtue hereof and by direction of the Plaintiff's attorney, I made a diligent search throughout my precincts to locate the within named Defendant, Richard P. Andrew, 329 Lakeside Blvd., Rockville, Connecticut 06066, but could not make service upon said Defendant at the address on file at the office of the Motor Vehicle Commissioner of the State of Connecticut, being 329 Lakeside Blvd., Rockville, Connecticut 06066 or anywhere else in my precinct. And afterwards on the 11th day of May, 1998, in the Town of Wethersfield, County of Hartford, State of Connecticut, I made due and legal service upon the within named Defendant, Richard P. Andrew, 329 Lakeside Blvd., Rockville, Connecticut 06066 by leaving a true and attested copy of the original Writ, Summons and Complaint, with my doings thereon endorsed, at the office of the Commissioner of Motor Vehicles of the State of Connecticut at least twelve days before the return date. Said Commissioner of Motor Vehicles of the State of Connecticut is the duly authorized agent and attorney for the within named resident Defendant.

       And afterwards on the 11th day of May, 1998, at least 12 days before the return date, I deposited in the Post Office at Vernon, Connecticut, postage paid, and certified, return receipt requested, a true and attested copy of the within original Writ, Summons and Complaint, with my doings thereon endorsed, addressed to the within named Defendant, Richard P. Andrew, 329 Lakeside Blvd., Rockville, Connecticut 06066, that being the address on file at the office of the Motor Vehicle Commissioner of the State of Connecticut.

       The within and foregoing is the original Writ, Summons and Complaint, with my doings thereon endorsed.

Fees:

Service	20.00	ATTEST:
Travel	32.50	
Endorsement	2.40	
Pages	24.00	
DMV	5.00	
Cost to Mail	2.75	
	$105.45	Alex J. Zaniewski
		Deputy Sheriff

11 *Pleadings: Defendant's Request to Revise, Plaintiff's Response and Amending Pleadings*

Introduction

Requests to Revise are commonly filed by Defendants and are directed to the Plaintiff's Complaint. In addition, Plaintiffs may file a Request to Revise a Defendant's Answer and/or Special Defenses. Counterclaims and Cross Complaints as well as Plaintiff's Special Defenses to a Counterclaim are also not immune. These requests can be minor, such as correcting spelling or numeric errors, or may go as far as deleting certain portions of a pleading.

Amended pleadings are also permitted. Pursuant to certain rules, a Plaintiff can amend the Complaint to correct errors, add counts, etc. In addition, the parties may request to amend any pleadings they have filed.

I. GROUNDS FOR A REQUEST TO REVISE

A. *A Request to Revise a Complaint, Counterclaim or Cross Complaint*

Pbs 147 provides four distinct reasons to request to revise an adverse party's pleading:

1. to obtain a more complete or particular statement of the allegations;

2. to delete any unnecessary, repetitious, scandalous, impertinent, immaterial or otherwise improper allegations in an adverse party's pleading;

3. to separate cause of actions which may be improperly combined in one count;

4. to obtain any other appropriate revision.

B. *A Request to Revise Special Defenses*

A Request to Revise Special Defenses is appropriate to separate two or more grounds of defense that are improperly combined in one defense, and to obtain any other appropriate revision.

II. DRAFTING A REQUEST TO REVISE

Pbs 148 explains how to draft a Request to Revise. For each portion of the pleading:

1. number and restate the specific provision to be revised;

2. underneath each provision, explain the reasons for the request e.g., any of the grounds stated in Pbs 147 and case law if available; and

3. leave appropriate space underneath each reason for objections from the opposing party.

III. FILING A REQUEST TO REVISE

Pursuant to Pbs 149, after drafting a Request to Revise, the original should be filed in court with a certification of service that a copy was sent to all other parties of record. No order is needed.

IV. RECEIVING A REQUEST TO REVISE

Pursuant to Pbs 149, a party who receives a Request to Revise should take the following action within *30 days* of the date the request was filed:

1. file an objection to the Request to Revise or any part thereof; or

2. comply with all the requests.

As we said earlier, requests do not need a judge's ruling, unless the opposing party files an objection. Therefore, the request is automatically deemed granted unless an objection is filed within 30 days from the date the request was filed in court. A party who decides not to object should file a *revised pleading*, complete with all the requested changes, preferably within the 30-day period. In addition, many parties attach a *Notice* to the revised pleading, indicating that they have complied with the Request to Revise.

V. OBJECTING TO A REQUEST TO REVISE

We will refer to the following example throughout the remainder of this chapter: If a Defendant files a Request to Revise a Complaint on February 3, 1997, the Plaintiff has until 5:00 p.m. on March 5, 1997 to file an objection to any of the requests. The Plaintiff can object to all or some of the Defendant's requests. Any requests not objected to must be incorporated into a Revised Complaint after the objections are resolved.

The reasons for a Plaintiff's objections must be clearly stated in the space provided by the Defendant in the Request to Revise. This can be accomplished by simply photocopying the Defendant's Request to Revise, then, inserting "Objection to" above or on the same line as the title. For example: OBJECTION TO REQUEST TO REVISE

Next, the Plaintiff will simply insert the objections and reasons in the spaces provided, continuing on another sheet if necessary.

VI. THE COVER SHEET AND OBJECTIONS

Pursuant to Pbs 149, the Plaintiff must also attach a **cover sheet** to the objections. The cover sheet should contain the following:

1. case caption;
2. title, "COVER SHEET, RE: OBJECTION TO REQUEST TO REVISE";
3. contents specifically stating the numbers of the specific requests the Plaintiff objects to;
4. necessary signature and related information;
5. order;
6. certification;
7. "Oral Argument Not Requested
Testimony Not Required."

VII. SHORT CALENDAR

Pursuant to Pbs 149, an objection to a Request to Revise will be placed on the next available Short Calendar as nonarguable. If a party wants oral argument, follow the instructions on the applicable Short Calendar. In most cases, the deciding judge will take the matter on the papers, rather than allow argument.

VIII. REVISED PLEADINGS: DEADLINE TO FILE

Pursuant to Pbs 149, if the court overrules one or more of the Plaintiff's objections, the Plaintiff has *15 days* from the court's order to file a Revised Complaint that contains all the revisions ordered by the court. In addition, the Plaintiff must include any requested revisions he or she did not object to.

IX. AMENDED PLEADINGS

An amended pleading is exactly what it sounds like. It is a corrected or modified version of a previously filed pleading.

A. *Plaintiff's Right to Amend Complaint*

Within *30 days* after the return date, Pbs 175 permits a Plaintiff to file an **Amended Complaint** to address any "defect, mistake or informality" in the original Summons or Compliant, without additional costs or permission from the court or the opposing party. See also C.G.S. sec. 52-128.

B. *Amendments by Either Party: Request to Amend Pleading*

Pbs 176 allows *either* party to amend any pleading under the circumstances listed below. This includes a Plaintiff who decides to amend the Complaint after the30 days mentioned above. These circumstances include:
1. by court order;
2. by written consent from the opposing party;
3. by filing a Request for Leave to Amend, and attaching the amended pleading.

C. *Objecting to a Request to Amend*

If the opposing party wishes to object to a Request to Amend, Pbs 176(c) requires an objection to be filed within *15 days* from the date the request was filed. If no objection is filed within 15 days, the court treats the request as having been consented to by the opposing party. See also C.G.S. sec. 52-130.

D. *Drafting an Objection to Request to Amend*

The objection procedure is similar to an Objection to Request to Revise, except a cover sheet does not appear to be necessary. Instead, Pbs 177(c) indicates that the objecting party should state the paragraph(s) at issue, followed by the reasons for the objection. Once filed, the objection will be placed on the next available Short Calendar.

E. *Reasons to Object to a Request to Amend*

A common reason to object to an amended pleading, especially an Amended Complaint, is because the content of the amendment may further delay the litigation process or inconvenience or cause surprise to the opposing party. In such situations the court may limit the amendment, or allow it but award the opposing party costs for any inconvenience or delay caused by the amendment. On the other hand, the amendment could be denied altogether.

F. Pleading to an Amended Pleading

Pursuant to Pbs 177, if an opposing party has not responded to the original pleading when the amended version is filed, he or she should respond to the amended version in accordance with Pbs 114: *30 days* after the return date and in *15-day* increments thereafter.

If the opposing party has already responded to the original pleading, he or she may respond to the amended pleading within *ten days* after the amendment becomes part of the file. This is, however, voluntary. If the opposing party fails to respond to the amendment, his or her original response will be considered applicable, as far as possible, to the amendment.

X. CONCLUSION

A. Key Issues in This Chapter Include:

1. Requests to Revise: Time Limits
> **a.** A party who objects to a Request to Revise must file an objection within *30 days* of the date the Request to Revise was filed in court. Otherwise, the request is granted.
> **b.** If the court overrules the objections, a revised pleading that complies with the court's order must be filed within *15 days* of that order.

2. Requests to Amend: Time Limits
A party who opposes a Request to Amend a pleading must file an objection within *15 days* of the date the Request was filed. Otherwise the request is granted.

3. Oral Argument at Short Calendar
There is no right to oral argument to address objections to a Request to Revise. If you want oral argument, be sure to follow the instructions found on the applicable Short Calendar. Remember, the court has discretion to grant or deny a request for oral argument.

B. Relevant Connecticut Practice Book Sections Include:

Pbs 147: Request to Revise
Pbs 148: Request to Revise--Reasons
Pbs 149: Request to Revise--Granting of and Objection to Request to Revise

Example 1, Request to Revise

DOCKET NO. CV 98-0555555 S	:	SUPERIOR COURT
SHEILA WILKENSON	:	JUDICIAL DISTRICT
	:	OF FAIRFIELD
VS	:	AT BRIDGEPORT
RYAN KEEGAN	:	MAY 4, 1998

REQUEST TO REVISE

Pursuant to Connecticut Practice Book Section 147 et seq., the Defendant in the above-captioned case hereby requests the Plaintiff to revise her Complaint dated March 2, 1998 in the following ways:

1. Portion of Pleading Sought to be Revised:

11. The Defendant acted negligently and is responsible for the Plaintiff's injuries for one or more of the following ways in that he:

a) knew or should have known that the door to the bathroom was not constructed in accordance with building codes and created a hazard to those attempting to open it;

b) knew or should have known that the light switches were not constructed and located according to the building codes and created a hazard to those persons upstairs who seek to use them to light the hallway.

Requested Revision:

The Defendant requests the Plaintiff to specify what building code provisions were allegedly not complied with.

Reasons for Request:

It is unknown if the Plaintiff is referring to the local or state building code. Both codes are voluminous and it would be extremely burdensome on the Defendant to try to figure out which provisions of which code the Plaintiff claims were violated.

It is up to the Plaintiff to plead facts sufficient to place the Defendant on notice as to the facts claimed. See Connecticut Practice Book Section 108. Further, absent specificity as to the facts of which housing code sections were allegedly violated, it will be difficult for the Defendant to investigate and respond to these two allegations.

Finally, with such open-ended and broad allegations, it will be difficult for the court to rule on objections relating to them at trial. See <u>Bourquin v. Melsungen</u>, 40 Conn. App. 302 (1996). Objections at trial on the ground that evidence is outside the scope of the allegations of the Complaint will be difficult to sustain if the Complaint is open-ended and vague. <u>Id</u>.

Plaintiff's Objection and Reasons: (to be filled in by Plaintiff)

2. Portion of Pleading Sought to be Revised:

11. The Defendant acted negligently and carelessly and is responsible for the Plaintiff's injuries in one or more of the following ways in that he:

d). failed to make and keep his property safe for persons, such as the Plaintiff, who were invited onto the property.

Requested Revision:

The Defendant requests the Plaintiff to delete the reference to "property" and "persons."

Reasons for Request:

The Plaintiff claims that she allegedly fell down the stairs adjacent to the bathroom. The allegations indicate that the negligence of the Defendant involved the placement of the bathroom door relative to the stairs, and locations of the light switches. Therefore, the only alleged defects appear to involve the placing of the bathroom relative to the stairway, and the locations of the light switches, not the "property" generally.

To allow the Complaint to proceed as framed would allow for the introduction of any and all evidence concerning the property, although it is unrelated to the Plaintiff's claim. It will be difficult if not impossible for the court to rule on objections on this issue at trial. See <u>Bourquin v. Melsungen,</u> 40 Conn. App. 302 (1996). Objections at trial on the ground that evidence is outside the scope of the allegations of the Complaint will be difficult to sustain if the Complaint is open-ended and vague. <u>Id</u>.

Additionally, there is only one Plaintiff in this case. Therefore the reference to "persons" is inappropriate and should be deleted.

Plaintiff's Objection and Reasons:

THE DEFENDANT

BY _____

Glen Lutley, Esq.,
Lutley & Associates,
his attorneys
906 Park Plaza
Bridgeport, CT 04530
Tele. #(203) 555-5555
Juris #464646

CERTIFICATION

I hereby certify that a copy of the above Request to Revise was mailed on May 4, 1998 to all counsel and pro se parties of record, namely: Attorney Ann Lambert, of Lambert and Smith, P.C., 529 Corporate Place, Fairfield, CT 04540.

_____
Commissioner of Superior Court

Example 2, Cover Sheet and Objections to Request to Revise

DOCKET NO. CV 98-0555555 S	:	SUPERIOR COURT
SHEILA WILKENSON	:	JUDICIAL DISTRICT
	:	OF FAIRFIELD
VS.	:	AT BRIDGEPORT
RYAN KEEGAN	:	MAY 28, 1998

COVER SHEET: PLAINTIFF'S OBJECTIONS TO DEFENDANTS' REQUEST TO REVISE

Pursuant to Connecticut Practice Book Section 149, the Plaintiff hereby objects to requested revisions, #1 and #2 stated by the Defendant in his May 4, 1998 Request to Revise, for the reasons set forth in the attached objections.

THE PLAINTIFF

BY_____

Ann Lambert, Esq.,
Lambert and Smith, P.C.,
her attorneys
529 Corporate Place
Fairfield, CT 04540
Tele. #(203) 777-7777
Juris #545454

ORAL ARGUMENT NOT REQUESTED
TESTIMONY NOT REQUIRED

ORDER
The foregoing objection having been considered by the Court, it is hereby ORDERED: SUSTAINED/OVERRULED.

_____
BY THE COURT

CERTIFICATION OF SERVICE

I hereby certify that a copy of the foregoing Cover Sheet and the attached Objections were mailed on May 28, 1998 to all counsel and pro se parties of record, namely: Attorney Glen Lutley, of Lutley & Associates, 906 Park Plaza, Bridgeport, CT 04530.

_____
Commissioner of the Superior Court

DOCKET NO. CV 98-0555555 S	:	SUPERIOR COURT
SHEILA WILKENSON	:	JUDICIAL DISTRICT
	:	OF FAIRFIELD
VS.	:	AT BRIDGEPORT
RYAN KEEGAN	:	MAY 28, 1998

OBJECTION TO REQUEST TO REVISE

Pursuant to Connecticut Practice Book Section 147 et seq., the Defendant in the above-captioned case hereby requests the Plaintiff to revise her Complaint dated March 2, 1998 in the following ways:

1. Portion of Pleading Sought to be Revised:

11. The Defendant acted negligently and carelessly and is responsible for the Plaintiff's injuries in one or more of the following ways in that he:

a) knew or should have known that the door to the bathroom was not constructed in accordance with building codes and created a hazard to those attempting to open it;

b) knew or should have known that the light switches were not constructed and located according to the building codes and created a hazard to those persons upstairs who seek to use them to light the hallway.

Requested Revision:

The Defendant requests the Plaintiff to specify what building code provisions were allegedly not complied with.

Reasons for Request:

It is unknown if the Plaintiff is referring to the local or state building code. Both codes are voluminous and it would be extremely burdensome on the Defendant to try to figure out which provisions of which code the Plaintiff claims were violated.

It is up to the Plaintiff to plead facts sufficient to place the Defendant on notice as to the facts claimed. See Connecticut Practice Book Section 108. Further, absent specificity as to the facts of which housing code sections were allegedly violated, it will be difficult for the Defendants to investigate and respond to these two allegations.

Finally, with such open-ended and broad allegations, it will be difficult for the court to rule on objections relating to them at trial. See <u>Bourquin v. Melsungen</u>, 40 Conn. App. 302 (1996). Objections at trial on the ground that evidence is outside the scope of the allegations of the Complaint will be difficult to sustain if the Complaint is open-ended and vague. <u>Id</u>.

Plaintiff's Objection and Reasons:

The Plaintiff objects to the above-requested revision for the following reasons:

a. In paragraphs 11 a) and b), the Plaintiff specifically informs the Defendant that she believes the construction of the door and the light switches caused her injuries. Therefore, any local and state building codes that apply to the construction of doors and light switches apply and the court will have no difficulty ruling on this issue at trial.

b. The Complaint, read in its entirety, fully apprises the Defendant of what the Plaintiff intends to prove at trial. In addition, pleadings are to be construed "broadly and realistically, rather than narrowly and technically." <u>Dornfried v. October Twenty-Four, Inc.</u>, 230 Conn. 622, 629, 1994. Therefore, the Defendant is not subject to surprise or prejudice regarding the Plaintiff's claims.

c. Pursuant to an agreement between the parties, the Plaintiff's expert engineer will be inspecting the Defendant's property and the Defendant indicates he has retained his own expert engineer to conduct its own inspection. As a result, each party will have the opportunity to consult with its expert and to depose the opposing expert regarding the Defendant's concerns, as stated in this requested revision.

2. Portion of Pleading Sought to be Revised:

11. The Defendant acted negligently and carelessly and is responsible for the Plaintiff's injuries in one or more of the following ways in that he:

d) failed to make and keep his property safe for persons, such as the Plaintiff, who were invited onto the property.

Requested Revision:

The Defendant requests that the Plaintiff delete the reference to "property" and "persons."

Reasons for Request:

The Plaintiff claims that she allegedly fell down the stairs adjacent to the bathroom. The allegations indicate that the negligence of the Defendant involved the placement of the bathroom door relative to the stairs, and locations of the light switches. Therefore, the only alleged defect appear to involve the placing of the bathroom relative to the stairway, and the locations of the light switches, not the "property" generally.

To allow the Complaint to proceed as framed would allow for the introduction of any and all evidence concerning the property although it is unrelated to the Plaintiff's claim. It will be difficult if not impossible for the court to rule on objections on this issue at trial. See Bourquin v. Melsungen, 40 Conn. App. 302 (1996). Objections at trial on the ground that evidence is outside the scope of the allegations of the Complaint will be difficult to sustain if the Complaint is open-ended and vague. Id.

Additionally, there is only one Plaintiff in this case. Therefore, the reference to "persons" is inappropriate and should be deleted.

Plaintiff's Objection and Reasons:

The Plaintiff objects to the above-requested revision for the following reasons:
The Complaint, read in its entirety, fully apprises the Defendant of what "persons" and what "property" are at issue. Pleadings are to be construed "broadly and realistically, rather than narrowly and technically." Dornfried v. October Twenty-Four, Inc., 230 Conn. 622, 629, 1994. Therefore, the Defendant is not subject to surprise or prejudice regarding the Plaintiff's claims and the court will have no difficulty ruling on evidence that could lead to expanding the meaning of "persons" or "property" at trial.

THE PLAINTIFF

BY_____

Ann Lambert, Esq.,
Lambert and Smith, P.C.,
her attorneys
529 Corporate Place
Fairfield, CT 04540
Tele. #(203) 777-7777, Juris #545454

COURT NOTICE

DOCKET NO. CV 98-0555555 S
SHEILA WILKENSON VS. RYAN KEEGAN

The Plaintiff's Objection to Request to Revise dated May 28, 1998 is hereby ordered :
1. Overruled as to Objection #1;
2. Sustained as to Objection #2;   Notice sent June 15, 1998.

Example 3, Notice of Filing Revised Complaint

DOCKET NO. CV 98-0555555 S	:	SUPERIOR COURT
SHEILA WILKENSON	:	JUDICIAL DISTRICT
	:	OF FAIRFIELD
VS.	:	AT BRIDGEPORT
RYAN KEEGAN	:	JUNE 29, 1998

NOTICE OF FILING REVISED COMPLAINT

  The Plaintiff in the above-captioned case hereby gives notice that she is filing the Revised Complaint attached hereto in accordance with the Defendant's Request to Revise dated May 4, 1998 and the court's subsequent order, by deleting the phrase "building codes" found in Paragraph 11 (a) and (b) of her original Complaint.

THE PLAINTIFF

BY_____

    Ann Lambert, Esq.,
    Lambert and Smith, P.C.,
    her attorney
    529 Corporate Place
    Fairfield, CT 04540
    Tele. #(203) 777-7777
    Juris #545454

CERTIFICATION

  I hereby certify that a copy of the above Notice and attached Revised Complaint was mailed on June 29, 1998 to all counsel and pro se parties of record, namely, Attorney Glen Lutley, Lutley and Associates, 906 Park Plaza, Bridgeport, CT 04530.

_____
Commissioner of the Superior Court

Example 4, Request to File Amended Complaint

DOCKET NO. CV 98-0444444 S	:	SUPERIOR COURT
GEORGE SKILLMAN, ET AL	:	JUDICIAL DISTRICT OF
	:	HARTFORD/NEW BRITAIN
VS.	:	AT HARTFORD
AUTO SERVICE CENTER, INC.	:	MAY 8, 1998

REQUEST TO FILE AMENDED COMPLAINT

Pursuant to Connecticut Practice Book Section 176 (c), the Plaintiffs in the above-captioned case hereby request to file the Amended Complaint. Specifically, the Plaintiffs seek to correct the amount of the monthly payments claimed due in Paragraph 3 of the original Complaint.

According to terms of the promissory note at issue, the Defendant is obligated to pay the Plaintiffs $10,500.00 per month, which includes interest. Not $10,000.00, as stated in the Complaint. An Amended Complaint containing this correction is attached hereto.

THE PLAINTIFF

BY_____

Kenneth I. Marcus, Esq.,
Friedman & Marcus, P.C.,
their attorneys
27 Main Street
Bristol, CT 00000
Tele. #(826) 955-9595
Juris #424242

CERTIFICATION

I hereby certify that a copy of the above Notice and the attached Amended Complaint was mailed on May 8, 1998 to all counsel and pro se parties of record, namely: Mark Peters, Esq., Mark Peters and Associates, P.C., 1001 Sanberg Street, Manchester, CT 06660.

_____
Commissioner of the Superior Court

12 *Pleadings: Defendant's Motion to Strike and Plaintiff's Response*

Terminology

> Substitute Complaint

Pbs: 152, 153, 154, 155, 156, 157, 158, 204

Introduction

The grounds for a Motion to Strike appear more complex than a Motion to Dismiss. In most cases, the purpose of this motion is to require the Plaintiff to remove (strike) a portion of the Complaint, or the entire Complaint itself, because the allegations at issue are not legally recognized by our courts. Therefore, the Defendant believes the court has no basis to award any damages to the Plaintiff.

In addition to attacking a Plaintiff's Complaint, a Motion to Strike may be used to challenge Answers, Special Defenses, Counterclaims, Cross Complaints and prayers for relief.

I. GROUNDS FOR A MOTION TO STRIKE

Pursuant to Pbs 152, a Motion to Strike is appropriate when a party challenges:
1. the legal sufficiency of a Complaint, Counterclaim or Cross Complaint to state a claim upon which relief can be granted;
2. the legal sufficiency of a prayer (demand) of relief in a Complaint;
3. the legal sufficiency of a Complaint because it lacks a necessary party;

4. a Complaint that contains two or more causes of action that can't properly be united in one Complaint, even if they are stated more than one count;

5. the legal sufficiency of an Answer or part thereof to a Complaint, including Special Defenses.

A Motion to Strike can be directed against an entire pleading or a portion of the pleading. In addition, Pbs 154 requires each claim of legal sufficiency to be set forth separately and include specific reasons. Last, like a Motion to Dismiss, Pbs 155 requires a Motion to Strike and an objection to be accompanied by a memorandum of law that cites the legal authority (case law, etc.) that is relied upon.

Once filed in court, a Motion to Strike will appear on the Short Calendar within two to three weeks.

II. OBJECTING TO A MOTION TO STRIKE

A. Time to Object

Pursuant to Pbs 155, a party who wishes to object to a Motion to Strike must file an objection and memorandum of law at least *five days* before the date the motion is scheduled to be heard on Short Calendar. (As you should recall, the rule is the same for objecting to a Motion to Dismiss.)

For instance, if the case appears on Short Calendar for Monday, February 16, 1998, the objection and memorandum of law must be filed no later than the previous Wednesday by 5:00 p.m.

B. Goal of the Objection

The goal of the objection is to provide the court with legal authority (case law, rules, statutes, regulations, etc.) to justify denying the Motion to Strike. In some cases it may be sufficient for the party to simply amend the pleading to include the language and facts necessary to prove that a real cause of action exists.

For example, a Plaintiff may have forgotten to include an applicable statute in the Complaint or may not have realized that such statute exists. Or, the Plaintiff may have omitted certain facts which support applying a specific statute, or rule, regulation or case. In this situation, the Plaintiff has three choices:

1. Amend the Complaint and obtain the opposing party's agreement not to go forward on the Motion to Strike;

2. File an objection and memorandum of law, based upon the new Amended Complaint, which is attached;

3. Allow the court to grant the Motion to Strike and file the new pleading within *15 days* of that decision. See Section IV below.

III. SHORT CALENDAR

Pursuant to Pbs 211, the court will hear oral argument on a Motion to Strike and an objection, if requested by one or more of the parties.

IV. IF A MOTION TO STRIKE IS GRANTED

Sometimes, no matter how unfair it may seem, a Plaintiff may have no real basis to sue a Defendant. Therefore, the court will strike the entire Complaint against the Defendant In other cases, only one or more of the Defendants listed in the Complaint will be affected. Therefore, the court will strike those counts that apply to those Defendants.

Pursuant to Pbs 157, if the court grants a Defendant's Motion to Strike pertaining to only a portion of the Plaintiff's Complaint, the Plaintiff may replead within *15 days* after the motion is granted, either deleting that portion or drafting the pleading to address the defect. In this situation, the new pleading is often entitled a **Substitute Complaint**, rather than an Amended Compliant.

Caution: Pbs 157 also provides that if the *entire* Complaint is stricken, the Plaintiff *must* file a Substitute Complaint within *15 days* after the court's decision. If this deadline is missed, the Defendant may file a Motion for Judgment against the Plaintiff which the court may grant. This same provision applies to Counterclaims and Cross Complaints.

V. CONCLUSION

A. *Key Issues in This Chapter Include:*

As you've probably already noticed, Motions to Strike can be quite technical and complicated. Fortunately, if the motion is granted, a party has the opportunity to correct the defects by filing a substitute pleading. If the entire Complaint, Counterclaim or Cross Complaint is stricken, a Substitute Complaint must be filed within *15 days* of the court's order. Otherwise, the party who filed the Motion to Strike may obtain judgment.

B. *Relevant Connecticut Practice Book Sections Include:*

Pbs 152: Motion to Strike--In General
Pbs 153: Motion to Strike--Date for Hearing
Pbs 154: Motion to Strike--Reasons
Pbs 155: Motion to Strike--Memorandum of Law
Pbs 156: Motion to Strike--When Memorandum of Decision Is Required
Pbs 157: Motion to Strike--Substitute Pleading
Pbs 158: Motion to Strike--Stricken Pleading Part of Another Cause or Defense
Pbs 204: Memorandum of Law Required

Example 1, Motion to Strike

DOCKET NO. CV 98-0777777 S	:	SUPERIOR COURT
SAMSON ZANEWCHIO	:	JUDICIAL DISTRICT
	:	OF MIDDLESEX
VS.	:	AT MIDDLETOWN
HERMAN SHEPPERD, ET AL.	:	JANUARY 7, 1999

MOTION TO STRIKE

Pursuant to Connecticut Practice Book Section 151 et seq., the Defendant, Oakmont Terrace Condominium Association, hereby moves to strike the Sixth and Seventh Counts of the Plaintiff's Complaint dated October 19, 1998 on the grounds that said counts fail to state a claim upon which relief can be granted and are insufficient as a matter of law.

A memorandum of law in support of this motion is attached hereto.

THE DEFENDANT,
OAKMONT TERRACE
CONDOMINIUM ASSOCIATION

BY_____

Heidi Zimmerman, Esq.
Law Office of Heidi Zimmerman,
its attorney
P.O. Box 256
Middletown, CT 09870
Tele. #(860) 334-1212
Juris #123789

ORAL ARGUMENT REQUESTED
TESTIMONY NOT REQUIRED

ORDER

The foregoing Motion having been duly presented and heard by the Court, it is hereby ORDERED: GRANTED/DENIED

_____

BY THE COURT

CERTIFICATION

I hereby certify that a copy of the above was mailed on January 7, 1999 to all counsel and pro se parties of record as follows: Joshua A. Graham, Esq., of Mahoney & Tyler, P.C., P.O. Box 145, Middletown, CT 09870.

_____

Commissioner of the Superior Court

DOCKET NO. CV 98-0777777 S   :   SUPERIOR COURT
SAMSON ZANEWCHIO   :   JUDICIAL DISTRICT
    :   OF MIDDLESEX
VS.   :   AT MIDDLETOWN
HERMAN SHEPPERD, ET AL.   :   JANUARY 7, 1999

MEMORANDUM OF LAW
IN SUPPORT OF MOTION TO STRIKE

FACTS

The Plaintiff, Samson Zanewchio, claims he was injured when he was allegedly bitten by a dog on October 24, 1997. The Plaintiff has sued five separate Defendants.

The Defendant, Herman Shepperd, owns the dog in question. The Defendant, Oakmont Terrace Condominium Association (hereinafter referred to as "Oakmont") is the location in which the Defendant, Herman Shepperd, resides with the dog in question.

The Plaintiff's Complaint contains seven counts. The first two counts are directed against Herman Shepperd. The third through fifth counts are directed at Defendant, New Haven Savings Bank. The remaining sixth and seventh counts are directed at the Defendant, Oakmont, alleging negligence, presumably pursuant to Connecticut General Statutes Sec. 22-357, known as the Dog Bite Statute.

The Defendant, Oakmont, files this instant Motion to Strike on the ground that the allegations set forth in the sixth and seventh counts against it fail to state a cause of action.

In his Complaint, the Plaintiff alleges that the Defendant, Oakmont, owned and controlled the area where the alleged attack took place. In paragraph two of the sixth count, the Plaintiff alleges that the Defendant, Oakmont, knew or should have known of the dog's dangerous propensities. It appears that the Plaintiff believes these two allegations are sufficient to hold the Defendant, Oakmont, liable for the Plaintiff's injuries. The Defendant, Oakmont, disagrees.

ARGUMENT

Paragraph two of the Sixth Count of the Plaintiff's Amended Complaint claims the Defendant, Oakmont, was negligent, and therefore liable for the Plaintiff's injuries. This allegation, however, does not justify holding the Defendant, Oakmont, liable under C.G.S. Sec. 22-357, the dog bite statute, which states:

> If any dog does any damage to either the body or property of any person, the <u>owner or keeper</u>, or if the owner or keeper is a minor, the parent or guardian of such minor, shall be liable for such damage, except when such damage has been occasioned to the body or property of the person who, at the time such damage was sustained, was committing a trespass or other tort, or was teasing, tormenting or abusing such dog."

The Statute defines keeper as: "any person, other than the owner, harboring or having in his possession any dog."

In addition, in order for a duty to arise under C.G.S. Sec. 22-357, some degree of control over the dog must be exercised. <u>Buturla v. St. Onge, Et Al.</u>, 9 Conn. App. 495, 496, cert. denied, 203 Conn. 803 (1987).

There is no dispute that the Defendant, Oakmont, is not the owner or keeper of the dog. Nor did the Plaintiff claim that the Defendant, Oakmont, had any degree of control over the dog at any time of the alleged attack. Therefore, the Defendant, Oakmont, can not be found liable for the Plaintiff's injuries.

Pursuant to Connecticut Practice Book Section 152, a Motion to Strike tests the legal sufficiency of a cause of action or defense. In this case, there is no authority to hold the Defendant, Oakmont, liable for the Plaintiff's claims.

CONCLUSION

Accordingly, the allegations in the sixth and seventh counts of the Plaintiff's Amended Complaint fail to state a cause of action against the Defendant, Oakmont, under Conn. Gen. Stat. Sec. 22-357 or any case law, and should be stricken.

THE DEFENDANT,
OAKMONT TERRACE
CONDOMINIUM ASSOCIATION

BY _____

Heidi Zimmerman, Esq.,
Law Office of Heidi Zimmerman,
its attorney
P.O. Box 256
Middletown, CT 09870
Tele. # (860) 334-1212
Juris #123789

Example 2, Objection to Motion to Strike

DOCKET NO. CV 98-0777777 S	:	SUPERIOR COURT
SAMSON ZANEWCHIO	:	JUDICIAL DISTRICT
	:	OF MIDDLESEX
VS.	:	AT MIDDLETOWN
HERMAN SHEPPERD, ET AL.	:	JANUARY 19, 1999

OBJECTION TO MOTION TO STRIKE

In accordance with Connecticut Practice Book Section 155, the Plaintiff hereby objects to the Motion to Strike filed by the Defendant, Oakmont Terrace Condominium Association, dated January 7, 1999. The Plaintiff makes this objection on the grounds that he has stated a cause of action upon which relief can be granted, against the Defendant, Oakmont Terrace Condominium Association. Therefore, this Objection to the Defendant's Motion to Strike should be sustained.

THE PLAINTIFF

BY _____

Joshua A. Graham, Esq.,
Mahoney & Tyler, P.C.,
ORAL ARGUMENT REQUESTED   his attorneys
TESTIMONY NOT REQUIRED   P.O. Box 145
Middletown, CT 09870
Tele. #(860) 344-5151
Juris # 70598

ORDER

The foregoing Objection having been presented to the Court, it is hereby ORDERED: GRANTED/DENIED.

_____
BY THE COURT

CERTIFICATION

I hereby certify that a copy of the foregoing objection and attached memorandum of law were mailed on January 19, 1999 to all counsel and pro se parties of record, namely: Heidi Zimmerman, Esq., P.O. Box 256, Middletown, CT 09870.

_____
Commissioner of the Superior Court

DOCKET NO. CV 98-0777777 S	:	SUPERIOR COURT
SAMSON ZANEWCHIO	:	JUDICIAL DISTRICT
	:	OF MIDDLESEX
VS.	:	AT MIDDLETOWN
HERMAN SHEPPERD, ET AL	:	JANUARY 19, 1999

MEMORANDUM OF LAW
IN SUPPORT OF
OBJECTION TO MOTION TO STRIKE

FACTS

The Plaintiff in the above-captioned case brought suit for injuries he sustained as a result of being viciously attacked by a dog owned by the Defendant, Herman Shepperd.

The Plaintiff was a resident of the Defendant, Oakmont Terrace Condominiums, at the time of the incident at issue. The Defendant, Herman Shepperd, was also a resident of the Defendant condominium complex at the time of the incident.

On or about October 24, 1997, the Plaintiff was jogging in the jogging path located on the common areas of the condominium complex. While the Plaintiff was jogging, a large German Shepherd mix chased and viciously attacked the Plaintiff. The Plaintiff was then rushed to the hospital where he was subsequently treated for his injuries.

In October 1998, the Plaintiff instituted this action against the owner of the dog and the condominium association. In his Complaint, the Plaintiff asserts that the condominium association was negligent in that it owned and controlled the condominium complex where the Defendant dog owner resided and:

a. it knew or should have known the dog lived with the Defendant owner at the condominium complex;

b. the Defendant condominium association permitted the Defendant dog owner to have the animal, although the condominium association charter clearly states no dogs are allowed and several residents have filed written Complaints about the dog with the Defendant condominium association;

c. the Defendant condominium association knew or should have known of the animal's dangerous propensities because it attacked other residents, including children, before attacking the Plaintiff.

As a result of the attack, the Plaintiff was knocked to the ground by the dog, received several sutures as a result of bite marks, broke his tibia, and tore several ligaments which required surgery and will require additional surgery in the future, all of which has resulted in permanent injury.

LAW AND ARGUMENT

In its Motion to Strike, the Defendant condominium association incorrectly asserts that the Plaintiff's action against it is based on the Dog Bite statute, C.G.S. Sec. 22-357. It is not. The Plaintiff's cause of action against the Defendant condominium association rests solely on negligence.

A claim for negligence is based on a breach of duty by the Defendant to the Plaintiff and the causal connection between the Defendant's breach of duty and the resulting harm to the Plaintiff. Catz v. Rubenstein, 201 Conn. 39, 44 (1986).

In this instant case, the Defendant condominium association breached its duty to the Plaintiff by permitting the dog to live at the condominium complex although it knew the dog's presence was a violation of the condominium association charter and that the dog had dangerous propensities. Hence, the Plaintiff has stated a cause of action in which relief can be granted against the Defendant condominium association.

CONCLUSION

Based on the foregoing, the Plaintiff's Objection to Motion to Strike should be sustained.

THE PLAINTIFF

BY _____

Joshua A. Graham, Esq.,
Mahoney & Tyler, P.C.,
his attorneys
P.O. Box 145
Middletown, CT 09870
Tele. #(860) 344-5151
Juris # 70598

13 Pleadings: Defendant's Answer, Special Defenses, Counterclaims and Plaintiff's Response

Terminology

Contested Issues	Reply to Special Defenses	Burden of Proof
Admit	Counterclaim	Deny
Special Defenses	Insufficient Knowledge	Impleader
Contributory Negligence	Comparative Negligence	Joinder

Pbs: 7KK, 83, 116, 117, 160, 161, 162, 164, 165, 166, 167, 168, 171
C.G.S. sections: 52-101 et seq. 52-114

Introduction

At this point, a year or more has passed since the Plaintiffs in our three sample cases filed their Complaints. During this time, the Plaintiffs survived the Defendants' Motion to Dismiss, a Request to Revise, and most recently, the judge denied the Defendant's Motion to Strike in another case. Now, at long last, the 15-day deadline is swiftly approaching for the Defendants to file their Answers, and if applicable, any Special Defenses or Counterclaims. Soon, the pleadings will be closed and the cases will be claimed to the Trial List.

I. THE DEFENDANT'S ANSWER

A. *Purpose of the Answer*

The Defendant's Answer is the response to the Plaintiff's Complaint. Up until this point, the Defendant has been permitted to challenge the Complaint on form and technical issues. Now, the Defendant must face the music, so to speak, and present a defense against the wrongdoing the Plaintiff claims he or she committed.

The Defendant's Answer is extremely important because it defines specifically what allegations the Plaintiff must focus on at trial to meet his or her burden of proof at trial.

B. *Content of the Defendant's Answer*

In comparison to the preceding pleadings, the Answer is an uncomplicated document. Pbs 161 and 162 require that it be direct, precise and specific. It must not be argumentative, hypothetical or stated in the alternative.

In practice, Defendants must read all the allegations set forth in each paragraph of the Plaintiff's Complaint and respond to them in one of the following ways:

1. admit the entire truth of each paragraph that is true; or

2. deny the entire truth of each paragraph that is false; or

3. claim that they have **insufficient knowledge or belief to either admit or deny the truth of the paragraph and leave the Plaintiff to his or her burden of proof**. This response is treated as a denial.

In addition:

4. If a Defendant finds one portion of a paragraph true and another portion untrue, this should be explained in the Answer to that paragraph.

5. If a Defendant finds he or she has insufficient knowledge or belief to admit or deny a portion of a paragraph, this should be stated. The remainder of the paragraph should be either admitted or denied.

6. If a Defendant intends to deny each paragraph in the Complaint, the Answer may consist of one sentence: "The Defendant hereby denies each and every paragraph in the Plaintiff's Complaint." The same holds true if the Defendant intends to admit every paragraph in the Complaint: "The Defendant hereby admits each and every paragraph in the Plaintiff's Complaint." (Of course this rarely occurs.)

At trial, each allegation a Defendant admits to will be treated as true by the trier of fact. Therefore, both parties need to concentrate only on those allegations a Defendant denies (or claims to have insufficient knowledge.) These denied allegations are often referred to as the **contested issues.**

At the end of this chapter, you will find sample Answers to two Complaints found in Chapter 4 that demonstrate the Defendant's options as described above. Once the Defendant's Answer is filed, either party may claim the case to the Trial List, *unless* the Defendant also files **Special Defenses** and/or a **Counterclaim**.

II. SPECIAL DEFENSES

When drafting an Answer, the Defendant must decide whether or not to include any Special Defenses.

A. *What Are Special Defenses?*

Special Defenses are *legally recognized reasons* Defendants may rely upon to claim that they should not be found liable for all or some of the Plaintiff's injuries.

In essence, Special Defenses permit a Defendant to take an offensive, rather than a solely defensive position in the case. Their goal is to prevent the Plaintiff from obtaining any type of judgment or to reduce the amount of the judgment.

Pbs 164 provides a list of many Special Defenses a Defendant can claim:

1. Accord and Satisfaction: The parties previously reached an agreement which wiped out a cause of action adjacent to their original agreement.

2. Arbitration and Award: A prior proceeding took place that resolved the issues.

3. Duress: The Defendant was forced by the Plaintiff to enter into the agreement (usually applies in contract cases).

4. Fraud: The Plaintiff used false or illegal information or methods to cause the Defendant to enter into the contract (usually applies in contract cases).

5. Illegality not apparent on the face of the pleading: For instance, if a promissory note that is being sued on does not state that the interest charged was higher than legally permitted.

6. Infancy: The Defendant was not legally old enough to enter into the agreement and therefore the agreement cannot be enforced.

7. Non Compos Mentis: The Defendant was not of sound mind while involved in the incident.

8. Payment (even though the Plaintiff alleges nonpayment): The Plaintiff already received any payment due.

9. Release: The parties already resolved this issue and the Plaintiff agreed that the Defendant is no longer responsible

10. Set Off: If the Plaintiff owes money to the Defendant, the Defendant may claim he or she is entitled to a credit for that sum, against the sum the Plaintiff is seeking in the Complaint. (See also Pbs 168.)

11. Statute of Limitations: The deadline to file this lawsuit against the Defendant expired before this action was brought.

12. Res Judicata: The issue has already been decided by the court in a prior proceeding.

13. Statute of Frauds: The terms of the contract are not in writing as required (in contract cases).

14. Title in a Third Person to What the Plaintiff Sues upon or Alleges to Be His Own: The Defendant does not own or have what the Plaintiff wants.

In addition, Pbs 167 and C.G.S. sec. 52-114 permit a Defendant to allege **contributory negligence** as a special defense. This special defense claims that the Plaintiff's actions contributed to his or her injuries in some way. As a result, the Defendant will want the trier of fact to determine a percentage which reflects the Plaintiff's negligence, if any. If such percentage is determined, the trier of fact will deduct that percentage from the verdict.

Similarly, **comparative negligence** requires the trier of fact to find in favor of the Defendant and not award any damages to the Plaintiff if it determines that the Plaintiff was more than 50 percent negligent.

B. Pleading Special Defenses

Pbs 164 requires Defendants to plead their Special Defenses. They cannot simply admit or deny the allegations in the Answer and expect to elaborate on the issue during the trial. Hence, as you can see from the example at the end of this chapter, Special Defenses are made part of the Defendant's Answer.

If a Defendant has more than one Special Defense, each must be designated separately, in accordance with Pbs 165. For instance, FIRST SPECIAL DEFENSE, SECOND SPECIAL DEFENSE, etc.

If the Plaintiff's Complaint contains more than one count, the Defendant must indicate which count the Special Defense(s) applies to. For instance, FIRST SPECIAL DEFENSE TO FIRST COUNT.

C. Burden of Proof and Plaintiff's Response to Special Defenses

The burden of proving a Special Defense rests with the Defendant. As a result, Pbs 171 requires the Plaintiff to reply to each of the Defendant's Special Defenses. This **Reply to Special Defenses** is very similar to the Defendant's Answer: The Plaintiff has the option of admitting, denying, or if applicable, claiming he or she has insufficient knowledge to either admit or deny the Special Defenses.

Last, as we've discussed in previous chapters, prior to filing a Reply to Special Defenses, the Plaintiff has the right to file a Request to Revise and Motion to Strike the Special Defenses. Those Special Defenses that survive these pleadings and are denied by the Plaintiff are treated as contested issues which the Defendant must prove at trial.

III. COUNTERCLAIMS

A. A Defendant's Lawsuit against a Plaintiff

In addition to Special Defenses, the Defendant has the right to brings a own lawsuit against the Plaintiff. This lawsuit is called a **Counterclaim**. Like Special Defenses, a Counterclaim should be filed with the Defendant's Answer.

B. Relationship between Complaint and Counterclaim

Pursuant to Pbs 116, in order to be valid, a counterclaim must relate to the events that are the subject of the Plaintiff's Complaint. When filed, the Plaintiff's role and the Defendant's role are reversed: The Defendant bears the burden of proving the Counterclaim and the Plaintiff will present a defense. The following example comes to mind: An attorney sues a former client for failing to pay legal bills. In response, the client turns around and files a Counterclaim against the attorney for legal malpractice pertaining to legal work the attorney wants to be paid for.

According to Pbs 168, a Plaintiff may utilize all the pleadings in the Pleading Stage to defend against the Defendant's Counterclaim. In addition, both sides will conduct discovery. The Counterclaim's case caption, including the docket number, will be the same as that of the Complaint. In addition, the Counterclaim must include a Statement of Amount in Demand.

Once a Counterclaim survives a Request to Revise and a Motion to Strike, the Plaintiff must finally file an Answer to the Defendant's Counterclaim. This Answer may can contain the Plaintiff's own Special Defenses, which the Defendant must address, as described in Section II above.

IV. IMPLEADING PARTIES: THIRD-PARTY PLAINTIFFS AND THIRD-PARTY DEFENDANTS

If a Defendant believes a third party is liable for the Plaintiff's claims, the Defendant may file a motion and memorandum of law under Pbs 204 to implead that third party. If the motion is granted, the Defendant will become a third-party Plaintiff and the new party will become the third-party Defendant. See Pbs 117 and C.G.S. sec. 51-102a for more details.

V. JOINDER

If more than one Plaintiff has an action against a single Defendant as a result of the same dispute, these Plaintiffs may be joined together in the same case. For instance, if a Defendant allegedly defrauded several unrelated consumers, these consumers may join together and bring suit against the Defendant. Or, if they had already filed their own lawsuits individually, the court may consolidate the cases into one trial, providing it would not cause embarrassment or delay the trial. See Pbs 83 et seq. and C.G.S. sec. 52-101 et seq. for more details.

VI. CONCLUSION

A. Key Issues in This Chapter Include:

1. Defendant's Pleadings
In this chapter, we discussed the Defendant's Answer, Special Defenses, and Counterclaims.

2. Plaintiff's Responsive Pleadings
In addition to the above, we've discussed the Plaintiff's responsive pleadings:
    a. Request to Revise Special Defenses,
    b. Motion to Strike Special Defenses,
    c. Reply to Special Defenses, and
    d. The remaining pleadings applicable to Complaints, through to the Answer.

3. Begin to Consider Closing the Pleadings
Once all of the above pleadings are filed and responded to, either side may notify the court that the pleadings are closed and that the case can be placed on the trial list. This is an easy procedure which involves filing a form, entitled Certificate of Closed Pleadings, discussed in Chapter 28.

Before filing the certificate, however, each side should first assess how much discovery they still need to complete before they will be ready to go to trial.

B. Relevant Connecticut Practice Book Sections Include:

Pbs 83:	Joinder of Parties--Interested Persons As Plaintiffs
Pbs 116:	Counterclaims
Pbs 117:	Impleading of Third Party by Defendant in Civil Action
Pbs 7KK:	Form of Pleading
Pbs 160:	The Answer--General and Special Denial
Pbs 161:	The Answer--Evasive Denials
Pbs 162:	The Answer--Pleadings to Be Direct and Specific
Pbs 164:	The Answer--Denials; Special Defenses
Pbs 165:	The Answer--Several Special Defenses
Pbs 166:	The Answer--Admissions and Denials in Special Defense
Pbs 167:	The Answer--Pleading Contributory Negligence
Pbs 168:	The Answer--Pleading Counterclaim and Set Off
Pbs 171:	Subsequent Pleadings--Plaintiff's Response to Answer
Pbs 204:	Requirement That Memorandum of Law Be Filed with Certain Motions

C Relevant Connecticut General Statutes Include:

C.G.S. sec. 52-101.:   Joinder of interested persons as plaintiffs.
C.G.S. sec. 52-114.:   Pleadings of contributory negligence.

Example 1, Answer and Special Defenses

DOCKET NO. CV 98-0333333 S	:	SUPERIOR COURT
SARAH A. DONAHUE	:	JUDICIAL DISTRICT
	:	OF TOLLAND
VS.	:	AT ROCKVILLE
RICHARD P. ANDREW	:	SEPTEMBER 30, 1998

ANSWER

1. The Defendant admits that the Plaintiff was traveling in a westerly direction along Manor Avenue as stated in Paragraph 1 of the Plaintiff's Complaint. The Defendant has insufficient knowledge as to the remainder of Paragraph 1 and leaves the Plaintiff to her proof.

2. The Defendant admits that he was traveling in a westerly direction along Manor Avenue as stated in Paragraph 1 of the Plaintiff's Complaint. The Defendant denies the remainder of Paragraph 1.

3. The Defendant denies Paragraphs 3 through 7 of the Plaintiff's Complaint.

DEFENDANT'S SPECIAL DEFENSES

DEFENDANT'S FIRST SPECIAL DEFENSE

1. Any injuries, losses or damages sustained by the Plaintiff were caused by her own negligence and/or carelessness in one or more of the following ways:

a. She failed to maintain her automobile in a safe and reasonable manner to prevent the automobile from stalling out in the middle of the road while in operation.

b. She operated her automobile on Manor Avenue and Wolcott Street, which are public highways, although she knew or should have known that it was in need of repairs and/or it was unsafe to operate on said public highways.

c. She operated her automobile in a negligent and in an unsafe manner on said public highways.

DEFENDANT'S SECOND SPECIAL DEFENSE

1. The Plaintiff was contributorily negligent in causing the collision and any injuries she claims in that she:

a. failed to maintain her automobile in a safe and reasonable manner to prevent the automobile from stalling out in the middle of the road while in operation;

b. operated her automobile on a public highway, although she knew or should have known that it was in need of repairs and/or it was unsafe to operate on said public highways;

c. operated her automobile in a negligent and unsafe manner.

THE DEFENDANT

BY_____

       Neil E. Clifford, Esq.,

       Michaels, and Sabrina & Alexander, P.C.,

       his attorneys

       259 Sage Road, Suite 200

       West Hartford, CT 08080

       Tele. # (860) 111-1111

       Juris #626262

CERTIFICATION

I hereby certify that a copy of the above was mailed on September 30, 1998 to all counsel and pro se parties of record, namely: Attorney Christine Kulas, Esq., P.O. Box 2005, Ellington, CT 06000.

_____

Commissioner of Superior Court

Example 2, Reply to Special Defenses

DOCKET NO. CV 98-0333333 S	:	SUPERIOR COURT
SARAH A. DONAHUE	:	JUDICIAL DISTRICT
	:	OF TOLLAND
VS.	:	AT ROCKVILLE
RICHARD P. ANDREW	:	OCTOBER 11, 1998

REPLY TO SPECIAL DEFENSES

The Plaintiff hereby denies each of the Defendant's Special Defenses, dated September 30, 1998.

THE PLAINTIFF

BY_____

       Christine Kulas, Esq.,

       Law Offices of Christine Kulas,

       her attorney

       P.O. Box 2005

       Ellington, CT 06066

       Tele. # (860) 222-2222

       Juris #989898

CERTIFICATION

I hereby certify that a copy of the above was mailed on October 11, 1998 to all counsel and pro se parties of record namely: Attorney Neil E. Clifford, of Michaels, Sabrina and Alexander, 259 Sage Road, Suite 200, West Hartford, CT 08080.

_____

Commissioner of Superior Court

Example 3, Answer and Special Defenses

DOCKET NO. CV 98-0555555 S	:	SUPERIOR COURT
SHEILA WILKENSON	:	JUDICIAL DISTRICT
	:	OF FAIRFIELD
VS.	:	AT BRIDGEPORT
RYAN KEEGAN	:	AUGUST 28, 1998

ANSWER

1. Paragraphs 1 through 5, inclusive, of the Plaintiff's Complaint, are hereby admitted.

2. With respect to Paragraphs 6 and 7, the Defendant has insufficient knowledge or information upon which to form a belief and therefore leaves the Plaintiff to her proof.

3. With respect to the portion of Paragraph 8 that states, "The Plaintiff attempted to open the bathroom door," the Defendant has insufficient knowledge or information upon which to form a belief and therefore leaves the Plaintiff to her proof. The remainder of Paragraph 8 is admitted.

4. Paragraph 9 is denied.

5. The Defendant admits that portion of Paragraph 10 which states, "...the Defendant was transported by ambulance to the hospital." The Defendant has insufficient knowledge or information upon which to form a belief with respect to the remainder of Paragraph 10 and leaves the Plaintiff to her proof.

6. Paragraph 11 is denied.

7. Paragraphs 12, 13, 14, and 15 are denied.

DEFENDANT'S SPECIAL DEFENSES

FIRST SPECIAL DEFENSE

1. Any injuries, losses or damages sustained by the Plaintiff were caused by her own negligence and/or carelessness in one of more of the following ways:

a. She neglected to use reasonable care in watching where she was walking and stepping;

b. She voluntarily consumed alcoholic beverages to the extent that her equilibrium, balance, vision and sense of place were impaired;

c. She attempted to step and walk in a careless manner;

d. She was blissfully oblivious to her surroundings.

SECOND SPECIAL DEFENSE

1. The Defendant was contributorily negligent in causing any injuries she claims in that:

a. She neglected to use reasonable care in watching where she was walking and stepping;

b. She voluntarily consumed alcoholic beverages to the extent that her equilibrium, balance, vision and sense of place were impaired;

c. She attempted to step and walk in a careless manner;

d. She was blissfully oblivious to her surroundings.

THIRD SPECIAL DEFENSE

The claims presented by the Plaintiff are barred by C.G.S. Sec. 52-584 and any other applicable provisions regarding limitations of actions.

RESPECTFULLY SUBMITTED
THE DEFENDANT

BY_____

Glen Lutley, Esq.,
Lutley & Associates,
his attorneys
906 Park Plaza
Bridgeport, CT 04530
Tele. # (203) 555-5555
Juris #464646

CERTIFICATION

I hereby certify that a copy of the above was mailed on August 28, 1998 to all counsel and pro se parties of record, namely: Attorney Ann Lambert, Lambert and Smith, P.C., 529 Corporate Place, Fairfield, CT 04540.

_____
Commissioner of Superior Court

Example 4, Reply to Special Defenses

DOCKET NO. CV 98-0555555 S	:	SUPERIOR COURT
SHEILA WILKENSON	:	JUDICIAL DISTRICT
	:	OF FAIRFIELD
VS.	:	AT BRIDGEPORT
RYAN KEEGAN	:	SEPTEMBER 10, 1998

<u>**REPLY TO SPECIAL DEFENSES**</u>

1. The Plaintiff hereby denies each of the Defendant's Special Defenses, dated August 28, 1998.

THE PLAINTIFF

BY _____

Ann Lambert, Esq.,
Lambert and Smith, P.C.,
her attorneys
529 Corporate Place
Fairfield, CT 04540
Tele. # (203) 777-7777
Juris #545454

<u>**CERTIFICATION**</u>

I hereby certify that a copy of the above was mailed on September 10, 1998 to all counsel and pro se parties of record, namely: Attorney Glen Lutley, of Lutley & Associates, 906 Park Plaza, Bridgeport, CT 04530.

_____
Commissioner of Superior Court

14 *Pleadings: Motions against Defendants Who Do Not File an Appearance*

Terminology

Default	Affidavit of Debt	Military Affidavit
Bill of Costs	Open Default	Notice of Judgment
Foreclosure	Set Aside Judgment	Hearing in Damages
Open Judgment	Set Aside Default	Order of Notice

Pbs: 7Q, 123, 199, 352, 353, 354, 356, 357, 358, 359, 360, 361, 362, 364, 369, 377
C.G.S. sections: 52-68, 52-87, 52-220 et seq., 52-259c

Introduction

Understandably, people who are being sued are not always cooperative. Some wait until the last minute to hire an attorney or forward the Complaint to their insurance company. Others totally ignore the action against them. Maybe they don't have insurance, or the money to hire an attorney. Instead of defending, they decide to risk a judgment being entered against them. Finally, a small few may not even know about the action because they were served abode while they were away on a month-long vacation, or in the military, or they moved and the officer was unable to contact them directly.

Regardless of the reasons, this chapter deals with how a Plaintiff may obtain a quick judgment against a Defendant who has failed to file an Appearance and what a Defendant can do if this occurs.

I. MOTION FOR DEFAULT FOR FAILURE TO APPEAR: TWO DIFFERENT TYPES

A Plaintiff may file one of two types of a Motion for Default for Failure to Appear against any Defendant who has not filed an Appearance in an action:

1. A Motion for Default for Failure to Appear, pursuant to Pbs 352. This type is discussed in Section II below.

2. In contract cases for a liquidated sum, a Motion for Default for Failure to Appear and Judgment, pursuant to Pbs 357 et seq. This type is discussed in Section III below.

II. MOTION FOR DEFAULT FOR FAILURE TO APPEAR

As you can see from the example on page 149, this motion is very short and to the point. Pbs 352(b) requires a Plaintiff who files this motion to serve a copy by mail or hand delivery to the Defendant at his or her last known address. Pursuant to Pbs 352(c), the motion will not be placed on the Short Calendar. Instead, it will be granted by the clerk as of the day it was filed, if the Defendant's Appearance is not in the file at that time.

When a Motion for Default for Failure to Appear is granted, the Defendant is deemed **defaulted** or **in default**. A **default** acts as a disadvantage against the Defendant because it has the effect of confirming a Defendant's liability to a Plaintiff. The only issue that remains in the case is to determine the amount of the Plaintiff's damages and obtain judgment against the Defendant in that amount. (See Hearing in Damages below.) As a result, a defaulted Defendant's smartest recourse is to act quickly to have the default **opened** or **set aside** (they mean the same thing) so that he or she may proceed with the case in the usual manner.

A. Opening or Setting Aside a Default

Pursuant to Pbs 369, when the clerk enters a default against the Defendant, he or she will mail a notice of the default to the Defendant's last known address. The clerk will also record the date the notice was sent.

Pbs 352(c) permits the clerk to open or set aside a default automatically, if the Defendant files an Appearance **before** the Plaintiff obtains judgment. (See also Pbs 7Q.) When the default is opened or set aside, the case proceeds as if the Defendant timely filed an Appearance. (Note: This differs from opening or setting aside a *default judgment* which is much more complicated. See Section IV below.)

B. When a Defendant Fails to Appear after Default: Judgment

If a Defendant fails to file an Appearance within *15 days* after notice of the default is sent, the Plaintiff may then file a Certificate of Closed Pleadings and claim the case to the **Hearing in Damages** list or take steps to obtain judgment without a Hearing in Damages.

1. *Hearing in Damages: C.G.S. sec. 52-220 et seq.*

Pursuant to Pbs 352(c), Plaintiffs who need to provide testimony in order to prove their damages should claim their cases to the Hearing in Damages list 15 days after the default is granted. (See Pbs 352(c).) This is accomplished by completing the Certificate of Closed Pleadings form and marking the Hearing in Damages box for a Jury or the Court, whichever the Plaintiff prefers. (Note that this is the same form used to close pleadings and claim a case to the Trial List. It is discussed in detail in Chapter 28.)

The Hearing in Damages list is similar to the Trial List. It is, however, a much shorter list than the Trial List and a hearing will be scheduled much sooner. The hearing is like a mini-trial. Since the Defendant's liability has already been established, the trier of fact will simply determine the amount of the Plaintiff's damages, based upon the evidence presented. Providing the Plaintiff can provide a current **Military Affidavit**, judgment will then enter against the Defendant. (See Pbs 353 and Section III, A(b) below.)

2. *Motion for Judgment instead of a Hearing in Damages*

In certain cases, such as foreclosures, summary process actions and contract cases for a liquidated sum (see Section III below), Pbs 365 allows a Plaintiff to file a Motion for Judgment, along with a Motion for Default for Failure to Appear, or after the default has been granted. Providing all the requirements are met, the court will grant the Motion for Judgment. As a result, a Hearing in Damages is not necessary.

III. MOTION FOR DEFAULT FOR FAILURE TO APPEAR AND JUDGMENT

In accordance with Pbs 357, this motion is great for Plaintiffs in cases like *Skillman Et. Al. v. Auto Service Inc.* (Complaint 3). There, the Plaintiff brought suit against the Defendant because he or she failed to pay a specific sum of money, as promised in a contract. As a result, the Plaintiff should be able to obtain judgment against the Defendant based solely upon documents, rather than at a Hearing in Damages.

A successful Plaintiff may accomplish this goal in less than one month's time, providing the Defendant is not in the military or naval service of the United States. See Pbs 356. In addition to the sum due, Pbs 357 allows the judgment to include interest, attorney's fees and other lawful charges, as stated in the contract.

A. *Required Documents*

A Motion for Judgment must be accompanied by the following documents:
1. Affidavit of Debt;
2. Military Affidavit;
3. Bill of Costs;
4. Proposed Judgment;
5. Two copies of a Notice of Judgment, to be sent to the Defendant, pursuant to Pbs 354;
6. A copy of the contract is usually attached and incorporated into the Complaint; if not, it should be attached to the Affidavit of Debt, pursuant to Pbs 358.

Before we discuss each document, note that most clerk's offices at the courthouses have forms for each of the above. These forms, made in duplicate, make the procedures very easy to accomplish.

a. *Affidavit of Debt*

Along with a sample form motion, a sample form Affidavit of Debt is found at the end of this chapter. This document is an affidavit that states how much the Plaintiff claims is due from the Defendant. It must be signed and sworn to by the Plaintiff and includes interest, lawful charges and attorney's fees.

If *interest* is claimed, it must be separately stated and specify the date it was computed through. This date cannot be later than the date judgment is entered. A per diem (per day) interest charge should also be included.

Lawful charges are those charges a Plaintiff is entitled to, pursuant to the terms of the contract. They can include late charges, returned check charges, etc. If applicable, the Plaintiff must state the terms of the contract that permit such charges in the Affidavit of Debt, and the amount claimed.

Many contracts also permit the Plaintiff to recover attorney's fees from the Defendant. The amount must be reasonable (determined by the court). In addition, the Plaintiff must state the reasons for the specific amount requested, breaking down the fees and the actual costs incurred for bringing the action, etc.

b. *Military Affidavit*

Pursuant to Pbs 352(e), the Plaintiff must obtain a current Military Affidavit from someone who has been able to determine that the Defendant is not currently in the military. In many cases, the officer who serves the Summons and Complaint will ask the Defendant if he or she is in the military or has plans to join, etc. Hence, the officer can provide you with this document, as long as the inquiry was within *30 days* of filing the motion.

If the officer did not make the inquiry, or if the inquiry is more than 30 days old, anyone can complete this task. The information can be obtained from the Defendant, or anyone who knows him or her, or from records that demonstrate he or she would be ineligible due to age or disability, etc.

c. *Bill of Costs*

These are costs incurred by the Plaintiff for bringing the lawsuit. They include the sheriff's fees, the entry fee required by the court, etc.

d. *Proposed Judgment*

This form specifies the terms of the judgment the Plaintiff seeks against the Defendant.

e. *Notice of Judgment*

Pursuant to Pbs 354, the Plaintiff has **ten days** from the date of the judgment to send notice of the judgment to the Defendant. Therefore, along with the other documents, the court will complete the notice provided by the Plaintiff, according to the terms of the judgment. Once judgment enters and the Plaintiff receives this back from the court, the Plaintiff must serve a copy to the Defendant, in accordance with Pbs 123. Afterward, a copy of the Notice must also be sent back to the clerk.

B. Filing the Motion for Default for Failure to Appear and Judgment

Pursuant to Pbs 354, the Plaintiff should serve a copy of this motion and the attachments to the Defendant by mail or hand delivery at the last known address. Once the original version is received by the clerk, it will not be placed on the Short Calendar. Instead, the clerk will bring it to the attention of the court. If granted, the clerk will complete the Proposed Judgment and the Notice to all parties, as stated above. One copy of the judgment will then be sent to the Defendant.

C. 20-Day Delay to Enforce Judgment

Pursuant to Pbs 361, the Plaintiff is not permitted to attempt to collect the money stated in the judgment from the Defendant until **20 days** after the Defendant is served a copy of the Notice of Judgment.

IV. MOTION TO OPEN JUDGMENT UPON DEFAULT: FOUR MONTH DEADLINE

Pbs 377 allows a Defendant up to **four months** from the date Notice of Judgment was sent, to ask the court to open the judgment and allow him or her to present a defense against the action in the regular manner. If granted, the judgment is void and the case usually begins again at the Pleadings Stage. (Note that summary process cases often go directly to trial.)

A. *Contents of a Motion to Open Judgment upon Default*

In this motion, the Defendant must state and demonstrate:
1. that a good defense existed at the time of the judgment; and
2. at the time of the judgment, the Defendant was prevented from filing an Appearance by:
>   a. mistake;
>   b. accident; or
>   c. other reasonable cause.
3. In addition, the Defendant should ask the court to prevent the Plaintiff from enforcing the judgment until after the court rules on this motion; and
4. include a $60 filing fee, via check, money order or cash, pursuant to C.G.S. sec. 52-259c, with this motion; and
5. include an Appearance; and
6. include an affidavit that states generally:
>   a. the nature of the defense; and
>   b. the reason (the mistake, accident or other reasonable cause) why the Defendant did not appear.

The affidavit must be signed by the Defendant's attorney or the Defendant client, whichever is more appropriate for the situation.

V. APPEARANCE DEADLINE IS POSTPONED UNDER CERTAIN CIRCUMSTANCES

Pursuant to C.G.S. sec. 52-87, a Defendant who is out of state may receive a continuance to file an Appearance before a default is granted.

A. *The Connecticut Resident Who Is Out-of-State: 30-Day Continuance*

Under C.G.S. sec. 52-87(a), if the Plaintiff filed a Motion for Default for Failure to Appear, with or without a Motion for Judgment, and the Defendant:
1. is an inhabitant of Connecticut; and
2. is "absent" from Connecticut at the time the action is commenced, and continues to be absent until after the return date; and
3. has not filed an Appearance as required,

the court may continue or postpone the matter for 30 days for the Defendant to file an Appearance and also order the Plaintiff to provide the Defendant with additional notice of the pending action against him or her, pursuant to an **Order of Notice**. Afterward, if no Appearance is filed and there is no special reason to justify additional delay, a default and possibly judgment, may be rendered against the Defendant.

B. The Nonresident or Noninhabitant Defendant: Three-Month Continuance

The court may order a three-month continuance for a nonresident or noninhabitant Defendant to file an Appearance. Again, the court may order the Plaintiff to give additional notice of the action to the Defendant pursuant to an **Order of Notice**.

If the Defendant does not file an Appearance after the three-month continuance and there is no known special reason to justify a further delay, the court many render a default (and possibly judgment) against the Defendant.

C.G.S. sec. 52-87 does not apply to actions under the following:
1. C.G.S. sec. 47-33, Actions to Settle Title to Land Belonging to Estate of Deceased Person;
2. C.G.S. sec. 52-69, Notice to Representatives, and Creditors, Widows or Widowers and Heirs; or
3. If service is made pursuant to C.G.S. sec. 52-59b(a)(4): if the Defendant owns, uses or possesses any real property situated in Connecticut.

VI. ORDERS OF NOTICE

Before granting a Motion for Default for Failure to Appear or Judgment, the court may require the Plaintiff to provide the Defendant with additional notice of the lawsuit through an **Order of Notice**.

A. When a Defendant's Out-of-State Address is Known

An Order of Notice will permit a Connecticut sheriff or constable to serve, by certified mail, a copy of the Summons and Complaint, alone or along with any other pleadings, such as a Motion for Default for Failure to Appear, to the Defendant at that address.

B. When a Defendant's Whereabouts Are Unknown

If the Defendant's whereabouts are unknown, the court may order the Plaintiff to publish notice of the lawsuit in certain newspapers.

C. Procedures

Refer to Pbs 199 et seq. for specific details concerning how to obtain an Order of Notice. In general, the Plaintiff needs to file an *Application for Order of Notice* and attach an *Order of Notice* for the court or clerk to sign, if the application is granted.

Specifically:

    1. The application must be made in writing; and

    2. include the name and residence of the Defendant the Plaintiff is attempting to contact; or

    3. that "all reasonable efforts have been made to ascertain the residence and have failed"; and

    4. state the type of notice most likely to come to the Defendant's attention and why.

The Plaintiff should include in the attached Order of Notice, the type of notice requested in the application. See also C.G.S. sec. 52-68 for the court's authority to act on a motion if service is sufficient or to require additional notice.

VII. CONCLUSION

A. Key Issues in This Chapter Include:

1. Default and Judgment Against Any Nonappearing Defendant in a Case

In cases that have multiple Defendants, the Plaintiff may default and move for judgment against any nonappearing Defendant. The case against the remaining Defendants will progress in the usual manner.

2. Calling the Court

Prior to filing the *Motion for Default for Failure to Appear*, many law offices prefer to call the court to verify that no Appearance has been filed. This prevents wasting time drafting the motion, if in fact the Appearance is there and your notification from the court is being processed.

3. If You Represent the Plaintiff, Keep the Following in Mind:

    a. After filing a Summons, Complaint, Return of Service and entry fee at the proper court, double check to be sure the Defendant's deadline to file the Appearance is diaried.

    b. A day or two after the Appearance deadline passes, call the court to verify that an Appearance has not been filed.

    c. If no Appearance is filed, draft a Motion for Default for Failure to Appear and include the Defendant's last known address in the certification of service. If the case involved a contract for a specific sum, include *and Judgment* in the title of the motion. In addition, attach an *Affidavit of Debt*, a *Military Affidavit*, a *Bill of Costs*, a *Proposed Judgment* and a *Notice of Judgment*. (Court-issued forms are available.)

    d. File the motion and required documents and send a copy to the Defendant.

e. Call the court or wait for notice by mail to find out if the motion was granted.

f. If the Defendant files an Appearance anytime before judgment is entered, the default is automatically set aside and the case continues.

g. If the Defendant fails to file an Appearance within *15 days* after notice of the default is sent, claim the case on the *Hearing in Damages* list, or if applicable, file a *Motion for Judgment*.

h. At the Hearing in Damages, provide a Military Affidavit to the court and present your evidence and witnesses as they pertain to determining damages.

i. If the Defendant files a *Motion to Open Judgment upon Default*, many courts do not permit oral argument on this issue. Therefore, if you intend to object, make certain the objection reaches the court file before the Short Calendar date.

4. *If You Represent the Defendant, Keep the following in Mind:*

a. File an Appearance within the time limits.

b. A Motion to Open Judgment upon Default may be filed within *four months* of notice of a default judgment.

c. When filing a Motion to Open Judgment upon Default be sure to include an affidavit, the filing fee and an Appearance.

B. *Relevant Connecticut Practice Book Sections Include:*

Pbs 7Q:	Time to File Appearance
Pbs 123:	Proof of Service
Pbs 199, et seq.:	Applications for Orders of Notice
Pbs 352:	Motion for Default and Nonsuit for Failure to Appear
Pbs 353:	Motion for Default and Nonsuit for Failure to Appear-Defaults under Soldiers' and Sailors' Relief Act
Pbs 354:	Motion for Default for Nonsuit Failure to Appear-Notice Judgments of Nonsuit and Default for Failure to Enter an Appearance
Pbs 356:	Contract Actions; Judgment after Default for Failure to Appear-Limitations
Pbs 357:	Contract Actions; Promise to Pay a Liquidated Sum
Pbs 358:	Contract Actions; Affidavit of Debt; Military Affidavit; Bill of Costs; Debt Instrument
Pbs 359:	Contract Actions; Order of Weekly Payments
Pbs 360:	Contract Actions; Entry of Judgment
Pbs 361:	Contract Actions; Enforcement of Judgment
Pbs 362:	Contract Actions; Default Motion Not on Short Calendar
Pbs 364:	When Judgment May Be Rendered after a Default
Pbs 377:	Opening Judgment upon Default or Nonsuit

C. Relevant Connecticut General Statutes Include:

C.G.S. sec. 52-68.:   Notice to nonresident adverse or interested parties and
                             interested parties unknown to plaintiff.
C.G.S. sec. 52-87.:   Continuance on account of absent or nonresident defendant.
C.G.S. sec. 52-220 et seq.: Hearing in Damages; when to a jury.
C.G.S. sec. 52-259c.:   Fee to open, set aside, modify, extend or reargue judgment.

Example 1, Motion for Default for Failure to Appear

DOCKET NO. CV 98-0555555 S	:	SUPERIOR COURT
SHEILA WILKENSON	:	JUDICIAL DISTRICT
	:	OF FAIRFIELD
VS.	:	AT BRIDGEPORT
RYAN KEEGAN	:	APRIL 8, 1998

MOTION FOR DEFAULT FOR FAILURE TO APPEAR

Pursuant to Connecticut Practice Book Section 352(a), the Plaintiff in the above-captioned case hereby moves that a Default be entered against the Defendant, Ryan Keegan, for failing to file its Appearance in this case. The return date in this case is March 31, 1998.

THE PLAINTIFF

BY_____

Ann Lambert, Esq.,
Lambert and Smith, P.C.,
her attorneys
529 Corporate Place
Fairfield, CT 04540
Tele. # (203) 777-7777
Juris #545454

ORAL ARGUMENT NOT REQUESTED
TESTIMONY NOT REQUIRED

ORDER

The foregoing Motion having been considered by the Court, it is hereby ORDERED: GRANTED/DENIED.

_____

BY THE COURT

CERTIFICATION

I hereby certify that a copy of the above was mailed on April 8, 1998 to the party against whom the Default for Failure to Appear is claimed, namely: Ryan Keegan, 43 Camelot Court, Bridgeport, CT 02360.

_____

Commissioner of the Superior Court

Example 2, Motion to Open Judgment of Default for Failure to Appear

DOCKET NO. CV 98-0444444 S	:	SUPERIOR COURT
GEORGE SKILLMAN, ET AL.	:	JUDICIAL DISTRICT OF
	:	HARTFORD/NEW BRITAIN
VS.	:	AT HARTFORD
AUTO SERVICE CENTER, INC.	:	APRIL 9, 1998

MOTION TO OPEN JUDGMENT OF
DEFAULT FOR FAILURE TO APPEAR

Pursuant to Connecticut Practice Book Section 377, the Defendant in the above-captioned case hereby respectfully requests the court to open the judgment entered against it on March 13, 1998, on the following grounds:

I. FACTS: A Mistake

Joseph Kelly, president of the Defendant corporation, contacted an attorney almost immediately aafter being served the Writ, Summons and Complaint in this action. An appointment to meet with the attorney was scheduled for February 18, 1998.

On February 17, 1998, Mr. Kelly received an emergency telephone call from family in Scotland. His father had suffered a serious heart attack. Mr. Kelly left immediately for Scotland, forgetting about the meeting with the attorney. Mr. Kelly did not return from Scotland until March 27, 1998.

Mr. Kelly is the sole director and the president of the corporation. The corporation's secretary is his wife, who accompanied him to Scotland. The corporation has only one part-time office assistant who was unaware of this lawsuit. As a result of Mr. Kelly's mistake and his and his wife's absence, judgment entered against the Defendant corporation.

II. ARGUMENT: A Good Defense Exists

The Defendant respectfully asserts that a good defense exists in that the Defendant believes it was misled by the Plaintiff who agreed to purchase Auto Service Center, Inc. and signed the promissory note at issue. In any event, since April 2, 1998, Mr. Kelly and the Plaintiffs, Mr. and Mrs. Skillman have been working diligently to reach a settlement.

Based on the foregoing, although the Defendant feels confident a settlement will be reached shortly, finalizing such agreement could exceed the four months permitted under Connecticut Practice Book Sec. 377 to open a judgment. Furthermore, if there is

ORAL ARGUMENT NOT REQUESTED
TESTIMONY NOT REQUIRED

no settlement, the Defendant wishes to be heard on the merits of the case and to be given the opportunity to present its defenses.

Attached hereto is an affidavit from Mr. Kelly in support of this Motion to Open and an Appearance from the undersigned counsel.

III. CONCLUSION

WHEREFORE, the Defendant respectfully requests the following:

1. That the Plaintiff be enjoined from enforcing said Judgment until the court renders its decision on this instant motion;

2. That said Default Judgment be opened in accordance with Connecticut Practice Book Section 377;

3. that the attached Appearance from the undersigned counsel be filed in this case.

RESPECTFULLY,
THE DEFENDANT

BY_____

Mark Peters, Esq.,
Mark Peters & Associates, P.C.,
its attorneys
1001 Sanberg Street
Manchester, CT 06666
Tele. # (860) 648-0000
Juris #246135

ORDER

The foregoing Motion having been considered by the Court, it is hereby ORDERED: GRANTED/DENIED

_____
BY THE COURT

CERTIFICATION

I hereby certify that a copy of the foregoing Motion and attached Affidavit and Appearance were mailed on April 8, 1998 to all counsel and pro se parties of record, namely: Kenneth I. Marcus, Esq., Friedman & Marcus, P.C., 27 Main Street, Bristol, CT 00000.

_____
Commissioner of Superior Court

Example 3, Affidavit to be filed with Motion to Open Judgment upon Default

DOCKET NO. CV 98-0444444 S	:	SUPERIOR COURT
GEORGE SKILLMAN, ET AL.	:	JUDICIAL DISTRICT OF
	:	HARTFORD/NEW BRITAIN
VS.	:	AT HARTFORD
AUTO SERVICE CENTER, INC.	:	APRIL 8, 1998

AFFIDAVIT

I, the undersigned, being duly sworn, do hereby depose and say:

1. I am over the age of eighteen years and understand the obligation of an oath and have personal knowledge of the above-captained case.

2. I am the President of Defendant, Auto Service Center, Inc., a Connecticut corporation.

3. On February 17, 1998, my wife and I were notified that my father had suffered a serious heart attack in Scotland. We left immediately to be with him and did not return until March 27, 1998.

4. Unfortunately, before I left, I forgot to contact the attorney I spoke with who I intended to hire to represent the corporation in this instant lawsuit. As a result, judgment had already entered against the corporation by the time I returned.

5. I believe that the Defendant corporation has a good defense to this action. Specifically, on behalf of the corporation I had several meetings and discussions with the Plaintiffs within a month of buying the corporation because I began to suspect that the value placed on the company at the time of the purchase was significantly higher than what it was worth. There are not nearly as many credit card holders as represented, nor have the Plaintiffs made improvements to the building or assisted in its operating for the first six months as they had promised.

6. Since April 2, 1998, the Plaintiffs and I have made great efforts to resolve this matter. I feel confident that we will resolve this issue soon, however I am not certain we can finalize everything before the four-month period to open the judgment expires. Furthermore, if we can not settle this matter, I wish to have the opportunity to have the case tried on its merits and for me to present my good defenses.

7. Based on my mistake and the fact I believe the Defendant corporation has a good defense, I respectfully request the court to open the judgment against the Defendant and enjoin the Plaintiff from enforcing the judgment until the court renders its decision on this instant motion.

_____
Joseph Kelly

Subscribed and sworn to before me this 8th day of April, 1998.

_____
Commissioner of the Superior Court

15 *Pleadings: Motions against Defendants Who Do Not File Pleadings*

Pbs: 114, 128, 326, 363, 363A, 365, 375, 376, 377
C.G.S. sections: 52-259c, 52-220 et seq.

Introduction

What should a Plaintiff do if a Defendant fails to file any of the optional pleadings, or an Answer, as required under Pbs 112 and 114? The Plaintiff can then file a Motion for Default for Failure to Plead.

I. MOTION FOR DEFAULT FOR FAILURE TO PLEAD

A. *Applicable Sections*

This motion is a favorite among many Plaintiffs and is permitted pursuant to Pbs 128, 363 and 363A. It's a very simple motion as you can see from the example at the end of this chapter.

B. *No Short Calendar*

Like a Motion for Default for Failure to Appear, if the Defendant has not filed a pleading within the time stated in Pbs 114, Pbs 363A allows the clerk to grant the Plaintiff's Motion for Default for Failure to Plead, as of the day it was filed, without the delay of Short Calendar.

C. After the Default Is Granted

According to Pbs 363A, if the default was granted and the Defendant fails to plead within **15 days** after notice of the default, the Plaintiff may file a Motion for Judgment or claim the case to the Hearing in Damages list.

II. TWO WAYS TO OPEN A DEFAULT

A. By the Clerk

Pursuant to Pbs 363A, a Default may be set aside by the clerk, automatically, if:
1. The Defendant files an Answer, rather than any other pleading permitted under Pbs 112 (Motion to Dismiss, Motion to Strike or Request to Revise.) Along with the Answer, the Defendant may include Special Defenses and a Counterclaim, if appropriate; *and*
2. The Plaintiff has not already filed a Motion for Judgment or claimed the case to the Hearing in Damages list.

Requiring the Defendant to Answer, rather than file another Pbs 112 pleading, can significantly reduce the duration of the lawsuit. Providing there is no Counterclaim or Special Defenses, either party may file a Certificate of Closed Pleadings and place the case on the Trial List.

B. When Opening a Default Requires a Court Order

If the Defendant wishes to file a pleading other than an Answer, or if the Plaintiff has already filed a Motion for Judgment or claim to the Hearing in Damages list, the Defendant should file a Motion to Open Default under Pbs 376. (This is sometimes called a Motion to Set Aside Default.) Pursuant to Pbs 363A, only the court can grant this motion. If the motion is granted, either party should file a Motion to Strike the case from the Hearing in Damages list.

III. JUDGMENT UPON DEFAULT

As we discussed in Chapter 14, if the Defendant does not file a Motion to Open Default or the court denies the motion, and the Plaintiff obtains Judgment upon Default, Pbs 377 gives a Defendant **four months** after notice of the judgment to file a Motion to Open Judgment upon Default. The contents of this motion are similar to those found in a Motion to Open Judgment upon Default for Failure to Appear. Don't forget the $60 filing fee under C.G.S. sec. 52-259c.

IV. HEARING IN DAMAGES

If a case remains on the Hearing in Damages list, it will eventually be scheduled for a hearing, or mini-trial. The Defendant's liability has already been determined. Therefore, the purpose of the hearing is to determine the Plaintiff's damages. See Pbs 365 et seq. and C.G.S. sec. 52-220 et seq., for more information.

V. CONCLUSION

Did you notice the lack of new terminology in this chapter? By now, many of the terms should be second nature to you.

A. Key Issues in This Chapter Include:

1. As a Plaintiff:

a. Keep checking your diary. If a Defendant has not filed a pleading, promptly file a *Motion for Default for Failure to Plead.*
b. Be prepared to file a Motion for Judgment or Hearing in Damages, whichever is appropriate. Remember, a Hearing in Damages is necessary only if the trier of fact needs to determine the Plaintiff's damages, such as in a personal injury case. Damages for many debt collection and contract cases can be determined by an Affidavit of Debt. Therefore, a Motion for Judgment is sufficient.

2. As a Defendant:

a. File pleadings when they are due. Otherwise, be prepared to file an Answer, immediately upon receipt of the Plaintiff's Motion for Default for Failure to Plead.
b. A *Motion to Open Default* is needed if:
    i. you want to file a pleading under Pbs 112, other than an Answer; or
    ii. the Plaintiff has already filed a Motion for Judgment that has not yet been decided; or
    iii. the Plaintiff has already claimed the case to the Hearing in Damages list and you want it returned to the regular docket.

B. Relevant Practice Book Sections Include:

Pbs 114:	Time to Plead
Pbs 128:	Penalty for Failing to Plead
Pbs 326:	Setting Aside or Opening Judgments
Pbs 363:	Procedure Where Party Is in Default
Pbs 363A:	Where Defendant Is in Default for Failure to Plead

Pbs 365 et seq.:   Hearing in Damages
Pbs 375:   Relief Permissible on Default
Pbs 376:   Opening Defaults Where Judgment Has Not Been Rendered
Pbs 377:   Opening Judgment upon Default or Nonsuit

C. Relevant Connecticut General Statutes Include:

C.G.S. sec. 52-220 et seq.: Hearing in damages; when to a jury.
C.G.S. sec. 52-259c.:   Fee to open, set aside, modify, extend or reargue judgment.

Example 1, Motion for Default for Failure to Plead

DOCKET NO. CV 98-0555555 S	:	SUPERIOR COURT
SHEILA WILKENSON	:	JUDICIAL DISTRICT
	:	OF FAIRFIELD
VS.	:	AT BRIDGEPORT
RYAN KEEGAN	:	AUGUST 12, 1998

MOTION FOR DEFAULT FOR FAILURE TO PLEAD

Pursuant to Connecticut Practice Book Section 128, the Plaintiff in the above-captioned case hereby moves that a Default be entered against the Defendant, for his failure to plead in accordance with Connecticut Practice Book Section 114. Specifically, the Defendant has failed to respond to the Plaintiffs' Revised Complaint dated June 29, 1998 and no previous Answer has been filed.

THE PLAINTIFF,

BY_____

Ann Lambert, Esq.,
Lambert and Smith, P.C.,
her attorneys
529 Corporate Place
Fairfield, CT 04540
Tele. #(203) 777-7777
Juris #545454

ORAL ARGUMENT NOT REQUESTED
TESTIMONY NOT REQUIRED

ORDER

The foregoing Motion having been duly presented to the Court, it is hereby ORDERED: GRANTED/DENIED

_____

BY THE COURT

CERTIFICATION

I hereby certify that a copy of the above was mailed on August 12, 1998 to all counsel and pro se parties of record namely: Attorney Glen Lutley of Lutley & Associates, 906 Park Plaza, Bridgeport, CT 04530.

_____

Commissioner of Superior Court

16 *Pleadings: Motions against Plaintiffs Who Do Not Comply with the Rules of Court*

Terminology

Nonsuit	Stay	Dormancy	Dismissal

Pbs: 7WW, 128, 149, 206, 250B, 251, 326, 354, 351, 352, 353, 354, 363, 363A, 377
C.G.S. sections: 51-84, 52-259c, 52-592

Introduction

Plaintiffs bear the burden of proving their case. They also have their share of problems during a lawsuit. Clients disappear, they stop paying their legal bills, they lose interest in prosecuting their case, etc. In addition, Plaintiff's attorneys sometimes get bogged down with too many cases and aren't always able to keep on top of them. As a result, they may miss deadlines or court appearances.

In this chapter, we will address what Defendants can do when it appears that Plaintiffs are failing to timely prosecute their cases.

I. NONSUITS VERSUS DEFAULTS

At times, our practice book appears to use **nonsuit** and default interchangeably. In practice, however, it has been my experience that defaults are used against Defendants and nonsuits are used against Plaintiffs. As a result, much of this chapter will be devoted to the reasons why a nonsuit may be filed against a Plaintiff.

II. WHEN A NONSUIT IS GRANTED

When a Motion for Nonsuit is granted, the Plaintiff's case is over. The Plaintiff is out of luck. The only hope is to file a Motion to Open Judgment, pursuant to Pbs 377, and comply with all of its requirements. If this doesn't work, the Plaintiff may be able to start the action again, under C.G.S. sec. 52-592, the Accidental Failure of Suit Statute. Note, however, that Defendants often challenge cases filed under this statute, so be prepared for a fight.

III. FAILURE TO PLEAD: REQUEST TO REVISE

When a Defendant files a Request to Revise, the Plaintiff must eventually take some action.

A. Overruled Objections

If a Plaintiff files objections, and the court overrules one or more of them, Pbs 149 requires the Plaintiff to file a Revised Complaint which incorporates the necessary changes within *15 days* of the court's order.

B. Failure to Object

If the Plaintiff fails to object, he or she must file a Revised Complaint, which incorporates all of the Defendant's requests, within *30 days* after the Request was filed.

C. Failure to File the Revised Complaint

If the Plaintiff fails to file either of the above, or if he or she files a Revised Complaint that does not incorporate all of the requests of the court order, a Defendant may file a Motion for Nonsuit pursuant to Pbs 351 if the Plaintiff is violating a court order, or Pbs 363.

IV. MOTION TO STRIKE

A Plaintiff may have similar court orders to comply with pursuant to a Defendant's Motion to Strike. If the entire Complaint is not stricken, the Plaintiff must make certain revisions, either deleting or adding language, etc. A Plaintiff who fails to timely comply will eventually face a Motion for Nonsuit.

Furthermore, remember that if a Plaintiff's entire Complaint is stricken, the Plaintiff must file a new Complaint within *15 days* of the court's order, pursuant to Pbs 157. Otherwise, the Defendant can file a Motion for Judgment.

V. REPLY TO SPECIAL DEFENSES

If the Defendant filed Special Defenses, the pleadings cannot be closed until the Plaintiff files a Reply to Special Defenses. According to Pbs 114, the Plaintiff has *15 days* from the date the Defendant filed an Answer and Special Defense, to file a reply. Otherwise, the Defendant could file a Motion for Nonsuit for Failure to Plead.

VI. FAILURE TO APPEAR AT TRIAL OR PRETRIAL

Sometimes, for whatever reason, a Plaintiff client will fail to appear at a court-ordered appearance. This includes pretrials, scheduling conference, or even the actual trial itself. Pbs 351 and 352(d) permit a Plaintiff to be nonsuited for this mistake. In addition, the court may use Pbs 251 to dismiss the action. See Section IX below.

If an attorney (for the Plaintiff or the Defendant) fails to appear at court for a scheduled hearing or trial, or delays the case without good cause, Pbs 7WW permits the court to invoke C.G.S. sec. 51-84 and fine the attorney and otherwise discipline him or her.

VII. OTHER REASONS FOR A NONSUIT

Nonsuits as well as defaults are used when any party fails to comply with discovery requests. This will be discussed in later chapters. Other reasons for a nonsuit can involve any other rule or court order, not mentioned here, that the Plaintiff has failed to comply with.

VIII. SHORT CALENDAR

Most nonsuits will appear on the Short Calendar before they are granted by the court. This will give the Plaintiff the opportunity to remedy the mistakes, hopefully to the opposing party's satisfaction. Other nonsuits, especially those that involve missing a court-ordered appearance, may be ordered from the bench. In most cases the Plaintiff will receive a court notice of the nonsuit in the mail.

IX. DISMISSAL FOR LACK OF DILIGENCE

Pursuant to Pbs 251, either a party or the court, on its own, may seek to dismiss a case that has not been pursued with reasonable diligence.

A. A Party's Motion

Clearly, a Plaintiff is not going to file a Motion for Dismissal for Lack of Diligence against his or her own case. Hence, this motion is usually filed by the

Defendant, unless the Defendant has filed a Counterclaim. Then the Plaintiff may file a Motion for Nonsuit against the Counterclaim as needed.

Pbs 251 requires a Plaintiff to receive at least two weeks' notice before a case will be dismissed. This should give the Plaintiff time to file an objection to the motion that demonstrates to the court that the case is being reasonably prosecuted.

B. The Court's Motion

Our courts have been known to dismiss a case, instantly, in certain circumstances. For example, if a Plaintiff fails to appear at trial without explanation, as stated above, an instant nonsuit (having the result of a dismissal) is permitted under Pbs 251 because at this stage, the case already appears on the Trial List, which is an "assignment list for final adjudication."

X. THE DORMANCY PROGRAM

The court also dismisses cases pursuant to Pbs 251, based upon the **Dormancy Program.** The purpose of this program is to strongly encourage Plaintiffs to immediately take all necessary steps to close the pleadings and file the Certificate of Closed Pleadings. Once this form is filed, the case is placed on the Trial List and there is no danger of dormancy.

Keep in mind that Defendants would like nothing more than to have a case dismissed. Hence, the burden of this program rests heavily on the Plaintiff.

A. Why the Dormancy Program?

The program prevents cases from sitting idle, year after year, and clogging up the court docket.

B. How Does the Dormancy Program Work?

In recent years, all the courthouses in this state have simultaneously mailed out one or more Short Calendars containing lists of cases that are not on the Trial List and have not been acted upon for approximately six months.

There are three reasons why a case may be subject to the Dormancy Program:
1. When a Defendant has failed to file an Appearance in a case and approximately six months or more have passed since the return date; or
2. When a Defendant has appeared, but approximately six months or more have passed since that appearance and no action has taken place and the pleadings are not closed; or
3. Approximately six months or more have passed since any action has taken place on the case, regardless of its age, and the pleadings are still not closed.

Customarily, these "Dormancy Calendars" are printed two times per year:
> **a.** Each September or October. This calendar usually gives a Plaintiff until sometime in December to take appropriate action. If no such action is taken, the case will be dismissed, pursuant to Pbs 251.
> **b.** Each March or April. This calendar usually gives Plaintiffs until sometime in June to take appropriate action. Again, if no such action is taken, the case will be dismissed.

C. What Plaintiffs Should Do if Their Cases Appears on the Dormancy Calendar

In many instances, a Plaintiff can realistically close the pleadings and file a Certificate of Closed Pleadings before the dismissal date. On the other hand, there are many other instances when this may not be possible. Therefore, the Plaintiff must attempt to have the case exempted from the Dormancy Program.

1. Claim for Exemption from Dormancy Program by Reason of Bankruptcy

Under the federal Bankruptcy rules, when any party files a petition for bankruptcy protection, any action that party may be involved with, in any state court, must come to an immediate halt. This is known as a **stay**.

Pbs 250B acknowledges the stay and will prevent a state court case from being dismissed for any reason, including Dormancy, until permitted otherwise by the bankruptcy court.

Hence, if one of the parties is in bankruptcy, Pbs 250B directs the Plaintiff to file a "Claim for Exemption from the Dormancy Program." Along with that claim, the Plaintiff must file an affidavit that includes the following information:
> **a.** The date the bankruptcy petition was filed;
> **b.** The district of the bankruptcy court in which the petition was filed;
> **c.** The address of the bankruptcy court;
> **d.** The name of the bankruptcy debtor;
> **e.** The docket number of the bankruptcy case.

The affidavit must be sworn to by the party making the claim or the party's attorney. Last, the Plaintiff must update the affidavit every six months.

2. Motion for Exemption from Dormancy Program

Upon receiving the court calendar, immediately read the instructions or call the court to determine the dismissal date and its procedure, if any, for exempting cases from the Dormancy Program.

In recent years, many of the courthouses throughout the state have handled the dormancy program in their own way. Some will address each case on an individual basis by permitting a Plaintiff to file a Motion to Exempt from Dormancy. In this motion,

Plaintiffs should explain why they will not be able to file the Certificate of Closed Pleadings before the dismissal date. The motion will appear on the Short Calendar and the court may or may not permit oral argument.

If the court permits, a Plaintiff should file a Motion to Exempt from Dormancy as soon as possible after receiving the calendar. This way, if the motion is denied, there is usually still time to determine how to close the pleadings before the dismissal date.

Other courts require all Plaintiffs who want an exemption to appear in court on a specified date. In addition, they may or may not require a written Motion for Exemption. Once in court, the Plaintiff is then provided with the opportunity to explain the circumstances to the judge.

Some courts, like Hartford Superior Court in recent years, will not dismiss the case, or will require oral argument, providing the Plaintiff files a specific form and it is the first time the case has appeared on the Dormancy Calendar. A motion and/or oral argument, if permitted, may be needed if the case has been on the list more than once.

In addition to seeking an exemption, or if the Motion to Exempt was denied, here are some helpful hints. (Mind you, I can't guarantee they will work.)

If the Defendant has not appeared:
> **a.** ***Immediately*** file a Motion for Default for Failure to Appear and Judgment, if appropriate.
> **b.** If testimony is required, and the Defendant has still not appeared, wait the required 15 days, then file the Certificate of Closed Pleadings form and mark the box entitled "Hearing in Damages to the Court" or "Hearing in Damages to the Jury." This will close the pleadings and remove the case from the Dormancy Program.

If the Defendant has failed to plead:
> **a.** First of all, Plaintiffs must make sure they have no outstanding pleadings of their own that are due. If so, get them filed as soon as possible.
> **b.** The Plaintiff should then determine whether there are any outstanding pleadings already filed in court that must be decided in order to close the pleadings. If the answer is yes, Pbs 206 permits either the Plaintiff or the Defendant to reclaim the pleading because the case in on the Dormancy List.
> **c.** Presuming all outstanding pleadings have been decided by the court, if the Defendant fails to file a pleading within 15 days of the court's last decision, the Plaintiff should file a Motion for Default for Failure to Plead, in accordance with Pbs 128. Because the case is on the Dormancy List, Pbs 251 requires the Defendant to file a pleading that will close the pleadings, such as an Answer.

As stated earlier, if the Defendant has not filed an Answer after 15 days from the date notice of the default was sent, Pbs 363A allows the Plaintiff to file a Motion for Judgment or claim the case to the Hearing in Damages list. This will save the case from dismissal.

d. The Defendant may, however, file Special Defenses and a Counterclaim, along with the Answer. (See Pbs 363A.) In that instance, the Plaintiff should immediately file a Reply to Special Defenses and an Answer, if necessary, along with the Certificate of Closed Pleadings. Note, however, that if a Request to Revise, Motion to Strike or Special Defenses is appropriate, the Plaintiff may not be able to close the pleadings and claim the case to Trial List by the dismissal deadline, unless the case is exempted from Dormancy.

XI. CONCLUSION

A. *Key Issues in This Chapter Include:*

As you can see, our practice book rules make every effort to be fair to both offending Plaintiffs and Defendants. In many instances, where there's a penalty for failing to comply, there is also a remedy. But remember, these remedies do not always work and using them clearly places the offending party at the mercy of the court. Be careful! Don't rely upon them! You'll be flirting with malpractice!

B. *Relevant Connecticut Practice Book Sections Include:*

Pbs 7WW: Sanctions for Counsel's Failure to Appear
Pbs 128: General Rules of Pleading--Penalty for Failing to Plead
Pbs 149: Request to Revise--Granting of and Objection to Request to Revise
Pbs 204: Requirement That Memorandum of Law Be Filed With Certain Motions
Pbs 206: Short Calendar List
Pbs 250B: Claim for Exemption from Dormancy Program by Reason of Bankruptcy
Pbs 251: Dismissal for Lack of Diligence
Pbs 326: Setting Aside or Opening Judgment
Pbs 351: Procedure Where Party Fails to Comply with Order of Court or to Appear for Trial
Pbs 352: Motion for Default and Nonsuit for Failure to Appear
Pbs 354: Notice of Judgments of Nonsuit and Default for Failure to Enter an Appearance
Pbs 363: Procedure Where Party Is in Default

Pbs 363A: Where Defendant Is in Default for Failure to Plead
Pbs 377:   Opening Judgment upon Default or Nonsuit

C. Relevant Connecticut General Statutes Include:

C.G.S. sec. 51-84.:   Attorneys subject to rules.
C.G.S. sec. 52-259c.:   Fee to open, set aside, modify, extend or reargue
judgment.
C.G.S. sec. 52-592.:   Accidental failure of suit; allowance of new action.

17 *Prejudgment Remedies*

Terminology

Prejudgment Remedy	Commercial Transaction	Garnishee
Fraudulent Conveyances	Mechanic's Lien	Lien
Offer of Proof	Attachment	PJR
Commercial Waiver	Consumer Transaction	
Lis Pendens	Judgment Proof	
Ex-Parte PJR		

Pbs: 230A
C.G.S. sections: 46b-80, 49-33 et seq., 52-259, 52-278a-n, 52-280, 52-325 et seq.

Introduction

What can Plaintiffs do if they win a million-dollar judgment against a Defendant, but the Defendant does not have any assets, cash or insurance to pay the judgment? The answer is, not much. A judgment is usually valid for 20 or more years. If, however, the Defendant is unemployed during that time, or out of business and has no other assets, such as a house, car, expensive equipment, money in the bank, etc., the Plaintiff may be out of luck. These Defendants are labeled **judgment proof.**

No Plaintiff's attorney wants to take a case if the Defendant is or will be judgment proof. Why bother? After all the time and money spent on litigation, the judgment will be worthless. Prejudgment Remedies (known as **PJR**s) help Plaintiffs avoid this situation. If a Defendant has any assets at the time the suit is brought, a PJR allows a Plaintiff to **attach** (also known as freeze or lien) a Defendant's assets *before and during* a lawsuit. (Hence, the name: *prejudgment.*) If a Plaintiff obtains a Prejudgment Remedy against a Defendant, that Defendant will not be able to spend, sell, transfer, give away, destroy and sometimes use any assets listed in the Prejudgment Remedy while the lawsuit is ongoing. At the end of the lawsuit, if the Plaintiff wins, the court will direct the attached assets to be turned over directly to the Plaintiff to pay the judgment. If the Defendant wins, he or she will get the assets back.

166

Prejudgment Remedies are serious business. In many situations, there's no better way to bring Defendants to their knees than to attach all of their assets. Settlements tend to occur much more quickly when Defendants need the thousands of dollars in a bank account to operate a business. They won't have time to toss the dice and hope to win in court several years later. If they don't resolve the dispute now, they could be ruined forever.

I. DEFINITION OF A PJR REMEDY

C.G.S. sec. 52-278a(d) defines a Prejudgment Remedy as "any remedy...that enables a person by way of attachment...to deprive the Defendant in a civil action or affect the use, possession or enjoyment by such Defendant of his property right, prior to final judgment, but shall not include a temporary restraining order."

II. TYPES OF PJRs

A. *Four Types of PJRs*

There are four types of PJRs under C.G.S. sec. 52-278a-n:
1. A *regular PJR* brought prior to suit, which requires a hearing and a court order *before* any assets may be frozen.
2. A *regular PJR*, as described above, brought *after* suit has already started or after judgment. It still requires a hearing and a court order before any assets may be frozen.
3. A PJR, pursuant to a **commercial waiver**, which does not require a hearing or court order. The assets are frozen as soon as the PJR is served.
4. An **ex parte PJR** obtained before or during the suit without first notifying the opposing party. This type of PJR requires a court order.

III. WHO MAY OBTAIN A PJR UNDER C.G.S. SEC. 52-278a-n AND DEFENDANT'S RIGHTS

PJRs are most commonly sought by Plaintiffs and we will refer to this scenario throughout the remainder of this chapter. Defendants, however, may seek a PJR if they file a Counterclaim in an action. Any other party (such as a third-party Plaintiff) who is seeking damages from another party in the action may also seek a PJR.

If a PJR is granted, a Defendant may ask the court to order the Plaintiff to post a bond, under C.G.S. sec. 52-278(d)(e) and (f), to protect the Defendant's interest in the attached property.

IV. DEFINITIONS THAT APPLY TO A PJR

A. Consumer Transaction: C.G.S. sec. 52-278a(b) defines this term as "transaction(s) in which a natural person obligates himself to pay for goods sold or leased, services rendered or moneys loaned for person, family or household purposes."

B. Commercial Transaction: C.G.S. sec. 52-278a(a) defines this term as "a transaction which is not a consumer transaction."

C. Person: C.G.S. sec. 52-278a(c) defines this term to include "individuals, partnerships, associations, limited liability companies and corporations."

D. Property: C.G.S. sec. 52-278a(e) defines this term as "any present or future interest in real or personal property, goods, chattels or chose in action, whether such is vested or contingent."

V. REQUIREMENTS UNDER C.G.S. SEC. 52-278a-n

Due to the serious nature of PJRs, C.G.S. sec. 52-278b directs the court to strictly enforce each C.G.S. section that applies. This means a Plaintiff must specifically follow each relevant statute. Otherwise, the court must deny the PJR and the Defendant may go off and spend or give away all of the assets to prevent the Plaintiff from trying again. Though there is a remedy for such **fraudulent conveyances**, it is usually extremely time-consuming and expensive to prove. As a result, it's best to follow all the requirements the first time and get the PJR granted.

VI. WHAT CAN BE ATTACHED WITH A PJR

It's up to the Plaintiff to somehow identify all of the Defendant's attachable assets and include them in the PJR. Almost anything the Defendant has a right in can be attached.

A. What Can Be Attached

The following assets may be attached:
1. Bank accounts, joint or in the Defendant's name exclusively;
2. Stocks and bonds in the Defendant's name, in part or joint;
3. Cars, boats, planes, motorcycles, etc., in the Defendant's name in part or joint;
4. Equipment, in the Defendant's name in part or joint;
5. Real estate: Although the Defendant will be allowed to live or work in the attached real estate, a lien is placed on the land records to prevent someone from purchasing the property without knowledge of the lien. If someone purchases it anyway, and a judgment is rendered, the purchaser will be compelled to turn the property over to the Plaintiff. (See also **Notice of Lis Pendens**.)

B. Garnishees

A garnishee is a person or entity who owes or may owe a Defendant money or who has possession of a Defendant's assets. For example, a garnishee can be a bank in which a Defendant's accounts are located, a company in which a Defendant owns stock, or even an insurance company that may owe a Defendant insurance proceeds from another matter. In addition, if a Defendant is a contractors, the people who owe the contractor money can be garnishees.

When a PJR is granted, the court orders a garnishee not to pay a Defendant the amount he or she owes, or not to return any funds or assets to a Defendant, until the court orders otherwise. This is called garnishing, or attaching or liening the funds or assets. In most instances, the court will order the funds or assets to be held in escrow pending the resolution of the case. If the garnishee disregards the court order to withhold a Defendant's funds or assets, the garnishee will be responsible to the Plaintiff for the amount of value of the funds or assets not garnished and up to the amount of the judgment if the Plaintiff wills his or her case, and may face other consequences determined by the court.

When preparing the necessary PJR documents, the Plaintiff will need to bring two sets of original documents to court, and make enough copies for his or her own file and each Defendant and the garnishees.

C. Substitute Assets

If a PJR is granted, the Defendant may be permitted to post a bond or provide any other type of security which is sufficient to meet the purposes of the PJR, as a substitute for the attached assets. This request can be made by filling out the bottom portion of the Notice of Application of Prejudgment Remedy for regular and ex parte PJRs.

D. Motion to Disclose Assets: Pbs 230A

Pursuant to Pbs 230A(b), a Plaintiff may file a Motion to Disclose Assets with the Application for Prejudgment Remedy, or anytime afterward. If the PJR is granted, the court will order the Defendant to disclose his or her assets at a specific date and time. In the alternative, pursuant to Pbs 230A(d), the Defendant may ask the court to allow him or her to post a bond or provide other security (money, property, etc.) in an amount that is sufficient to meet the purposes of the PJR.

VII. REGULAR PJR, PRIOR TO SUIT

A. Plaintiffs Seeking a Regular PJR Prior to Suit Must Draft the Following Documents, Most Of Which Are Listed in C.G.S. sec. 52-278c:

1. *Notice of Application for Prejudgment Remedy/Claim for Hearing to Contest Application or Claim Exemption.* This is a court-issued form and contains the required notice to Defendants.

2. Proposed, *unsigned* (Writ) *Summons and Complaint* the Plaintiff intends to use to serve the Defendant and start the lawsuit.

3. An *Application for Prejudgment Remedy*, directed to the Superior Court where the lawsuit will be filed.

4. An *Affidavit*, sworn to by the Plaintiff or any competent affiant, which sets forth a statement of facts to show:

"that there is probable cause that a judgment in the amount of the Prejudgment Remedy sought, or in an amount greater than the amount of the Prejudgment Remedy sought, taking into account any known defenses, counterclaims or set-offs, will be rendered in favor of the Plaintiff."

5. An *Order for Hearing and Notice*, stating that a hearing will be held at a certain time and date and at a specific court, to determine whether or not the PJR should be granted. (The clerk will determine the date and time.)

6. An *Order, after Hearing in Which the Defendant Appeared*; and

7. An *Order, after Hearing in Which the Defendant Failed to Appear*.

For items 6 and 7, the Plaintiff drafts the order and includes all the attachments he or she wants the court to grant after the PJR hearing.

8. A Summons, called a **Summons and Direction for Attachment**, which will be needed for the proper officer after the PJR is granted. This Summons and Direction for Attachment provides instructions for the officer to serve a *signed* copy of the Summons and Complaint, along with the Order after Hearing and all the other documents, on the Defendant and any garnishee listed in the documents and the Order. In addition, if real estate is involved, the Plaintiff will need a **Notice of Attachment** to be filed on the land records. The attachments are in effect as soon as service is made. (See C.G.S. sec. 52-280 regarding service.)

9. A **Summons**, to a proper officer, commanding him or her to serve the Defendant all of the above-listed unsigned documents. This Summons is used initially to serve the Defendant, after the documents are filed and the clerk schedules a hearing date on the PJR.

B. Procedure to Obtain a Hearing and Provide Notice to the Defendant

1. After the Plaintiff drafts all of the above, he or she usually must go to the court where the suit will be brought (where the action is made returnable) and bring the following:

a. two original sets of all the documents; (I suggest originals because the clerk will keep one set and the other will be given back to the Plaintiff to give to the officer, along with copies, to make service on the Defendant and any garnishees.)

b. the fee, which is $235. (A new bill was passed in June 1997, amending the $200 fee stated in C.G.S. sec. 52-259.)

2. While the Plaintiff waits, the clerk will usually carefully review the documents. If they are correct, the clerk will sign the Order for Hearing and Notice and assign the case a hearing date. This hearing date and time will also be written on the Order for Hearing and Notice in both sets of documents. In most instances, the hearing date is approximately two weeks away, although it never hurts for the Plaintiff to ask for the earliest date possible. The clerk will then take the fee, file one set of documents and return the other to the Plaintiff.

3. The Plaintiff must then photocopy the signed Order for Hearing and Notice and attach it to the set of copies to be served upon the Defendant.

C. Type of Service

Any proper sheriff or constable may serve the above-listed documents, in the same manner as a regular Summons and Complaint are served.

D. Time for Service: C.G.S. sec. 52-278c(4)

After all of the above is filed and the clerk assigns a hearing date, the Defendant must be served at least *four days* before the hearing date.

E. Officer's Return of Service

The Return of Service must be available at the hearing to demonstrate that the Defendant had proper notice of the hearing.

F. Short Calendar

If the hearing date is two or more weeks away, the Plaintiff should receive a Short Calendar, showing the case is scheduled for that date. In this circumstance, the court may require the Plaintiff to call the court with an off or ready marking. Check the Short Calendar's instructions.

If the hearing is scheduled sooner than two weeks, the case will probably be a **write-in**. This means the clerk will write the name of the case on the Short Calendar for that date. The Plaintiff should contact the court to confirm it is scheduled.

In addition, some courts do not hold an actual hearing on this date. Instead, the instructions on the Short Calendar will require the parties to appear and mark the case over for two weeks. During this two-week time, they must exchange an **Offer of Proof**. An offer of proof contains each parties' reasons for granting or denying the PJR. A hearing will then be held at the next court date.

G. *After the Hearing: PJR Granted: C.G.S. sec. 52-278d*

If, after a hearing, the court grants the Prejudgment Remedy, the court or clerk will sign the Order and give it to the Plaintiff, along with the unsigned, proposed Writ, Summons and Complaint. Then, the Plaintiff must:

1. Sign the Summons (which includes Directions for Attachment) and Complaint, photocopy the Order, and have sufficient copies of all the documents made for all Defendants and any garnishees, as well as the Plaintiff's files.
2. Within *30 days* of the PJR being granted, a proper officer must serve the Defendant and garnishees with the following:

    a. a copy of the signed Summons and Complaint;

    b. a copy of the Order granting the PJR and attachments)

Then, the original set of documents must be returned (filed), along with a Return on Service, to the court *within the same 30 days* in which the PJR was granted. The return date on the original documents may be changed as needed. If the 30-day deadline is missed, the case will be dismissed and the Plaintiff will have to start all over again. (See C.G.S. sec. 52-278j.)

G. *After the Hearing: PJR Denied: C.G.S. sec. 52-278d(b)*

If the PJR is denied, C.G.S. sec. 52-278(b) a Plaintiff who still wants to bring suit will serve only the signed copy of the Summons and Complaint on the Defendant, like any other lawsuit. Again the 30-day deadline to serve and file applies under C.G.S. sec. 52-278j. If it is missed, the Plaintiff must pay another $185 entry fee to file the lawsuit.

VIII. REGULAR PJR, WHILE SUIT IS IN PROGRESS

C.G.S. sec. 52-278h, m and n apply to Plaintiffs who decide to seek a PJR after they have started an action, or Defendants who have filed a Counterclaim or right to set-off.

When seeking a PJR in an action that has already started, the same documents are used. Note, however, the following:

A. *Filing Fee*

When filing the PJR document, be prepared to pay a $50 filing fee, pursuant to C.G.S. sec. 52-259.

B. Service

If the Defendant has already appeared, personal service by an officer will not be needed, unless the court determines otherwise. Instead, certification of service, pursuant to C.G.S. sec. 120 et seq., is sufficient. Each party will receive a Short Calendar to inform them when the hearing is scheduled to occur.

IX. THE EX PARTE PJR

C.G.S. sec. 52-278e allows an ex parte PJR to be sought prior to or during suit. This means that the court may grant a PJR, with or without a hearing, without the Defendant's knowledge.

A. Reasons to Seek an Ex Parte Prejudgment Remedy

C.G.S. sec. 52-278e provides four reasons to seek an ex parte PJR:
If there is a reasonable likelihood that the Defendant:
> **1.** has hidden or will hide so that process cannot be served; or
> **2.** is about to leave Connecticut or remove attachable property from Connecticut; or
> **3.** is about to fraudulently dispose of or has fraudulently disposed of attachable property with intent to hinder, delay or defraud creditors; or
> **4.** has fraudulently hidden or withheld money, property or effects which should be liable to satisfy debts.

B. Documents Needed

Many of the same documents are used as for a regular PJR sought prior to suit:
> **1.** Notice: Like a regular PJR, this is a court-issued form. It is entitled: *Notice of Ex-Parte Prejudgment Remedy/Claim for Hearing to Dissolve or Modify;*
> **2.** Application for PJR;
> **3.** The *Affidavit:* C.G.S. sec. 52-278e requires the Plaintiff to state the reasons, as stated above, for the ex parte PJR in an affidavit, along with the other information required in a regular PJR;
> **4.** A *signed Complaint;*
> **5.** An *Order* (to be signed by the court);
> **6.** A *Summons and Direction for Attachment*, directing the officer to serve all of the above to the Defendant and garnishees listed in the Order (item 5) in which the court granted the ex parte PJR.

The initial fee is $50.00. If the ex parte PJR is granted, the Plaintiff must then pay the $185 entry fee.

C. The Procedures

Time is of the essence when an ex parte PJR is sought. As a result, the Plaintiff must go to the courthouse and find a judge willing to give the Plaintiff a hearing, either that day or soon after, or to take the matter on the papers within the next few hours. Don't forget to bring at least two sets of documents and the total fee of $235.

D. The Courts and Defendant's Rights

If the ex parte PJR is granted, the court-issued Notice form permits the Defendant to ask the court for a hearing to dissolve or modify the PJR. If the Defendant makes this request, a hearing will take place within seven days.

Though some ex parte PJRs are granted, many courts are reluctant to grant them. They are more willing to schedule a hearing within a few days, or sooner, providing the Plaintiff is able to serve the Defendant with an Order for Hearing and Notice and all the documents described above.

X. PJR WITH COMMERCIAL WAIVER

A. Definition of a Commercial Waiver

In accordance with C.G.S. sec. 52-278f, a PJR pursuant to a **commercial waiver** takes effect at the time the documents are served. A **commercial waiver** is specific language which may be included in any contract involving a commercial transaction. Defendants who sign contracts containing this specific language waive their rights to a hearing, in the event they default, and permit the Plaintiff to immediately, and without prior warning, attach their assets. As a result, a PJR of this type takes place automatically, without a hearing and court order, usually at the same time suit is brought.

B. To Benefit from a Commercial Waiver

To benefit from a commercial waiver, the Plaintiff must do the following:
1. Be sure the specific language necessary is stated in the promissory note or contract signed by the Defendant, and
2. Be sure that a copy of the waiver is included in the Plaintiff's Complaint. The promissory note or contract should also be incorporated into the Complaint by reference and a copy attached to the Complaint. For example: Paragraph 2 of the *George Skillman Et Al. v. Auto Service Center, Inc.* Complaint reads:

2. On or about September 1, 1997, the Defendant, through its duly authorized President, Joseph Kelly, executed a promissory note promising to pay the Plaintiffs the sum of ONE HUNDRED THOUSAND DOLLARS ($100,000), plus interest, pursuant to the terms of said promissory note, a copy of which is attached hereto and incorporated herein.

Paragraph 7 of the *Skillman Et Al. v. Auto Service Center, Inc.* Complaint demonstrates the necessary commercial waiver language. It reads:

7. Pursuant to Paragraph 11 of said promissory note, the Defendant as Maker, acknowledges that the loan evidenced by this note is a Commercial Transaction and waives its rights to notice and hearing under Chapter 903a of the Connecticut General Statutes, with respect to any Prejudgment Remedy which the Plaintiff Lender may desire to use.

C. Documents Required

When a commercial waiver is involved, the documents and procedure are much simpler. All the Plaintiff needs are the following:

1. A *signed Complaint*, with a copy of the promissory note or contract at issue, which contains a commercial waiver. Like a regular lawsuit, the Plaintiff selects the return date, etc.
2. A court-issued form entitled: *Notice of Ex Parte Prejudgment Remedy/Claim for Hearing to Dissolve or Modify.*
3. An *Affidavit*, like the Affidavit described above for regular PJRs.
4. A *Summons and Direction for Attachment*, as described for Ex Parte PJRs.

D. Procedure Required

1. Service

The officer will make service on the Defendant and all garnishees in the same manner as any other Complaint: at least 12 days before the return date. Note that in my experience, I have found it best to serve the garnishees first and the Defendant last. This prevents the Defendant from obtaining the assets from the garnishees before the garnishees are served.

2. Return to Court

As in a regular lawsuit, the original documents and the officer's Return of Service, which will include the names of the garnishees served, must be filed in court at least six days before the return date, with a $185 entry fee. (Note that the $50 PJR fee is not needed when the PJR is based on a commercial waiver.)

E. Defendant's Rights

The *Notice of Ex Parte Prejudgment Remedy and Claim for Hearing to Dissolve or Modify* contains directions for a Defendant who wants a hearing before the court to challenge the attachment. The attachment stays in effect until the court orders otherwise.

XI. OTHER TYPES OF LIENS: MECHANIC'S LIENS

In addition to Prejudgment Remedies under C.G.S. sec. 52-278a-n, parties may attempt to protect their interests by placing a lien against real estate that is in some way involved in the dispute with an opponent. The purpose of the lien is to prevent the opponent from selling or transferring the real estate until the dispute has been resolved.

One type of lien that can accomplish this goal is called a **Mechanic's Lien.** However, be sure to carefully read and comply with the applicable Connecticut General Statutes before you record and serve them.

A. Who May File a Mechanic's Lien

Plaintiffs may place a lien on a piece of real estate with a Mechanic's Lien without bringing suit. Pursuant to C.G.S. sec. 49-33 et seq., the purpose of a Mechanic's Lien is to protect Plaintiffs who are owed money for work performed on a building or piece of real estate. In general terms, Mechanic's Liens may be utilized by those Plaintiffs who are in construction or a similar type of profession that involves, but is not limited to, building, improving, removing and repairing real estate or any type of structure on the real estate.

Plaintiffs who have claims against owners of a building or real estate for more than ten dollars for services or materials relating thereto may protect their interests by filing a Mechanic's Lien at the town or city hall where the real estate is located. As a result, one of two scenarios may occur:

1. If the owner sells the property, he or she must first pay the Plaintiff the amount of money claimed due in the Mechanic's Lien. Otherwise, the new owner will become liable to the Plaintiff; or

2. If the owner of the real estate still fails to pay the sum due, the Plaintiff may bring a lawsuit to attempt to foreclose on the real estate, just like a bank or other lender may foreclose on a mortgage, to collect the money that is owed.

B. How to File a Mechanic's Lien

C.G.S. sec. 49-33 et seq. provides explicit instructions regarding Mechanic's Liens. In addition, note that there are specific provisions for subcontractors and materialmen. For our purposes, keep in mind the following:

1. The Mechanic's Lien can only lien the property in the amount claimed due by the Plaintiff. If there is more than one Mechanic's Lien on the property, their

total amount cannot exceed the total amount the Defendant agreed to pay the original contractor.

2. The Mechanic's Lien must include a legal property description of the property at issue. A copy can be obtained from the clerk's office in the town or city hall where the applicable land records are available.

3. C.G.S. sec. 49-33 requires a Mechanic's Lien to be "lodged" (recorded) with the town clerk in the town (or city) where the real estate is located (land records office), *within 90 days* after the Plaintiff ceased performing services or furnishing materials for the building or real estate. The Mechanic's Lien is then deemed recorded and made part of the town or city land records and public knowledge to anyone who cares to look up the property. See C.G.S. sec. 49-34 and 49-35. The Mechanic's Liens may be filed by a sheriff or constable in their respective precincts or jurisdictions, or by an indifferent person.

4. In addition, all owners of record (listed in the land records) of the building or real estate must be served, in hand or abode, with a true and attested copy of the Mechanic's Lien *before* it is recorded on the land records, or *at the same time, or no later than 30 days* after the lien is recorded on the land records. Otherwise, the lien is invalid. To be safe, I interpret the statutes to require that the land owners be served and the Mechanic's Lien be recorded on the land records within the 90-day deadline. Service can be accomplished by a proper sheriff, constable, or indifferent person. (A sheriff or constable may act as an indifferent person to record and serve Mechanic's Liens in any Connecticut jurisdiction.)

C. Releasing a Mechanic's Lien

If the owner of the property pays the debt owed to the Plaintiff, the Plaintiff must release the Mechanic's Lien by filing a Release on the land records where the Mechanic's Lien is filed. If the lien is not released, the owner may file an Application for Discharge with the court, asking the court to discharge the lien. See C.G.S. sec. 49-35a.

XII. ANOTHER TYPES OF LIEN: NOTICE OF LIS PENDENS

C.G.S. sec. 52-325 permits Plaintiffs and those Defendants who plead an affirmative cause of action and "demand substantive relief" in their Answer to file a **Notice of Lis Pendens** in those cases that are "intended to affect real property... ." In many instances, these are foreclosure and dissolution of marriage cases.

In a foreclosure action, the real estate is at issue because the Defendant allegedly defaulted on the mortgage which is secured by the real estate. The Plaintiff sues to receive the property and sell it in order to pay off the Defendant's mortgage. In dissolution of marriage actions, real property such as the marital home and other real property often make up the majority of the parties' assets. Therefore, its value is a major component in an equitable distribution of the marital estate.

A. Effect of a Lis Pendens

The purpose of a Notice of Lis Pendens is to prevent one party from selling or transferring the property to a third party, to defeat a judgment. A Notice of Lis Pendens places all potential purchasers of the property on notice that they will be bound by the court's decision regarding the property as if they were a party to the action. This can include being ordered to transfer the property to one or more of the parties and not receiving a refund for the purchase price, without bringing a separate lawsuit.

B. Contents of a Notice of Lis Pendens

Like a Mechanic's Lien, a Notice of Lis Pendens contains a legal description of the property at issue and must be recorded at the land records office in the town or city where the real property is located. In addition, it should include:
1. the names of the parties;
2. the nature of the case;
3. the court that has jurisdiction over the matter (include the return date or the docket number);
4. the date of the Complaint.

C. Serving a Notice of Lis Pendens

Like Mechanic's Liens, a true and attested copy of the Notice of Lis Pendens must be served upon all owners of record no later than *30 days* after the recording. Service may be made by any proper officer including an indifferent person. (See C.G.S. sec. 46b-80(a)(2) and C.G.S. sec.52-325(c).) Unlike Mechanic's Liens, a Notice of Lis Pendens is not appropriate until the lawsuit is brought, or afterward.

D. Releasing a Lis Pendens

At the conclusion of the case, a Lis Pendens is no longer valid or necessary. Therefore, the party who placed a Notice of Lis Pendens on the property must release it by filing a "Release of Lis Pendens" on the land records where the Notice of Lis Pendens is filed. Otherwise, the party who obtains title to the property will have difficulty transferring the property in the future because it will appear that the lien is still in effect.

If the Notice of Lis Pendens was filed but the case was never filed in court, see C.G.S. sec. 52-325a et seq., which permits a party to ask the court to discharge the Lis Pendens.

XIII. CONCLUSION

A. *Key Issues in This Chapter Include:*

1. *Prejudgment Remedies*

Prejudgment Remedies are great when they work. They are also quite time-consuming to prepare. Be sure to carefully read and comply with each applicable statute. In addition, some courts handle the scheduling or the hearing process differently from others. Therefore, it never hurts to call the court at issue beforehand and speak with the clerk who handles PJRs to verify the procedures.

2. *Mechanic's Liens*

Mechanic's Liens are applicable when the Plaintiff has performed some type of work upon a piece of land, or a building thereon, or has supplied materials for such work, and has not been paid by the owner for such services or materials. A Mechanic's Lien must be recorded with the town clerk where the real property is located within *90 days* of the Plaintiff ceasing to perform service or furnish materials. In addition, the owner of the property must be timely served a copy of the Mechanic's Lien no later than 30 days after it is recorded. In addition, I suggest making sure that service also occurs during the original 90 days mentioned above.

3. *Notice of Lis Pendens*

A Notice of Lis Pendens also protects real property. It is commonly used in foreclosure and dissolution of marriage actions. Like a Mechanic's Lien, it must be recorded on the applicable land records and a copy must be served on the property owners within *30 days* of being recorded.

4. *Service*

Keep in mind that a sheriff or constable can act as an indifferent person to record and serve a Mechanic's Lien or Notice of Lis Pendens in any jurisdiction in Connecticut.

B. *Examples*

C.G.S sec. 52-278a et seq. contains examples of the forms needed to file a PJR. In addition, samples of a court-issued Notice of Application for PJR/Claim for Hearing to Contest Application or Claim Exemption and Notice of Ex Parte PJR/Claim for Hearing to Dissolve or Modify are found at the end of this chapter. You will also a Motion for Disclosure of Assets, a Mechanic's Lien, and a Notice and Release of Lis Pendens.

C. Completing the "Notice of Application for Prejudgment Remedy/Claim for Hearing to Contest Application or Claim Exemption"

This is a basic form which requests the following information from the Plaintiff:

1. type of court;
2. address of court;
3. indicate if temporary restraining order is requested;
4. name of case;
5. indicate amount in demand;
6. indicate if sheets are attached for additional parties;
7. case type: major and minor;
8. number of counts in Complaint;
9. name and address of Plaintiff;
10. name and address of Defendant;
11. name and address of garnishees, if any;
12.-14. Plaintiff's appearance: name and address of attorney, law firm, pro se, telephone number, Juris Number;
15. attorney's signature;
16. date signed.
17. The clerk fills in this information to inform the Defendant of the date, time and courtroom where the hearing will be held.
The Defendant should complete the remainder of the form if he or she decides to challenge the PJR:
18. check the box that applies;
19. date the Defendant mailed/delivered copies of the Notice to all other parties in the case (service under Pbs 120 et seq.);
20. Defendant's signature;
21. date signed;
22. name and address of the Defendant;
23. name of each party the Defendant served a copy of the Notice;
24. address where service was made.

D. Completing the "Notice of Ex Parte Prejudgment Remedy/Claim for Hearing to Dissolve or Modify"

This form is identical to the regular PJR form above, except there is no place for the clerk to place the date, time and room number for a hearing (item 17).

E. Relevant Connecticut Practice Book Sections Include:

Pbs 230A: Disclosure of Assets in Cases in Which Prejudgment Remedy Sought

F. Relevant Connecticut General Statutes Include:

C.G.S. sec. 46b-80.:   Prejudgment remedies available; Lis Pendens, notice and effect.

C.G.S. sec. 49-33 et seq.: Mechanic's Lien. Precedence. Rights of subcontractors.

C.G.S. sec. 52-259.:   Court fees.

C.G.S. sec. 52-278a-n.:   Prejudgment remedies.

C.G.S. sec. 52-280.:   Service of writ of attachment.

C.G.S. sec. 52-325 et seq.: Notice of Lis Pendens.

Example 1, Motion to Disclose Assets

DOCKET NO. CV 98-0444444 S	:	SUPERIOR COURT
GEORGE SKILLMAN, ET AL.	:	JUDICIAL DISTRICT OF
	:	HARTFORD/NEW BRITAIN
VS.	:	AT HARTFORD
AUTO SERVICE CENTER, INC.	:	MARCH 23, 1998

MOTION FOR DISCLOSURE OF ASSETS

Pursuant to Connecticut Practice Book Section 230A, the Plaintiff in the above-captioned case hereby respectfully requests the court to order the Defendant, Auto Service Center, Inc. to disclose its assets.

By Complaint dated February 2, 1998, the Plaintiff filed suit against the Defendant and obtained a Prejudgment Remedy pursuant to a commercial waiver contained in the contract between the parties. The value of the assets attached at that time is insufficient to meet the Plaintiff's damages.

WHEREFORE, the Plaintiff requests the court to order Joseph Kelly, sole shareholder, director, and the president of the Defendant, to appear at the office of the undersigned within 60 days of the granting of this order, to disclose under oath during a deposition, all of its assets.

THE PLAINTIFF
BY_____
Kenneth I. Marcus, Esq.,
Friedman & Marcus, P.C.
his attorney
27 Main Street
Bristol, CT 00000
Tele. #(860) 955-9595
Juris #424242

ORDER

The foregoing Motion having been considered by the Court, it is hereby
ORDERED: GRANTED /DENIED.   _____
Judge/Clerk

CERTIFICATION

I hereby certify that a copy of the above was mailed on March 23, 1998 to all counsel and pro se parties of record, namely: Mark Peters, Esq., 1001 Sanberg Street, Manchester, CT 06660.

_____
Commissioner of Superior Court

Example 2, Mechanic's Lien

MECHANIC'S LIEN

THIS IS TO CERTIFY THAT ABC Buildings, Inc., of the City of New Britain, County of Hartford and State of Connecticut, its heirs, successors and assigns, in accordance with a certain contract between ABC Buildings, Inc., the Contractor, and Jack Mason, of the City of New Britain, County of Hartford and State of Connecticut has a lien under the Connecticut General Statutes in such cases made and provided, on the premises, owned by said Jack Mason, and described in Exhibit "A" attached hereto and to other buildings standing thereon, to the amount of Six Thousand ($6,000.00) Dollars as nearly as the same can be ascertained.

THE LIEN is for services rendered and materials furnished in the construction, erecting, raising and removal of said building and for repairs thereon, commencing the July 15, 1997 and ending on March 14, 1998.

THE SAID PREMISES are situated in the City of New Britain, County of Hartford and State of Connecticut, recorded in the name of Jack Mason, of the City of New Britain, in Vol. 27, Page 458, are bounded and described in Exhibit "A" attached hereto.

The name and names against whom this lien is being filed is: Jack Mason.

THIS CERTIFICATE is made and filed within ninety days from the time of ceasing to render services and furnish material, as aforesaid.

IN WITNESS WHEREOF, I have hereunto set my hand this 30th day of April, 1998.

_____   BY_____

Mary Steward   Walter Martin,
                                                President and duly authorized
_____   agent of ABC Buildings, Inc.

Gerald Murry

STATE OF CONNECTICUT)
)   ss. NEW BRITAIN
COUNTY OF HARTFORD   )

PERSONALLY APPEARED, Walter Martin, Signer and Sealer of the foregoing Certificate, and made solemn oath to the truth of the same and that the amount above named is justly due to the said ABC Buildings, Inc., as nearly as the same can be ascertained. Before me.

                                    _____
                                    Commissioner of the Superior Court
                                    Notary Public, Justice of the Peace

Received:

    Town Clerk

    (*Be sure to include or attach the property description.)

Example 3, Notice of Lis Pendens

RETURN DATE: MARCH 4, 1998:	:	SUPERIOR COURT
DELILAH FARRARA	:	J.D. OF HARTFORD/NEW BRITAIN
	:	AT HARTFORD
MAXWELL FARRARA	:	FEBRUARY 18, 1998

NOTICE OF LIS PENDENS

Notice is hereby given of the pendency of a civil action between the above-named parties by a Complaint made returnable to the Superior Court at Hartford, Connecticut, within and for the Judicial District of Hartford/New Britain, at Hartford, on March 4, 1998, which action is brought claiming a dissolution of marriage and an equitable distribution of the parties' marital assets. Such marital assets include real property known as 506 South Logan Way, Bloomfield, Connecticut and is bounded and described as set forth in Exhibit A, attached hereto.

Dated in Hartford, this 18th day of February 18, 1998.

THE DEFENDANT

BY_____

Felicia Sullivan, Esq.,
his attorney
P.O. Box 105
(*Be sure to attach the property description)   Rocky Hill, CT 06067
Tele. No. (860) 333-9999
Juris No. 888888

Example 4, Release of Lis Pendens

DOCKET NO. FA 98-999999 S	:	SUPERIOR COURT
DELILAH FARRARA	:	J.D. OF HARTFORD/NEW BRITAIN
VS.	:	AT HARTFORD
MAXWELL FARRARA	:	JANUARY 24, 1999

RELEASE OF LIS PENDENS

Notice is hereby given that the Notice of Lis Pendens found in Volume 290, Page 1098, pertaining to real property known as 506 South Logan Way, Bloomfield, Connecticut, as described in Exhibit A attached hereto, and the above-captioned case, is hereby released.

Dated in Hartford, this 24th day of January, 1999.

THE DEFENDANT

BY_____

Felicia Sullivan, Esq.,
his attorney
P.O. Box 105
Rocky Hill, CT 06067
Tele. No. (860) 333-9999
Juris No. 888888

18 *Discovery: An Overview*

Terminology

Interrogatories	Requests for Production	Requests for Admission
Deposition	Protective Order	Disclosure of Expert Witnesses
Stipulation	Request to Inspect Property	

Request for Mental/Physical Exam

Pbs: 216, 218, 221, 232, 249, and generally Chapter 8, Discovery and Depositions

Introduction

The purpose of **discovery** is to assist the parties in preparing their cases and to prevent any surprises at trial. Discovery permits each party in a lawsuit to formally investigate allegations and defenses, strengths and weaknesses. Armed with this information, they formulate strategies for trial.

Unlike on television, once a civil trial starts, there should be no last-minute surprise witnesses running into the courtroom, excitedly waving a piece of paper containing new information vital to the case. Instead, each party should have the names of all witnesses both sides expect to testify, and should have a pretty good idea what these witnesses will say. In addition, the parties should see, prior to trial, any photographs, documents, etc., their opponent has in their possession.

Having said that, it's important to understand that discovery is optional and expensive. No one can force a party to prepare a case for trial. Most often, a client's financial resources, along with the strengths and value of the case, will determine how much and what type of discovery will be pursued. The risk, of course, is that the case will go to trial and both the unprepared attorney and the client will look like fools. To avoid that, many cases settle the evening before, or on the actual day the trial is scheduled to begin.

As you read this and the other discovery chapters, keep the following in mind: The *requesting party* is the party that serves the Interrogatories on the opposing party. The opposing party who receives the discovery requests is called the *responding party*.

I. FORMS OF DISCOVERY

As I stated above, discovery permits each party in a lawsuit to formally investigate allegations and defenses, strengths and weaknesses. How? By asking the right questions of the right persons, according to the applicable practice book rules.

Chapter 8 of the Connecticut Practice Book permits each party to ask these questions in one or more of the following formats:

1. Interrogatories: written questions answered in writing, under oath;

2. Requests for Production: written requests to inspect or copy documents, statements, photographs or other tangible items in the opposing party's control;

3. Request for Inspection of Property: a written request to enter onto land to inspect, take measurements, take photographs, etc.;

4. Requests for Admissions: written statements the opposing party must admit or deny;

5. Request for Mental and/or Physical Exam: a written request to allow a qualified physician to perform a mental or physical examination of the opposing party;

6. Deposition: an oral examination of the opposing party, witnesses and expert witnesses, under oath and recorded by a court reporter (also called a stenographer), video, etc.

In addition, each party is required to file a **Disclosure of Expert Witnesses**: a formal pleading filed by any party to disclose the name and proposed testimony of any expert witnesses he or she intends to call to testify at trial. All these types of discovery are discussed in the next several chapters.

II. DISCOVERY LIMITATIONS

A. *Discovery Cannot Be Used As a Fishing Expedition or to Harass*

Regardless of which type of discovery is used, Pbs 218 requires the following:

1. That the information sought:

    a. relates to the subject matter of the pending action, and

    b. assists requesting parties to prove their case or defend themselves, and

    c. must not be considered privileged between the attorney and his or her client, or the attorney's work product, preparation in anticipation of litigation or trial.

2. The responding party must be able to obtain the information sought with "greater facility than the requesting party." In other words, the information must be available and/or easier for the responding party to provide than it would be for the requesting party to obtain the information.

Discovery cannot be used as a fishing expedition to seek answers to irrelevant questions or to harass someone. Any party who believes a question is inappropriate may file an objection or a **protective order**. If necessary, the court will decide whether the question must be answered.

B. Protective Order

1. Purpose of a Protective Order
According to Pbs 221, any party may file a Motion for Protective Order. The purpose of a protective order is to ask the court to relieve a party of his or her obligation to comply with specific discovery requests which may be inappropriate, or to establish parameters for such discovery requests.

2. Grounds for a Protective Order
Pbs 221 permits a Protective Order "to protect a party from annoyance, embarrassment, oppression or undue burden or expense."

3. Relief Requested in a Motion for Protective Order
Pursuant to Pbs 221, for "good cause," a party may request the court to:
>**a.** not permit the discovery;
>**b.** specify the terms and conditions, including time and place to provide discovery;
>**c.** allow the discovery, but in a different form;
>**d.** limit the scope of discovery;
>**e.** limit the persons present at the time the discovery is disclosed;
>**f.** allow a deposition, after being sealed by the court reporter, to be opened only by the court;
>**g.** rule that trade secrets or other confidential research, development or other commercial information not be disclosed or be disclosed only in a specified manner;
>**h.** rule that the parties both file specific discovery, in sealed envelopes, to be opened only upon court order.

III. TO WHOM DISCOVERY IS DIRECTED

A. Parties and Nonparties

A party can request discoverable information from three sources:
1. Pursuant to Pbs 216, *an opposing party* that is:
>**a.** a pro se;
>**b.** a client, in the presence of his or her attorney;
>**c.** an agent, employee, officer or director of a public or private corporation, partnership, association or governmental agency;

2. *Witnesses*: individuals who are not parties but who observed the incident at issue, or have special knowledge of the incident. Note, however, that because the parties will testify as witnesses at the trial, the term *nonparty* may be used to distinguish the two.

3. *Expert witnesses*: individuals who are not parties and who provide expert opinions based upon their expertise and the facts of the case. (Experts are included as nonparties in this text.)

B. Only Depositions Apply to Parties and Nonparties

The following types of discovery apply only to parties:

Interrogatories	Requests for Production
Depositions	Requests for Inspection of Property
Requests for Admission	Requests for Mental or Physical Exam
Disclosure of Expert Witnesses	

A *deposition* is the only type of discovery that apply to all parties, as well as nonparties. Thus, either party can depose the other and any nonparties who may potentially testify at trial.

IV. CONTINUING DUTY TO DISCLOSE

Each type of discovery must be conducted and responded to according to specific parameters and deadlines. According to Pbs 232, this includes a "continuing duty to disclose" new or additional information that may come to light, after a party has responded to an opposing party's discovery requests. Hence, neither party can claim, "I told you the truth when you asked me the question. I didn't know until later that my answer was wrong." Or, "I didn't know about this new witness when you asked me. She came out of the woodwork just a few days ago."

V. STIPULATIONS

Pbs 249 permits the parties to reach agreements to modify the discovery procedures and deadlines set forth in Chapter 8 of the Practice Book, so long as the court does not order otherwise. These agreements are called **stipulations**. In most cases, it's best to confirm stipulations in writing and file them in court, to prevent a future misunderstanding.

Stipulations are not limited to discovery issues. The parties can agree to almost anything: pleading deadlines, specific photographs and documents that will be introduced at trial, etc., so long as the purpose of the stipulation is not to intentionally and unduly delay a proceeding, or otherwise interfere with courthouse procedures.

An agreement to settle a lawsuit is often referred to as a stipulation. Either side will put the agreement in writing for the clients or the attorneys or both to sign. It is then filed in court.

VI. WHEN A PARTY FAILS TO COMPLY WITH DISCOVERY REQUESTS

Pbs 231, 351 and 363 permit a requesting party to ask the court to penalize a party who fails to timely comply with discovery requests by filing a Motion for Order of Compliance, Motion for Sanctions, Motion for Nonsuit, Motion for Default or even a Motion for Dismissal. Future chapters will address these pleadings in more detail.

VII. CONCLUSION

A. *Key Issues in This Chapter Include:*

As you explore the various types of discovery described in the next several chapters, keep the following in mind:

Regardless of which side you represent, you will encounter many clients who are unwilling to spend the thousands of dollars necessary for you to adequately prepare their cases. They may not have the money, or the actual damages involved may be small in comparison to the costs of proper discovery.

For example, if a case is worth $10,000, many clients (both Plaintiffs and Defendants) will not want to pay even $1,000 for discovery and court costs. It's just not worth it to them. In addition to the money, there are the aggravations of waiting years for a trial date and missing time from work to attend depositions and the trial. Plaintiffs face the additional possibility that the Defendant will not or cannot pay a $10,000 judgment. Defendant clients are worse off: Whether they win or lose at trial, they're stuck with a legal bill for the cost of their defense.

B. *Relevant Connecticut Practice Book Sections Include:*

Pbs 216: Definitions
Pbs 218: Scope of Discovery--In General
Pbs 221: Scope of Discovery--Protective Order
Pbs 232: Continuing Duty to Disclose
Pbs 249: Stipulations Regarding Discovery and Deposition Procedure

19 *Discovery: Interrogatories*

Terminology

Discovery Conference	Interrogatories
Motion for Extension of Time	Discovery Affidavit

Pbs: 223, 224, 225

Introduction

Interrogatories are the most common, and often the least costly, form of discovery. They are no filed in court. Instead, they are served (by mail or hand delivery) on opposing parties. Most personal injury cases are limited to standardized sets of Interrogatories that are found in the Connecticut Practice Book.

I. INTERROGATORIES

Pursuant to Pbs 223, Interrogatories are written questions *from one party, to his or her opponent*. They may be requested any time after the return date.

A. *Drafting Interrogatories: Pbs 223*

Like Requests to Revise,
1. each interrogatory must be numbered;
2. each interrogatory must be followed by sufficient space for the responding party to insert an answer. If more space is needed, the responding party may attach a separate sheet of paper;
3. a certification of service must be inserted at the end of the document, stating when the documents were mailed or hand delivered to the opponent's attorney;
4. the requesting party should not file Interrogatories in court.

B. *Personal Injury Cases vs. Other Types of Cases*

Our rules provide for a standard set of specific Interrogatories found in Forms 106.10A and 106.10B for both Plaintiffs and Defendants in personal injury cases that do not involve death or product liability. In addition, the Interrogatories found in Form 106.10C are specifically designed for Plaintiffs to use in premises liability (fall down) cases.

Note that the standardized Interrogatories may be expanded. Pursuant to Pbs 223 (Interrogatories) and 227 (Requests for Production), a party may ask the court to broaden the scope of standardized sets, if they are "inappropriate or inadequate in a particular action." Therefore, parties may file a Motion for Additional Discovery, stating in the motion what information they seek and why.

In all other types of cases, there is no limit to the type or number of Interrogatories a party may ask his or her opponent. In fact, in some cases it's common to send out one set of Interrogatories, followed by one or more additional sets. The only criteria is that the Interrogatories must relate to the subject matter of the case and assist the requesting party in proving or defending the case.

As with motions, I strongly suggest that you avoid reinventing the wheel when it comes to drafting Interrogatories. Your firm's forms file is bound to contain several types of Interrogatories you will want to ask your opponent. In addition, the law libraries contain numerous texts on discovery that you will find helpful.

C. *Responding to Interrogatories: Pbs 224*

Pbs 224 mandates that all Interrogatories must be:
1. answered under oath;
2. answered by the party they are directed to, meaning the client;
3. signed by the answering client, and witnessed by a Notary Public or Commissioner of the Superior Court;
4. returned within *30 days* after the date stated in the requesting party's certification of service, unless the party receives an extension of time;
5. Preceded by a *cover sheet*. This cover sheet is very similar to the one drafted in response to a Request to Revise: If there are no objections, the cover sheet should state that all the Interrogatories have been answered. Any objections should be listed on the sheet. Do not file anything in court.

D. *Stipulations and Motions for Extension of Time, Pbs 224 and 249*

If a party is unable to respond to the Interrogatories within 30 days, Pbs 224 allows the responding party to file a Stipulation (if the parties can agree on a new deadline) or a Motion for Extension of Time in court. There are two types of Motions for Extension of Time.

1. Motions for Extension of Time That Are Automatically Granted

If the responding party is simply seeking an additional 30 days in which to respond to all the Interrogatories, Pbs 224 permits a party to file a **Motion for Extension of Time** within the initial 30-day period and certify that the case has not been assigned for trial. The motion is treated like a request and is granted automatically so long as the party who served the Interrogatories does not object within *ten days* of the request being filed. A responding party is entitled to one such extension for each set of Interrogatories he or she receives.

2. Motions for Extension of Time That Require a Court Order

Parties who need more than an additional 30 days to respond should file a Motion for Extension of Time under Pbs 224(c). In many instances, the information the Interrogatories seek can be quite detailed and time-consuming to prepare. Therefore, the party can request the court to extend the deadline for a longer period and should specifically state how long he or she will need. In addition, the motion should also state that the case has not been assigned for trial. As long as the request is reasonable and no objection is filed, this motion is usually granted.

II. OBJECTIONS TO INTERROGATORIES

A. *Personal Injury Cases*

According to Pbs 225, Plaintiffs and Defendants in personal injury cases, excluding death or product liability, are not permitted to object to any of the court-ordered, standardized Interrogatories previously mentioned.

Not too long ago, it was customary for both Plaintiffs and Defendants in personal injury cases to serve each other countless Interrogatories and Requests for Production that almost always raised numerous objections. Rather than require a discovery conference, as described below, the court permitted these numerous objections to appear on the Short Calendar, and to be argued orally, at the discretion of the attorneys.

As you can imagine, the Short Calendar was a mess. Every Monday or other Short Calendar day, different attorneys would argue similar objections, over and over again, all day long, in almost every available courtroom in every courthouse. Because the judges were different, the rulings were different.

Accordingly, standardized set of Interrogatories and Requests for Production were created for Plaintiffs and Defendants in all personal injury cases, except those involving death or product liability. Neither party may object to any portion of these standardized sets. See Pbs 225 and 228.

B. Objections to Nonstandard Interrogatories: Deadline

Parties who wish to object to one or more nonstandard Interrogatories must do one of the following:

1. Serve the objection(s) on the requesting party within the initial 30 days pursuant to Pbs 224 (d); or

2. Specify in the Motion for Extension of Time that more time is needed to answer and/or object to the Interrogatories; or

3. If the party is requesting more than one additional 30-day extension, file the Motion for Extension of Time, and specify that more time is needed to answer and/or object; or

4. Obtain a stipulation from the requesting party on this issue.

Otherwise, the court may require the party to answer Interrogatories that could have been successfully objected to.

C. Reasons to Object to Nonstandard Interrogatories

The following is a list of reasons why a party may object to Interrogatories: of this action.

1. The Interrogatory is beyond the permissible scope of discovery.
2. It is not material to the subject matter of the instant action.
3. It would not be of assistance in the prosecution
4. The answer is neither admissible nor reasonably calculated to lead to the discovery of admissible evidence.
5. It is designed to annoy, embarrass or oppress the respondent Defendant, or have the effect thereof.
6. It is unduly burdensome to answer.
7. The requesting party has not demonstrated a substantial need for said information in the preparation of his or her case.
8. The responding party does not have access to the information sought and that information can be obtained with substantially greater facility by the requesting party.
9. The interrogatory is unclear and unduly vague.
10. The interrogatory seeks information that is the responding party's opinion, rather than fact.
11. The interrogatory seeks information that has been prepared in anticipation of litigation for trail.
12. The interrogatory seeks information that consists of mental impressions, conclusions or legal theories of the responding party's attorney, which is the attorney's work product.
13. The interrogatory seeks information that is privileged.
14. The interrogatory is beyond the scope permitted under the Practice Book rules.

In addition, be sure to check in the law library for examples of other types of objections that may apply to your case.

D. Drafting Objections

Like objections to Requests to Revise, all objections must be listed by number on the cover sheet. In addition, Pbs 225 requires the party to restate the Interrogatories objected to, followed by the reason for the objection directly below. The original cover sheet, along with the attached Interrogatories and objections, must be filed in court. A copy, along with all answers to the remaining Interrogatories, must be sent to the requesting party.

E. Discovery Conferences

The cover sheet and objections will not be placed on the Short Calendar. Instead, pursuant to Pbs 225, the parties must first make a "bona fide attempt" to resolve the objections themselves. In essence, this means the attorneys should hold some type of conference, often referred to as a **discovery conference**, usually by telephone, to discuss the objections and try to reach an agreement concerning what information, if any, the responding party should provide.

Often, the attorneys will settle most if not all of their disputes during the discovery conference. Therefore, there is no need for the court to rule on the objections. In these situations, the attorneys reach an agreement as to a deadline for the responding party to provide the information agreed upon, and the case moves on.

If the parties still have unresolved objections, either attorney must then file an affidavit, notifying the court of the outstanding objections.

F. The Discovery Affidavit

This affidavit, which is also known as the **discovery affidavit**, may be filed by either side and must include the following:

1. the attorney must certify that *bona fide attempts* have been made to resolve the differences concerning the subject matter of the objection(s) and that counsel have been unable to reach an agreement;
2. the date of the objection(s);
3. the name of the party who filed the objection(s);
4. the name of the party to whom the objection(s) was addressed;
5. the date, time and place of any conference held to resolve the differences;
6. the names of all persons who participated in the discovery conference;
7. the specific number of the Interrogatories still objected to;
8. if a discovery conference did not occur, the reasons why it did not take place.

After the affidavit is filed in court, the case will be placed on the Short Calendar. There will be no oral argument allowed, unless it is requested and the court agrees.

G. Overruled Objections

If the court overrules any of the responding party's objections, the responding party must provide the answers to those Interrogatories within *20 days* of the court's decision.

III. CONCLUSION

A. Key Issues in This Chapter Include:

1. Interrogatories are directed to parties only.

2. Interrogatories may be served at any time after the return date and are not filed in court.

3. Parties in most personal injury cases are limited to the Interrogatories contained in the standard sets found in Form 106.10A, B and C. Parties may file a motion asking the court for permission to file additional Interrogatories if they believe the forms are inappropriate or inadequate.

4. For standard Interrogatories, the responding party must answer each interrogatory within *30 days* of service, unless he or she files a Motion for Extension of Time before the 30-days deadline expires.

5. The first Motion for Extension of Time for an additional 30 days should be granted automatically, as long as the case is not yet assigned for trial and no objection is filed within *10 days*. Note, however, for nonstandard Interrogatories, you may want to use the following terminology in the motion: "The Plaintiff hereby requests an additional 30 days to *answer and/or object...*" Otherwise, the party will still be required to serve all objections within the initial 30 days.

6. If timely objections are not made, the court will order a party to answer the objectionable Interrogatories.

7. If the court overrules an objection, the interrogatory must be responded to within 20 days after the court's ruling.

8. A Motion for Order of Compliance under Pbs 231 is appropriate if a party fails to properly respond to Interrogatories.

9. In many cases, Interrogatories are served along with Requests for Production.

B. Relevant Connecticut Practice Book Sections Include:

Pbs 223: Interrogatories--In General
Pbs 224: Interrogatories--Answers to Interrogatories
Pbs 225: Interrogatories--Objections to Interrogatories
Pbs 249: Stipulations Regarding Discovery and Deposition Procedure
Forms 106.10A, B and C: Standard Set of Interrogatories for Plaintiff and Defendants

---

Example 1, Notice of Serving Interrogatories and Requests for Production (which are commonly served together.)

DOCKET NO. CV 98-0333333 S	:	SUPERIOR COURT
SARAH A. DONAHUE	:	JUDICIAL DISTRICT
	:	OF TOLLAND
VS.	:	AT ROCKVILLE
RICHARD P. ANDREW	:	AUGUST 5, 1998

NOTICE OF SERVING INTERROGATORIES
AND REQUESTS FOR PRODUCTION

The Plaintiff, Sarah A. Donahue, hereby gives notice that she has served, this date, upon the Defendant, Richard P. Andrew, Interrogatories and Requests for Production by mailing a copy of the same to: Attorney Neil E. Clifford, of Michaels, Sabrina and Alexander, P.C., 259 Sage Road, Suite 200, West Hartford, CT 08080.

THE PLAINTIFF

BY_____

Christine Kulas, Esq.,
her attorney
Law Offices of Christine Kulas
P.O. Box 2005
Ellington, CT 06066
Tele. #(860) 222-2222
Juris #989898

CERTIFICATION

I hereby certify that a copy of the foregoing and attached Interrogatories and Requests for Production were mailed on August 5, 1998, to all counsel and pro se parties of record, namely: Attorney Neil E. Clifford, of Michaels, Sabrina and Alexander, P.C., 259 Sage Road, Suite 200, West Hartford, CT 08080.

_____
Commissioner of the Superior Court

Example 2: Heading for Interrogatories

DOCKET NO. CV 98-0333333 S	:	SUPERIOR COURT
SARAH A. DONAHUE	:	JUDICIAL DISTRICT
	:	OF TOLLAND
VS.	:	AT ROCKVILLE
RICHARD P. ANDREW	:	AUGUST 5, 1998

INTERROGATORIES

Pursuant to Connecticut Practice Book Section 223 et seq., the Plaintiff, Sarah A. Donahue, hereby propounds the following Interrogatories to be answered by the Defendant, Richard P. Andrew, under oath, within 30 days of August 5, 1998. The disclosure sought will be of assistance in the prosecution of this action and can be provided by the Defendant with substantially greater facility than it could otherwise be obtained.

Example 3, Motion for Extension of Time (30-Day Extension)

DOCKET NO. CV 98-0333333 S	:	SUPERIOR COURT
SARAH A. DONAHUE	:	JUDICIAL DISTRICT
	:	OF TOLLAND
VS.	:	AT ROCKVILLE
RICHARD P. ANDREW	:	AUGUST 10, 1998

<u>**MOTION FOR EXTENSION OF TIME**</u>

Pursuant to Connecticut Practice Book Sections 224(b) and 228(b), the Defendant hereby respectfully requests an extension of time of 30 days to and including October 5, 1998 within which to answer and/or object to the Plaintiff's first set of Interrogatories and Requests for Production dated August 5, 1998.

The Defendant seeks this additional time in order to properly comply with the Plaintiff's requests.

This is the Defendant's first request for extension of time. The undersigned hereby certifies that this case has not been assigned for trial as of the date of this request.

THE DEFENDANT

BY_____

Neil E. Clifford, Esq.,
Michaels, Sabrina and Alexander, P.C.
his attorneys
259 Sage Road, Suite 200
ORAL ARGUMENT NOT REQUESTED   West Hartford, CT 08080
TESTIMONY NOT REQUIRED   Tel. (860) 111-1111
Juris #626262

<u>**ORDER**</u>

The foregoing Motion having been considered by the Court, it is hereby ORDERED: GRANTED/DENIED.

_____

BY THE COURT

<u>**CERTIFICATION**</u>

I hereby certify that the above was mailed on August 10, 1998 to all attorneys and pro se parties of record, namely: Attorney Christine Kulas, P.O. Box 2005, Ellington, CT 06066.

_____

Commissioner of the Superior Court

Example 4, Motion for Extension of Time (More Than 30 Days)

DOCKET NO. CV 98-0333333 S	:	SUPERIOR COURT
SARAH A. DONAHUE	:	JUDICIAL DISTRICT
	:	OF TOLLAND
VS.	:	AT ROCKVILLE
RICHARD P. ANDREW	:	AUGUST 25, 1998

MOTION FOR EXTENSION OF TIME

The Plaintiff in the above-captioned case hereby requests this court to grant her a ninety (90) day extension of time, to and including December 20, 1998, within which to answers and/or object to the Defendant's Request for Interrogatories and Requests for Production dated August 20, 1998.

In support of the motion, the Plaintiff represents that the Interrogatories and Production Requests propounded are lengthy, containing more than 35 questions, with detailed subsections. In addition, the information requested requires time and preparation, as well as additional investigation. In addition, the medical records, bills and reports that will be included are extremely voluminous.

To the best of the Plaintiff's knowledge, this case has not been assigned for trial, as of the date of this motion.

Wherefore, the Plaintiff respectfully requests the court to grant this motion, for the reasons stated above.

THE PLAINTIFF

BY_____

Christine Kulas, Esq.,
her attorney
Law Offices of Christine Kulas
P.O. Box 2005
Ellington, CT 06066
ORAL ARGUMENT NOT REQUESTED   Tele. #(860) 222-2222
TESTIMONY NOT REQUIRED   Juris #989898

ORDER

The foregoing Motion having been considered by the Court, it is hereby ORDERED: GRANTED/DENIED

_____

BY THE COURT

CERTIFICATION

I hereby certify that a copy of the above was mailed on August 25, 1998 to all attorneys and pro se parties of record, namely: Attorney Neil E. Clifford, Michaels, Sabrina and Alexander, P.C., 259 Sage Road, Suite 200, West Hartford, CT 08080.

_____

Commissioner of the Superior Court

Example 5, Cover Sheet: Discovery Responses

DOCKET NO. CV 98-0333333 S	:	SUPERIOR COURT
SARAH A. DONAHUE	:	JUDICIAL DISTRICT
	:	OF TOLLAND
VS.	:	AT ROCKVILLE
RICHARD P. ANDREW	:	OCTOBER 3, 1998

COVER SHEET RE: DISCOVERY RESPONSES

Pursuant to Connecticut Practice Book Sections 224 and 228, the Defendant, Richard P. Andrew, hereby states that he has answered all the Interrogatories and permitted all copying, inspections, etc., as requested by the Plaintiff in her Interrogatories and Requests for Production dated August 5, 1998.

THE DEFENDANT

BY_____

Neil E. Clifford, Esq.,
Michaels, Sabrina and Alexander, P.C.
his attorneys
259 Sage Road, Suite 200
West Hartford, CT 08080
Tel. (860) 111-1111
Juris #626262

CERTIFICATION

I hereby certify that the above Cover Sheet and attached responses were mailed on October 3, 1998 to all attorneys and pro se parties of record, namely: Attorney Christine Kulas, P.O. Box 2005, Ellington, CT 06066.

_____
Commissioner of the Superior Court

20 *Discovery: Requests for Production, Inspection and Examination*

Pbs: 227, 228

Introduction

Requests for Production and Requests for Inspection and Examination are similar to Interrogatories in that they seek information. Such information, however, comes in the form of documents, photographs, tangible objects, etc., rather than written answers to written questions. It is common to include one or both of these requests with a set of Interrogatories.

I. REQUESTS FOR PRODUCTION VS. REQUESTS FOR INSPECTION AND EXAMINATION

A. Requests for Production

Pursuant to Pbs 228, Requests for Production ask the responding party to provide actual tangible objects. These objects include:
1. photographs;
2. copies of specific documents. These documents include but are not limited to writings, reports, statements, drawings, graphs, charts, photographs, etc.

B. Requests for Inspection and Examination

Pursuant to Pbs 229, Requests for Inspection and Examination pertain to:
1. other objects in the possession, custody or control of the responding party that the requesting party may *inspect, copy, test or sample.* for instance: a request to inspect and test an automobile involved in a collision;
2. permission to enter a parcel of land which is in the possession, custody or control of the responding party, for the purpose of inspecting, measuring, surveying, photographing, testing or sampling, or to perform these tasks on a specific object or operation that is located on the land.

II. DRAFTING REQUESTS FOR PRODUCTION AND REQUESTS FOR INSPECTION AND EXAMINATION

Both requests are quite similar in format to Interrogatories:
1. They should not be filed in court.
2. They are directed to a specific party, rather than anyone who is not a party.
3. They are drafted in the same manner: numbered, with sufficient space after each one for a response and are followed by a certification of service.
4. They can be mailed or hand delivered to the party any time after the return date.
5. Our court rules provide standard Requests for Production for personal injury cases, except those involving death or product liability. Parties in personal injury cases may file a motion asking permission to make Requests for Production that are in addition to the standard requests.
6. There are no limitations for other types of cases.
7. The same 30-day time limits apply.
8. The objection process is the same.
Furthermore, for Requests for Inspection and Production, each request must:
      a. specifically designate the items to be provided and/or inspected; and
      b. state a reasonable time, place and manner of making the inspection.

III. METHODS OF PRODUCTION OR INSPECTION AND EXAMINATION

In requests that seek only copies of documents, it is customary for the responding party to provide these copies within the 30-day time period, by mail or hand delivery, unless he or she objects or files a stipulation or Motion for Extension of Time.

Items that need to be inspected or tested are a bit more complicated to actually produce. The same concerns exist for arranging an entry upon land. As a result, the requesting party should state how and when he or she wishes the production or inspection to occur. Often times it's easier to make the request by telephone in order to coordinate schedules, then confirm the agreed upon date and time etc. in a stipulation.

IV. GROUNDS FOR OBJECTIONS

The same reasons used to object to nonstandard Interrogatories apply to non-standard Requests for Production, as well as Requests for Inspection and Examination.

V. OVERRULED OBJECTIONS

Objections to Requests for Production are handled in the same manner as Objections to Interrogatories: file a cover sheet containing the objections, participate in a discovery conference and, if necessary, file a discovery affidavit which will place the matter on the Short Calendar to be decided by the court. Pursuant to Pbs 228, if the court overrules an objection, it will also determine the time in which the responding party must comply with the request.

VI. CONCLUSION

A. Key Issues in This Chapter Include:

The rules for Interrogatories and Requests for Production are practically identical. Remember that parties in most personal injury cases are limited to the Requests for Production contained in the standard sets found in Form 106.11A, B and C. Parties may file a motion asking the court for permission to file additional Requests for Production if they believe the forms are inappropriate or inadequate.

B. The Relevant Connecticut Practice Book Sections Include:

Pbs 227: Requests for Production, Inspection and Examination--In General
Pbs 228: Requests for Production, Inspection and Examination--Responses to Requests for Production; Objections
Forms: 106.11A, B and C

Example 1, Heading for Requests for Production

DOCKET NO. CV 98-0333333 S	:	SUPERIOR COURT
SARAH A. DONAHUE	:	JUDICIAL DISTRICT
	:	OF TOLLAND
VS.	:	AT ROCKVILLE
RICHARD P. ANDREW	:	AUGUST 5, 1998

REQUESTS FOR PRODUCTION

Pursuant to Connecticut Practice Book Section Pbs 227, the Plaintiff, Sarah A. Donahue, requests that the Defendant, Richard P. Andrew, provide Plaintiff's counsel with copies of the documents described in the following Requests for Production, or afford Plaintiff's counsel the opportunity or, if necessary, sufficient written authorization to inspect, copy, photograph or otherwise reproduce said documents within thirty days of August 5, 1998.

*See Chapter 19 for examples of a Notice of Serving Interrogatories and Requests for Production, Motion for Extension of Time and Cover Sheet Re: Discovery Responses.

21 *Discovery: Request for Physical or Mental Examination*

Terminology

Independent Medical Examination (IME)

Pbs: 229
C.G.S. sections: 52-178a

Introduction

A request for a physical or medical examination is common in cases in which a party's physical or mental condition is at issue. Personal injury cases are good examples. There, the Plaintiff is seeking to recover damages for his or her physical injuries.

I. PURPOSE OF A REQUEST FOR PHYSICAL OR MENTAL EXAMINATION

Pbs 229 provides that a Defendant may request a Plaintiff to submit to an examination by a physician selected by the Defendant. This type of examination is often called an IME: independent medical examination. The Defendant, as the requesting party, is responsible for the IME's expense.

The purpose of an IME is similar to the reason people often get second opinions regarding their own medical conditions: to provide the Defendant with an impartial medical opinion from a physician who has not treated the Plaintiff for his or her alleged injuries.

After the examination, the Defendant will usually compare the IME physician's report to the report produced by the Plaintiff's own physician(s). Specifically, the Defendant will look for inconsistencies in the two reports and for indications that the Plaintiff's injuries are not really as significant as the Plaintiff claims.

II. DRAFTING A REQUEST FOR A PHYSICAL OR MENTAL MEDICAL EXAMINATION

A. Personal Injury Cases

IMEs are automatically permitted in personal injury cases. All that is needed is a written request in the form of a pleading that is filed in court and includes a certification of service. Because it is a request, no order is needed.

B. All Other Cases

In other types of cases, the Defendant must first file a motion (including an order) asking permission from the court to authorize such exam. The motion will be granted only if the Defendant can convince the court he or she has "good cause" for such an examination.

C. Content and Filing Requirements

Pursuant to Pbs 229, the request or motion must include the following:
1. time and date;
2. place;
3. names of the physician conducting the exam;
4. manner, conditions and scope of the exam;
5. "good cause" (for motions).

III. OBJECTING TO A REQUEST FOR A PHYSICAL EXAMINATION

Pbs 229 specifically states that "no Plaintiff will be compelled to undergo a physical examination by any physician to whom he objects in writing." This rule applies to personal injury cases as well as other types of cases.

The Plaintiff's objection must be filed in court within *ten days* of the filing of the request and will appear on Short Calendar. The objection must specify:
1. which portion(s) of the request the Plaintiff objects to; and
2. the reasons for the objection(s).

A common reason to object to a physician is because the Plaintiff believes the physician is defense-oriented or a "Defendant's doctor." Therefore, he or she will produce a report that is inaccurate and will tend to minimize the Plaintiff's injuries.

Another reason to object may have nothing to do with the named physician. Instead, the Plaintiff objects to the scheduled date because of a conflict with work, or vacation, etc.

IV. OBJECTING TO A REQUEST FOR A MENTAL EXAMINATION

The time and content of an objection to a mental examination is the same as for a physical examination. Note, however, that Pbs 229 does not appear to give a Plaintiff the right to base an objection solely upon the physician selected to perform the examination.

V. THE IME REPORT

After the examination, the Plaintiff may request a copy of the examining physician's written report. That report should include the physician's finding, "including the results of all tests made, diagnosis and conclusions, together with like reports of all earlier examination of the same condition."

If necessary, either party can make a motion to the court to receive a copy of these reports. In addition, if a physician fails to provide such a report, the court may not permit him or her to testify at the trial.

VI. CONCLUSION

A. Key Issues in This Chapter Include:

1. Requests to inspect property and for medical exams are quite straightforward. If agreements cannot be reached, the requesting party will usually file a Motion for Order of Compliance, pursuant to Pbs 231.
2. Don't forget: unlike Interrogatories and Requests for Production and Inspection, a request or motion for a physical or mental examination must be filed in court.

B. Relevant Connecticut Practice Book Sections Include:

Pbs 229: Requests for Production, Inspection and Examination-Physical or Mental Examination

C. Relevant Connecticut General Statutes Include:

C.G.S. sec. 52-178a.: Physical examination of plaintiff. When.

Example 1, Objection to Motion for Order of Compliance

DOCKET NO. CV 98-0555555 S	:	SUPERIOR COURT
SHEILA WILKENSON	:	JUDICIAL DISTRICT OF FAIRFIELD
VS.	:	AT BRIDGEPORT
RYAN KEEGAN	:	AUGUST 5, 1998

OBJECTION TO MOTION FOR ORDER OF COMPLIANCE

Pursuant to Connecticut General Statutes Section 52-178a and Practice Book Section 229, the Plaintiff, Sarah A. Donahue, hereby objects to the Defendant's Motion to Compel dated August 3, 1998 in which the Defendant seeks to have the court order the Plaintiff to submit to a medical examination by Dr. Daffy Duck.

The Plaintiff will submit herself for an independent medical examination for the purpose of obtaining an unbiased opinion of her injuries, but requests that the physician selected be one who actively treats patients, rather than one who is retired and/or makes a substantial living performing IMEs for insurance companies. The Plaintiff objects to Dr. Duck because he makes a substantial amount of his living working for insurance companies and therefore may not be objective. Furthermore, the Plaintiff objects to any doctors who are in Old England Orthopedic or any related groups such as IME, Inc., for the same reasons stated above.

Connecticut General Statutes Section 52-178a provides:

> "In any action to recover damages for personal injuries, the court or judge may order the Plaintiff to submit to a physical examination by one or more physicians or surgeons. No party may be compelled to undergo a physical examination by any physician to whom he objects in writing submitted to the court or judge."

Connecticut Practice Book Section 229 essentially provides for the same requirements in actions to recover damages for personal injuries.

The Defendant claims, in its Motion to Compel, that "[t]he instant action is not a negligence personal injury claim. It is a claim for contract benefits." Therefore, the Defendant argues that the Plaintiff must comply with the language of the insurance contract which requires her to submit to a medical examination by a physician chosen by the Defendant.

Neither C.G.S. Sec. 52-178a nor Conn. Prac. Book Sec. 229 requires that the action be a "negligent personal injury claim." Nor can there be any dispute that the amount of contract benefits in this case will be based upon damages for the personal injuries the Plaintiff sustained in the automobile accident due to the negligent driving of another individual. Therefore, both the statute and the practice book apply to this instant action and permit the Plaintiff to object to the physician selected by the Defendant.

To require a Plaintiff to submit herself to a physical examination by a physician she objects to certainly flies in the face of public policy as well as C.G.S. Sec. 52-178a,

ORAL ARGUMENT REQUESTED
TESTIMONY REQUIRED

Conn. Prac. Book Sec. 229 and case law. "It is not unreasonable to object because the physician designated by the Defendant devotes a large portion of his or her practice to examining Plaintiffs for insurance companies." <u>Rosenfield v. Milner's Cafe, et al.</u>, 10 Conn. L.R., vol. 14, 454, 456 (1994). Moreover, policies must follow regulations and statutes. <u>Loika v. Aetna Casualty & Surety, Co.</u>, 44 Conn. Sup., 59, 66 (1995). "Where certain terms of a contract have been, in effect, legislatively dictated, it is appropriate to consider legislative intent in interpreting those terms." <u>Gaudet v. Safeco Ins. Co.</u>, 219 Conn. 391, 397 (1991).

Clearly, the legislature was concerned about forcing Plaintiffs to undergo the highly intrusive act of a physical examination by a doctor they object to, and our courts have recognized that certain doctors who obtain a significant amount of their income performing IMEs may not be objective. See <u>Rosenfield v. Milner's Cafe, et al.</u>, supra, and <u>LeBlanc v. Cambo</u>, 26 Conn. Sup. 338 (1966). Accordingly, the specific provision of the policy which the Defendant relies upon, to wit, that the Plaintiff is required to submit to a physical examination by a physician of its choosing, is contrary to Connecticut law and therefore should be interpreted to comply with C.G.S. Sec. 52-178a and Conn. Prac. Book. Sec. 229.

Based on the foregoing, the Plaintiff respectfully requests the court to deny the Defendant's Motion to Compel her to be examined by Dr. Daffy Duck, or anyone in Old England Orthopedic or any related groups such as IME, Inc., or who is retired and makes his or her living performing IMEs for insurance companies.

THE PLAINTIFF

BY_____

        Ann Lambert, Esq.
        Lambert and Smith, P.C.
        her attorney
        529 Corporate Place
        Fairfield, CT 04540
        Tele. #(203) 777-7777
        Juris #545454

ORDER

The foregoing Objection having been considered by the Court, it is hereby ORDERED: SUSTAINED/DENIED

_____

BY THE COURT

CERTIFICATION

I hereby certify that a copy of the foregoing was mailed on August 5, 1998 to all counsel and pro se parties of record, namely: Attorney Glen Lutley, of Lutley & Associates, 906 Park Plaza, Bridgeport, CT 04530.

_____

Commissioner of the Superior Court

22 *Discovery:*
Requests for Admission

Pbs: 238, 239, 240, 241

Introduction

Although Requests for Admission may be used in any type of civil case, they are my personal favorites to use in contract and debt collection cases. These requests require a party to either *admit* or *deny* certain statements in writing. Their purpose is to streamline contested issues and attempt to compel a Defendant to admit his or her liability.

I. REQUESTS FOR ADMISSION VS. THE ANSWER

Don't confuse Requests for Admissions with the Answer. Remember, all types of discovery are optional and either party may elect to use them. An Answer, on the other hand, is a required pleading that must be filed in response to a Complaint, Counterclaim, Cross Complaint etc., in order to place the case on the Trial List. You will notice other important differences throughout this chapter.

A. *Time to Service Requests for Admission*

These requests may be served any time after the return date and the Defendant's Appearance.

B. *Unlimited Requests*

According to Pbs 238, there is no limit to how many Requests for Admission a party may serve on another. The scope, however, must still comply with Pbs 218. See Section II below.

210

C. *Response Time: Unanswered Requests Are Treated As True*

A party has *30 days* from the date a Notice of Requests for Admission is filed in court, to respond to all the requests. Pursuant to Pbs 239, every request that is not answered or objected to that within 30 days is treated as true, unless the responding party files a stipulation or Motion for Extension of Time within that time period.

D. *Admitted Requests*

Pursuant to Pbs 240, all admissions are treated as true, and therefore, do not have to be proven at trial. Furthermore, a party can use such admissions to attempt to obtain judgment now, through Summary Judgment (Pbs 379 et seq.), rather than wait for a trial.

II. THE SCOPE OF REQUESTS FOR ADMISSION

Like all other types of discovery, the purpose of Requests for Admission must be to assist a party in proving or defending his or her case. Specifically, Pbs 238 requires that Requests for Admissions must be:
1. relevant to the subject matter of the pending action; and
2. related to statements or opinions of fact, or application of law to fact, including the existence, due execution and genuineness of any documents described in the request.

Compare the Requests for Admission found at the end of this chapter with the allegations set forth in the *Skillman Et Al. v. Auto Service Center, Inc.* (Complaint #3). As you can see, these requests force Joseph Kelly, the Defendant corporation's president, to admit or deny that Exhibit A is the contract he entered into and to acknowledge his signature. If the Defendant admits all of the requests, he will not later be permitted to deny the allegations of the Complaint in his Answer, or, later at trial. Nor can he claim that the signature on the contract is a forgery.

What if the Defendant does deny these requests? Then the Plaintiff knows he or she is in for a lot of work to prepare for trial.

III. HOW TO DRAFT REQUESTS FOR ADMISSION

Unlike Interrogatories, Requests for Admissions are not questions. Instead, they are actual statements. However, like Interrogatories, Requests for Production, and Requests to Revise, Pbs 238(a) requires there to be sufficient space after each request for the responding party to inset her or her response. Also, be sure to attach copies (not originals) of any documents that are mentioned in the requests.

IV. HOW TO SERVE REQUESTS FOR ADMISSION

Pursuant to Pbs 238(b), the Requests for Admission are not filed in court. Instead, a **Notice of Serving Requests for Admission** must be filed in court. The Notice must include:

1. that Requests for Admission have been served on another party;
2. the name of the party served;
3. the date service was made;
4. the signature of the serving party's attorney or pro se;
5. a certification of service, which states that the Notice and the Requests for Admission were mailed or hand delivered on a certain date to all counsel and pro se parties of record.

V. RESPONDING TO REQUESTS FOR ADMISSION

A. *Answers to Requests for Admission*

1. Directly under each Request
Like Interrogatories, the responding party must insert his or her admission, denial or objection directly under each request.

2. Types of Responses

    a. If an objection is made, the reasons must be stated.

    b. A denial must address the substance of the request. For example, the responding party must admit and specify which portion of a request is true, if any, and which portion he or she denies.

    c. If the responding party cannot admit or deny a request, he or she must state why. Unlike Answers, parties may not fail to admit or deny a request by claiming they lack sufficient information or knowledge. Instead, they must state that they "made reasonable inquiry and that the information known or readily obtainable is insufficient to enable [him or her] to admit or deny."

    d. Parties may not object or fail to admit or deny a request on the ground that "the request presents a genuine issue for trial." Instead, they must deny the request or state the reasons why they can't admit or deny.

If more room is needed, attach an additional sheet.

B. *The Cover Sheet*

Pursuant to Pbs 239, this cover sheet follows the same format as the one used for responses to Interrogatories and Requests for Production: Specify which requests were answered and which were objected to. Next, attach the actual requests and responses to the cover sheet.

C. Filing Requirements

Pursuant to Pbs 239, the responding party must file his or her cover sheet and responses in court, and mail or hand deliver a copy to all other counsel and pro se parties of record in accordance with Pbs 120 et seq.

VI. CHALLENGING OBJECTIONS AND OTHER RESPONSES: DISCOVERY CONFERENCE AND AFFIDAVIT

Pbs 239 permits the requesting party to challenge the sufficiency of a party's answer and objection(s) in court. Unlike Interrogatories, etc., this challenge must come in the form of a motion. The motion, however, will not be placed on Short Calendar until either party files an affidavit certifying that "bona fide attempts have been made to resolve the differences...and that counsel have been unable to reach an accord." Hence, they are handled similarly to objections to Interrogatories, Requests for Production, etc.

VII. THE COURT'S RULING ON OBJECTIONS AND ANSWERS

A. Objections

According to Pbs 239, if the court overrules an objection, it will order the party to respond within a specified time period.

B. Insufficient Answers

If the court determines that an response does not comply with the requirement of Pbs 239, it may order:
1. that the matter is admitted, or
2. that an amended answer be served, or
3. that the matter will be resolved at a later time, prior to trial.

VIII. WITHDRAWING OR AMENDING ADMISSIONS

Admissions by a responding party may only be used in the instant action. They cannot be used in any other proceedings. In addition, pursuant to Pbs 240, a party may file a motion to withdrawal or amend an admission.

IX. PENALTIES FOR FAILING TO ADMIT

Under Pbs 241, a responding party's failure to admit a document or request must be reasonable. Otherwise, a requesting party who later proves the document or request should have been admitted may ask the court to order the responding party to pay reasonable expenses, including attorney's fees, incurred to make this proof.

X. CONCLUSION

A. Key Issues in This Chapter Include:

1. The purpose of *Requests for Admission* are to narrow down the contested issues in a case and if appropriate, file a Motion for Summary Judgment, based upon the Respondent's answers.

2. A party must respond to Requests for Admission within *30 days* of being served or the requests are deemed admitted.

3. In Chapter 27, you will discover how responses to Requests for Admission can be used to establish grounds for a Motion to Summary Judgment. There, the Defendant did not file objections or seek an extension of time to respond to the Requests for Admission found on the following pages. Instead, he simply failed to respond to the requests. As a result, the requests are deemed admitted and enable the Plaintiffs to claim that there are no contested issues in the case. Therefore, they are entitled to Summary Judgment.

B. Relevant Connecticut Practice Book Sections Include:

Pbs 238: Admission of Facts and Execution of Writing--Requests for Admission
Pbs 239: Admission of Facts and Execution of Writing--Answers and Objections to
     Requests for Admission
Pbs 240: Admission of Facts and Execution of Writing--Effect of Admission
Pbs 241: Admission of Facts and Execution of Writing--Expenses on Failure to Admit

Example 1, Notice and Requests for Admission

DOCKET NO. CV 98-0444444 S	:	SUPERIOR COURT
GEORGE SKILLMAN, ET AL.	:	JUDICIAL DISTRICT OF
	:	HARTFORD/NEW BRITAIN
VS.	:	AT HARTFORD
AUTO SERVICE CENTER, INC.	:	MAY 18, 1998

NOTICE OF PLAINTIFF'S SERVICE OF REQUESTS FOR ADMISSION

Pursuant to Connecticut Practice Book Section 237 et seq., the Plaintiff in the above-captioned case has served Requests for Admission upon Mr. Joseph Kelly, President and sole shareholder and director of the Defendant, Auto Service Center, Inc.

Service was made by mail to the Defendant's attorney of record, Mark Peters, Esq., 1001 Sanberg Street, Manchester, CT 06660 on May 18, 1998, in accordance with Connecticut Practice Book Section 120 et seq.

THE PLAINTIFF

BY_____

Kenneth I. Marcus, Esq.,
Friedman & Marcus, P.C.,
his attorney
27 Main Street
Bristol, CT 00000
Tele. #(860) 955-9595
Juris #424242

CERTIFICATION

I hereby certify that a copy of the above was mailed on May 18, 1998 to all counsel and pro se parties of record, namely: Mark Peters, Esq., 1001 Sanberg Street, Manchester, CT 06660.

_____
Commissioner of Superior Court

DOCKET NO. CV 98-0444444 S   :   SUPERIOR COURT
GEORGE SKILLMAN, ET AL.   :   JUDICIAL DISTRICT OF
     :   HARTFORD/NEW BRITAIN
VS.   :   AT HARTFORD
AUTO SERVICE CENTER, INC.   :   MAY 18, 1998

PLAINTIFF'S REQUESTS FOR ADMISSION

Pursuant to Connecticut Practice Book Section 237 et seq., the Defendant through its President, Mr. Joseph Kelly, is hereby requested to either admit or deny the truth of each matter asserted below, within thirty days of the filing of the Notice of Plaintiff's Service of Requests for Admission, dated May 18, 1998.

1. The Defendant, through its President, Mr. Joseph Kelly, agreed to purchase Auto Service Center, Inc., located at 126 Maple Street, Hartford, CT from the Plaintiffs, George Skillman and Barbara Skillman, for the sum of One Hundred Thousand Dollars ($100,000.00).

RESPONSE: (Mr. Kelly would insert his response in this space.)

2. On behalf of the Defendant, Mr. Joseph Kelly signed a promissory note, dated September 1, 1995 in the amount of One Hundred Thousand Dollars ($100,000.00), plus interest, in favor of the Plaintiffs, George Skillman and Barbara Skillman, which specifies the terms in which the Defendant would pay for Auto Service Center, Inc..

RESPONSE:

3. A copy of the same promissory note Mr. Kelly signed pertaining to Request for Admission #2 above is attached hereto as Exhibit A.

RESPONSE:

4. Mr. Kelly acknowledges that a copy of his signature appears on the copy of the promissory note which is attached hereto as Exhibit A.

RESPONSE:

5. Pursuant to the terms of the promissory note, attached hereto as Exhibit A, in the event the Defendant fails to make any of the payments stated therein, the Defendant is responsible to pay the Plaintiff for all of its costs and reasonable attorney's fees incurred in the collection of said $100,000.00 or any part thereof.

RESPONSE:

6. Pursuant to the terms of said promissory note, the Defendant promised to pay the Plaintiff the sum of Ten Thousand ($10,000.00) Dollars on the first of the month commencing January 15, 1998 and Ten Thousand ($10,000.00) Dollars each month thereafter with a final payment being made on October 15, 1998.

RESPONSE:

7. Pursuant to the terms of said promissory note, should the Defendant fail to pay any one or more of the payments specified therein, the entire balance of the promissory notice remaining, plus interest, would become immediately due and owing to the Plaintiff.

RESPONSE:

8. The Defendant has failed, refused, and/or neglected to make any payments whatsoever specified in said promissory note to the Plaintiff, as of the date of these instant Requests for Admission.

RESPONSE:

Personally appeared, Joseph Kelly, being duly sworn, deposes and says: that the answers to the preceding Requests for Admission are true and accurate to the best of his knowledge and belief.

Subscribed and sworn to before me this _____ day of _____, 199_.

_____

Notary Public (or)
Commissioner of Superior Court

23 Discovery: Depositions of Parties

Terminology

Deponent   Notice of Deposition   Court Reporter   Transcript
Indifferent Person

Pbs: 243, 244, 245, 246, 247, 248, 249
C.G.S. sections: 51-60 et seq., 51- 61, 51-74, 52-148a et seq., 52-178

Introduction

As discussed in Chapter 18, depositions go beyond the parties themselves. Any party in a lawsuit may take the deposition of any other *party,* and/or any other *person* (known as a nonparty) who is not a party in the lawsuit, but who has information relevant to the case.

Though the principles involved in deposing a party and deposing other persons are similar, there are also distinct differences. Therefore, this chapter will address deposing a party. If the party is a corporation, its officers, directors and managing agents may be deposed as a party. The next chapter will address deposing nonparties.

I. WHAT IS A DEPOSITION?

Pursuant to Pbs 243, a deposition involves obtaining testimony of a party through an **oral examination**, i.e., orally answering questions. The party being deposed is known as the **deponent** or **party deponent**.

Deposition procedures are quite similar to those procedures used during a trial. The difference is that depositions usually take place at an attorney's office, rather than a courtroom, and there is usually no judge present. Like a trial, however:

1. All the attorneys and pro ses in an action may attend and participate.
Clients who are not deponents are also welcome.

218

2. The deponent is placed under oath, by an appropriate individual, i.e., a notary public, a judge, a clerk of any court or Commissioner of Superior Court.

3. During the deposition, a **court reporter** is present and records every word said. See C.G.S. sec. 51-60 et seq.

4. The party (pro se or attorney) taking the deposition begins by asking questions which the deponent must answer truthfully. (The discussion in Chapter 30 regarding direct and cross examination during trial applies to depositions as well.)

5. The deponent's attorney may object to certain questions, when appropriate.

6. When the party taking the deposition is finished, the deponent's attorney may ask questions that relate to the questions and answers just discussed, to clarify the deponent's previous answers, and ask his or her own related questions.

7. In cases involving more than one Plaintiff and Defendant who have their own attorneys or represent themselves pro se, these attorneys and pro ses may also ask the deponent questions.

8. After the deposition, if requested, the court reporter will create a written document of the testimony. This document is called a **transcript**. Every party is entitled to receive a copy of the transcript. See C.G.S. sec. 51-61.

9. In some cases, a party may decide to serve the deponent written questions in a sealed envelope, rather than meet face to face. The deponent will give the sealed envelope to an officer (usually a court reporter) who will ask the questions and record the answers. (This might be done for an out-of-state party to save everyone the expense of traveling, etc.) See also C.G.S. sec. 52-148a et seq. regarding Depositions.

II. PURPOSE OF DEPOSITIONS

As stated earlier, the purpose of discovery is to prevent surprises at trial. Depositions are one of the best ways to prevent such surprises because they permit a party to ask the deponent questions, including those questions that will be asked at trial. The parties then have the opportunity to not only hear the answers, but observe the demeanor of the deponent. This enables the parties to determine what type of witness the deponent will make at trial. Will he or she be strong and convincing, or weak and timid or unbelievable? All parties who attend the deposition will use the information obtained and their observations to prepare their cases for trial.

If the deponent who becomes a witness at the trial changes his or her testimony at trial, the deposition transcript can be used to inform the trier of fact of this change. This can cause the trier of fact to question the witness's credibility and possibly choose to disbelieve everything the person says. (See Pbs 248.) Hence, depositions can be extremely useful discovery tools.

III. WHEN A DEPOSITION MAY TAKE PLACE

A. *When Court Orders Are Necessary*

At first glance, Pbs 243 seems to indicate that a deposition may be taken "any time after the commencement of the action...." There are, however, certain limitations and procedures that must be followed if the deponent is in jail, or if the party wishes to take a deposition within *20 days* after the return date. For example:

1. Pursuant to Pbs 243, if a deponent is confined in prison, the party wishing to take the deposition must first file a motion and obtain the court's permission. It must then conduct the deposition according to the court's terms.

2. Pbs 244(d) allows the court, for good cause shown, to increase or decrease the time for taking a deposition.

3. Court permission for a Deposition before the expiration of the 20 days does not appear to be needed if:

   a. the deponent has already started the discovery process; or

   b. the deponent is about to go out of this state, or on a sea voyage and will not be available for a deposition unless the deposition occurs before the expiration of the 20 days; and

   c. the party seeking to take the deposition must certify that this information is true, to the best of his or her knowledge, and include it in the **Notice for Deposition** described below.

B. *The Time of Day*

Depositions usually take place during regular business hours. If all the parties agree, however, a deposition can take place during the evening and on weekends. This request is made when a party has difficulty taking time off from work, or does not have day care for children, etc.

IV. WHERE A DEPOSITION MAY TAKE PLACE

A. *Party Deponents Who Reside in Connecticut*

Pbs 246(a) states that parties who are residents of this state may be deposed at any place, (usually a law office):

1. within the county of their residence; or

2. within 30 miles of their residence; or

3. any other location the court determines;

4. if the deponent is a Plaintiff, at any place in the county where the action is commenced or pending.

B. *Nonresident Plaintiff Deponents*

According to Pbs 246(b), nonresident Plaintiff deponents may be deposed, (usually at a law office):
1. in the Connecticut county where the action is commenced or pending (at his or her own travel expense);
2. any place within 30 miles of their residence;
3. within the county of their residence; or
4. at any location ordered by the court.

C. *Nonresident Defendant Deponents*

Pursuant to Pbs 246(c), nonresident Defendants may be deposed (usually at a law office):
1. by *subpoena*, in any county in this state where they are personally served the subpoena requiring them to attend the deposition (see Chapter 24);
2. by Notice of Deposition, pursuant to Pbs 244(a), any place within *30 miles* of their residence or within the county of their residence or at any location ordered by the court.

For the purpose of determining where to hold a deposition, Pbs 246(f) says to treat the residence of the deponent (including an officer, director or managing agent of the corporate Plaintiff or Defendant) as the residence of the party.

V. WHO MUST BE PRESENT DURING A DEPOSITION

In addition to the parties (meaning the deponent, other clients, attorneys and any pro ses,) Pbs 245(a) states that a deposition must be taken before one of the following:
1. a judge (not usually necessary);
2. a clerk of any court;
3. a notary public; or
4. a Commissioner of the Superior Court (an attorney licensed in Connecticut).

As I said earlier, in most cases depositions take place in an office rather than a courthouse. Therefore, since the court reporter is a notary public, he or she may administer the oath, as well as fulfill the Pbs 245 requirement.

Be aware, however, that some deponents may choose to be difficult and refuse to answer one or more of the questions asked. Or, a deponent may claim that the attorney or pro se conducting the deposition is acting in bad faith, to harass or annoy him or her, etc., pursuant to Pbs 247(c).

In these situations, depositions may end up taking place in a conference room in the courthouse, or in a courtroom with a judge or clerk present, in order to ensure that the deponent and party or attorney conducting the deposition properly conduct themselves.

VI. RECORDING A DEPOSITION: COURT REPORTER OR VIDEO TAPE AND FEES

A. Purpose of a Court Reporter

As stated above, most depositions are recorded by a court reporter who is present. Regardless of the title, these men and women are specially trained and certified to record testimony, by typing into a specialized computer or stenographic machine, in court and at depositions, to provide an accurate transcript of every word said during the proceeding. See Pbs 247(e)(1).

B. The Transcripts

When the transcript is complete, a copy may be given to the deponent to review to review for errors, unless the parties stipulate otherwise. Pbs 247(d) requires the deponent to notify the court reporter of any necessary changes or inaccuracies, within *30 days* of receiving the transcript.

C. How to Find a Court Reporter

Court reporters can be found in the yellow pages of the telephone book, in legal publications, at courthouses, etc. In addition, most offices that handle a lot of litigation usually have a list of court reporters they use frequently.

When scheduling a deposition, be sure to contact a court reporter and make sure he or she is available. In addition to regular business hours, most court reporters will agree to work during evenings and on weekends, if requested. Be sure to remember to promptly notify the court reporter if a deposition is postponed or canceled.

D. Fees

The party taking the deposition is responsible to pay the court reporter's fee. This fee includes the time at the proceeding and the cost of producing a transcript. In addition, pursuant to Pbs 247(f), the party is responsible for paying for sufficient copies of the transcript to be given to all pro ses or attorneys in the action.

E. Video Taping a Deposition

Pursuant to Pbs 244(e), a party may wish to have a deponent's deposition video taped, instead of recorded by a court reporter. If so, the party must file a motion in court. If granted, the court will order how the deposition shall take place, to assure that the recorded testimony will be accurate and trustworthy. Any party attending the deposition may also make arrangements for a court reporter to record the testimony and produce a transcript, at his or her own expense.

VII. NOTICE OF DEPOSITION

Pbs 244(a) requires any party who wishes to take the deposition of any other party to send written notice of the pending deposition to all parties in the action.

This **Notice of Deposition** must provide each party with reasonable time in which to make arrangements to attend and participate and should include the following:

1. case caption and title;
2 name of the party taking the deposition;
3. name and address of the party to be deposed;
4. the date and time of the deposition;
5. the address where the deposition will take place;
6. that the deposition will be taken under oath before an authorized officer;
7. signature of the deposing party's attorney or pro se;
8. certification of service to all counsel and pro se parties of record.

VIII. PRODUCTION OF MATERIALS AT A DEPOSITION

In addition to testimony, the party seeking to take a deposition may request the deponent to bring certain materials to the deposition. Pursuant to Pbs 244(f), these materials may include designated books, papers, documents, or tangible things to be inspected or copied that fall within the scope of permissible discovery. Often, these materials include originals or copies of specific bank or telephone records, medical records, photographs, contracts, etc. Pbs 244(f) allows the party taking the deposition to include with the Notice of Deposition, a Request for Production that complies with Pbs 226 et seq. See also Pbs 247(e)(2).

IX. SERVING A NOTICE OF DEPOSITION: SPECIAL REQUIREMENTS

This notice should not be filed in court. Nor is simple mail or hand delivery sufficient. Instead, Pbs 244(a) requires that a Notice of Deposition be served upon each party or each parties' attorney in one of the following ways:

1. personal service (in hand),
2. abode service,
3. registered or certified mail.

If the party deponent is represented by an attorney, I suggest serving the Notice of Deposition upon the attorney or his or her law firm. Certified or registered mail to the law firm is often the easiest way.

Unlike Complaints, personal or abode service need not be done by a proper officer like a sheriff or constable. Instead, service may be accomplished by an **indifferent person**. An indifferent person is any person who is not related to the action or the parties or their attorneys. In addition, a sheriff or constable can act as an indifferent person to serve a Notice of Deposition outside of his or her precinct.

Regardless of the way service is made, the party will have proof of service, such as a receipt from the post office or a Return of Service, in the event the party deponent fails to appear for the deposition. Last, it's also a good idea to state precisely how service was made in the certification of service on the Notice of Deposition.

X. WHEN A PARTY FAILS TO COOPERATE

A. Stipulations and Postponements

As with all discovery, Pbs 249 allows the parties to reach agreements (stipulations) as to scheduling depositions. If the date originally selected is inconvenient for the deponent party or attorney, a prompt telephone call to reschedule will often resolve the situation.

In addition, a party may disappear or perhaps go on a long vacation. Although the attorney received the Notice of Deposition, he or she may be unable to reach the client in time to inform him or her of the pending deposition. In this situation, the attorney will eventually have to inform the other attorneys and reach some sort of agreement. Otherwise, a Motion for Order of Compliance may be needed under Pbs 231.

B. When a Party Does Not Appear at His or Her Deposition

Furthermore, there are situations when a party or his or her attorney (or both) will simply fail to appear for a deposition. The reasons vary. Sometimes, it's a mistake. Other times, an attorney may be detained in court, or either the attorney or deponent is ill, a car broke down, or a party refuses, for whatever reason, to attend.

In any of the above situations, the attorney who arranged deposition ends up sitting at a conference table, usually with his or her annoyed client who took time off from work, and a court reporter who still expect to be paid for the time spent. The situation worsens if other attorneys and parties (except the deponent) are also in attendance.

If the failed deposition is due to sudden illness, accident, etc., the attorney involved will usually call the opposing attorney to reschedule and agree to pay the costs of the court reporter. If, on the other hand, a party simply refuses to be deposed, a court order compelling the party (or his or her officers, agents, employees in cases involving corporations) to testify may be necessary. See Chapter 26 and C.G.S. sec. 52-178.

XI. CONCLUSION

A. *Key Issues in This Chapter Include:*

1. This chapter discussed deposing a party. Chapter 24 will discuss deposing *nonparties*.

2. *Notice of Depositions* must be served upon each party or their attorney in one of the following ways:

        a. personal; or

        b. abode; or

        c. by certified or registered mail.

If the party is represented by counsel, it is easiest to send the Notice of Deposition to the attorney's office by certified mail.

3. Be sure the location of the deposition falls within Pbs 246.

4. Be sure to arrange for a qualified *court reporter* to record the deposition and remember to notify the court reporter as soon as possible if the deposition is postponed or rescheduled.

5. Conducting depositions of parties can be costly, but they are great discovery tools because they force the parties to meet face to face answer questions they often prefer to avoid. In addition, depositions allow the parties to size up one another and determine what kind of witnesses they will make at trial.

B. *Relevant Connecticut Practice Book Sections Include:*

Pbs 243: Depositions--Depositions Generally

Pbs 244: Depositions--Notice of Deposition; General Requirements; Special Notice; Nonstenographic Recording; Production of Documents and Things; Depositions of Organizations

Pbs 245: Depositions--Subpoenas

Pbs 246: Depositions--Place of Deposition

Pbs 247: Depositions--Deposition Procedure

Pbs 248: Depositions--Use of Depositions in Court Proceedings

Pbs 249: Depositions--Stipulations Regarding Discovery and Deposition Procedure

C. *Relevant Connecticut General Statutes Include:*

C.G.S. sec. 51-60 et seq.:	Appointment of official court reporters.
C.G.S. sec. 51-60:	Court Reporter to be sworn. Duties. Transcript.
C.G.S. sec. 51-74.:	Use of shorthand writing machine or recording device.
C.G.S. sec. 52-148a et seq.:	Taking of depositions. When court order necessary.
C.G.S. sec. 52-178.:	Adverse party of officer, agent or employee thereof may be compelled to testify.

Example 1, Notice of Deposition (of a Party)

DOCKET NO. CV 98-0333333 S	:	SUPERIOR COURT
SARAH A. DONAHUE	:	JUDICIAL DISTRICT
	:	OF TOLLAND
VS.	:	AT ROCKVILLE
RICHARD P. ANDREW	:	DECEMBER 1, 1998

NOTICE OF DEPOSITION

Pursuant to Connecticut Practice Book Section 242 et seq., the Plaintiff, Sarah A. Donahue, hereby gives notice that her counsel intends to take the deposition of the Defendant, Richard P. Andrew, regarding his knowledge of the above-captioned case, on December 18, 1998 at 10:00 a.m., before Rogers and Associates, court reporters or other competent authority, at the law offices of the Plaintiff's counsel located at 21 North Street, Ellington, CT.

THE PLAINTIFF

BY_____

Christine Kulas, Esq.,
Law Offices of Christine Kulas,
her attorney
P.O. Box 2005
Ellington, CT 06066
Tele. #(860) 222-2222
Juris #989898

CERTIFICATION

I hereby certify that a copy of the above was mailed, certified, return receipt requested, on December 1, 1998 to all counsel and pro se parties of record namely: Neil E. Clifford, Esq., Michaels, Sabrina and Alexander, P.C., 259 Sage Road, Suite 200, West Hartford, CT 08080.

_____
Commissioner of Superior Court

24 Discovery: Depositions of Persons Who Are Not Parties

Terminology

Subpoena   Capias   Witness

Subpoena Duces Tecum   Nonparty Deponent   Motion to Quash

Pbs: 243, 244, 245, 246, 247, 248
C.G.S. sections: 4-104, 52-143, 52-144, 52-260

Introduction

In the last chapter, we discussed deposing a party to a lawsuit. Now we will decipher the same practice book rules as they apply to deposing individuals who are not parties, but who have information that is relevant to a case. In previous chapters we called them nonparties.

I. NONPARTY DEPONENTS

Like all other discovery, Pbs 218 applies to depositions. Only nonparties who may shed some light on the case should be deposed. These individuals are called **nonparty deponents.** They may also be referred to as **witnesses** because in most situations, they will be called as witnesses to testify at the trial.

Nonparty deponents include, but are not limited to:

1. individuals who observed the events that led to the dispute, such as a bystander who watched an automobile accident take place;

2. individuals who have knowledge or are involved in the events that led up to the dispute;

3. physicians who have examined the Plaintiff in a personal injury action;

4. experts who have been hired by a party to form an opinion pertaining to a crucial issue in the case and to testify at trial.

II. PURPOSE OF DEPOSING A NONPARTY

Nonparties often have new or additional information pertaining to a case that a party may be unaware of. Rather than wait for trial and the inevitable surprises that are sure to follow, deposing a witness enables the parties to better evaluate and prepare their cases. In addition, the parties will have the opportunity to determine how believable an individual will be as a witness at trial.

III. SUBPOENAS

Parties in a lawsuit are subject to the court's jurisdiction and must permit themselves to be deposed by opposing parties. Nonparty deponents, unless they are agents of the party, are not under the court's jurisdiction. As a result, they must be served a **subpoena** which commands them to appear at their deposition. Once served, these nonparty deponents are subject to the court's jurisdiction, including fines and possible incarceration if they fail to comply with the terms of the subpoena.

A subpoena is a written document and may be used for two types of proceedings:

1. to command a person to appear at court, on a specific date and time, to testify at a hearing or trial; or

2. to command a person to appear at court or at a specific location, on a specific date and time, to testify at a deposition.

A subpoena places a person under the court's jurisdiction for *60 days*. If the person fails to obey the subpoena, he or she could be arrested and fined. (See Section XII below.)

Pbs 245(b) states that a subpoena may be issued (drafted and signed) by any of the following:

1. a judge; or

2. a clerk of any court; or

3. a notary public; or

4. a Commissioner of the Superior Court.

In most cases, the attorney for one of the parties who wishes to depose a nonparty will issue the subpoena in his or her capacity as Commissioner of the Superior Court. Pro ses wishing to depose a nonparty should draft the subpoena and then ask any of the above to sign it. (Court-issued forms are available for this purpose.)

IV. SUBPOENA DUCES TECUM: PRODUCTION OF MATERIALS

A. *A Subpoena Duces Tecum*

A **subpoena duces tecum** is a type of subpoena that commands a person to appear and testify at a deposition or at trial *and* commands him or her to produce specific documents or materials at the deposition or at trial. The specific documents or materials are listed in the subpoena duces tecum.

As you can see from the samples at the end of this chapter, the two types of subpoenas look quite similar. In addition, they command the same compliance and are served in the same manner.

B. *Types of Materials*

Pursuant to Pbs 245(c), the materials requested in a subpoena duces tecum include but are not limited to specific books, papers, documents, or tangible things to be inspected or copied that fall within the scope of permissible discovery. Often, these materials include originals or copies of specific bank or telephone records, medical records, photographs, contracts, etc.

V. DRAFTING SUBPOENAS

Legal supply stores provide subpoena and subpoena duces tecum forms that contain the required information with appropriate blanks to fill in the names, date, time and location of the deposition. In addition, many firms have this basic format on their computer systems.

In accordance with C.G.S. sec. 52-144 and Pbs 245(b), the content of a subpoena and subpoena duces tecum include:

1. the name of the party seeking to take the deposition;

2. the name and address of the person to be deposed. If the name is not known, include a general description sufficient to identify the individual person, or a particular group or class to which he or she belongs;

3. the date and time of the deposition; and

4. the address where the deposition will take place.

In addition, the subpoena or subpoena duces tecum should state:

> **a.** that the deposition will take place before an officer authorized to administer oaths within this state; and
>
> **b.** the deponent will give testimony concerning what he or she knows about a case between the Plaintiff and the Defendant; and
>
> **c.** that the deponent is commanded to appear at the designated time or within 60 days thereof, and at the designated place;
>
> **d.** if it is a subpoena duces tecum, list the materials requested;

e. the words: HEREOF FAIL NOT, UNDER PENALTY OF THE LAW IN THAT CASE PROVIDED.

Thus, even if a deposition is postponed, as long as it is rescheduled to take place within 60 days from that original date, the deponent named in the subpoena or subpoena duces tecum is still compelled to attend.

VI. SERVING SUBPOENAS

A. Notice to Other Parties

In addition to serving a deponent with a subpoena or subpoena duces tecum, the party seeking to take the deposition must send a Notice of Deposition to all other parties in the action, pursuant to Pbs 243. In addition, attach a copy of the subpoena or subpoena duces tecum to the Notice of Deposition.

B. Serving the Subpoena or Subpoena Duces Tecum

1. Who May Serve Subpoenas

Sheriffs and constables may serve all types of subpoenas in their precincts. In addition, an indifferent person may serve any type of subpoenas anywhere in Connecticut. See Pbs 52-143(a). Remember that sheriffs and constables can also make service outside their precincts as an indifferent person.

2. Method of Service

All subpoenas must be served, *in hand, to the person named in the document, and read out loud to that person.* The only exceptions are as follows:

> **a.** pursuant to C.G.S. sec. 52-143(b), a subpoena directed to a police officer may be served on the chief of police or any person designated by the chief of police at the station to act as an agent for the officer named in the subpoena;
>
> **b.** pursuant to C.G.S. sec. 52-143(c), a subpoena directed to a correctional officer may be served on the Commissioner of Corrections or any person designated by the Commissioner to act as an agent for the officer named in the subpoena.

3. Time to Serve

> **a.** Hospital Records Departments: Pursuant to C.G.S. sec. 4-104, a subpoena deuces tecum for hospital medical records must be served not less than **24 hours** before the time designated for compliance.
>
> > **i.** Note, however, that it is a good idea to provide as much notice as possible. Therefore, in addition to a courtesy

telephone call, before service, you may notify the hospital by sending the appropriate person in the records department a *Notice of Intent to Serve Subpoena* which lists all the documents you are requesting in the subpoena duces tecum. As long as this notice is received no later than 24 hours before the designated time for appearance and compliance, actual service may be made after that 24 hour deadline.

ii. Hospital records regarding a mentally ill person are not subject to disclosure under C.G.S. sec. 4-104.

iii. Hospital records produced pursuant to a subpoena are delivered directly to the court in sealed envelopes. These envelopes may not be opened without permission from the court. See Pbs 7TTT.

b. Bank records should be subpoenaed at least *10 days* before the date designated for appearance and compliance.

c. Pursuant to Pbs 52-143(a), all other subpoenas must be served at least *18 hours* before the designated time for appearance and compliance.

4. Witness Fees

In addition to serving the subpoena, the officer must give the nonparty **witness fees** to cover travel expenses. It is a nominal amount. See C.G.S. sec. 52-260.

5. Return of Service

After service, the officer or indifferent person must draft a Return of Service, similar to a Return of Service used for a Complaint. This return will be needed as proof of service if the deponent witness fails to attend the deposition.

VII. MOTIONS TO QUASH, MODIFY AND OBJECTIONS

Pbs 245(d) and (e) permit a nonparty who is served any type of subpoena to take action to prevent a deposition from taking place, or object to producing or copying requested materials, or modify the terms of the subpoena.

A. *Purpose of a Motion to Quash and Motion to Modify or Objection*

It appears that a Motion to Quash may be used to challenge a subpoena or a subpoena duces tecum. A Motion to Modify appears to be directed at a subpoena duces tecum. Specifically, their purpose is to:

1. obtain a court order that prevents a nonparty from being compelled to testify at a deposition; and/or

2. attempt to prevent the production of materials; or

3. modify the terms of the subpoena to meet the nonparty's concerns.

B. Grounds for Motion to Quash, Modify or Objection

1. The subpoena is unreasonable or oppressive; and/or
2. The subpoena duces tecum seeks the production of materials that are not subject to production under Pbs 245(c); and/or
3. The nonparty will agree to comply on the condition that the party taking the deposition pay the reasonable costs of producing the requested materials.

C. Drafting and Filing a Motion to Quash, Motion or Objection

Pbs 245(e) states that the motion should be filed promptly, at or before the time of the deposition. Pbs 245 does not provide specific directions to draft or file a Motion to Quash or Motion to Modify. However, Pbs 245(d) addresses how to draft an objection to a subpoena which I believe also applies to motions to quash and motions to modify. Accordingly, these pleadings should be:
    1. in writing;
    2. served on the authority who issued the subpoena or subpoena duces tecum (Commissioner of the Superior Court, notary, judge or clerk);
    3. made within *15 days* of being served the subpoena or subpoena duces tecum; or
    4. if the deposition is to occur less than 15 days from service, made before the time stated for the deposition.

D. Who May Draft and File a Motion to Quash, Modify or Objection

The nonparty is not a party in the action. He or she may not even have an attorney. In some cases, the opposing party who considers the nonparty as his or her witness will draft and serve the objection on behalf of the deponent. In other cases, the nonparty will retain an attorney to handle the matter. If the nonparty retains an attorney, that attorney should file an Appearance in court, strictly for the purpose of addressing the motion or objection.

VIII. WHEN A DEPOSITION OF A NONPARTY MAY TAKE PLACE

A deposition of a nonparty deponent may take place under the same circumstances and times as a deposition of a party. As a result, Pbs 243, 244(b)(c) and (d) apply.

IX. WHERE A DEPOSITION OF A NONPARTY MAY TAKE PLACE

Pursuant to Pbs 246(d), a nonparty deponent's deposition may occur in the following locations:

1. If the deponent is served a subpoena in this state, the deposition may take place:

    a. within the county of the deponent's residence; or

    b. within 30 miles of the county of the deponent's residence.

2. If the deponent is not a resident of this state, the deposition may take place:

    a. within any county in this state where the deponent was personally served the subpoena; or

    b. at a place ordered by the court.

X. WHO MUST BE PRESENT

Like depositions of parties, pursuant to Pbs 245, a deposition of a nonparty deponent must be taken before either a judge, a clerk of any court, a notary public or a Commissioner of the Superior Court. Moreover, under Pbs. 247(c), a deposition may be stopped or moved to the courthouse if either party believes the other party or the nonparty deponent is acting in bad faith.

XI. RECORDING A DEPOSITION: COURT REPORTER OR VIDEO TAPE

The use of a court reporter, transcripts and fees are the same for depositions of parties as well as nonparties. In addition, either party is free to ask the court to permit a video tape of the deposition, instead of or in addition to a court reporter.

XII. WHEN A NONPARTY DEPONENT FAILS TO COOPERATE

In accordance with C.G.S. sec. 52-143(e) and Pbs 245(f), if a subpoenaed nonparty fails to obey the subpoena and appear at the deposition, the court may fine the individual, require him or her to pay all damages relating to the lack of compliance or, if necessary, issue a **capias**.

A capias is similar to an arrest warrant. It is a court order that directs the police to take the subpoenaed person into custody until he or she appears before the court. Once before the court, if the subpoenaed person still refuses to comply with the subpoena, the court may commit him or her to jail until he or she indicates they are willing to comply.

Proper service is satisfied by the Return of Service on the subpoena, and possibly the testimony of the officer who made the service.

XIII. CONCLUSION

A. Key Issues in This Chapter Include:

1. One significant difference between deposing parties and nonparties is that nonparties should be subpoenaed to attend their deposition. This way, if they change their mind about attending, they are under the court's jurisdiction and may be compelled to cooperate.

2. A nonparty who does not want to be deposed, but who has been served with a subpoena, may file a Motion to Quash and ask the court to prevent the deposition or a Motion to Modify the Subpoena if he or she objects to producing certain materials.

3. Not every witness who will testify at a trial is deposed. Sometimes statements made to a private investigator are enough to inform a party what the witness will say. Experts, however, are another story. Due to the often technical nature and importance of their testimony, it's good practice to know ahead of time what they will say.

4. In most instances, a deponent must be served with a subpoena at least *18 hours* before the scheduled court appearance or deposition.

5. A subpoena duces tecum for bank records should be served at least *10 days* before the scheduled court appearance or deposition.

6. A subpoena duces tecum for hospital medical records should be served at least *24 hours* before the scheduled court appearance or deposition, unless a *Notice of Intent to Serve Subpoena* is received by the proper person at least *24 hours* before the scheduled court appearance or deposition.

7. The rules and statutes pertaining to subpoenaing nonparty deponents to attend a deposition are the same as for subpoenaing witnesses to testify at trial. See Chapter 30.

B. Relevant Connecticut Practice Book Sections Include:

Pbs 243:   Depositions--Depositions Generally
Pbs 244:   Deposition--Notice of Deposition; General Requirements; Special Notice; Nonstenographic Recording; Production of Documents and Things; Depositions of Organizations
Pbs 245:   Deposition--Subpoenas
Pbs 246:   Deposition--Place of Deposition
Pbs 247:   Deposition--Deposition Procedure
Pbs 248:   Deposition--Use of Depositions in Court Proceedings

C. Relevant Connecticut General Statute Sections Include:

C.G.S. sec. 4-104.:	Inspection and subpoena of hospital records.
C.G.S. sec. 52-143.:	Subpoenas for witnesses. Penalty for failure to appear and testify.
C.G.S. sec. 52-144.:	Form of Subpoena.
C.G.S. sec. 52-260.:	Witness Fees.

Example 1, Notice of Deposition (of a Nonparty)

DOCKET NO. CV 98-0333333 S	:	SUPERIOR COURT
SARAH A. DONAHUE	:	JUDICIAL DISTRICT
	:	OF TOLLAND
VS.	:	AT ROCKVILLE
RICHARD P. ANDREW	:	NOVEMBER 2, 1998

NOTICE OF DEPOSITION

Pursuant to Connecticut Practice Book Section 243, the Defendant, Richard P. Andrew, hereby gives notice that his counsel intends to take the deposition of Mr. Thomas O'Neill regarding his knowledge of the above-captioned case, on November 19, 1998 at 10:00 a.m., before Matthews and Associates Reporting Service or other competent authority, at the law offices of the Defendant's counsel located at 259 Sage Road, Suite 200, West Hartford, CT 08080.

Mr. O'Neill was served a (subpoena or subpoena duces tecum, whichever is applicable), a copy of which is attached hereto.

THE DEFENDANT

BY_____

Neil E. Clifford, Esq.,
Michaels, Sabrina and Alexander, P.C.,
his attorneys
259 Sage Road, Suite 200
West Hartford, CT 08080
Tel. # (860) 111-1111
Juris #626262

CERTIFICATION

I hereby certify that a copy of the Notice of Deposition and the attached (subpoena or subpoena duces tecum) were mailed certified, return receipt requested, on November 2, 1998 to all counsel and pro se parties of record namely: Attorney Christine Kulas, P.O. Box 2005, Ellington, CT 06066.

_____
Commissioner of the Superior Court

Example 2, A subpoena, used to compel testimony only. No documents are required.

SUBPOENA

JUDICIAL DISTRICT OF TOLLAND
DOCKET NO. CV 98-0333333 S

TO: Mr. Thomas O'Neill, 251 Pepperbush Court, South Windsor, CT 06074

BY THE AUTHORITY OF THE STATE OF CONNECTICUT, you are hereby commanded to appear at a deposition taken by a Commissioner of the Superior Court, before a proper officer from Matthews & Associates Reporting Service who is authorized to administer oaths within this state, to be held at the law firm of Michaels, Sabrina and Alexander, P.C., 259 Sage Road, Suite 200, West Hartford, CT 08080 on November 19, 1998 at 10:00 a.m., then and there to testify what you know in a certain cause therein pending, wherein

Sarah A. Donahue is the Plaintiff and

Richard P. Andrew is the Defendant

or to such day thereafter and within 60 days thereof on which said action is legally to be tried.

HEREOF FAIL NOT, UNDER PENALTY OF THE LAW IN THAT CASE PROVIDED.

Dated at Ellington, this 2nd day of November, 1998.

To any proper officer or indifferent person to serve and return.

_____
Commissioner of the Superior Court

Example 3, A subpoena duces tecum, used when documents are required, in addition to testimony.

SUBPOENA DUCES TECUM

JUDICIAL DISTRICT OF TOLLAND
DOCKET NO. CV 98-0333333 S

TO: Mr. Thomas O'Neill, 251 Pepperbush Court, South Windsor, CT 06074
BY THE AUTHORITY OF THE STATE OF CONNECTICUT, you are hereby commanded to appear at a deposition taken by a Commissioner of the Superior Court, before a proper officer from Matthews & Associates Reporting Service who is authorized to administer oaths within this state, to be held at the law firm of Michaels, Sabrina and Alexander, P.C., 259 Sage Road, Suite 200, West Hartford, CT 08080 on November 19, 1998 at 10:00 a.m., then and there to testify what you know in a certain cause therein pending, wherein
Sarah A. Donahue is the Plaintiff and
Richard P. Andrew is the Defendant
or to such day thereafter and within 60 days thereof on which said action is legally to be tried, **AND YOU ARE FURTHER COMMANDED TO BRING WITH YOU AND PRODUCE AT THE SAME TIME AND PLACE:**

1. Legible copies of all invoices, bills, etc., indicating any type of repairs and/or maintenance made or provided by you or your employees at Tommy's Auto Repair Service, to a 1995 Honda Civic, owned by Sarah A. Donahue, during the years 1996, 1997 and 1998.

HEREOF FAIL NOT, UNDER PENALTY OF THE LAW IN THAT CASE PROVIDED.

Dated at Ellington, this 2nd day of November, 1998.

To any proper officer or indifferent person to serve and return.

_____
Commissioner of the Superior Court

25 *Discovery: Disclosure of Experts*

Terminology

    Expert Witness

Pbs: 220

Introduction

Expert witnesses are perfect examples of nonparty deponents. Both parties may obtain their own experts to support their case and testify at trial.

The purpose of an expert is twofold: to explain to the trier of fact technical issues that are relevant to the specific facts in a case, and to provide the trier of fact with an opinion, based upon the expert's knowledge and experience.

Deposing an expert is the best means to determine what he or she will say at trial.

I. WHY EXPERTS?

Experts are usually necessary in any case that involves technical or specialized issues that are not commonly known to the average person. For instance, in personal injury cases, it is doubtful that the judge or all six members of a jury are also physicians. Yet, how then can they, as the triers of fact, understand the full scope and impact of the Plaintiff's injuries?

To address this predicament, each side usually obtains an expert physician who specializes in the Plaintiff's condition to testify at trial. Now you can see why independent medical exams are permitted. In most situations, the physician who performs the IME will testify at trial as the Defendant's expert witness.

238

Other cases in which experts are common include product liability, medical and legal malpractice, situations involving a dangerous condition, such as the construction of a stairwell, faulty elevator installation, etc. An expert will explain what went wrong to the trier of fact.

II. WHO MAY BE AN EXPERT

An expert may be any objective individual who does not know either the Plaintiff (client) or the Defendant (client) and has sufficient knowledge, education and experience in the subject he or she will testify to. Before an expert witness is permitted to testify, the court must *qualify the witness as an expert*. This entails a party providing the court with the witness' qualifications. The opposing party may object to a witness being qualified as an expert at that time. If the objection is sustained, the witness will still be permitted to testify, but his or her testimony will not include providing an "expert opinion" concerning the issue in dispute.

III. HOW TO FIND AN EXPERT

Individuals who wish to testify in court often advertise their services in various trade magazines relating to their field of expertise and in legal publications, such as the *Connecticut Law Tribune*. In addition, many physicians are well recognized in their field and can be contacted directly from area hospitals and medical institutions.

A. Issues to Keep in Mind

When obtaining an expert, keep two issues in mind:

1. Experts cost money. A doctor who is accustomed to earning over a thousand dollars a day will expect to be paid that same amount to spend a day in court. In addition, they often charge hundreds of dollars for the time they take to examine the Plaintiff, prepare their written reports and comply with discovery requests described below.

2. Each party wants an expert who will testify in his or her favor. Why would any party pay an expert thousands of dollars to ruin the case? At the same time, each party must be careful to find an expert who is considered impartial or unbiased. For example, physicians who often testify in court, rather than practice medicine full-time, and testify only for Plaintiffs or only for Defendants, quickly develop a questionable reputation for themselves in the legal community. This reputation may lead to being labeled an "expert for hire," or a "Plaintiff's expert" or a "Defendant's expert." In many instances, the opposing side will inform the trier of fact of this reputation, in hopes of persuading it to discount or totally ignore the opposing expert's opinion.

B. Criteria to Consider

The best experts:
1. are well respected in their field;
2. actually work in their occupation on a full-time basis;
3. review all the facts and make all the necessary examinations and inspections;
4. objectively formulate their opinions;
5. clearly explain their opinions and reasoning to the trier of fact in a way it can understand; and
6. form an impartial and unbiased opinion in one party's favor.

As a result, when each party obtains an expert, the expression, "It's a war between the experts" often comes to mind. This means that the trier is faced with opposite or contrary expert opinions and must decide which expert to believe. This can be a tough decision.

IV. DISCLOSING AN EXPERT

Pbs 220 permits opposing parties to conduct discovery relating to experts, even if this information was acquired or developed in anticipation of litigation or for trial.

An opposing party's expert's opinions and the facts relied upon to form these opinions are discoverable through Interrogatories and a pleading entitled "Disclosure of Expert Witnesses."

A. Interrogatories

A party may use Interrogatories at any time after the return date to obtain the following information:
1. to identify each person who is expected to be called as an expert witness at trial;
2. to state the subject matter to which the expert is expected to testify;
3. to state the substance of the facts and opinions to which the expert is to testify;
4. to provide a summary of the grounds for each opinion.

It's possible that the responding party may not have obtained an expert(s) within the time frame required by the Interrogatories. In addition to filing a stipulation or Motion for Extension of Time, it is appropriate for the responding party to state something like:
"No expert has been obtained at this time. The requested information will be timely disclosed when it is determined."

This response is appropriate pursuant to Pbs 220(D) which states that once this information becomes available, it must be timely disclosed in response to Interrogatory requests. In addition, as you already know, Pbs 232 requires each party to continually and promptly supplement new, corrected or additional responses to his or her original Interrogatory and production responses.

B. Disclosure of Expert Witnesses: Required Information and Time Limits

1. Plaintiff's Disclosure of Expert Witnesses

In addition to Interrogatories, Pbs 220(D) requires any Plaintiff who expects to call an expert witness at trial to disclose this information to all parties, "within a reasonable time prior to trial." This requirement is accomplished by filing a Disclosure of Expert Witnesses.

The Disclosure of Expert Witnesses is very similar to what is requested in the Interrogatories. It should include:

> **a.** the name of the expert;
>
> **b.** the subject matter on which the expert is expected to testify;
>
> **c.** the substance of the facts and opinions to which the expert is expected to testify;
>
> **d.** a summary of the grounds for each opinion.

2. Defendant's Disclosure of Expert Witnesses

Defendants must disclose the same information regarding their experts "within a reasonable time from the date the Plaintiff disclosed its experts, or, if the Plaintiff does not have experts, within a reasonable time prior to trial."

3. Within a Reasonable Time

"Within a reasonable time prior to trial" or "from the date the Plaintiff disclosed its experts" seems somewhat vague. Undoubtedly, the purpose is to ensure that each party has the opportunity to fully investigate the expert and retain his or her own experts, if necessary.

Pbs 220(D) offers some assistance by requiring that "any expert disclosed within six months of the trial date shall be made available for the deposition within *30 days* of the date of such disclosure, unless otherwise agreed by the parties."

This time requirement would presumably allow the deposing party sufficient time to obtain his or her own expert or an additional expert to address the newly disclosed expert's testimony. If such new or additional expert is needed, he or she must also be available to the other party for a deposition within *30 days* of disclosure, unless otherwise agreed by the parties.

C. Motion to Preclude Expert Testimony

Pbs 220(D) permits any party to file a Motion to Preclude Expert Testimony, to prevent an expert from testifying at trial, if he or she believes the expert was not timely disclosed. The grounds for this motion include:
1. the testimony will cause undue prejudice to the party filing the motion; or
2. the testimony will cause undue interference with the orderly progress of the trial; or
3. the delay in disclosing the expert was caused by bad faith on the part of the disclosing party.

V. DEPOSITIONS

As stated in the previous chapter, either party may take the deposition of the opposing party and any nonparty who has information that is relevant to the lawsuit. Pursuant to Pbs 220(B), this includes an opposing party's expert witnesses who are disclosed by Interrogatories or a Disclosure of Expert Witnesses.
As with other depositions, Pbs 242 et seq. applies. The purpose of the deposition is to learn firsthand what an expert will say and determine what type of a witness he or she will make at trial.

VI. CONCLUSION

A. Key Issues in This Chapter Include:

1. If you intend to depose the opposing party's experts, be sure to serve them with a subpoena or subpoena duces tecum. Otherwise, they are under no obligation to be deposed.
2. Remember that expert witnesses must be disclosed "within a reasonable time" prior to trial. Otherwise, the court may not permit them to testify at trial.

B. Relevant Connecticut Practice Book Sections Include:

Pbs 220: Scope of Discovery--Experts

Example 1, Disclosure of Expert Witnesses

DOCKET NO. CV 98-0333333S	:	SUPERIOR COURT
SARAH A. DONAHUE	:	JUDICIAL DISTRICT OF TOLLAND
VS.	:	AT ROCKVILLE
RICHARD P. ANDREW	:	JANUARY 18, 1999

DISCLOSURE OF EXPERT WITNESSES

Pursuant to Connecticut Practice Book Section 220(D), the Plaintiff hereby discloses the following experts she intends to call as witnesses at trial:

I. Names of Experts

Dr. Andrew Hall, professor of orthopedic surgery at New Haven Hospital.

II. Subject Matter

This expert will testify regarding the injuries the Plaintiff sustained as the result of the Defendant's negligence, as mentioned in the Plaintiff's Complaint. In addition, each expert will testify as to reasonable and necessary past, present and future treatments the Plaintiff has undergone and will be required to undergo as a result of her injuries, and the nature and extent of permanent impairment she sustained.

III. Substance of Facts and Opinions

The Plaintiff sustained injuries to various parts of her body as a result of the Defendant's negligence. She has undergone one regimen of conservative therapy and may require medical/surgical treatment in the future. She has been left with a permanent partial disability of some parts of her body as a consequence of such injuries which may increase in the future. These injuries, the treatments and past, present and future disability are proximately caused by the Defendant's negligent operation of his motor vehicle, as stated in the Plaintiff's Complaint.

IV. Summary of the Grounds for Opinion

This expert will rely upon its examination, observation and evaluation of the Plaintiff, based upon his education, training certification, and professional experience.

THE PLAINTIFF

BY_____

Christine Kulas, Esq.,
Law Offices of Christine Kulas,
her attorney
P.O. Box 2005
Ellington, CT 06066
Tele. #(860) 222-2222
Juris #989898

CERTIFICATION

I hereby certify that a copy of the foregoing was mailed on January 18, 1999 to all counsel and pro se parties of record, namely: Attorney Neil E. Clifford of Michaels, Sabrina and Alexander, P.C., 259 Sage Road, Suite 200, West Hartford, CT 06080.

_____
Commissioner of the Superior Court

26 *Discovery: Motions for Order of Compliance*

Terminology

Sanctions

Pbs: 7X, 7Y, 231, 351, 363
C.G.S. sections: 52-259c, 52-592

Introduction

A party who fails to respond to requested discovery, or who responds falsely or to mislead his or her opponent, may be subjected to a Motion for Order of Compliance, a Motion for Nonsuit or a Motion for Default.

I. MOTION FOR ORDER OF COMPLIANCE PURSUANT TO PBS 231

A. Discovery Deadlines

The purpose of a Motion for Order of Compliance is to ask the court to order a party to comply with specific discovery requests. In addition, a party may request the following:

1. a court order requiring a party to respond to specific discovery requests by a certain date, or face a nonsuit or default if he or she fails to comply;

2. to punish the noncomplying party by asking the court to enter a default or a nonsuit or dismissal;

3. to order **sanctions** against the noncomplying party. Sanctions are costs and attorney's fees incurred as a result of a party's failure to comply with specific discovery requests. For example, when a party fails to appear for his or her deposition without notice to the other party. Sanctions may also include attorney's fees for drafting the Motion for Order of Compliance as well as preparing for depositions, court reporter's fees, etc.;

4. to obtain orders relating to the information sought which are in favor of the requesting party at trial;

5. to obtain orders to prevent the uncooperative party from introducing certain matters into evidence at trial.

B. Objections

Parties who object to a Motion for Order of Compliance may not claim they failed to comply because the requests were objectionable, unless a proper, written objection to the discovery request had been filed and not yet ruled upon.

See below for Short Calendar procedures pursuant to Pbs 363.

C. Motion to Compel

A Motion for Order of Compliance is often called a Motion to Compel. Don't be confused. They accomplish the same goal.

II. MOTION FOR NONSUIT OR DEFAULT PURSUANT TO PBS 351

When a Motion for Order of Compliance is filed under Pbs 231, the court may order a noncomplying party to comply with discovery requests by a specified date, rather than grant a nonsuit or default. If, however, the party still does not comply, he or she may be subject to a nonsuit or default under Pbs 351.

Pbs 351 specifically states that "a party who fails to comply with an order of the court...may be subject to a nonsuit or default by the court."

This section also applies if a party fails to appear for trial without a proper excuse or fails to comply with any other court order.

III. MOTION FOR NONSUIT, MOTION FOR DEFAULT, MOTION FOR ORDER OF COMPLIANCE, PURSUANT TO PBS 363

A. Pbs 363 and Pbs 231

Pbs 363 authorizes a party to file a Motion for Nonsuit or Motion for Default, or a Motion for Order of Compliance under Pbs 231, if any party fails to comply with certain practice book rules.

Commonly, motions for nonsuit or default are used for violations of Pbs 114: Time to Plead, and Pbs 147, Request to Revise.

A Motion for Order of Compliance is used for discovery violations:

1. Pbs 222, Interrogatories;

2. Pbs 226, Requests for Production;

3. Pbs 229, Request for a Mental or Physical Examination.

B. Procedure: Compliance

Under Pbs 363, once a Motion for Nonsuit or Motion for Default (other than for a Pbs 114 violation) or Motion for Order of Compliance is filed, the clerk will hold the motion for ten days. During this time, if the noncomplying party complies, the motion will not be ruled on.

C. Procedure: Noncompliance

If the party does not comply, the party who filed the motion must file a Short Calendar claim slip which will then place the motion on the next available Short Calendar. This procedure usually gives the noncomplying party an additional two weeks to make the necessary disclosures.

IV. UNCOOPERATIVE CLIENTS

At times, clients simply refuse to cooperate with discovery requests. In those situations, their attorney's best course of action is to explain, in writing, that the case will be nonsuited or defaulted, and what the result of either will be, if the client does not change his or her attitude. Moreover, under Pbs 7Y an attorney can ask the court for permission to withdraw from the case if the client continues to be uncooperative.

V. REMEDIES FOR NONSUIT AND DEFAULT JUDGMENT

As stated earlier in this text, Pbs 377 permits a party who is nonsuited or who had a default judgment entered against him or her to file a Motion to Open Nonsuit or Default Judgment. Note, however, that in most instances the court will require the party to comply with the outstanding pleadings or discovery requests before granting the motion. If the motion is denied, C.G.S. sec. 52-592 may allow a new action.

VI. CONCLUSION

A. Key Issues in This Chapter Include:

1. A *Motion for Order Compliance* may be avoided by reaching an agreement and entering into a written stipulation with the opposing party regarding the dates compliance is due.

2. If a Motion for Order of Compliance is granted, which results in a default judgment or nonsuit, the party should file a Motion to Open Judgment under Pbs 377, along with an affidavit, the $60 filing fee, and a statement that the party is now able to comply. Don't forget the four-month deadline.

B. Relevant Connecticut Practice Book Sections Include:

Pbs 7X: Appearance--Withdrawal of Appearance
Pbs 7Y: Motion to Withdrawal Appearance
Pbs 231: Order for Compliance; Failure to Answer or Comply with Order
Pbs 351: Procedure Where Party Fails to Comply with Order of Court or to Appear at
    Trial
Pbs 363: Procedure Where Party Is in Default

C. Relevant Connecticut General Statutes Include:

C.G.S. sec. 52-259c.:   Fee to open, set aside, modify, extend or reargue judgment.
C.G.S. sec. 52-592.:   Accidental failure of suit; allowance of new action.

Example 1, Motion for Order of Compliance and Nonsuit

DOCKET NO. CV 98-0333333 S	:	SUPERIOR COURT
SARAH A. DONAHUE	:	JUDICIAL DISTRICT
	:	OF TOLLAND
VS.	:	AT ROCKVILLE
RICHARD P. ANDREW	:	JANUARY 15, 1999

MOTION FOR ORDER OF COMPLIANCE AND NONSUIT

The Defendant in the above-captioned case respectfully represents the following:

1. On August 20, 1998, he served the Plaintiff Interrogatories and Requests for Production pursuant to Connecticut Practice Book Section 223 et seq.

2. On or about August 25, 1998, the Plaintiff moved for an extension of time until December 20, 1998 to respond to said discovery requests. Said motion was granted by the court on September 7, 1998.

3. As of the date of this instant Motion for Order of Compliance and Nonsuit, the Plaintiff has failed to respond to said discovery requests.

4. The information sought in the above-mentioned discovery requests is necessary for the Defendant to prepare his defense.

WHEREFORE, pursuant to Connecticut Practice Book Section 231, the Defendant respectfully requests the court to order one or more of the following sanctions to be imposed on the Plaintiff for her noncompliance:

a. Nonsuit;

b. Dismissal of her action;

c. Award of attorney's fees and costs incurred by the Defendant to bring this instant motion;

d. A final order by the court for compliance on a date certain, with an automatic dismissal if the Plaintiff fails to comply by such date.

RESPECTFULLY SUBMITTED
THE DEFENDANT

BY _____

Neil E. Clifford, Esq.,
Michaels, Sabrina and Alexander, P.C.,
his attorneys
259 Sage Road, Suite 200
West Hartford, CT 08080
Tele. # (860) 111-1111
Juris #626262

ORDER

The foregoing Motion having been duly presented and heard by the Court, it is hereby ORDERED: GRANTED/DENIED.

_____
BY THE COURT

CERTIFICATION

I hereby certify that a copy of the above was mailed on January 15, 1999 to all counsel and pro se parties of record as follows: Attorney Christine Kulas, P.O. Box 2005, Ellington, CT 06066.

_____
Commissioner of the Superior Court

*The Plaintiff complied with all discovery requests prior to this motion appearing on the Short Calendar.

27 *Motion for Summary Judgment*

Terminology

Summary Judgment   Material Fact

Pbs: 204, 379, 380, 381, 382, 383, 384, 385

Introduction

A Motion for Summary Judgment may be filed by either party and is another attempt to end a lawsuit before it goes to trial. Parties usually file a Motion for Summary Judgment after they have conducted what they believe to be sufficient discovery to prove that their version of the facts is true and there are no other contested issues. Hence, they will claim that there is no need for a trial. Instead, they are entitled to judgment now.

I. GROUNDS FOR SUMMARY JUDGMENT

Pbs 384 states that Summary Judgment is appropriate "if the pleadings, affidavits and any other proof submitted show that there is *no genuine issue as to any material fact* and that the moving party is entitled to judgment as a matter of law." (Emphasis added.)

In other words, parties who believe they are entitled to Summary Judgment should attach the following to the motion and memorandum of law:

1. the pleadings;

2. affidavits and sworn to, or certified copies of, relevant documents that are not part of the court file;

3. certified transcripts of testimony under oath, such as deposition testimony;

4. disclosures, such as responses to Interrogatories and Requests for Production;

and

5. written admissions, etc. (Responses to Requests for Admission or admissions to a Complaint or Counterclaim in an Answer.)

The purpose of this documentation is to convince the court that it is quite clear what the truth is and what really happened during the dispute in question. As a result, there is no need for a trier of fact to waste its time determining the facts during a trial. See also Pbs 380 et seq.

II. TIME TO FILE A MOTION FOR SUMMARY JUDGMENT

Pursuant to Pbs 379, this motion may be filed at any time before the case is scheduled for trial. Furthermore, with the court's permission, it may be filed even after a trial date is assigned. This flexibility enables a party to file the motion early, during the Pretrial Stage, or later, after the pleadings are closed and in-depth discovery is completed. It depends upon the facts of each case and how much documentation is necessary to prove the party's version of the facts.

III. OBJECTING TO A MOTION FOR SUMMARY JUDGMENT

In their objection, parties opposing a Motion for Summary Judgment must convince the court that some real (genuine) issue of material fact still exists, which questions liability or damages. As a result of this unresolved issue(s), the moving party is not entitled to judgment as a matter of law. Instead, there must be a trial to determine the facts.

Pursuant to Pbs 380, the opposing party must file an Objection and Memorandum of Law in Support of Objection, "prior to the day the case is set down for Short Calendar." In addition, he or she must attach any affidavits and other documents needed to prove a genuine issue of material fact exists. In the event the opposing party needs more time to obtain these documents, Pbs 382 allows him or her to ask the court for a continuance.

IV. THE PLAINTIFF AND MOTIONS FOR SUMMARY JUDGMENT

As I mentioned in Chapter 3, a civil lawsuit consists of two issues:

1. The Defendant's **liability** to the Plaintiff, if any; and
2. The amount of **damages** due to the Plaintiff from the Defendant, if any.
Both issues are determined by the facts of each lawsuit.

At trial, a Plaintiff who intends to win on the Complaint must be able to prove both liability and damages. As a result, the same is true if a Plaintiff intends to prevail on a Motion for Summary Judgment. This is possible in certain types of cases; in others it is not.

A. Contract/Debt Collection Cases

Contract or debt collection cases such as *Skillman, Et Al. v. Auto Service Center, Inc.,* in this text, are fairly simplistic: The Defendant promised to pay a certain sum of money to the Plaintiff, by a certain date.

The Defendant's *liability* to the Plaintiff is established by the Defendant's signature on a written contract: the promissory note. The *damages* owed to the Plaintiff are established by how much, if anything, the Defendant has already paid to the Plaintiff. This amount can be proven by written receipts, canceled checks, bank statements, etc. Likewise, any interest and attorney's fees allowed under the terms of the note can also be established by documentation.

Accordingly, the Plaintiff may file a Motion for Summary Judgment, along with a memorandum of law, and attach the appropriate documents to prove the Defendant's liability and damages due to the Plaintiff. Based upon this information, he or she will claim that there is no genuine issue as to any material fact. Therefore, the court should enter Summary Judgment now, as a matter of law.

In response, the Defendant may assert Special Defenses that are stated in his or her Answer, to demonstrate that liability is not absolute. In addition, he or she should attach contrary documentation to an objection and provide proof to support the claim that genuine issues of material fact still exist. As a result, a trial is necessary to determine these issues.

B. Negligence Cases, Intentional Torts, Breach of Contract without a Specified Sum, etc.

It is difficult to prove liability and damages in negligence cases without a trial. Both depend very much upon the credibility of witnesses and the content of their testimony, rather than just on documents.

1. Proving Liability Only: Interlocutory in Character

Liability is a bit easier to prove than damages because witness statements can be reduced to writing, such as affidavits, depositions, etc. As a result, many Plaintiffs who file Motions for Summary Judgment will follow Pbs 385: Summary Judgments-Triable Issue as to Damages Only. The pleading itself is often called a *Motion for Summary Judgment Interlocutory in Character with Respect to Liability.* If the Plaintiff wins the motion, the trial will consist only of a Hearing in Damages.

Through documentation, the Plaintiff will attempt to establish the Defendant's liability. In response, a Defendant will claim that even liability cannot be proven by documents. Instead, a trier of fact needs to observe each witness and determine his or her credibility, in order to determine the facts necessary to prove whether or not the Defendant is liable. The court often agrees.

If the Plaintiff is successful, the court will do the following:

      a. Grant Summary Judgment in favor of the Plaintiff, as to liability;

      b. Order an immediate Hearing in Damages, before a judge or jury, to determine the amount of damages the Plaintiff is entitled to from the Defendant.

2. Damages

Damages in personal injury cases, specifically, are extremely difficult to prove through documentation because someone who is qualified must place a dollar amount on a Plaintiff's pain and suffering. But who? The Plaintiff? No. At least at trial, the trier of fact will have the opportunity to listen to the entire story, from both the Plaintiff and the Defendant, their witnesses, as well as their experts, before it places a dollar amount that is appropriate to address the Plaintiff's losses.

V. THE DEFENDANT AND MOTIONS FOR SUMMARY JUDGMENT

A. Contract/Debt Collection Cases, Sum Specific Cases: Liability

Defendants who attempts Summary Judgment must only prove that they are not liable to the Plaintiff. If there is no liability, there can be no damages. As a result, Defendants may rely upon Special Defenses (even if they have not yet filed an Answer) in order to prove that they are not liable. For instance, they can present documentation which proves one or more of the following:

1. They are not liable, because they did not sign the contract or promissory note or enter into the agreement the Plaintiff claims.

2. They are not liable because they paid the Plaintiff the entire amount due.

3. The Plaintiff released them from the obligation.

4. The agreement was illegal.

5. The agreement was made while the Defendant was an infant (under legal age).

6. The agreement was made while the Defendant was Non Compos Mentis;

7. This dispute was resolved during arbitration, or another proceeding (res judicata).

8. The agreement was created as a result of the Plaintiff's fraud or duress.

9. The statute of limitations has expired.

B. Contract/Debt Collection Cases, Sum Specific Cases: Damages

If a Defendant is in fact liable, he or she may still contest the amount of damages the Plaintiff claims due. Again, this can be accomplished through documentation to support any applicable Special Defenses as stated above, or documentation that proves he or she owes an amount that is less than what the Plaintiff claims.

Pursuant to Pbs 386, a defense may apply to only a part of the Plaintiff's claim. In that situation, Summary Judgment may be granted in favor of the Plaintiff for issues not applicable to the Defendant's defenses.

C. Negligence Cases, Intentional Torts, Breach of Contract without a Specified Sum, Etc.

For the same reasons stated above, it is difficult for a Defendant to demonstrate through a Motion for Summary Judgment that he or she is not liable in these types of cases. As a result, it is often difficult to prevail on such a motion.

VI. AFFIDAVITS MUST BE MADE IN GOOD FAITH

Pursuant to Pbs 383, the affidavits mentioned above must be made in good faith. If not, or if they were created to purposely delay the case, the court may order the offending party to pay the opposing party's reasonable expenses, including attorney's fees, incurred due to such bad faith. In addition, the offending party may be found in contempt and, if appropriate, the attorney involved may be disciplined by the court.

VII. WHEN THERE IS MORE THAN ONE PLAINTIFF OR DEFENDANT

Like Motions to Strike, when there is more than one Plaintiff or Defendant, one or more of either party may seek Summary Judgment for those counts in the Complaint that apply to them.

VIII. COUNTERCLAIMS AND CROSS COMPLAINTS

In addition to Complaints, pursuant to Pbs 380, any party may file a Motion for Summary Judgment with respect to Counterclaims and Cross Complaints filed in an action.

IX. CONCLUSION

A. Key Issues in This Chapter Include:

Summary Judgment prevents a party from having his or her day in court at trial. As a result, courts are often reluctant to grant a Motion for Summary Judgment in cases where the Defendant has appeared and actively participated in the litigation process. Instead, the courts prefer the case to go to trial and be decided by a trier of fact who has heard all the evidence. Nevertheless, these motions are occasionally granted.

B. Relevant Connecticut Practice Book Sections Include:

Pbs 204: Requirement That Memorandum of Law Be Filed with Certain Motions
Pbs 379: Summary Judgment--Scope of Remedy
Pbs 380: Summary Judgment--Proceedings upon Motion
Pbs 381: Summary Judgment--Form of Affidavits
Pbs 382: Summary Judgment--When Appropriate Documents Are Unavailable
Pbs 383: Summary Judgment--Affidavits Made in Bad Faith
Pbs 384: Summary Judgment--Judgment
Pbs 385: Summary Judgment--Triable Issue as to Damages Only

Example 1, *Motion for Summary Judgment Interlocutory in Character*

DOCKET NO. CV 98-0333333 S	:	SUPERIOR COURT
SARAH A. DONAHUE	:	JUDICIAL DISTRICT
	:	OF TOLLAND
VS.	:	AT ROCKVILLE
RICHARD P. ANDREW	:	FEBRUARY 16, 1999

MOTION FOR SUMMARY JUDGMENT INTERLOCUTORY IN CHARACTER, WITH RESPECT TO LIABILITY

Pursuant to Connecticut Practice Book Section 385, the Plaintiff, Sarah A. Donahue, hereby respectfully submits that there is no genuine issue as to any material fact with respect to the Defendant's liability. Therefore, the Plaintiff respectfully moves for Summary Judgment in its favor on the issue of liability.

Furthermore, the Plaintiff respectfully moves for an Order for an Immediate Hearing before a jury, pursuant to Connecticut Practice Book Section 385, to determine the amount of damages suffered by the Plaintiff.

The Plaintiff submits the following documents in support of her Motion for Summary Judgment, an affidavit of the Plaintiff, Sarah A. Donahue, the police accident report and a memorandum of law.

THE PLAINTIFF,
SARAH A. DONAHUE

BY_____

ORAL ARGUMENT REQUESTED
TESTIMONY NOT REQUIRED

Christine Kulas, Esq.,
Law Offices of Christine Kulas,
her attorney
P.O. Box 2005
Ellington, CT 06066
Tele. #(860) 222-2222
Juris #989898

ORDER

The foregoing Motion having been duly presented and heard by the Court, it is hereby ORDERED: GRANTED/DENIED

_____
BY THE COURT

CERTIFICATION

I hereby certify that a copy of the above was mailed on February 16, 1999 to all counsel and pro se parties of record as follows: Neil E. Clifford, Esq. of Michaels, Sabrina and Alexander, P.C., 259 Sage Road, Suite 200, West Hartford, CT 06080.

_____
Commissioner of the Superior Court

*A memorandum of law in support of this motion is not included here but would be needed if this motion was filed in court.

Example 2, Objection to Motion for Summary Judgment Interlocutory in Character

DOCKET NO. CV 98-0333333 S	:	SUPERIOR COURT
SARAH A. DONAHUE	:	JUDICIAL DISTRICT
	:	OF TOLLAND
VS.	:	AT ROCKVILLE
RICHARD P. ANDREW	:	FEBRUARY 27, 1999

OBJECTION TO MOTION FOR SUMMARY JUDGMENT

The Defendant, in the above-captioned action, hereby objects to the Plaintiff's Motion for Summary Judgment Interlocutory in Character with Respect to Liability dated February 16, 1999. The Defendant respectfully submits that there are genuine issues as to material facts with regard to liability and the Plaintiff is not entitled to judgment as a matter of law. A memorandum of law and an affidavit are attached hereto, in support of this objection.

THE DEFENDANT,
RICHARD P. ANDREW

BY_____

Neil E. Clifford, Esq.,
Michaels, Sabrina and Alexander, P.C.,
his attorneys

ORAL ARGUMENT REQUESTED
TESTIMONY REQUIRED

259 Sage Road, Suite 200
West Hartford, CT 06080
Tele. # (860) 111-1111
Juris #626262

ORDER

The foregoing Objection having been duly presented and heard by the Court, it is hereby ORDERED: SUSTAINED/OVERRULED.

_____

BY THE COURT

CERTIFICATION

I hereby certify that a copy of the above objection, a memorandum of law and an affidavit were mailed on February 27, 1999 to all counsel and pro se parties of record as follows: Attorney Christine Kulas, P.O. Box 2005, Ellington, CT 06066.

_____

Commissioner of the Superior Court

*A memorandum of law in support of this objection is not included here but would be needed if this motion was filed in court.

Example 3, Motion for Summary Judgment and Memorandum of Law

DOCKET NO. CV 98-04444444 S	:	SUPERIOR COURT
GEORGE SKILLMAN, ET AL	:	JUDICIAL DISTRICT OF
	:	HARTFORD/NEW BRITAIN
VS.	:	AT HARTFORD
AUTO SERVICE CENTER, INC.	:	AUGUST 3, 1998

MOTION FOR SUMMARY JUDGMENT

The Plaintiffs in the above-captioned action hereby respectfully move that the Court grant Summary Judgment in their favor in the amount of ONE HUNDRED THOUSAND DOLLARS ($100,000.00), plus interest, costs and attorney's fees.

The Plaintiffs make this motion on the ground that no genuine issues of material fact exist and therefore, they are entitled to judgment as a matter of law.

The Plaintiffs have attached a memorandum of law, Requests for Admission, George Skillman's affidavit, and an Affidavit of Debt in support of this motion.

THE PLAINTIFFS

BY_____

ORAL ARGUMENT REQUESTED
TESTIMONY NOT REQUIRED

Kenneth I. Marcus, Esq.,
Friedman & Marcus, P.C.,
their attorneys
27 Main Street
Bristol, CT 00000
Tele. #(860) 955-9595
Juris #424242

ORDER

The foregoing Motion having been presented and heard by the court, it is hereby ORDERED: GRANTED/DENIED.

_____

BY THE COURT

CERTIFICATION

I hereby certify that a copy of the foregoing motion, memorandum of law, **Requests for Admission, and Affidavit of Debt were mailed on August 3, 1998 to all counsel and pro se parties of record, namely: Mark Peters, Esq., 1001 Sanberg Street, Manchester, CT 06660.

_____

Commissioner of the Superior Court

*Rather than object to this motion, the Defendant in this case settled with the Plaintiffs. See the sample Stipulated Judgment at pages 270-271.

**Note that the Requests for Admission are found in Chapter 22.

DOCKET NO. CV 98-0444444 S	:	SUPERIOR COURT
GEORGE SKILLMAN, ET AL.	:	JUDICIAL DISTRICT OF
	:	HARTFORD/NEW BRITAIN
VS.	:	AT HARTFORD
AUTO SERVICE CENTER, INC.	:	AUGUST 3, 1998

MEMORANDUM OF LAW IN SUPPORT OF
MOTION SUMMARY JUDGMENT

FACTS

On or about September 1, 1997, the Plaintiffs, George Skillman and Barbara Skillman, entered into a Purchase and Sale Agreement to sell all of their interest in Auto Service Center, Inc. to Joseph Kelly. According to said Agreement, the Defendant agreed to purchase from the Plaintiffs a business known as Auto Service Center, located at 126 Main Street, Hartford, CT, for the sum of One Hundred Thousand Dollars ($100,000.00).

On September 1, 1997, the Defendant signed a promissory note in the amount of One Hundred Thousand Dollars ($100,000.00) payable to the Plaintiffs, representing the agreed-upon price for Auto Service Center, Inc. Pursuant to the terms of the promissory note, the Defendant was to pay said sum in ten monthly installments, commencing January 15, 1998. A copy of the promissory note is attached hereto and incorporated herein as Exhibit A.

Contrary to the terms of said promissory note, as of the date of this instant motion, the Defendant has failed to make any payments at all to the Plaintiffs. As a result, according to said terms, the entire amount of One Hundred Thousand Dollars ($100,000.00), plus interests, costs and attorney's fees, is now due and owing to the Plaintiffs from the Defendant.

On May 18, 1998, the Plaintiffs served a set of Requests for Admission upon the Defendant, through its attorney of record. A copy of the required Notice and the Requests for Admission are attached hereto and incorporated herein as Exhibit B.

Pursuant to Connecticut Practice Book Section 239, the Defendant was required to answer said Requests within thirty (30) days of the filing of the Plaintiff's Notice of Service of Requests for Admissions. As of the date of this motion, more than sixty days have passed, and still, the Defendant has failed to respond to said Requests.

The Plaintiff, George Skillman, has attached his affidavit hereto as Exhibit C. In that affidavit he affirms that in spite of the terms of the Purchase and Sale agreement, the promissory note and the Defendant's oral promises, the Defendant has failed to pay any of the money due.

ARGUMENT

A party is entitled to Summary Judgment "if the pleadings, affidavits and other proof submitted show that there is no genuine issue as to any material fact and that the moving party is entitled to Judgment as a matter of law." Connecticut Practice Book section 384; Strada v. Connecticut Newspaper, Inc., 193 Conn. 313, 316-317 (1984).

In this instant case, the Plaintiffs have the burden of showing that there was no genuine issue of material fact. See Amendola v. Geremia, 21 Conn. App. 35, 37 (1990).

The court defines the material fact as a fact which will make a difference in the result of a case. Yanow v. Teal Industry, Inc., 178 Conn. 262, 268 (1979). Hence, the Plaintiffs must satisfy this burden by showing that "it is quite clear what the truth is, and that excludes any real doubt as to the existence of any genuine issue of material fact." Dougherty v. Grapheme, 161 Conn. 248, 250 (1971); Fogarty v. Rashaw, 193 Conn. 442 (1984).

Pursuant to Connecticut Practice Book Section 239, each Request for Admission the Defendant failed to respond to within thirty (30) days of the filing of the Plaintiffs' Notice, is deemed admitted, unless the Defendant obtained an extension of time to respond or has an objection pending.

In this case, the Defendant neither requested an extension for time or objected to any of the Requests. Therefore, each admission is now deemed truth.

Accordingly, the Defendant has admitted the following:

1. Through its president, and sole director and shareholder, Joseph Kelly, it agreed to purchase a business known as Auto Service Center, Inc. from the Defendant.

2. Pursuant to that agreement, Joseph Kelly signed a promissory note agreeing to pay the Plaintiffs the sum of One Hundred Thousand Dollars ($100,000.00) representing the purchase price of Auto Service Center, Inc.

3. Pursuant to the terms of the promissory note, the Defendant was to make ten monthly installments of Ten Thousand Dollars ($10,000.00) to the Plaintiffs, commencing January 15, 1998.

4. The Defendant has failed to make any payments at all to the Plaintiffs, although said payments are past due.

5. Pursuant to the terms of the promissory note, in the event the Defendant fails to make any payments when due, the entire remaining balance of the note becomes due and owing.

6. In addition, pursuant to the terms of the promissory note, the Defendant must pay the Plaintiffs all of their costs and reasonable attorney's fees incurred in the collection of the sum due.

"In a summary judgment motion, the parties are entitled to consideration, not only of the facts presented by their affidavits, but of the inferences which could be reasonably and logically be drawn from them as well." DeDominicis v. American Fire Insurance Co., 2 Conn. App. 686, 687 (1984).

In the present case, the facts, the unanswered Requests for Admissions, the promissory note and the Plaintiff's affidavit leave no doubt what the facts are in this case. Hence, the Plaintiffs have met their burden of proof.

CONCLUSION

Accordingly, the Plaintiffs are entitled to Summary Judgment against the Defendant in the amount of $113,179.00, representing the principal, interest, attorney's fees and costs due, as demonstrated by the attached Affidavit of Debt.

THE PLAINTIFF

BY_____

Kenneth I. Marcus, Esq.,
Friedman & Marcus, P.C.,
their attorneys
27 Main Street
Bristol, CT 00000
Tele. #(860) 955-9595
Juris #424242

28 *Closing the Pleadings and Pretrial*

Terminology

Pretrial Conference	Privileged Cases	State Trial Referee
Jury List	Jury Claim	Withdrawal
Court List	Pretrial Memo	Closed Pleadings
Trial List	Bench Trial	Stipulated Judgment
Attorney Trial Referee	Satisfaction of Judgment	

Pbs: 7BBB, 258, 259, 260. 263, 264, 265, 268, 273, 274A, 306, 377
C.G.S. sections: 52-215, 52-258

Introduction

The Defendant has filed an Answer, the Plaintiff has responded to any Special Defenses, there is no counterclaim and discovery is well under way. Now it's time to close the pleadings and claim the case to the **Trial List**. A trial date may soon be hovering over the horizon.

I. CERTIFICATE OF CLOSED PLEADINGS

The Certificate of Closed Pleadings is the same court-issued form mentioned previously to claim a case to the Hearing in Damages list. Now, pursuant to Pbs 258, *either party* may file the form to notify the court that the pleadings are closed and to place the case on the Trial List. Once this form is filed, the case is no longer subject to the Dormancy List. It will be placed on the Trial List, which is also called the Trial Docket.

A. The Trial List: Court or Jury

When completing the form, a party must decide if he or she wants a judge or jury to act as the *trier of fact* and decide the case.

1. A Court Trial versus a Jury Trial

In a trial to the court, called a **bench trial**, there is no jury. Instead, a judge will determine all issues of law that apply to the case, as well as issues of fact, in reaching a decision.

In a trial to a jury, the judge will preside over the case, to maintain order and proper decorum. In addition, according to Pbs 306, it will decide the following:

a. all issues of law; and

b. questions of law that arise during the trial and relate to any issue of fact.

The court will then explain the applicable law to the jury and that the jury alone must determine the facts of the case. This determination must be based upon the law, as it was explained by the judge, and upon the jury's observations of the evidence presented during the trial.

2. Two Types of Trial Lists

Most courthouses have at least two separate trial lists:

a. the Court Trial List; and

b. the Jury Trial List.

B. The Court Trial List

Cases placed on the Court Trial List (**Court List**) tend to be scheduled for trial much sooner than cases placed on the Jury Trial List (**Jury List**). The Court List is often smaller than the Jury List and the trial itself tends to be shorter in duration than a trial to a jury. All that's needed are the parties and their attorneys, a judge, a court reporter and a courtroom.

1. Types of Cases Placed on the Court Trial List

Contract cases, including debt collection cases, appear on the Court List much more frequently than on the Jury List. The issues in these cases are more clear-cut and focus on the terms of the contract, the law and the facts. On the other hand, personal injury cases tend to be more subjective. One eye witness account may differ from another eye witness's account. In addition, the degree of pain and suffering a Plaintiff experiences depends upon many different elements. Some attorneys believe a jury may be more sympathetic to all of this subjective evidence and render a higher damage award than a judge who hears cases day in and day out, as part of its job.

2. State Trial Referees

Retired judges who still hear cases and perform other judicial duties are called **State Trial Referees**. A case may be tried before a State Trial Referee, providing all parties in the case agree. Agreeing to a State Trial Referee may permit a case to be scheduled for trial sooner than waiting for an available judge. State Trial Referees may also preside over cases tried to juries.

3. Fact Finders and Attorney Trial Referees

Some courthouses have **Fact Finders** or **Attorney Trial Referee** programs as part of the Court List, or on a separate list. If each party consents, an attorney who meets certain qualifications may hear and decide a case instead of a judge. There is no jury and usually the cases involve contract disputes up to a certain dollar amount. The advantage is that a case will often be scheduled for trial much sooner than if it were to be tried to a judge or jury.

C. The Jury Trial List

1. How to Assign a Case to the Jury Trial List

A case can be assigned to the Jury Trial List in three ways:

> **a.** The party who files the Certificate of Closing Pleadings may mark the box next to "Jury" on the form and include a check for $300 which is the required jury fee. (A new bill passed in June 1997 increasing the $250 fee stated in C.G.S. sec. 52-258.)
>
> **b.** If a court trial is requested on the Certificate of Closed Pleadings, Pbs 260 and C.G.S. sec. 52-215 permit the opposing party to file a **Jury Claim** form within *ten days* of the certificate being filed and pay the jury fee.
>
> **c.** Pursuant to C.G.S. sec. 52-215, if both parties consent in writing, a case claimed to the Court List can be placed on the Jury List at any time.

2. Length of the Jury Trial List

Jury trials require a jury to be selected and tend to last much longer than court trials. In addition, more parties prefer a case to be heard and decided by a jury, rather than the court. As a result, the waiting list can be quite long. At a busy court, a case may be on the Jury List for as long as two or more years before it is scheduled for trial. During this time, the parties may attend **pretrial conferences**, complete discovery and attempt to settle their dispute.

To obtain a quicker trial date, the parties could ask if a State Trial Referee would be available sooner than a nonretired judge. Or, the parties could agree to change their minds and ask the court to place the case on the Court List. Finally, a case should receive a quicker trial date if it is **privileged**.

D. Privileged Cases

Pbs 259 lists 20 different reasons why a case may receive a quick trial date, regardless of whether it is on the Court List or the Jury List, because it is privileged.

For our purposes, these reasons include:

1. any case brought by or against any party who is sixty-five years old or will be sixty-five years old while the case is pending;

2. cases in which a verdict was set aside;

3. cases in which a new trial was granted;

4. cases in which a mistrial was declared;

5. Hearing in Damages cases to the court on damages, based upon a Default;

6. Hearing in Damages cases on damages, due to Summary Judgment as to Liability; see Pbs 385;

7. cases remanded for a new trial by the Appellate or Supreme Court.

Look to Pbs 273 for other reasons why a case may be privileged. In addition, Pbs 273 permits the court to order an immediate trial under extraordinary circumstances.

E. Completing the Certificate of Closed Pleadings

This form should be typewritten and include the following information:

1. the name of the case;

2. the docket number;

3. type of court, JD, GA or Housing Session;

4. the address of the court;

5. the certification:

    a. name of person making the certification;

    b. his or her signature;

    c. check the Plaintiff or attorney for Plaintiff box; or

    d. check the Defendant or attorney for Defendant box.

6. type of proceeding: check the box in front of one of the following:

    a. jury;

    b. Hearing in Damages to Court;

    c. Hearing in Damages to Jury;

    d. Administrative Appeals;

    e. Court Trials.

7. if case is privileged, select the box in front of the appropriate reason;

8. check the box in front of the relief requested;

9. complete the certification of service:

    a. the date copies were served;

    b. signed by attorney or pro se party;

c. the address of signing attorney or pro se;
d. the telephone number;
e. the name and address of each party served.

II. PRETRIAL CONFERENCES

A pretrial conference (pretrial) is a court appearance that permits the parties to discuss the case with each other, face to face, in front of a judge or qualified attorney. The purpose of a pretrial is to assist the parties in settling their dispute now, rather than going to trial later. If the case does not settle, the parties will address issues they believe will arise during the trial and create a discovery schedule. More than one pretrial may take place while the case waits on either the Court List or the Jury List.

A. Settlement

Pursuant to Pbs 263(a), once a case is placed on either the Court List or Jury List, it will usually be scheduled for a pretrial within a few weeks or months. The judge or attorney assigned to the pretrial will point out the strengths and weaknesses on both sides and assist in narrowing the issues. If damages are appropriate, it may place a dollar value on the case which it believes a court or jury would award, if the case were to go to trial.

Clients are usually required to attend the pretrial in order to be available to discuss settlement figures. Sometimes, they simply wait in the hallway while the judge or attorney and the parties' attorneys meet in another room. At other times, the clients are directly involved in the discussions. It depends upon each case, and the preferences of the individual conducting the pretrial.

Parties may agree to settle the case during the pretrial. This can be accomplished in one or more ways, such as:

1. handwriting a **Stipulated Judgment** which all the parties and attorneys sign, which is then filed in court;

2. handwriting and signing a Stipulated Judgment as described above, then reading it into the record to a court reporter;

3. withdrawing the Complaint or a part of it against one or more Defendants by filing a court-issued, blue Withdrawal form;

4. informing the court that the case is settled and filing a Withdrawal form within *30 days*, pursuant to Pbs 274A.

The parties may also agree to discuss the settlement proposal in more detail with their clients and contact one another by a certain date. If a settlement is reached, it is usually written, signed and filed with the court as a Stipulated Judgment.

If the case settles and the parties file a Stipulated Judgment, the Plaintiff should subsequently file a **Satisfaction of Judgment** with the court, pursuant to Pbs 7BBB, after the Defendant has met all the terms of the stipulation.

B. Discovery Schedule and Trial Date

According to Pbs 264, 265 and 268, if a case does not settle during the pretrial, the parties and the judge or attorney presiding over the pretrial will usually determine deadlines for all parties to complete discovery and take any other steps necessary to prepare the case for trial. In addition, a trial date may be assigned.

C. The Pretrial Memo

The Pretrial Memo is a court-issued form which provides a summary of the case and the parties' claims for the judge or attorney presiding over the pretrial. Pursuant to Pbs 265, the party seeking damages or another kind of relief fills out the form. Many courts, however, require all parties to complete the form and some firms prefer to do so, regardless of which side they represent. The form and sufficient copies for all the attorneys or pro ses must be brought to the pretrial and distributed.

The following information should be typewritten on the Pretrial Memo:

1. docket number;
2. date of completing form;
3. Plaintiff's name;
4. Defendant #1 name;
5. name of Defendant trial attorney;
6. telephone number of Defendant's trial attorney;
7. name of Plaintiff's trial attorney;
8. telephone number of Plaintiff's trial attorney;
9. Defendant #2's name, if applicable;
10. Defendant #2's trial attorney, if applicable;
11. telephone number of trial attorney for Defendant's #2, if applicable;
12. name of intervening trial counsel, if applicable;
13. telephone number of intervening trial counsel, if applicable;
14. Defendant #3's name, if applicable;
15. Defendant #3's trial attorney, if applicable;
16. telephone number of trial attorney for Defendant #3, if applicable;
17. return date;
18. date the case was claimed to the Trial List (the date Certificate of Closed Pleadings will be filed);
19. type of claim;
20. trial date, if known;
21. a short summary of the claim: date and time of accident, etc.;
22. intervenor's claims, if any;
23. summary of damages sought from Defendant;
24. date of Plaintiff's last medical exam;
25. permanency of injuries/life expectancy;
26. age of Plaintiff party;

27. specials:
>   **a.** doctors bills, the costs and explanation;
>   **b.** hospital bills, costs and explanation;
>   **c.** subtotal of doctor and hospital bills;
>   **d.** future medical bills expected;
>   **e.** wages:
>>   **i.** amount lost due to injuries; and
>>   **ii.** future earning capacity affected, etc.;
>>   **iii.** other damages: property, etc.;
>>   **iv.** total of specials
>   **f.** indicate whether copies of all medical bills and reports
>   have been given to Defendant;

28. summary of claims of law involved in case; include any evidentiary and procedural problems;

29. name of person who prepared Pretrial Memo (applicable attorney's name);

30. preparer's telephone number (law firm's telephone number);

31. attorney for Plaintiff or Defendant. (You may want to state the name of your client.)

III. CONTINUANCES

Pbs 263(c) permits either party to request to continue a pretrial to another date if he or she believes the case cannot be effectively pretried because damages are still not determined, or the attorney is unavailable because he or she is on trial in another case, or on vacation, or ill, etc. Many courts require the party asking for a continuance to first notify the opposing parties and ask whether or not they agree to the request. If there is no agreement, the pretrial may still be continued. It depends upon the policies of each court and the circumstances of each case.

In addition, if it is difficult for the client to attend the pretrial, its attorney may ask that the client be excused by writing a letter to the clerk or judge in charge of assigning pretrials. In these situations, this request will probably be granted as long as the client is available to discuss the case by telephone while the pretrial is in progress.

IV. FAILURE TO APPEAR AT A PRETRIAL

According to Pbs 265, if a Plaintiff fails to appear at the scheduled pretrial without obtaining a continuance or permission excusing the client, the court may order a nonsuit against the Plaintiff. Likewise, a Defendant who fails to appear risks a default. Furthermore, the absent party may be ordered to pay the appearing party's attorney's fees.

In either situation, the penalized party must file a Motion to Open Nonsuit or Judgment upon Default, pursuant to Pbs 377, in order to have the case reinstated on the docket.

V. CONCLUSION

A. *Key Issues in This Chapter Include:*

1. The pleadings are closed when the Defendant has filed an Answer and, if applicable, the Plaintiff has filed a Reply to Special Defenses. If there is a Counterclaim, the Plaintiff must file an Answer to the Counterclaim.

2. The pleadings must be closed and a *Certificate of Closed Pleadings* must be filed in court before a case will be placed on the Trial List. Either party may file the Certificate of Closed Pleadings.

3. If you want a jury trial and the opposing party has selected a court trial on the Certificate of Closed Pleadings, be sure to file a *Jury Claim* slip within *ten days* of the Certificate of Closed Pleadings being filed, and include the jury fee.

4. The parties can stipulate to remove a case from the *Jury List* and place it on the *Court List* and vice versa.

5. Each party in a lawsuit must consent if a *State Trial Referee* is assigned to a court or jury trial.

6. The purpose of a pretrial is to attempt to settle the case. If settlement is not possible at that time, a discovery schedule may be determined. If possible, a trial date is assigned.

B. *Relevant Connecticut Practice Book Sections Include:*

Pbs 7BBB:	Notation of Satisfaction
Pbs 258:	Trial Lists--Certifying That Pleadings Are Closed
Pbs 259:	Trial Lists--Privileged Cases
Pbs 260:	Trial Lists--Claims for Jury
Pbs 263:	Pretrial--Assignment for Pretrial
Pbs 264:	Pretrial--When Case Not Disposed of at Pretrial
Pbs 265:	Pretrial Procedure
Pbs 268:	Pretrial Procedure--Orders at Pretrial
Pbs 273:	Methods of Assigning Cases--Immediate Trial
Pbs 274A:	Method of Assigning Cases--Cases Marked Settled
Pbs 306:	Questions of Law and Fact
Pbs 377:	Opening Judgment upon Default or Nonsuit

C. Relevant Connecticut General Statute Sections Include:

C.G.S. sec. 52-215.: Dockets. Jury cases. Court Cases

C.G.S. sec. 52-258.: Jury fees

Example 1, Motion for Stipulated Judgment and Stipulated Judgment

DOCKET NO. CV 98-0444444 S	:	SUPERIOR COURT
GEORGE SKILLMAN, ET AL.	:	JUDICIAL DISTRICT OF
	:	HARTFORD/NEW BRITAIN
VS.	:	AT HARTFORD
AUTO SERVICE CENTER, INC.	:	OCTOBER 7, 1998

MOTION FOR JUDGMENT
IN ACCORDANCE WITH STIPULATION

The Plaintiffs and the Defendant request the court to enter judgment against the Defendant, Auto Service Center, Inc., in accordance with the stipulation attached hereto.

Respectfully,
The Plaintiffs and the Defendant

BY_____   BY_____
Kenneth I. Marcus, Esq.,   Mark Peters, Esq.,
Friedman & Marcus, P.C.,   Mark Peters & Associates, P.C.,
the Plaintiff's attorney   the Defendant's attorney
27 Main Street   1001 Sanberg Street
Bristol, CT 00000   Manchester, CT 06660
Tele. #(860) 955-9595   Tele. # (860) 648-0000
Juris #424242   Juris # 246135

ORAL ARGUMENT NOT REQUESTED
TESTIMONY NOT REQUIRED

ORDER

The foregoing Motion for Judgment having been considered by the Court, it is hereby ORDERED: GRANTED / DENIED.

BY THE COURT

CERTIFICATION

I hereby certify that a copy of the foregoing Motion for Judgment in Accordance with Stipulation and Stipulation were hereby hand delivered on October 7, 1998 to all counsel of record, namely: Mark Peters, Esq., Mark Peters & Associates, 1001 Sanberg Street, Manchester, CT 06660.

Commissioner of the Superior Court

DOCKET NO. CV 98-0444444 S   :   SUPERIOR COURT
GEORGE SKILLMAN, ET AL.   :   JUDICIAL DISTRICT OF
                                                       :   HARTFORD/NEW BRITAIN
VS.   :   AT HARTFORD
AUTO SERVICE CENTER, INC.   :   OCTOBER 7, 1998

STIPULATION

It is hereby agreed and stipulated that judgment may enter in accordance with the following stipulation:

By agreement of the parties, judgment may enter in favor the Plaintiffs and against the Defendant, Auto Service Center, Inc., in the amount of ONE HUNDRED AND TWENTY-SEVEN THOUSAND, ONE HUNDRED and SEVENTY-NINE DOLLARS (the "Principal Amount") payable as follows:

1. Five Thousand, Two Hundred, Ninety-Nine Dollars ($5,299.00) per month shall be paid by the Defendant to the Plaintiffs beginning October 15, 1998 and shall be payable on the 15th day of each month thereafter, through and including the last payment which shall be made on September 15, 1999. Upon making the final payment, the Plaintiffs shall provide the Defendant a release of judgment.

2. In the event that the Defendant does not make a payment as provided in paragraph one above, the entire remaining balance shall become due and payable immediately and paragraph one shall become null and void. Execution for said entire remaining balance shall issue immediately.

3. The Defendant shall make each payment by certified check or cash to the Plaintiff's attorney, Kenneth I. Marcus, Esq., Friedman & Marcus, P.C., 27 Main Street, Bristol, CT 00000.

THE PLAINTIFFS   THE DEFENDANT

_____   _____
George Skillman   Joseph Kelly, President of
                                                     Auto Service Center, Inc., its duly
                                                     authorized agent

_____
Barbara Skillman

29 *The Trial Stage: Preparations for Trial*

Terminology

Motion in Limine Offer of Judgment

Pbs: 248, 276, 279, 280, 284A, 342, 343, 344, 346, 347, 348, 349, 350, 351, 352, 353
C.G.S. section: 52-192a

Introduction

We've finally on the Trial List and yet there is still plenty of work to do. Be on your toes. Bench trials are usually scheduled for a specific date. Jury trials are sometimes different. Some courts place their jury cases on an alert list and the inform the attorneys to be prepared to start sometime during a specific week or month with 24 to 72 hours notice. Why? Because many cases on the list will settle as late as the day before, the morning of, or even in the middle of trial. As a result your case could be next!

Having received a ball park trial date, both parties must notify their clients and all of their witnesses to be available on that date and be sure all of their exhibits are ready to be introduced into evidence. At the same time, the parties should be considering whether they intend to file an Offer of Judgment or if a Motion in Limine is necessary. Last, if it's a jury case, the parties should be drafting their Requests to Charge, which are discussed in the next chapter.

I. REQUESTING A CONTINUANCE

Each court attempts to provide all parties in a case as much advance notice as possible regarding a trial date. If a continuance is needed, it should be requested as soon as a party realizes it is necessary.

A. *Reasons to Seek a Continuance*

Pursuant to Pbs 276, all clients and their attorneys on both sides of a lawsuit must be "present and ready to begin trial on the day and time specified by the court." What happens, however, if an important witness cannot be available to testify on the date of trial? Or, if an important document or other evidence cannot be made available on that date? Or, if one of the attorneys is already *on trial*, or a vacation is already scheduled, etc.?

Fortunately, Pbs 279 and 280 permit any party to ask the court to continue the trial to another date. In addition, if all the parties in the case agree to the continuance, some courts will grant this request over the telephone or pursuant to a letter from the requesting party. To be safe, the requesting party should call the court and ask which procedure the presiding judge requires.

B. *When a Witness or Other Evidence Is Not Available*

If the court requires a formal motion to request a trial continuance, Pbs 280 discusses making this motion when an important witness or evidence is not available on the date of trial. In addition to the motion, the court or the opposing party may require the requesting party to include an affidavit. This affidavit should:
1. identify the name of the witness or the evidence at issue; and
2. state the particular facts which, if believed, may be proved by the witness or the evidence; and
3. state the "grounds of such belief."

If the opposing party agrees to the continuance, that agreement should be included in the motion and affidavit.

The court may not grant the motion for a continuance if:
1. it believes the requesting party did not have a "good reason" why he or she did not properly prepare to have the witness or evidence available; or
2. if the opposing party is willing to stipulate to the affidavit regarding what the material witness would say if he or she were to testify at trial or the content of the evidence, if either were available. In these situations, the affidavit or a written stipulation would be introduced to the trier of fact at trial, instead of the actual witness or evidence.

In addition to the above, keep in mind that Pbs 248(d) allows a witness's deposition testimony to be read to the trier of fact by an individual agreed to by all parties, if the witness is unavailable to testify at trial.

C. Failure to Appear at Trial

Any party who fails to appear at trial without a proper excuse may face a nonsuit or default, pursuant to Pbs 351. See also Pbs 352 and 353.

II. MOTIONS IN LIMINE

A. Purpose of a Motion in Limine

The purpose of a Motion in Limine is to prevent an opposing party from introducing specific evidence at trial, or to limit its introduction to definite boundaries. In such cases, the party drafting the motion should claim that the evidence in question is irrelevant to the case and highly prejudicial. Therefore, it is not needed to support or to prove any issues and will unfairly affect the trier of fact's decision.

For instance, if the Plaintiff in a civil case served a short prison sentence after the motor vehicle accident at issue in the case, the Plaintiff may not want the jury to know about this criminal record or incarceration at the trial. Therefore, he or she may file a Motion in Limine, asking the court to prevent the Defendant from disclosing that information to the jury because it is irrelevant to the instant lawsuit and it may unfairly prejudice the jury against the Plaintiff.

As with all motions, the opposing party may object. In this situation, the Defendant may claim that the Plaintiff's incarceration aggravated the injuries claimed, due to riots in the prison and inadequate medical care the Plaintiff received during that time. As a result, the Defendant will argue that this information must be disclosed to the jury so that it may fairly determine what percentage, if any, of the Plaintiff's injuries the Defendant should be held liable for.

B. Time to File a Motion in Limine

A Motion in Limine is usually filed after the case has been assigned to a specific judge for trial, but before the trial begins. In addition, Pbs 284A permits the motion to be filed prior to that time, "for good cause shown."

C. The Court's Ruling

In accordance with Pbs 284A, the court may grant the Motion in Limine and order the relief the party requests or order some other kind of relief to address the situation. On the other hand, the court may grant or deny the motion, with or without prejudice.

Finally, the court may simply decide not to rule on the motion until later in the proceedings, after it has had the opportunity to hear a portion of the case and is better able to determine what prejudicial effect, if any, the questionable evidence may have.

III. OFFER OF JUDGMENT

Offers of Judgment apply in contract cases and other cases when the Plaintiff seeks money damages exclusively, or as part of other relief sought.

An Offer of Judgment is a written offer, from either party, to settle the case for a specific sum. Note that either party may file more than one Notice of Offer of Judgment, offering the same or different amounts, within the time frames stated below.

A. *Defendant's Offer of Judgment to Plaintiff*

1. *Time to File Notice of Offer of Judgment*

Pbs 342 permits a Defendant to file a Notice of Offer of Judgment anytime *before* evidence is offered during trial. Hence, the Defendant may make this offer early on in the case, or during the Pleadings Stage, or even as late as during jury selection.

2. *The Plaintiff's Response: Accepted*

Pursuant to Pbs 343, the Plaintiff has **ten days** after receiving the Defendant's Notice of the Offer of Judgment to accept the offer in writing, by filing an "Acceptance of Offer of Judgment." It appears, however, from the first sentence in Pbs 344, that if evidence is scheduled to start during the ten-day period, the Plaintiff must accept before evidence begins, unless the court is willing to delay the trial or permit the Plaintiff to accept after evidence begins.

If the Plaintiff accepts the Offer of Judgment, the case is over. The judgment against the Defendant is treated as a Default in the amount offered, plus the Plaintiff's costs that had been incurred up until the time the Offer of Judgment was made. Last, Pbs 349 requires the clerk to add the Offer of Judgment and the Acceptance to the record of the case.

3. *The Plaintiff's Response: Rejected*

Under Pbs 344, if the Plaintiff does not accept the Offer of Judgment as stated above, the offer is deemed withdrawn.

4. *Consequences for a Plaintiff Who Rejects an Offer of Judgment*

According to Pbs 344, if the verdict is in favor of the Plaintiff, and the damages awarded are more than the Offer of Judgment, the Plaintiff suffers no consequences. If, however, the damages awarded are equal to or less than the Offer of Judgment, the Plaintiff:

> **a.** shall not recover any costs from the Defendant which the Plaintiff incurred after receiving the Defendant's Notice of Offer of Judgment; and

b. shall pay all the Defendant's costs, which were incurred after the Plaintiff received the Defendant's Notice of Offer of Judgment. These costs may include up to $350 for reasonable attorney's fees.

As a result of these consequences, a Plaintiff who receives a small damage award could end up having to pay several hundred or even thousands of dollars in costs for both sides.

Pbs 344 states that its provisions do not apply in situations where "nominal damages were assessed upon a hearing after a default or after a Motion to Strike had been denied." Nor does it override any contract the parties may have entered into regarding attorney's fees.

B. Plaintiff's Offer of Judgment to Defendant

1. Time to File

Pbs 346 permits a Plaintiff to file a Notice of Offer of Judgment at any time before trial.

2. Defendant's Response: Accepted

Pursuant to Pbs 347, the Defendant has *30 days* after the Plaintiff's Notice of Offer of Judgment is filed *(*and before a jury or court reaches a verdict), to file a written Acceptance of Offer of Judgment. In this Acceptance, the Defendant agrees to stipulate to the amount stated in the Plaintiff's offer.

If the Plaintiff's Offer of Judgment is accepted, the case is over and judgment will be in the amount stated in the Plaintiff's offer.

3. Defendant's Response: Rejected

If the Plaintiff's Offer of Judgment is not accepted by the Defendant within the time stated above, Pbs 348 states that the offer is considered rejected.

4. Consequences for a Defendant Who Rejects an Offer of Judgment

If the damages awarded are equal to or greater than the Plaintiff's Offer of Judgment, Pbs 350 directs the court to increase the judgment against the Defendant by:

a. adding twelve (12) percent annual interest, to the amount of the verdict, which should be computed in accordance with C.G.S. sec. 52-192a; and

b. the court may add reasonable attorney's fees up to $350.

IV. CONCLUSION

A. Key Issues in This Chapter Include:

1. Promptly notify all clients and witnesses of trial dates. If a continuance is needed, try to obtain an agreement from the opposing party and include it in your request to the court.

2. Be sure to review your case thoroughly to determine if a Motion in Limine is appropriate.

3. An Offer of Judgment can create great inducement to settle a case.

4. As the trial date approaches, timely serve all necessary subpoenas.

B. Relevant Connecticut Practice Book Sections Include:

Pbs 248:	Depositions--Use of Depositions in Court Proceedings
Pbs 276:	Methods of Assigning Cases--Order of Trial
Pbs 279:	Methods of Assigning Cases--Motions to Continue or Postpone
Pbs 280:	Methods of Assigning Cases--Motion to Postpone; Absent Witness; Missing Evidence
Pbs 284A:	Motion in Limine
Pbs 342:	Offer of Judgment by Defendant--How Made
Pbs 343:	Offer of Judgment by Defendant--Acceptance of Offer
Pbs 344:	Offer of Judgment by Defendant--Offer Not Accepted
Pbs 346:	Offer of Judgment by Plaintiff--How Made
Pbs 347:	Offer of Judgment by Plaintiff--Acceptance of Offer
Pbs 348:	Offer of Judgment by Plaintiff--Offer Not Accepted
Pbs 349:	Offer of Judgment by Plaintiff--Offer of Judgment and Acceptance Included in Record
Pbs 350:	Offer of Judgment by Plaintiff-Judgment Where Plaintiff Recovers an Amount Equal to or Greater Than Offer
Pbs 351:	Procedure Where Party Fails to Comply with Order of the Court or to Appear at Trial
Pbs 352:	Motion for Default and Nonsuit for Failure to Appear
Pbs 353:	Motion for Default and Nonsuit for Failure to Appear--Defaults under Soldiers' and Sailors' Relief Act

C. Relevant Connecticut General Statute Sections Include:

C.G.S. sec. 52-192a.:	Offer of judgment by Plaintiff. Acceptance by Defendant. Computation of Interest

Example 1, Plaintiff's Offer of Judgment

DOCKET NO. CV 98-0555555 S	:	SUPERIOR COURT
SHEILA WILKENSON	:	JUDICIAL DISTRICT
	:	OF FAIRFIELD
VS.	:	AT BRIDGEPORT
RYAN KEEGAN	:	OCTOBER 9, 1998

NOTICE OF PLAINTIFF'S OFFER OF JUDGMENT

Pursuant to Connecticut Practice Book Section 346, the Plaintiff hereby offers to take judgment against the Defendant in the amount of One Hundred Thousand Dollars ($100,000.00).

THE PLAINTIFF

BY_____

Ann Lambert, Esq.,
Lambert and Smith, P.C.,
her attorneys
529 Corporate Place
Fairfield, CT 04540
Tele. #(203) 777-7777
Juris #545454

CERTIFICATION

I hereby certify that a copy of the foregoing was mailed on October 9, 1998 to all counsel and pro se parties of record, namely: Attorney Glen Lutley of Lutley & Associates, 906 Park Plaza, Bridgeport, CT 04530.

_____
Commissioner of the Superior Court

Example 2, Defendant's Acceptance of Plaintiff's Offer of Judgment

DOCKET NO. CV 98-0555555 S	:	SUPERIOR COURT
SHEILA WILKENSON	:	JUDICIAL DISTRICT
	:	OF FAIRFIELD
VS.	:	AT BRIDGEPORT
RYAN KEEGAN	:	OCTOBER 23, 1998

ACCEPTANCE OF OFFER OF JUDGMENT

The Defendant, Ryan Keegan, hereby accepts the Plaintiff's Offer of Judgment dated October 9, 1998, and agrees to stipulate to a judgment in the amount of One Hundred Thousand Dollars ($100,000.00), pursuant to Connecticut Practice Book Section 347.

THE DEFENDANT

BY_____

Glen Lutley, Esq.,
Lutley & Associates,
his attorneys
906 Park Plaza,
Bridgeport, CT 04530
Tele. #(203) 555-5555
Juris #464646

CERTIFICATION

I hereby certify that a copy of the foregoing was mailed on October 23, 1998 to all counsel and pro se parties of record, namely: Attorney Ann Lambert of Lambert and Smith, P.C., 529 Corporate Place, Fairfield, CT 04540.

_____
Commissioner of the Superior Court

30 *The Trial*

Pbs: 7D, 7NN, 7PP, 7QQ, 7RR, 7TT, 7UU, 230, 296, 297, 303, 303C, 304, 304A, 305, 305A, 305B, 306, 308A, 309A, 309B, 311, 312, 313, 315, 316, 317,318, 318A-K

C.G.S. sections: 52-215a, 52-216a, 52-216b

Introduction

Typically, the following individuals are present during a trial: the trial judge, the jury if it's a jury trial, all the attorneys involved in the case, all the clients involved in the case, at least one court sheriff to assist the witnesses and jurors, the court reporter and the courtroom clerk.

Pursuant to Pbs 7D, trial judges are available to open court and begin a case each week day at 10:00 a.m., unless ordered otherwise. Trials usually take place Tuesdays through Fridays. Mondays are often reserved for Short Calendar.

I. STAGES OF A TRIAL

The stages of a trial are described below. They include:
1. jury selection;
2. Plaintiff's opening argument;

3. Plaintiff's case-in-chief, during which evidence is presented through witnesses and exhibits;

4. Defendant's case, during which evidence is presented through witnesses and exhibits;

5. Plaintiff's Rebuttal;

6. Plaintiff's and Defendant's Closing Arguments;

7. judge's decision, if it is a bench trial;

8. judge's charge to the jury, if there is a jury;

9. jury deliberations;

10. jury's verdict.

II. JURY SELECTION

In cases tried to a jury, the members of the jury must be selected before the trial actually begins. C.G.S. sec. 52-215a states that a civil jury consists of six members. In addition, it is customary to select at least two additional jurors to act as alternates, to replace any juror who is not able to complete the entire trial.

A. Jury Duty and Voir Dire

Each day court is in session, several individuals are present at various courthouses throughout the state to serve jury duty. After a brief orientation, they are instructed to remain in one specific location in their respective courthouses, usually designated as the *jury room*, until they are called for a case.

When a new case is ready to start trial, the clerk will select a *panel* of potential jurors (also known as **veniremen**) and bring them to the courtroom. Pursuant to Pbs 303C, the trial judge will swear in the panel and briefly explain the nature of the case. The attorneys will then introduce themselves and their clients and read off the names of the witnesses they intend to call during the trial. A venireman who knows any of the attorneys, clients, or witnesses or who is familiar with the case may be excused **for cause** from serving on the jury for that case. (See explanation below.) Next, the panel will be led from the courtroom to another nearby location where the members will wait to be individually examined by the parties' attorneys.

Pursuant to Pbs 305, the parties are permitted to examine each member of the panel individually, outside the presence of the other members. This examination is called **Voir Dire**, and is similar to an interview.

B. Accepting and Excusing a Potential Juror

Members of the panel who are *accepted* by both sides become jurors. They will be sent back to the original jury room (away from the rest of the panel who have not yet been interviewed) until the entire jury is selected. Those members of the panel who are *excused* will also be sent back to the original jury room to wait to be called for another case.

Each individual Plaintiff and Defendant in a case is given four peremptory **challenges** to use to excuse an individual for any reason. If a case involves one Plaintiff and three Defendants, the Plaintiff will have four challenges and the Defendants will have a combined total of twelve. (But see Pbs 304A which permits the court to consider several Plaintiffs or Defendants as a single party.) When the Plaintiff runs out of challenges, he or she will be stuck accepting the next potential juror, unless the Defendants exercise one of their challenges, or the judge agrees to excuse the individual **for cause**.

Excused for cause usually means that the parties agree or the court determines that a potential juror should be disqualified to sit on a particular case. Therefore, neither party is required to use a challenge. The reasons can include a situation in which the individual's bias or prejudice toward or against one party is obvious, or, perhaps the individual is ill, or will be going into the hospital for major surgery during the trial. In some situations, a judge may completely excuse a person from the remainder of his or her jury duty. Note that pursuant to Pbs 304, neither deafness or hearing impairment alone will excuse a juror *for cause*.

In some courthouses, the trial judge and a courtroom clerk will preside over the Voir Dire. In other courts, only a clerk will be present. If the judge is present, it will be an easy matter to decide if someone should be excused for cause. If not, the parties will have to find an available judge to listen to their arguments and make a ruling.

Jury selection can take a day or as long as several weeks. It depends upon the type of case, the number of parties and the number of available challenges.

C. No Communications during Trial

In accordance with Pbs 305B, once the entire jury is selected, the trial judge will swear the panel in again and warn everyone to avoid and ignore all news reports of the case. In addition they must not discuss the case with anyone else until the judge tells them to begin deliberations. Then, they may discuss it only among themselves.

In addition, pursuant to Pbs 309A and 309C, until a jury has returned a verdict and the trial judge has dismissed the jury, "[n]o party or attorney, employee, representative or agent of any party or attorney shall contact, communicate with or interview any juror or alternate, or any relative, friend or associate of any jury or alternate juror" regarding the deliberations or verdict, unless the court grants permission. Any individual who violates this section could be charged and found in contempt of court.

D. Sequestering the Jury

To **sequester** a jury means that the jurors will not be permitted to go home or anywhere else until the trial is over. Instead, they will be required to attend the trial each day and reside at a specific motel or hotel, under the watchful eyes of sheriffs each evening and weekend. The purpose of sequestering a jury is to prevent the jurors from being contacted by the press or the public and to reduce their exposure to vast media coverage. Juries are rarely sequestered in civil cases. A party who wants the jury sequestered must bring the request to the trial judge's attention at the earliest possible time before jury selection begins.

III. OPENING STATEMENTS

Pbs 296 allows each party to make an **opening statement** to the jury (or the trial judge in a bench trial) regarding the nature of the case. Pursuant to Pbs 297, this opening statement should not take longer than one hour, unless otherwise ordered by the judge.

IV. PLAINTIFF'S BURDEN OF PROOF AND CASE-IN-CHIEF

A. Preponderance of Evidence

In order to win any case at trial, the Plaintiff must meet the required **burden of proof**. In most civil cases, this burden of proof is by **preponderance of the evidence**. By contrast, in criminal cases, the Plaintiff (being the State of Connecticut) must prove the case *beyond a reasonable doubt*. A small minority of civil cases involving family and juvenile matters require the Plaintiff to prove the case by *clear and convincing evidence*.

Over the years, I have heard these terms interpreted as follows:

1. Preponderance of the evidence: The Plaintiff must prove that the evidence weighs in his or her favor 51% or more, compared to the Defendant.

2. Clear and convincing evidence: The Plaintiff must prove that the evidence weighs in his or her favor 85% or more, compared to the Defendant.

3. Beyond a reasonable doubt: The Plaintiff must prove that the evidence weighs in his or her favor 95% or more, compared to the Defendant.

B. Plaintiffs Case-in-Chief

In every trial, the Plaintiff has the opportunity to present his or her case first. This is called the **Plaintiff's case-in-chief**. After the Plaintiff presents an opening argument, he or she must then present the evidence necessary to prove the case to the trier of fact.

The term **evidence** encompasses everything the parties introduce to the trier of fact during trial. Generally speaking, there are two types of evidence: testimony and exhibits.

1. Testimony

A witness's statements, made under oath, (pursuant to Pbs 7PP) to the trier of fact during a trial is called **testimony**. Witnesses include clients and are individuals who have knowledge pertaining to a case. (Don't forget to subpoena nonparty witnesses.

Otherwise, they are not subject to the court's jurisdiction if they fail to appear. The rules for subpoenaing nonparty witnesses to testify at trial are the same as for subpoenaing a nonparty witness to appear and testify at a deposition. See Chapter 24 and C.G.S. sec. 52-143 et seq. and 52-260.)

Some witnesses are permitted to wait in the courtroom to be called to testify. Other witnesses are sequestered. Unlike sequestered juries who are confined until the end of trial, sequestered witnesses are merely required to wait outside the courtroom until it is their turn to testify, unless they are under some type of protective custody. As a result, they are prevented from hearing the testimony of any other witnesses. The question of whether to sequester or not sequester witnesses should be addressed prior to the beginning of trial.

The Plaintiff calls witnesses, one at a time, to take the witness stand and asks them a series of questions through **direct examination**, in front of the trier of fact. The witness's responses are called **testimony**.

Direct examination involves questions that require an open-ended response, rather than a simple yes or no.

For instance:

Question 1: When did you first meet the Plaintiff? versus

Question 2. You met the Plaintiff the same day the Defendant collided into her car. Isn't that correct?

Question 1 is an open-ended question, appropriate to ask during direct examination. Question 2 is called a **leading question**: It requires merely a yes or no response, and is usually appropriate only during **cross examination**.

When the Plaintiff is finished with direct examination, the Defendant may then ask the witness questions about his or her testimony. This is called **cross examination**. Unlike direct examination, cross examination often involves a series of questions that require only a yes or no response.

When the Defendant is finished cross examining, the Plaintiff may again question the witness. This is called **re-direct examination.** Its purpose is to allow the witness to explain any issues raised or clouded during the cross examination. In many instances, the court will permit the Defendant to re-cross examine the Plaintiff's witness.

In many situations, an attorney will have another attorney, either from his or her law firm or from another firm, assist during the trial. According to Pbs 7QQ, however, only one attorney for each client may examine a witness.

2. Exhibits

Exhibits are tangible items that pertain to the case which a party introduces to the trier of fact through the witnesses. For instance, documents, photographs, medical reports, medical bills, etc. The clerk marks each exhibit that is introduced by each side, by number or letter, and keeps a list, pursuant to Pbs 7TT. The parties can stipulate, prior to trial, that specific documents or items will be entered as exhibits, or they can wait until trial.

When both parties have finished their examinations of a witness, the witness will be permitted to *step down*, meaning he or she is excused. The Plaintiff will then call the next witness and the process will begin again.

V. THE DEFENDANT'S CASE

When all of the Plaintiff's witnesses have been examined, the Plaintiff will **rest**. At that point, the Defendant will have the opportunity to present an opening argument and call his or her witnesses to the stand. Now, the Defendant will perform direct examination and the Plaintiff will perform cross examination, followed by re-direct and re-cross as described above.

VI. PLAINTIFF'S REBUTTAL

When the Defendant is finished presenting his or her case and rests, the Plaintiff will have the last word through rebuttal. **Rebuttal** is the Plaintiff's response to the evidence the Defendant presented. Witnesses called to testify during this time are called rebuttal witnesses.

VII. OBJECTING TO EVIDENCE

There are numerous rules that dictate if and in what matter testimony and exhibits should be introduced to the trier of fact. As with motions, a party who wishes to challenge specific evidence must object to it, in accordance with Pbs 7RR. The objection must take place at the time the evidence is being introduced. Pursuant to Pbs 7UU, only one attorney for each side may argue each issue as it arises, unless the court permits otherwise. After hearing both sides, the trial judge may rule on the issue or require the parties to brief the issue, pursuant to Pbs 7NN. (Note: consult the rules of evidence concerning taking an *exception* to a judge's ruling on an objection in order to preserve the right to appeal the ruling later.)

VIII. RULES REGARDING JURIES

A. *Note Taking*

Pbs 305A permits a trial judge to allow jurors to take notes and submit questions to be asked of witnesses during a civil trial.

B. *Insurance Coverage*

Pbs 230 states that a party's insurance coverage, or lack thereof, is not generally admissible at trial unless the dispute at issue specifically involves a contract for insurance. This matter depends upon the facts of each case and should be addressed prior to trial.

C. Viewing

In accordance with Pbs 308A, during the trial and before closing arguments, the trial judge may permit the jury to be brought to a specific location to view a scene or object, to assist the jury in determining a material factual issue in the case.

IX. CLOSING ARGUMENTS

After all the evidence is introduced and the parties have rested, each party may present a closing argument to the trier of fact. According to Pbs 297, each argument should not exceed one hour, unless the court orders otherwise. After the Defendant has completed his or her closing argument, the court often permits the Plaintiff to have one last opportunity to address the trier of fact.

According to Pbs 313, during closing arguments neither party may disclose to the jury the sum of damages the Plaintiff demanded in the Complaint (I presume this refers to the Statement of Amount in Demand) or any other specific amount of damages. Instead, any party may, during closing arguments, mention a lump sum or mathematical formula regarding damages claimed, subject to cautionary instructions made by the trial judge, pursuant to C.G.S. sec. 52-216b.

X. BENCH TRIAL DECISIONS

If the case is tried to the court, the trial judge may do one of the following:

1. Rule from the bench; or

2. Adjourn court and mail a memorandum of decision to the parties; or

3. Ask the parties to submit briefs, pursuant to Pbs 7NN, pertaining to the issues presented at trial. After the briefs are received the judge will then write a memorandum of decision and mail it to the parties.

XI. JURY TRIALS: INTERROGATORIES, REQUESTS TO CHARGE AND JURY INSTRUCTIONS

As stated in the previous chapter, in a jury trial, the judge's functions involve deciding issues and questions of law. When both parties have finished presenting their evidence and their closing arguments, the judge will then instruct the jurors on their role in the deliberations room and explain the principles of law that apply to the case. These instructions or the explanation are often referred to as **jury instructions** or the **judge's charge**. At this time, at the parties' request, the court will also submit **Interrogatories** (not related to any Interrogatories served as part of discovery) to the jury. During the Judge's Charge, the courtroom is usually locked, to prevent any interruptions or distractions.

A. Interrogatories

Pursuant to Pbs 312, the purpose of Interrogatories (these are different than those Interrogatories used as a discovery tool) is to ask the jurors to clarify their verdict by stating the *facts* (not the law) they determined to reach the verdict. As a result, Interrogatories may prevent the Plaintiff from unjustly receiving a **general verdict** in his or her favor on all of the counts or causes of action in the Complaint, if the facts determined by the jury only support a verdict for one count or cause of action.

Parties who want Interrogatories submitted to the jury must make this request in their **Requests to Charge**, to be discussed during the **charge conference**. (Both are described below.) If possible, the parties will work together to draft Interrogatories that are acceptable to everyone, and stipulate to them. The decision to submit Interrogatories is within the trial judge's discretion, although it appears that if there is more than one count or cause of action in the Plaintiff's Complaint, the Defendant's request should be granted.

B. Requests to Charge

Requests to Charge are a party's own written version of the jury instructions he or she wants the trial judge to use to explain the applicable law to the jury. Many judges already have their own jury instructions prepared, which they routinely use in civil cases. Other judges rely upon the parties to prepare this information. They will then review the information and make adjustments as they deem proper. Parties who draft a Request to Charge will find several texts in the law library that provide various versions of Requests to Charge that apply in civil cases.

C. Drafting a Request to Charge

Pbs 318 addresses Requests to Charge and includes the following:
1. Requests to Charge should not contain any more than 15 specific requests, unless the trial judge permits more for good cause shown.
2. Each request should be in paragraph form and numbered separately.
3. Each request should state the specific "proposition of law," clearly and concisely, *in only one way*, and include the authority (case law) to support the proposition and the evidence presented at trial that the proposition applies to.

In addition, pursuant to Pbs 317, the parties may amend their Requests to Charge in writing at any time before the beginning of the charge conference.

D. When Requests to Charge Are Mandatory

Pbs 316 states that Requests to Charge must be filed by any party who claims the benefit of any of the following:
1. supervening negligence;
2. superseding cause;
3. intervening cause;
4. assumption of the risk;
5. the provisions of any specific statute.

Requests to Charge are not required, but may be filed, in other types of cases.

E. Deadline to File Requests to Charge

In many cases, the judge will inform the parties when it wishes to receive their Request to Charge. Pbs 317 indicates that unless the judge orders otherwise, the requests should be hand delivered to the judge and a copy to opposing counsel, before the beginning of closing arguments.

F. Charge Conference

Pbs 318A permits either party to request a **charge conference**. During this conference, the trial judge will address the parties' Requests to Charge, if any, and disclose the general content of jury instructions (also known as the judge's charge) the jury will receive. This conference takes place out of the presence of the jury and before closing arguments. Any objections to the judge's proposed jury instructions should be made at this time and possibly resolved.

G. The Charge and Objections

After the trial judge charges the jury, the jury will be sent to a specific room to wait for further instructions. During this time, the judge will permit the attorneys to place their specific objections to the charge, and the grounds they rely upon, on the record. Pursuant to Pbs 318B and 318C, sometimes the judge will call the jury back and amend a portion of the charge. If not, the objecting attorney should take **exception** to the charge, pursuant to Pbs 315, in order to preserve the issue for appeal.

The purpose of an exception is to notify the judge that the attorney believes the judge's decision on a particular issue is wrong. As a result, the issue may be appealed to the Appellate Court or the Supreme Court after the trial.

According to Pbs 315, neither the Appellate Court nor the Supreme Court is required to consider alleged errors in a judge's charge unless:

1. the issue being appealed was addressed in the appealing party's written Requests to Charge; or

2. the appealing party took an exception to the issue, "immediately after the charge is delivered" to the jury (but out of the presence of the jury). In that exception, the attorney must state the "specific matter" he or she objects to and provide the grounds for the objection. (It will not hurt to still object and take exception, even if the issue was addressed in the Requests to Charge.)

XII. DELIBERATIONS

Jurors usually deliberate in a room adjacent to the courtroom they have been using each day while waiting for court to begin, during recesses and when the trial judge excuses them to listen to arguments from the attorneys that are not appropriate for them to hear. A court officer (often a deputy sheriff) is posted outside this room when the jury is inside, and especially during deliberations.

A. Beginning of Deliberations

At the start of deliberations, Pbs 309B directs the jury to receive all the exhibits accepted into evidence. In addition, at the court's discretion, the jury will receive:

1. the Complaint, Counterclaim and Cross Complaint and responsive pleadings thereto;

2. a copy or tape recording of the jury instructions (judge's charge);

3. upon the jury's requests, a copy or tape recording of an appropriate portion of the jury instructions.

B. During Deliberations: Review of Testimony and Request for Additional Instructions

During deliberations, the jury is permitted to request to review testimony of the trial under Pbs 318D. In addition, the jury may request the judge to reread a portion of the jury instructions or provide additional jury instructions to help reach a verdict. According to Pbs 318E, the judge will provide each party with the opportunity to make suggestions regarding this request for additional instructions.

XIII. THE VERDICT

A. Unanimous Verdict

Pursuant to Pbs 318G, in Connecticut, all six jurors must agree on the verdict. When the verdict is reached, the jury will contact the court officer guarding the room, who will notify the clerk, the judge and the parties. If the jury is unable to agree, Pbs

318F permits the judge to require it to continue deliberating, but will not threaten or require it to deliberate for unreasonable intervals or lengths of time. The judge may also provide instruction regarding disagreements.

B. Reconsideration

Pbs 311 permits a judge to send a jury back to deliberate further, up to three separate times, if it believes the jury has "mistaken the evidence in the cause and...brought in a verdict contrary to it" or brought in a verdict contrary to the court's direction on a matter of law.

C. Reading the Verdict

Once a verdict is reached, a member of the jury will write the verdict on a form and give the form to the court officer. The officer will give the form to the courtroom clerk who will hand it to the judge. After reviewing the verdict, the judge will give back the form to the clerk who will read the verdict aloud.

D. Polling the Jury

To be certain a jury verdict is unanimous, Pbs 318I permits either party to request that the jury be polled. This request must be made before the jury is discharged. In addition, the judge may proceed without a request.

To **poll the jury** means that the clerk will ask each individual juror, out loud, if the verdict announced was in fact his or her verdict. If the verdict was not unanimous, the jury will be sent back to continue deliberations or may be discharged.

E. Accepting the Verdict

Pursuant to Pbs 318H, if everything is in order, the judge will **accept the verdict** "without comment." Note, however, that the next chapter discusses motions that either party may make to challenge the verdict.

F. Discharging the Jury

After a verdict or a *mistrial*, Pbs 318J requires the judge to discharge the jury.

G. Impeachment of Verdict

Pbs 318K addresses impeaching a jury verdict due to jury misconduct.

XIV. CONCLUSION

A. Key Issues in This Chapter Include:

1. Two types of evidence are often introduced at trial: *exhibits* and *testimony* from witnesses.

2. Plaintiffs begin each case with their *case-in-chief.* When the Plaintiff *rests*, the Defendant presents his or her case, which is followed by the Plaintiff's *rebuttal.*

3. The Plaintiff's burden of proof is *preponderance of evidence.*

4. *Direct examination* takes place when a party questions his or her own witnesses. After direct examination, the opposing party will ask the witness questions through *cross examination. Re-direct, re-cross* and *rebuttal* will follow.

5. When submitting a *Request to Charge*, timely present it to the trial judge. Include *Interrogatories*, if applicable. In addition, ask the judge for a *charge conference*. During the conference, inform the judge of any objections you may have to the proposed jury instructions.

6. After the jury instructions are given, be sure to take *exception* on the record (outside the presence of the jury) to any portion objected to, in order to preserve the issue for appeal.

B. Relevant Connecticut Practice Book Sections Include:

Pbs 7D:	Court Opening
Pbs 7NN:	Trial Briefs
Pbs 7PP:	Administering Oath
Pbs 7QQ:	Examination of Witnesses
Pbs 7RR:	Objection to Evidence; Interlocutory Questions; Exceptions Not Required
Pbs 7TT:	Marking Exhibits
Pbs 7UU:	Interlocutory Matters
Pbs 230:	Disclosure of Amount and Provisions of Insurance Liability Policy
Pbs 296:	Argument by Counsel--Opening Argument
Pbs 297:	Argument by Counsel--Time Limit
Pbs 303C:	Preliminary Proceedings
Pbs 304:	Selection of Panel
Pbs 304A:	Peremptory Challenges
Pbs 305:	Conduct of Voir Dire
Pbs 305A:	Juror Questions and Note Taking
Pbs 305B:	Oath and Admonitions to Trial Jurors
Pbs 306:	Questions of Law and Fact
Pbs 308A:	View of Jury of Place or Thing Involved in Case
Pbs 309A:	Communications between Parties and Jurors

Pbs 309B:	Communications between Parties and Jurors--Materials to Be Submitted to Jury
Pbs 311:	Jury Returned for Reconsideration
Pbs 312:	Interrogatories
Pbs 313:	Reading of Statement of Amount in Demand or Statement of Claim: Argument Amount Recoverable
Pbs 315:	Requests to Charge and Exceptions--Necessity For
Pbs 316:	Requests to Charge and Exceptions--Request to Charge on Specific Claims
Pbs 317:	Requests to Charge and Exceptions--Filing Requests
Pbs 318:	Requests to Charge and Exceptions--Form and Content of Requests
Pbs 318A:	Requests to Charge and Exceptions--Charge Conference
Pbs 318B:	Modification of Instructions for Correction or Clarification
Pbs 318C:	Other Instructions
Pbs 318D:	Jury Request for Review of Testimony
Pbs 318E:	Jury Request for Additional Instructions
Pbs 318F:	Deadlocked Jury
Pbs 318G:	Verdict; Return of Verdict
Pbs 318H:	Acceptance of Verdict
Pbs 318I:	Poll of Jury
Pbs 318J:	Discharge of Jury
Pbs 318K:	Impeachment of Verdict

C. Relevant Connecticut General Statutes Include:

C.G.S. sec. 52-215a.: Jury of six in civil actions.

C.G.S. sec. 52-216a.: Reading of agreements or releases to jury prohibited. Adjustments for excessive and inadequate verdicts permitted.

C.G.S. sec. 52-216b.: Articulation to trier of fact of amount of damages claimed to be recoverable permitted.

31 *Motions Made During and After Trial*

Terminology

Bank Execution	Set Aside Verdict	Reduce Verdict	Mistrial
Remittitur	Prima Facie	Additur	Taxation of Costs
Judgment Lien	Wage Execution	Collateral Source	
Postjudgment	Property Execution	Stay of Execution	

Pbs: 320, 320A, 321, 322, 324, 325, 387, Chapter 14
C.G.S. sections: 52-216a, 52-225, 52-225a, 52-225b, 52-228, 52-228b,
52-240 et seq., 52-257 et seq., Chapter 906

Introduction

Under certain circumstances, the court may call a **mistrial** at any time during a trial and essentially end the case. In addition, at the end of the Plaintiff's case-in-chief, a Defendant may ask the court to end the trial and direct the verdict in his or her favor because the Plaintiff did not meet the burden of proof. Finally, after the jury reaches a verdict, the parties may file one or more of several motions that challenge the verdict within ten days of the judge's acceptance of the verdict.

I. MOTIONS MADE DURING TRIAL

A. *Mistrials*

A mistrial is appropriate at any time if it appears that the trial cannot or should not continue. Either party may make a motion, orally or in writing, for a mistrial, or the judge may call a mistrial on its own. A mistrial can be appropriate in bench trials and in jury trials. If a party is making a motion for a mistrial in a jury trial, the motion should be made outside the presence of the jury.

Examples of reasons for mistrials include: If the trial judge becomes ill in the middle of a long and complicated case and cannot complete the trial. Or, if one of the parties violates a rule or statute, such as inappropriately mentioning the availability of insurance to the jury, and the judge believes this reference will substantially interfere with and prejudice the jury's deliberations. Furthermore, if a jury cannot reach a unanimous verdict, regardless of its diligent efforts, the judge will call a mistrial. When a mistrial occurs, the case will be rescheduled to begin a new trial at another time.

B. *Motion for Dismissal: Bench Trials*

At the conclusion of the Plaintiff's case-in-chief, Pbs 302 permits the Defendant to make a motion to the court to dismiss the case, on the grounds that the Plaintiff failed to establish a **prima facie** case. In other words, the Defendant claims that the Plaintiff's evidence, if fully believed, would not permit the court to find in favor of the Plaintiff on the Complaint.

When deciding the motion, the court must treat the Plaintiff's evidence as true and draw every reasonable inference in the Plaintiff's favor. If a Motion for Dismissal is granted, the case is finished. If it is denied, the trial continues and the Defendant will present his or her case.

C. *Motion for Directed Verdict: Cases Tried to a Jury*

Pbs 321 makes reference to a Motion for Directed Verdict. This motion is appropriate in cases tried to a jury, not to the court. It is typically brought by the Defendant and should be made outside the presence of the jury, after the Plaintiff finishes his or her case-in-chief.

The purpose of a Motion for Directed Verdict is to ask the court to stop the trial, remove the case from the jury (discharge the jury), and render a verdict in the Defendant's favor. If the motion is denied, the trial will continue.

A Defendant making a Motion for a Directed Verdict must convince the court that the evidence presented by the Plaintiff, even if viewed in the Plaintiff's favor, will still cause the jury to reasonably and legally find in favor of the Defendant. Note that our courts do not grant a Motion for a Directed Verdict often. Instead, they prefer the jury to have the opportunity to hear the entire case and reach a verdict.

II. MOTIONS MADE AFTER VERDICT IS ACCEPTED

Pursuant to Pbs 320, unless the parties receive an extension of time, they have *ten days* from the day the verdict is accepted to file the following:

1. Motion to Set Aside Verdict: usually filed by the party who lost the case;
2. Motion for Remittitur: filed by the Defendant to reduce the verdict;

3. Motion for Additur: filed by a prevailing Plaintiff who wants the court to increase the verdict;

4. Motion for Reduction of Verdict: filed by the Defendant to reduce the verdict in the amount the Plaintiff has already received from **collateral sources**.

A. Motion to Set Aside Verdict

The grounds for a Motion to Set Aside Verdict must be stated in a written motion and assert that the evidence presented at trial does not support or justify the verdict. Therefore, the verdict must be set aside and a new trial must occur. See C.G.S. sec. 52-228b.

This motion is commonly filed by Plaintiffs in cases where the jury found in favor of the Defendant and did not award any damages to the Plaintiff. In addition, it is often filed if no damages are awarded on a Counterclaim or Cross Claim or to challenge a verdict in favor of the Plaintiff.

If the court grants the Motion to Set Aside Verdict, Pbs 322 requires it to file a memorandum of decision which states the grounds the court relied upon in reaching its decision.

B. Motion For Additur and Motion for Remittitur

These motions are authorized by Pbs 320 and are appropriate if the jury awards damages on a Complaint, Counterclaim or Cross claim.

1. A Motion for Additur permits the Plaintiff to ask the court to increase the amount of the jury's verdict, based upon the law and the evidence presented at trial.

2. A Motion for a Remittitur permits the Defendant to ask the court to reduce the jury's verdict, on the grounds of a mistake, clerical error or that the verdict is excessive, based upon the law and the evidence presented at trial. See also C.G.S. 52-216a, 52-228, and Pbs 325.

C. Motion to Reduce Verdict: Collateral Source Payments

A Motion to Reduce Verdict is appropriate if the jury awards damages to the Plaintiff and some or all of the Plaintiff's medical bills claimed in the lawsuit have already been paid by another source. This source is called a **collateral source** and usually involves payments made pursuant to medical insurance. In this situation, a Defendant is permitted to ask the court to reduce the jury's verdict by the amount of money the Plaintiff already received, either directly or on his or her behalf, from such collateral sources. See C.G.S. sec. 52-225a, 52-225b and Pbs 320. Note that verdicts in favor of Counterclaims and Cross Claims may also be reduced by the amount paid from a collateral source.

III. RENDERING JUDGMENT

A. *When No Motions Challenging the Verdict Are Filed*

Pursuant to Pbs 324, if no motions challenging the jury's verdict are filed within ten days after the judge accepts the verdict, the judge will render judgment on the verdict and include, if applicable, any adjustments required by statutes, with costs. The date of the judgment shall be the date the verdict was accepted.

B. *When Motions That Challenge the Verdict Are Filed*

After the court rules on one or more of these post-trial motions, it will render judgment according to its decision(s). The date of the judgment shall be the date the court decided the last motion. See C.G.S. sec. 52-225.

IV. TAXATION OF COSTS

Pursuant to C.G.S. sec. 52-240 et seq., 52-257 et seq., and Pbs 406 et seq., parties who win their cases at trial (not settlement) are entitled to be reimbursed by the opposing party for certain costs they expended in order to prosecute or defend the lawsuit. This is known an **taxation of costs**. Each case is addressed individually. Therefore, see the above-mentioned statutes and practice book rules for more information.

V. POSTJUDGMENT PROCEDURES: COLLECTING JUDGMENTS

Once a party (presume it's a Plaintiff) obtains a verdict in his or her favor, the next hurdles involve whether the Defendant will appeal, and if not, when and how the verdict (now called a judgment) will be paid. As stated back in Chapter 17, if a Plaintiff obtained a Prejudgment Remedy, the attached assets may be sufficient to pay the judgment, or if the Defendant is covered by sufficient insurance, the Plaintiff should have little difficulty being paid. If, on the other hand, the Defendant refuses to cooperate, or claims he or she is judgment proof, the Plaintiff must look to postjudgment procedures to determine how to collect from the Defendant.

Postjudgment procedures include filing a **judgment lien** against a Defendant's real estate (on the applicable land records) or, if appropriate, on his or her business (such as a corporation) at the Secretary of the State's Office.

Once a judgment lien is filed, the Defendant will not be able to sell or transfer the liened asset without first paying the judgment to the Plaintiff (because otherwise, the new buyer or transferee will become responsible for the Defendant's debt). In addition, the Plaintiff may foreclose on liened real estate and take the proceeds as payment of the judgment, or attempt to auction off other types of the liened assets belonging to a Defendant corporation.

A Plaintiff may also seek assistance from the court by filing a court-issued form which requests one of the following:

1. a **wage execution:** when the court orders the Defendant's employer to deduct a specific amount of money each pay period from the Defendant's paycheck and send it to the Plaintiff until the judgment is paid;

2. a **bank execution:** when the court orders a bank where the Defendant has an account to withdraw the funds in the account, up to the amount of the judgment (and permitted costs), and pay those funds to the Plaintiff;

3. a **property execution:** when the court orders the Defendant's assets (other than real estate) to be seized and sold at auction. The proceeds are paid to the Plaintiff, up to the amount of the judgment.

Note that bank, wage and property executions are usually handled by sheriffs or constables in their precincts. The money is paid first to them. They, in turn, will forward it to the Plaintiff. Their fee is usually 10 percent of the total amount received, above the amount of the judgment, and it is paid by the Defendant. Therefore, it does not cost the Plaintiff any additional money.

Because every case is different, see Pbs 387 and Chapter 906 of the Connecticut General Statutes for specific details.

VI. CONCLUSION

A. *Key Issues In This Chapter Include:*

1. A Motion for Mistrial and a Motion for Directed Verdict are made during the trial.

2. Parties who are dissatisfied with a verdict may file one or more of several motions within *ten days* of the trial judge accepting the verdict. If necessary, file a Motion for Extension of Time to file these motions, pursuant to Pbs 320.

B. *Appeal*

The trial is over. Now what? Either side who is aggrieved by the final judgment may appeal the case to the Appellate or Supreme Court. An appeal will **stay** the judgment. This means that if judgment entered for the Plaintiff, the Defendant will not be required to pay the judgment until after the appeal is decided. In the appeal, the aggrieved party will allege that the trial court made an error during the trial that was contrary to the law. As a result, the party is entitled to a new trial or to judgment in his or her favor.

C. Relevant Connecticut Practice Book Sections Include:

Pbs 320:	Motions after Verdict--Motions in Arrest of Judgment, to Set aside Verdict, for Additur or Remittitur, for New Trial or for Collateral Source Reduction
Pbs 320A:	Motions After Verdict--Motions to Reduce Verdict
Pbs 321:	Motions After Verdict--Reservation of Decision on Motion for Directed Verdict
Pbs 322:	Motions After Verdict--Memorandum of Decision on Setting Verdict Aside
Pbs 324:	Judgment on Verdict and Otherwise
Pbs 325:	Remittitur Where Judgment Too Large
Pbs 387:	Executions
Chapter 14:	Fees and Costs

D. Relevant Connecticut General Statutes Include:

C.G.S. sec. 52-216a.:	Reading of agreements or releases to jury prohibited. Adjustments for excessive and inadequate verdict permitted.
C.G.S. sec. 52-225.:	Judgment on verdict; assessment of damages when judgment rendered other than on verdict.
C.G.S. sec. 52-225a.:	Reduction in economic damages in personal injury and wrongful death actions for collateral source payments.
C.G.S. sec. 52-225b.:	"Collateral sources" defined.
C.G.S. sec. 52-228.:	Judgment too large; remittitur; correction.
C.G.S. sec. 52-228b.:	Setting aside of verdict in action claiming money damages.
C.G.S. sec. 52-240 et seq.:	Effect of damages on costs.
C.G.S. sec. 52- 257.:	Fees of parties in civil actions.
Chapter 906:	Postjudgment Procedures.

Example 1, Motion for Additur

DOCKET NO. CV 98-0333333 S	:	SUPERIOR COURT
SARAH A. DONAHUE	:	JUDICIAL DISTRICT
	:	OF TOLLAND
VS.	:	AT ROCKVILLE
RICHARD P. ANDREW	:	

MOTION FOR ADDITUR

Pursuant to Connecticut Practice Book Section 320, the Plaintiff, Sarah A. Donahue, hereby moves the court to increase the jury verdict accepted on _____, _____ on the ground that the award of noneconomic damages is inadequate as a matter of law, given the uncontroverted evidence at trial that the Plaintiff sustained permanent injuries.

Wherefore, the undersigned respectfully moves this court to increase the award of noneconomic damages consistent with the evidence at trial.

THE PLAINTIFF

BY_____

Christine Kulas, Esq.,
Law Offices of Christine Kulas,
her attorney
P.O. Box 2005
ORAL ARGUMENT REQUESTED
Ellington, CT 06066
TESTIMONY NOT REQUIRED
Tele. #(860) 222-2222
Juris #989898

ORDER

The foregoing Motion having been considered by the Court, it is hereby ORDERED: GRANTED/DENIED.

_____
BY THE COURT

CERTIFICATION

I hereby certify that a copy of the foregoing Motion for Additur was mail on _____ to all counsel and pro se parties of record, namely: Attorney Neil E. Clifford, of Michaels, Sabrina and Alexander, P.C., 259 Sage Road, Suite 200, West Hartford, CT 06080.

_____
Commissioner of the Superior Court

Example 2, Objection to Motion for Additur

DOCKET NO. CV 98-0333333 S	:	SUPERIOR COURT
SARAH A. DONAHUE	:	JUDICIAL DISTRICT
	:	OF TOLLAND
VS.	:	AT ROCKVILLE
RICHARD P. ANDREW	:	

OBJECTION TO MOTION FOR ADDITUR

The Defendant, Richard P. Andrew, hereby objects to the Plaintiff's Motion for Additur dated_____ on the grounds stated below.

The Plaintiff maintains that the verdict which awarded economic damages only is inadequate as a matter of law because the evidence introduced at trial demonstrated that she suffered permanent injuries. As a result, the Plaintiff is essentially asking the court to add noneconomic damages to the jury's verdict.

The evidence offered by the Plaintiff at trial indicated that she incurred medical bills in the amount of 9,035.00 and lost wages in the amount of $4,200. There was further evidence that she suffered a permanent partial disability to her _____.

In determining whether the verdict is inadequate as a matter of law, certain other evidence is pertinent. For instance, although Dr. Feller testified that the Plaintiff had been assessed with a permanent partial disability rating, the jury could have found that she nonetheless:

a. was capable of working at three different types of employment within six months after the accident;

b. earned $14,600 more during the year of her injury than she'd earned the previous year;

c. earned $23,000 more the year following the injury which she has maintained for the past two years before trial.

As a result, the jury could have reasonably found that the Plaintiff suffered minimal pain as a result of her injuries. It is also possible that the jury did not credit the evidence suggesting that the Plaintiff would be compelled to undergo future surgery.

It is the function of the jury to award fair, just and reasonable damages. If the verdict does not fall outside the limits of what amounts to reasonable compensation, it is improper for the court to increase the verdict pursuant to a Motion for Additur. Fox v. Mason, 189 Conn. 484, 489-490 (1983). Where the verdict does no go against the evidence and when there is no evidence that the jury was improperly influenced by prejudice, partiality, mistake or corruption, the verdict must stand. Ricket v. Fraser, 152

ORAL ARGUMENT REQUESTED
TESTIMONY NOT REQUIRED

Conn. 678, 682 (1965); Zarrelli v. Barnum Festival Society, Inc., 6 Conn. App. 322, 327 (1983). The jury had the right to accept part of the evidence presented and to reject the remainder. Ricket v. Fraser, supra, 581. Clearly, the jury in the instant case did not credit or believe that the Plaintiff's permanent partial injury justified noneconomic damages and the evidence introduced demonstrated that it could have reasonably and fairly reached the conclusion that it did.

Based upon the foregoing, the Defendant respectfully moves that his Objection to the Plaintiff's Motion for Additur be sustained.

THE DEFENDANT

BY_____

Neil E. Clifford, Esq.,
Michaels, Sabrina and Alexander, P.C.,
his attorney
259 Sage Road, Suite 200
West Hartford, CT 06080
Tele. # (860) 111-1111
Juris # 626262

ORDER

The foregoing Objection having been considered by the Court, it is hereby ORDERED: SUSTAINED/OVERRULED.

_____
BY THE COURT

CERTIFICATION

I hereby certify that a copy of the foregoing was mailed on _____ to all counsel and pro se parties of record, namely: Attorney Christine Kulas, Law Offices of Christine Kulas, P.O. Box 2005, Ellington, CT 06066.

_____
Commissioner of the Superior Court

32 *The Appeals Stage*

Terminology

Aggrieved Party   Notice of Intent to Appeal   Appellee

Appellant   Final Judgment   Rescript

Petition for Certification

Pbs: 204A, 204B, 4000, 4002A, 4002B, 4002C, 4002D, 4004, 4005 4009, 4010, 4017, 4023, 4024, 4027, 4040, 4120, 4182

C.G.S. sections: 51-197a, 51-199, 52-211, 52-592

Introduction

This chapter, along with Chapters 33 and 34, provides a broad overview of Appellate practice. Appellate practice is extremely specialized and the rules can be quite technical. In fact, entire texts have been devoted to appellate procedure and some law firms handle only appeals, and no other types of litigation. Therefore, be sure to read the rules found in the appellate practice section of the practice book beginning at Pbs 4000. It's a short section, compared to the Superior Court rules, but be careful. Follow the rules exactly as they are stated, consult other resources and call the Appellate Clerk's Office if you have any questions.

Reread the section in Chapter 2 pertaining to the Appellate and Supreme Courts. Also note that there is one clerk's office for both courts. It is located at 231 Capitol Avenue in Hartford. Last, like Superior Court rules, Appellate rules are to be liberally interpreted "to facilitate business and advance justice." See Pbs 4182.

I. THE SUPERIOR COURT AND APPEALS

A party who files an appeal disagrees with the outcome of his or her case in a lower court. In many instances, this lower court is the Superior Court and is usually referred to as the trial court when appeals are discussed. As a result, trial court judges constantly find themselves in the hot seat. Without warning, they are expected to make split-second decisions regarding all types of issues that arise. They don't have time to stop the trial and do hours of research or consult a law clerk. Instead, all eyes peer at these judges, expecting them to deliver instant pearls of wisdom. Afterward, if the case is appealed, the Appellate Court or Supreme Court will have several weeks or even months to review the trial record and the parties' briefs to determine if mistakes were made. Hence, trial court judges are at a significant disadvantage and work extremely hard to make proper rulings.

Appellate Court and Supreme Court decisions are released first in the *Connecticut Law Journal* which is delivered by mail each Monday to subscribers. Later, Appellate Court decisions are published in the *Connecticut Appellate Court Reports* and Supreme Court decisions are published in the *Connecticut Reports*. Both courts' decisions are also published in West's *Atlantic Reporters*. The **rescript**, which is a summary of the case, includes the name of the trial court judge at issue. See Pbs 4120.

II. THE PARTIES TO AN APPEAL

Pursuant to Pbs 4001A, the party who files an appeal is called the **Appellant**. The opposing party is called the **Appellee**. Pbs 4064, however, states that whenever possible, the parties are to be referred to as Plaintiffs and Defendants in their briefs and appendices. To avoid confusion here, we will use "Appellant" and "Appellee."

III. THE APPELLATE COURT AND THE SUPREME COURT: OVERVIEW

As you learned back in Chapter 2, Connecticut has a three-tiered court system. The Superior Court is the trial court and the lowest of the three tiers. The Appellate Court is often referred to as the intermediate court. It is not a trial court. Instead, each appeal is usually decided by a panel of three Appellate Court judges who refer only to the trial record, the parties' briefs and the law. These are no witnesses, exhibits and no new evidence presented. In Connecticut, any aggrieved party is entitled to appeal to the Appellate Court. See Chapter 33.

The Supreme Court is the highest court in the state. Only certain cases are decided by this court. C.G.S. sec. 51-199 provides a list of those cases that may be filed in the Supreme Court, directly from the Superior Court. The remainder must first be decided by the Appellate Court. If, after the appeal is decided, a party disagrees with the Appellate Court decision, he or she may file a **Petition for Certification** and ask the Supreme Court for permission to file an appeal. If the petition is granted, the appeal begins. If the petition is denied, the Appellate Court's decision stands. We will address the Supreme Court in greater detail in Chapter 34.

The court rules for both the Appellate Court and the Supreme Court are found in the appellate section of the Connecticut Practice Book. In many instances, the same rules apply to both courts.

IV. TRANSFERRING CASES

Before we begin, keep in mind that an appeal which is properly filed in the Appellate Court may be transferred to the Supreme Court. In addition, a proper Supreme Court appeal, filed directly from the Superior Court under C.G.S. sec. 51-199, may be transferred to the Appellate Court. The decision to transfer a case from one court to another rests solely with the Supreme Court. Furthermore, after filing an appeal in the Appellate Court, a party may file a Motion to Transfer the appeal to the Supreme Court. This motion should be directed to the Supreme Court and may be objected to by the opposing party. Last, cases that are filed in the wrong court will be transferred by the clerk, rather than dismissed. See Pbs 4023 et seq. for further details.

V. TYPES OF CIVIL CASES THAT MAY BE APPEALED: FINAL JUDGMENTS

Pursuant to Pbs 4000, "an *aggrieved party* may appeal from a **final judgment**, except as otherwise provided by law." (Emphasis added.) Typically, the aggrieved party is the party who loses his or his case in the Superior Court. A final judgment means that the trial court case has been decided and is now finished. See the examples stated below.

A. Judgment on an Entire Complaint

Pursuant to Pbs 4002A, the party who loses on an entire Complaint is an *aggrieved party* and may appeal that judgment to the Appellate Court. In these cases, the judgment is a *final judgment* because the case is over.

A final judgment on an entire Complaint may occur in one or more of the following ways:

1. after a trial, when a verdict is rendered in favor of either party;

2. when a Motion to Dismiss under Pbs 142 is granted;

3. when a Motion to Strike under Pbs 157 is granted;

4. when a Motion for Summary Judgment under Pbs 378 is granted.

B. Judgment on an Entire Counterclaim or Cross Complaint

Like a Complaint, a final judgment from a trial, a Motion to Dismiss, a Motion to Strike or a Motion for Summary Judgment can dispose of an entire Counterclaim or Cross Complaint. The case would then proceed at trial on the remaining Complaint.

C. Deferring an Appeal

This section gets complicated because it involves more than a simple Complaint. Take it slow.

According to Pbs 4002A, the aggrieved party *may* defer (delay) appealing a final judgment on a Counterclaim or Cross Complaint until after the entire case is concluded, instead of appealing the final judgment right away. Why? To see what happens in the remaining case. If the result of the case is favorable to the aggrieved party, he or she may not need to appeal the decision pertaining to the Counterclaim or Cross Complaint.

To defer the appeal, the aggrieved party must file a **Notice of Intent to Appeal** pursuant to Pbs 4002D. Note, however, that Pbs 4002D(2) allows any other party in the case to object to the deferment *if the objecting party is not a party to the remaining action.* Why? Because the result in the remaining case will not affect the objecting party. Therefore, he or she wants to get the appeal over with now, rather than waiting. If a timely objection is filed, the aggrieved party must file the appeal as described below in Section VI et seq.

On the other hand, if the aggrieved party is not a party to the remaining case and the final judgment resolved all the causes of action by or against that aggrieved party, the aggrieved party cannot file the appeal until the entire case is concluded. Instead, he or she **must** file a Notice of Intent to Appeal in order to preserve the rights to appeal after the entire case is concluded. See Pbs 4002D(1) for more details.

D. Judgment on Part of a Pleading

Pursuant to Pbs 4002B, a judgment that disposes of only a part of a pleading (a Complaint, Counterclaim or Cross Complaint) can still be a final judgment *if* the judgment disposes of all the causes of action in that pleading brought against or by a party or parties. This type of judgment usually occurs pursuant to a Motion to Dismiss, a Motion to Strike or a Motion for Summary Judgment that is granted as to part of the Complaint, Counterclaim or Cross Complaint, rather than as to the entire pleading.

According to Pbs 4002D(1), the aggrieved party *may* defer appealing this final judgment until the entire case is concluded by timely filing a Notice of Intent to Appeal. If an objection is filed by any party who is no longer a party in the remaining pleading, the aggrieved party must file the appeal.

On the other hand, Pbs 4002(2) *requires* a Notice of Intent of Appeal to be filed if the final judgment disposed of all the causes of action in the pleading "brought by or against a specific party or parties." Again, see the rules for further details.

E. Nonsuits, Default Judgments and Dismissals

1. *Nonsuits*

If a Superior Court judge grants a nonsuit against a Plaintiff, C.G.S. sec. 52-211 provides two courses of action:

a. appeal the nonsuit directly to the Appellate Court pursuant to C.G.S. sec. 51-197a (because the case is over); or

b. file a Motion to Set Aside Nonsuit pursuant to Pbs 377. If the motion is denied, that decision is a final judgment which may be appealed. If the motion is granted, the case will continue as if the nonsuit never occurred. (Don't forget that rather than appeal, it may be possible to file a new suit under C.G.S. sec. 52-592, the Accidental Failure of Suit statute.)

2. *Default Judgments and Dismissals*

The aggrieved party may appeal a Superior Court decision that denies a motion that asks it to set aside or open a judgment under Pbs 326 or 377. (Note that C.G.S. sec. 52-592 may be appropriate here also.)

F. Obtaining a Written Determination from the Appellate Court or the Supreme Court During a Trial

There are times when a trial court judge will permit a party to appeal a decision made during a trial because the issue is of "such significance to the determination of the outcome of the case." Once the issue is decided, the trial will continue and the trial court will follow the Appellate Court or Supreme Court's decision. See Pbs 4002C for more details.

VI. DEADLINE TO FILE AN APPEAL: 20 DAYS

Pursuant to Pbs 4009, an appeal must be filed within *20 days* from the date notice of the judgment or decision is "given." If a judge notified the parties of the judgment or decision in open court, the 20 days starts from that date. If the parties receive notice by mail, the 20 days starts from the date the notice was mailed.

A. Determining Deadlines

According to Pbs 4010, we do not count the day notice was given but we do count the 20th day. Therefore, be sure to file an appeal no later than 5:00 p.m. on the 20th day. If an appeal is due on a day that the court is closed, the appeal may be filed during the next day the court is open. This rule applies to all pleadings filed in the Appellate Court and the Supreme Court appeals (as well as the Superior Court).

B. Determining the Appeal Period: Motions for Waiver of Fees, Costs and Security

Any party in an appeal may file a Motion for Waiver of Fees, Costs and Security within *10 days* of the decision or judgment he or she wishes to appeal. If this motion is filed, the 20-day appeal period begins the day notice of the court's decision on the motion is given. See Pbs 4009 and 4017 for more details.

C. Determine the Appeal Period: A Decision or Judgment That Did Not Arise From a Jury Trial

The appeal period for decisions from a bench trial, or from granting a Motion to Dismiss, a Motion to Strike, or a Motion for Summary Judgment, begins from the date notice of the court's decision is given, as described above.

The appeal period for decisions granting a nonsuit or denying a Motion to Open Judgment upon Default or Nonsuit or Motion to Set Aside Dismissal begins from the date notice of the court's decision is given, as described above.

D. Determining the Appeal Period: After a Jury Trial

Pursuant to Pbs 4009(a), after a jury trial, the aggrieved party may file any of the motions listed below within *10 days* after the day the verdict is accepted by the court. These motions could render the final judgment ineffective if they are granted:
   1. Motion to Set Aside the Verdict (Pbs 320 and 321);
   2. Reduction of Verdict Due to Collateral Source Payments
   (C.G.S. sec. 52-225a).

If none of these motions are filed, the 20-day appeal period begins at the expiration of the 10 days as stated above. If the aggrieved party wants to file one or more of the above-stated motions, the 20-day appeal period begins as of the date notice of the court's decision on the last motion filed is issued (given). According to Pbs 4009(d), if more than one motion is to be filed, they should be filed simultaneously. In addition, keep in mind that if any of the above-stated motions are granted, the party who opposes the motion may become the aggrieved party and file an appeal.

According to Pbs 4009(b), the appeal period will also be delayed if a party files a **Motion for Remittitur** (Pbs 320) or a **Motion for Additur** (Pbs 320). If either motion is denied, the appeal period begins when notice of the denial is given. If either is granted, the appeal period begins at the earliest occurrence of:
   1. the court's acceptance of the additur or remittitur; or
   2. the expiration of the time set for acceptance.

E. Filing a Motion Which Delays the Commencement of the Appeal Period or Causes the Appeal Period to Begin Again

Pbs 204A requires these motions (listed above) to be decided by the trial judge involved in the judgment or decision at issue. The motion itself should include the following:

1. the judgment or decision that is being appealed;
2. the name of the judge who rendered the judgment or decision at issue;
3. the specific grounds the party relies on to file the motion;
4. at the bottom of the first page, "that the motion is a Sec. 204A motion."

F. Determining the Appeal Period: Motions for Extension of Time

Pbs 4009 and 4040 permit the aggrieved party to file a Motion for Extension of Time to file any of the above-stated motions (along with Pbs 320) and to file an appeal.

G. Motions Filed After the Appeal Is Filed

An Appellant may file an appeal within the 20-day period, and also file the motions listed above during that same 20-day period. See Pbs 4009(c) if you wish to take this course of action.

H. Motions to Reargue under Pbs 204B

According to Pbs 4009(d), a Motion to Reargue under Pbs 204B will not delay the time to file an appeal.

VII. JOINT AND CONSOLIDATED APPEALS AND CROSS APPEALS

Joint or Consolidated Appeals and Cross Appeals are addressed in Pbs 4004 and 4005.

VIII. CONCLUSION

A. Key issues in This Chapter Include:

1. Appeals may be taken from *final judgments* only.
2. The *Appellant* is the party who brings the appeal. The *Appellee* is the opposing party.
3. An appeal must be filed *within 20 days after notice of the final judgment or decision was given.* This deadline may be affected by motions which delay the commencement of the appeal period.

4. Remember: This chapter only highlights some of the more common issues that arise in appellate practice. Be sure to refer to the Rules of Appellate Procedure in the Connecticut Practice Book, the Connecticut General Statutes and case law before filing an appeal.

B. Relevant Connecticut Practice Book Rules Include:

Pbs 204A:	Motions Which Delay the Commencement of the Appeal Period or Cause the Appeal Period to Start Again
Pbs 204B:	Motion to Reargue
Pbs 4000:	Right to Appeal
Pbs 4002A:	Appeal of Judgment on Entire Complaint, Counterclaim or Cross Complaint
Pbs 4002B:	Appeal of Judgment on Entire Complaint, Counterclaim or Cross Complaint That Disposes of All Claims in That Pleading Brought By or Against One or More Parties
Pbs 4002C:	Appeal of Judgment on Entire Complaint, Counterclaim or Cross Complaint That Does Not Disposes of All Claims in That Pleading Brought By or Against One or More Parties
Pbs 4002D:	Deferring Appeal Until Judgment Rendered That Disposes of Case of All Purposes and as to All Parties
Pbs 4004:	Joint and Consolidated Appeals
Pbs 4005:	Cross Appeals
Pbs 4009:	Time to Appeal
Pbs 4010:	Expiration of Time Limitations
Pbs 4017:	Waiver of Fees, Costs and Security--Civil Cases
Pbs 4023:	Transfer of Cases--By Supreme Court
Pbs 4024:	Transfer of Cases-Motion for Transfer From Appellate Court to Supreme Court
Pbs 4027:	Transfer of Matters Brought to Wrong Court
Pbs 4040:	Extension of Time
Pbs 4120:	Opinions; Rescripts; Notice
Pbs 4182:	Rules to Be Liberally Interpreted

C. Relevant Connecticut General Statutes Include:

C.G.S. sec. 51-197a .:	Appeals to Appellate Court. Writs. Transfer of jurisdiction from appellate session.
C.G.S. sec. 51-199.:	Jurisdiction.
C.G.S. sec. 52-211. :	Refusal to set aside nonsuit; appeal.
C.G.S. sec. 52-592.:	Accidental failure of suit; allowance of new action.

33 *Appeals:*
The Appellate Court

Terminology

Amicus Curiae	Articulation	Rectification
Certificate of Completion	Preargument Statement	Brief
Reply Brief	Preargument Conference	Judgment File
Docketing Statement	Docket Sheet	Record
Transcript Order	Memorandum of Decision	Sanctions
Preliminary Statement of Issues		
Preliminary Designation of Specific Pleadings		

Pbs: 336, 4007, 4012, 4013, 4014, 4015, 4019, 4051, 4056, 4064, 4086, 4103, 4106 et seq, 4118 et seq., 4120, 4121 et seq., 4184A, 4184B, 4184C

Introduction

The Connecticut Appellate Court judges' chambers and courtrooms where appeals are heard are located on the fourth floor at 95 Washington Street in Hartford. Don't forget, however, that all paperwork must be filed at the Appellate Clerk's Office located at 231 Capitol Avenue in Hartford.

I. HOW TO FILE AN APPEAL IN THE APPELLATE COURT: A TWO-PART PROCESS

A. *Part One: The Appeal begins in Superior Court*

According to Pbs 4012, to begin an appeal, certain items must be filed in the *clerk's office of the trial court* (also known as the clerk's office in the Superior Court)

where the decision or judgment at issue was made, within *20 days* of the commencement of the appeal period. These items include:

1.The original appeal form, known as "Appeal to the Appellate Court" which can be obtained from the clerk's office in any Superior Court;

2. A certification of service, pursuant to Pbs 4014, that a copy of the appeal form has been served on all counsel of record, including pro ses. In the certification of service, include the names, addresses, telephone numbers, and fax numbers of everyone served.

3. A filing fee under Pbs 4015.

B. Part Two: Filing in The Appellate Clerk's Office

Pursuant to Pbs 4013, the Superior Court clerk will sign, date and stamp the original appeal form and make a copy to give to the Appellant, along with a **docket sheet** which lists all the pleadings filed in the Superior Court case. The Appellant must then "forthwith," file the copy of the appeal form and the docket sheet at the Appellate Clerk's Office in Hartford.

In addition, Pbs 4013 requires the Appellant to file an *original* and *one copy* of the following:

1. Preliminary Statement of Issues: the issues the Appellant intends to present on appeal. See Pbs 4013(a)(1).

2. Preliminary Designation of Specific Pleadings: pleadings that are part of the trial court record which the Appellant believes are necessary to be included in the record. Include the date each pleading was filed and the number as shown on the docket sheet. See Pbs 4013(a)(2).

3. A Copy of the **Transcript Order Form** or a **Certificate That No Transcript Is Necessary:** This form may be obtained from any court reporter's office in each courthouse. See Pbs 4013(a)(3). Section 1 of the Transcript Order Acknowledgment form must be completed by the court reporter.

4. Docketing Statement: To the best of the Appellant's knowledge, this statement lists:

a. names and addresses of all parties to the appeal;

b. names and addresses of all trial and appellate counsel;

c. names and addresses of any persons having a legal interest in the case on appeal, "sufficient to raise a substantial question whether a judge should be disqualified from participating in the decision on the case due to that judge's personal or financial interest in any persons";

d. docket numbers and case names of all pending appeals which "arise from substantially the same controversy as the cause on appeal, or involve issues closely related to those presented on appeal;"

e. if there are any exhibits in the trial court. See Pbs 4013(a)(4).

5. A Preargument Statement: a brief statement regarding the case which will to be read by the judge (who is usually a retired Appellate Court judge) who will schedule a **preargument conference** to attempt to settle the case. (See Pbs 4013(a)(5).

6. A draft **judgment file:** a document that states the terms of the judgment. The clerk at the Appellate Court will send this draft to the clerk of the trial court at issue. The trial court clerk then has 20 days to send the original judgment file to the Appellate Court. See Pbs 336 and 4013(a)(6).

7. If the Appellant is challenging the constitutionality of a state statute, he or she must identify that statute, and whether it was upheld by the trial court. See Pbs 4013(a)(7).

8. Signature on Papers and Certification of Service: Pursuant to Pbs 4030, all papers that are filed must be signed by the attorney of record. In addition, pleadings and other papers that are to be filed must also include the signer's address, telephone and fax number and Juris Number, if applicable.

Furthermore, Pbs 4014 requires that all documents contain a   certification of service: that a copy was served on all counsel of record (and pro ses). Include the names, addresses and telephone and fax numbers.

C. Appellee's Response

Within *20 days* of the Appellant filing the above-stated documents, the Appellee may:

1. File his or her own Preliminary Statement of Issues to present:
    a. alternative grounds for the Appellate Court to affirm the judgment;
    b. adverse rulings or decisions the trial court made, to be considered on appeal, in the event the Appellate Court orders a new trial;
    c. claim that if the appeal is successful, the Appellate Court should order a new trial, rather than direct judgment in the Appellant's favor. See Pbs 4013(a)(1).

2. Object to the Appellant's Preliminary Designation of the Specific Pleadings. See Pbs 4013(a)(2) and 4086.

3. Supplement the Appellant's Docketing Statement. See Pbs 4013(a)(4).

4. Object to or supplement the proposed judgment file. See Pbs 4013(a)(6).

To file any of the above, include the ***original*** and ***one copy***. In addition, be sure to include a certification of service that copies were sent to the opposing party.

In addition, the Appellee may file a Motion to Dismiss the appeal, if grounds exist. See Pbs 4056 and Sanctions, Section VIII for more details.

D. *Amendments*

Amendments may be made to the Preliminary Statement of Issues and the Preliminary Designation of Specific Pleadings before that party's brief is filed. The docketing statement may be amended at any time. If the Transcript Order Form needs to be amended, the party must first obtain permission from the Appellate Court to amend the form and notify the court reporter. See Pbs 4013(b).

II. TRANSCRIPTS

A. *The Appellant*

Pursuant to Pbs 4019(c), (d) and (e), once the Appellant's transcript order is completed, the Appellant will receive the transcript and a **Certificate of Completion**, which states the total number of pages in the entire transcript and the date of final delivery. Accordingly, the Appellant must then:

1. Immediately, send a copy of the completed transcript to all counsel of record in the appeal and file a certification of service with the Appellate Clerk's Office.

2. File a nonreturnable copy of the transcript at the Appellate Clerk's Office before or at the same time his or her brief is filed. Also include a copy of the court reporter's certification, which is found on the transcript order form filed at the beginning of the appeal.

3. When filing the copy of the transcripts, include a list of the number of volumes of transcripts and the dates involved, and send a copy of the list to all opposing counsel.

B. *The Appellee*

The Appellee must follow the same rules regarding transcripts as stated above except that he or she need not file copies of transcripts that the Appellant has already filed.

III. BRIEFS: Pbs 4064 et Seq.

Remember, there are no witnesses, no exhibits and no testimony presented in the Appellate Court. Instead, appeals are decided upon the trial court record, the party's briefs, oral argument and the law. Pbs 4064 et seq, provides directions for drafting and filing briefs.

A. How to File a Brief

Pursuant to 4064A, each party filing a brief must file, in the Appellate Clerk's Office, an *original* and *15 copies* of the brief, along with a certification of service that a copy has been sent to all counsel of record and the trial court judge whose decision is at issue in the appeal.

B. Size of Brief

Pursuant to Pbs 4064B, all briefs should be double spaced and printed on one side of the paper. In addition:

1. The Appellant's brief should be no more than *35 pages*.
2. The Appellee's brief should also be no more than *35 pages*.
3. The Appellant may file a **reply brief** containing no more than *15 pages*.
4. Either party may include an appendix. These pages will not count as part of the brief.
5. Either party may file a motion asking the court to extend the length of his or her brief.

C. Appearance of Brief: Firmly Bound with Cover Sheets

Pursuant to Pbs 4064A, each brief shall be firmly bound on the left side. In addition:

1. The Appellant must have a light blue cover sheet on each brief.
2. The Appellee must have a pink cover sheet on each brief.
3. The cover sheet for the Appellant's reply brief should be white.
4. The content of the cover sheets is stated in detail in Pbs 4064A.

D. When to File Briefs

1. The Appellant's Brief

Pursuant to Pbs 4064B, the Appellant's brief is due within *45 days* after the transcript is *delivered*. Pbs 4019(c) addresses this issue as follows:

> **a.** If the court reporter delivered the transcript by certified mail, the delivery date is the date of mailing.
>
> **b.** If the court reporter hand delivered the transcript, he or she should obtain a receipt acknowledging delivery on that date. The delivery date is the date the transcript was hand delivered.
>
> If no transcript is ordered, then the brief is due within *45 days* of filing the appeal.

2. *The Appellee's Brief*

According to Pbs 4064B, the Appellee's brief is due within *30 days* after the Appellant files his or her brief, or after the Appellee receives the transcripts he or she ordered, whichever is later.

3. *The Appellant's Reply Brief*

According to Pbs 4064B, the Appellant may file a **reply brief** within *20 days* after the Appellee files his or her brief.

4. *Extension of Time*

Either party may file a Motion for Extension of Time to file a brief pursuant to Pbs 4040.

E. *Content of the Brief for Both Parties*

Pbs 4064 (C) and (D), address the content and format of briefs. Review these sections carefully for important details. In general, each party's brief should contain the following:

1. For the Appellant: Statement of Issues; For the Appellee: Counter Statement of Facts
2. Table of Authorities cited in the brief;
3. For the Appellant: Statement of Facts; For the Appellee: Counter Statement of Facts
4. Argument;
5. Conclusion and Statement of Relief Requested;
6. Signature;
7. In the original only, a certification of service that a copy was sent to all counsel and the trial court that rendered the decision that is the subject matter of the appeal.

IV. PROVIDING AN ADEQUATE RECORD FOR THE APPELLATE COURT

A. *An Adequate Record*

Pursuant to Pbs 4007, the Appellant must provide an adequate record of the Superior Court proceedings for the Appellate Court to review in reaching its decision. This record includes:

1. transcripts of the trial or court proceeding at issue;
2. all exhibits introduced into evidence;
3. all trial court decisions;
4. any other pleadings or documents in the Superior Court file or introduced into evidence that will assist the Appellate Court in reaching its decision.

B. *Motion for Articulation: Pbs 4051*

Pursuant to Pbs 4051, a **Motion for Articulation** is appropriate when it is unclear how or why the trial court judge reached a decision. For instance, if a party receives a simple notice in the mail which states a trial court judge's decision, without an explanation, the party must file a Motion for Articulation and ask the trial court judge to explain its decision. Otherwise, the Appellate Court will have no idea how to determine if that decision was right or wrong. If there is no articulation, the Appellate Court will not address the issue and the entire appeal could end up being a total waste of time and money.

1. *When to File a Motion for Articulation*
   a. If necessary, a Motion for Articulation should be filed before a party's brief is filed, as described below. Specifically, the motion should be filed within *35 days* after the last portion of the trial transcript is delivered; or
   b. If no transcript has been ordered, within *35 days* after filing the appeal; or
   c. If a **memorandum of decision** was not filed by the trial court judge at the time the appeal was filed, but was filed afterward, and if a Motion for Articulation is still necessary because the decision is unclear, file the motion within *35 days* after the memorandum of decision was filed.
   d. A Motion for Extension of Time to file a Motion for Articulation may be granted for good cause.

2. *How to File a Motion for Articulation*
   File an *original* and *three copies* with the Appellate Clerk's Office.

3. *Objection to Motion for Articulation*
   If the Appellee opposes the Motion for Articulation, he or she must file an *original* and *three copies* of the objection with the Appellate Clerk's Office within *ten days* of the Appellant filing the Motion for Articulation.

4. *Other Motions to File to Correct the Record: **Motion for Rectification***
   Pbs 4051 permits a Motion for Rectification to correct any mistakes in a transcript to the Superior Court record. All the timelines and directions to file a Motion for Articulation apply to a Motion for Rectification. If further rectification or articulation is needed, a party has *20 days* from the issuance of notice of the trial court's decision to file a Motion for Further Articulation or Motion for Further Rectification.

5. When the Trial Court Does Not Cooperate

If the trial court refuses to articulate or correct the record or to further articulate, the party may file a **Motion for Review** with the Appellate Court clerk. If the motion is granted, the trial court will be directed to comply with the party's original motion.

Pursuant to Pbs 4054, a Motion for Review must be filed within *ten days* after the trial court's decision denying the Motion for Articulation or Motion for Articulation. If the Motion for Review is granted, the trial court will be directed to comply with the party's original motion

V. PREARGUMENT CONFERENCES

Like the Superior Court, the Appellate Court will schedule a conference for all the parties to attend in an attempt to settle the case and/or address important issues. As a result, this conference resembles pretrial conference. See Pbs 4103.

VI. ORAL ARGUMENT

After the briefs are filed, the Appellate Court clerk will notify the parties when to appear for oral argument. Again, keep in mind that this court appearance is to present oral argument regarding the facts of the case and the law to the Appellate Court. There are no witnesses, no evidence and no testimony presented. See Pbs 4106-4112.

The Appellate Court panel, which will consist of three judges, may ask questions but it will not inform the parties of its decision at the time of oral argument. Instead, the decision will be kept secret until it is released in print in the *Connecticut Law Journal*. Eventually, it will be reprinted in the *Connecticut Appellate Reports*.

VII. AMICUS CURIAE

This term is known as "friend of the court." This "friend" may be an individual or a government agency, such as the Office of the Connecticut Attorney General. It may ask the court's permission to submit a brief in a specific case to express its views. This usually occurs in cases that involve issues of broad public interest. See Pbs 4064F.

VIII. SANCTIONS

Pbs 4184A, 4184B and 4184C address sanctions a party may be subject to if he or she does not comply with the Appellate Court rules. For instance, parties who unduly delay the appellate process or who file unnecessary or unwarranted motions, or present a frivolous appeal or defense, may be subject to sanctions such as being prohibited from appearing in court or filing other motions for a specific period of time, or being fined or having their appeals dismissed. The court may order such sanctions on its own motion, or the motion may be made by the opposing party at any time. Pbs 4184C requires a hearing before the court imposes sanctions.

In addition to a Motion for Sanctions, Pbs 4056 permits the Appellee may file a Motion to Dismiss, based upon the Appellant's lack of compliance with the court's rules such as filing a late appeal.

IX. MOTIONS TO REARGUE

Motions to Reargue or Reconsider, or Motions for En Banc Reargument are addressed in Pbs 4121 et seq.

X. TAXATION OF COSTS

See Pbs 4118 et seq. to address the prevailing party's costs.

XI. CONCLUSION

A. *Key Issues in This Chapter Include:*

1. *Filing an Appeal*
File the court-issued Appeal form and $250 fee at the Superior Court where the final judgment occurred. Immediately after filing the appeal in the Superior Court, file the appeal form signed by the clerk and the *docket statement* at the Appellate Clerk's office along with an original and one copy of the following:

    a. *Preliminary Statement of Issues;*
    b. *Preliminary Designation of Specific Pleadings*;
    c. *Transcript Order Form or Certificate of No Transcript*;
    d. *Docketing Statement*;
    e *Preargument Statement* (a form);
    f. a draft *Judgment File.*

Be sure to appropriately sign and provide a certification of service on each document filed that a copy was properly delivered to the opposing party.

2. *Appellee's Response*
The Appellee may file an *original* and *one copy* of the following:

    a. *Preliminary Statement of Issues*;
    b. *Objection to the Designation of Specific Pleadings*;
    c. *Objection or Supplemental Docketing Statement*;
    d. *Objection to the Judgment File*;
    e. certification of service.

3. *Briefs: Both* parties must file one *original* and *15 copies* of their brief. In addition:

    a. The Appellant's brief is due within *45 days* from the date the transcripts are delivered. If no transcripts were ordered, the brief is due within *45 days* from the date the appeal was filed.

    b. The Appellee's brief is due within *30 days* after the Appellant files his or her brief, or within *30 days* after the Appellee's transcript is delivered, whichever is later.

    c. The Appellant's *reply brief* is due within *20 days* after the Appellee's brief is filed.

4. *Motion for Articulation*

    The Appellant must provide an adequate *record* for the Appellate Court to review. As a result, a *Motion for Articulation or a Motion for Rectification* may be filed to ask the trial court to clarify a decision or correct errors in the file. If necessary, the Appellant may file a *Motion for Further Articulation* or *Motion for Further Articulation*. Be sure to file the correct number of copies of these motions and any others that are filed, along with a certification of service.

5. *Motion for Review*

    If the trial court does not cooperate with a Motion for Articulation or a Motion for Rectification, the party may file a *Motion for Review*, asking the Appellate Court for assistance.

6. *Oral Argument*

    Oral argument does not include exhibits, testimony or any new evidence. Instead, it simply highlights the issues on the appeal, as addressed in the parties' briefs.

7. *Sanctions*

    The Appellate Court has the authority to punish a party who does not comply with its rules by ordering *sanctions*.

8. *Decisions*

    Appellate Court (and Supreme Court) decisions are released and printed each Monday in the *Connecticut Law Journal*. Eventually these decisions are reprinted in the *Connecticut Appellate Reports*.

B. Relevant Connecticut Practice Book Rules Include:

Pbs 336 et seq.:   Judgment Files
Pbs 4007:   Responsibility of Appellant to Provide Adequate Record

Pbs 4012: Filing Appeal--In General; Number of Copies

Pbs 4013: Filing Appeal--Additional Papers to Be Filed by Appellant and Appellee

Pbs 4014: Matters of Form; Filings; Number of Copies; Certification to Counsel

Pbs 4015: Fees

Pbs 4019: Ordering and Filing Transcript

Pbs 4051: Motion for Rectification; Motion for Articulation

Pbs 4056: Motion to Dismiss

Pbs 4064: Brief and Appendix

Pbs 4064A: Briefs and Appendix--Format; Copies

Pbs 4064B: Briefs and Appendix--Page Limitations; Time for Filing

Pbs 4064C: Brief and Appendix--The Appellant's Brief

Pbs 4064D: Brief and Appendix--The Appellee's Brief

Pbs 4064F: Brief and Appendix--The Amicus Curiae Brief

Pbs 4086: Record--Content of Record

Pbs 4103: Preargument Conference

Pbs 4106-4112: Right to Oral Argument

Pbs 4118 et seq.: Costs Included in Judgments

Pbs 4120: Opinions; Rescripts; Notice

Pbs 4121 et seq.: Motions for Reargument or Reconsideration; Motions for En Banc Reargument

Pbs 4184A: Lack of Diligence in Prosecuting or Defending Appeal

Pbs 4184B: Other Actions Subject to Sanctions

Pbs 4184C: Procedure on Sanctions

34 *Appeals:*
The Supreme Court

Terminology

Petition for Certification   Request for Certification
Justices   Statement in Opposition to Petition

Pbs: 4064A et seq., 4103 et seq., 4106 et seq., 4121 et seq., 4126, 4127,
    4129,4130,4131, 4135 et seq., 4136, 4138, 4184A et seq.

Introduction

This chapter will discuss petitioning the Supreme Court to file an appeal from a decision made by the Appellate Court. Judges who are appointed to the Supreme Court bench are called **justices**.

I. CERTIFICATION TO THE SUPREME COURT

A. *There Is No Right to a Supreme Court Appeal*

An appeal to the Supreme Court is not automatic. Instead, the party who is aggrieved by an Appellate Court decision must ask permission to file a Supreme Court appeal in a **Petition for Certification.**

B. *Possible Reasons Why the Supreme Court May Accept Certification*

Pbs 4127 lists the types of cases that may be taken by the Supreme Court. The list is not exhaustive, nor is the Supreme Court bound by this list. Instead, it has sole discretion to accept any appeal, for any reason.

The Supreme Court may grant a Petition for Certification in the following circumstances:

1. when the Appellate Court has determined an issue that has not been previously addressed by the Supreme Court, or decided a case in a way that may not follow applicable Supreme Court precedent;

2. when the Appellate Court decision conflicts with other Supreme Court decisions;

3. when the Supreme Court believes the Appellate Court may have acted in a manner that may require Supreme Court supervision;

4. when issues of great public importance are involved;

5. when the Appellate Court judges agree on the end result of a case, but do not agree on the grounds for that decision;

6. when, prior to deciding an appeal, the Appellate Court informs the Supreme Court that it believes a transfer to the Supreme Court is appropriate. This is known as a **Request for Certification** and is discussed in Pbs 4135 et seq.

II. FILING A PETITION FOR CERTIFICATION

A. Time to File

Pbs 4129 states that a Petition for Certification must be filed by the aggrieved party by the earlier of:

1. within *20 days* of the date the Appellate Court decision is officially released. This is the date the decision is published in the *Connecticut Law Journal*; or

2. within *20 days* of issuance of notice of any order or judgment by the Appellate Court that finally determines the case.

If a motion such as a Motion to Reargue under Pbs 4121 et seq., or a Motion for Waiver of Fees and Costs is filed within that initial 20-day period, a new 20-day period will begin to run, as of the date notice of a decision on the motion is issued by the court.

Pbs 4132 indicates that a party who needs more time may file a Motion for Extension of Time. See Pbs 4040 for more details.

B. What to File: Petition and Fee

1. Pbs 4129 requires one *original* petition and *one copy* to be filed with the clerk of the trial court.

2. At this time, the filing fee is $75 and is not needed if the case involves a worker's compensation appeal.

3. The trial court clerk will date stamp the *original* Petition for Certification and give it back to the petitioner.

4. the petitioner must then file the ***original*** and ***ten copies*** of the Petition for Certification, along with a certification of service, at the Appellate Clerk's Office.

If the petition and fee are filed at a trial court that was not the original trial court, the Appellant must send a copy to the original trial court clerk's office also.

C. Content of the Petition: Pbs 4130

A Petition for Certification should be no more than ***ten pages***, exclusive of the index, and shall contain the following sections, in the order listed:
1. Statement of the Questions Presented for Review;
2. Statement of the Basis for Certification;
3. Summary of the Case (material facts);
4. Argument: state the reasons relied upon to support the petition; no other memorandum of law will be accepted;
5. Index containing:
      a. copy of the Appellate Court opinion or order at issue;
      b. copy of any motion which would stay or extend the time for filing the petition;
      c. list of all parties to the appeal in the Appellate Court, including names, addresses, telephone and fax numbers, and Juris Numbers.

D. Opposition to Petition for Certification: Pbs 4131

1. Statement of Opposition to Petition
A party who opposes certification must file a Statement in Opposition to Petition. This pleading should disclose any reasons why the Supreme Court should not grant certification and respond to the Petition for Certification, in form and content. This is not a Motion to Dismiss, but any jurisdictional challenges should be included. No other memorandum of law on this issue will be accepted.

2. Where and When To File
The ***original*** Statement in Opposition to Petition and ***ten copies*** must be filed in the Appellate Clerk's Office within ***ten days*** of the Petition for Certification being filed in the trial court. It should not be more than ***ten pages*** long, except with permission from the court.

III. WHEN CERTIFICATION IS GRANTED OR DENIED

A. A Vote

According to Pbs 4136, a Petition for Certification will be granted by an affirmative vote of two or more Supreme Court justices. At this stage, the petitioner will become the Appellant. If the petition is denied, the Appellate Court's decision stands as the final decision.

B. The Appellant: Filing Fees and Notice to Counsel of Record

Pursuant to Pbs 4138, an Appellant who is granted certification must pay the applicable Supreme Court filing fees to the Appellate Clerk's Office within *20 days* of issuance of notice that certification was granted, and certify a notice to all counsel of record that the fees have been paid.

C. The Appellant: Docketing Statement

Also pursuant to Pbs 4138, the Appellant must file a docketing statement as mentioned in Pbs 4013(a)(4).

D. Other Documents to File

Within *14 days* from the time notice of certification was sent, the Appellee may file alternative grounds to affirm the judgment, if he or she had filed such alternative grounds during the Appellate Court appeal.

In addition, during that 14 day period, *any party* may raise adverse rulings or decisions to be considered in the event of a new trial, if such adverse rulings or decisions were raised in the Appellate Court appeal. If these matters were not raised, the party may ask the Supreme Court permission to raise them. Note, however, that Pbs 4140 states that such permission "will be granted only in exceptional cases... ."

Last, *any party* may raise any claim to modify the relief "afforded by the Appellate Court in its judgment" if the claim was raised to the Appellate Court in the party's brief or as part of a Motion to Reargue. See Pbs 4140.

IV. SUPREME COURT BRIEFS

A. Time to File

Pbs 4138 requires the Appellant's brief to be filed within *45 days* from the issuance of notice of certification.

The Appellee's brief and the Appellant's reply brief shall follow Pbs 4064B:
1. Appellee's brief: within *30 days* after Appellant's brief is filed;
2. Appellant's reply brief: within *20 days* after Appellee's brief is filed.

B. The Issues

Pursuant to Pbs 4138, the issues on appeal to the Supreme Court are limited to what was stated in the Petition for Certification, unless the Supreme Court further limited the issues when it granted certification, or unless the Supreme Court granted permission to address additional issues as discussed in Section III, D above.

C. Number of Copies and Pages of Briefs

1. The *original* brief and *25 copies* must be filed within the time limits stated above. In addition, the original must contain a certification of service that a copy was sent to all counsel of record and to the trial court that rendered the decision which is the subject of the appeal.
2. The page limitations are the same as for an Appellate Court brief.
3. Amicus Curiae briefs are permitted as in the Appellate Court.

V. PREARGUMENT CONFERENCE

According to Pbs 4103, parties to a Supreme Court appeal have the same opportunity to attempt to settle the case or address other relevant issues during a preargument conference, as stated in the previous chapter.

VI. ORAL ARGUMENT

Five justices sit at one time to hear oral argument. Again, there are no witnesses, no testimony, and no new evidence is presented. Instead, arguments presented refer to the facts of the case and the applicable law. See Pbs 4106 et seq.

VII. SANCTIONS

Pbs 4184 A, B, and C apply in the Supreme Court as well as to the Appellate Court.

VIII. MOTION TO REARGUE, RECONSIDERATION; MOTION FOR EN BANC REARGUMENT

These motions are addressed in Pbs 4121 et seq.

IX. MISCELLANEOUS SUPREME COURT MATTERS

Consult the applicable rules and statutes for appeals directly to the Supreme Court from the trial court, for writs of error, for reservations, etc.

X. CONCLUSION

A. *Key Issues in This Chapter Include:*

1. *Filing a Petition for Certification*
    a. An *original* and *one copy* of the Petition for Certification must be filed in the trial court clerk's office within *20 days* of the date the Appellate Court decision to be appeals is issued. Include the required fee.
    b. Afterward, the petitioner must file the *original* and *10 copies* of the Petition for Certification at the Appellate Clerk's Office.
    c. An opposing party may file an Opposition to Petition for Certification within *10 days* of the Petition for Certification being filed.

2. *When Certification is Granted*
    a. If the Petition for Certification is granted, the Appellant (who prior to this time was the petitioner) must pay the required Supreme Court filing fee within *20 days* and notify the opposing party.
    b. The Appellant's brief is due within *45 days* of the date the Petition for Certification was granted and should be no longer than *35 pages*.
    c. The Appellee's brief is due within *30 days* of the Appellant's brief being filed and should be no longer than *35 pages*.
    d. The Appellant's reply brief, if any, is due within *20 days* of the Appellee's brief being filed and should be no longer than *20 pages*.

B. Some Final Words

As I said in the first chapter of this text, the Connecticut Supreme Court dictates the law of the land. In spite of its selective discretion in accepting cases, the Supreme Court has plenty of work to do each September-through-July term.

When practicing litigation in any court, always double check the Practice Book and statutes. Laws and rules are amended every year and it's necessary to stay current.

Finally, good luck, keep your chin up and remember: Law is an argumentative profession. If everyone got along, there would be no need for attorneys. Don't fight the conflicts. Instead, allow them to stretch the limits of your imagination as you perfect the art of persuasion.

C. Relevant Connecticut Practice Book Sections Include:

Pbs 4064A et seq.:	Brief and Appendix-Format; Copies
Pbs 4103 et seq.:	Preargument Conference
Pbs 4106 et seq.:	Right to Oral Argument
Pbs 4121 et seq.:	Motions for Reargument or Reconsideration; Motions for En Banc Reargument
Pbs 4126:	Certification by Supreme Court
Pbs 4127:	Certification by Supreme Court--Basis for Certification
Pbs 4129:	Certification by Supreme Court--Petition; Time to File; Where to File; Service; Fee
Pbs 4130:	Certification by Supreme Court--Form of Petition
Pbs 4131:	Certification by Supreme Court--Statement in Opposition to Petition
Pbs 4135 et seq.:	Request for Certification by Appellate Panel--Determination of Request for Certification
Pbs 4136:	Grant or Deny Certification
Pbs 4138:	Proceedings after Certification by Supreme Court--Appeals Deemed Pending
Pbs 4140:	Proceedings after Certification by Supreme Court--Papers to Be Filed by Appellant and Appellee
Pbs 4184A:	Lack of Diligence in Prosecuting or Defending Appeal
Pbs 4184B:	Other Actions Subject to Sanctions
Pbs 4184C:	Procedure on Sanctions

APPENDIX A: LITIGATION CHECKLIST FOR SUPERIOR COURT

Name of Case:_____ Date of Incident:_____

Statute of Limitations: _____ Jurisdiction:_____

Trial Date and Court: _____ Conclusion:_____

I. THE COMPLAINT

Cause of Action:_____

Draft Complaint:_____ Return Date:_____

Judicial District:_____ Location:_____ Summons:_____

II. SERVE DEFENDANT

Name and Tele. # of Proper Officer:_____

Deadline to Make Service: _____ Approve Return of Service: _____

Type of Service and Location:_____

Deadline to File, Summons, Complaint, Return of Service and Filing Fee:_____

Receive Notice from Court Re: Docket No.:_____

III. DEFENDANT'S APPEARANCE

Deadline for Defendant to Appear:_____ Date Filed:_____

Name, Address, Telephone and Fax of Defense Attorney:_____

_____

IV. THE PLEADINGS: DEFENDANT'S FIRST PLEADING DUE:_____

A. Motion to Dismiss:_____ Obj. Due:_____

Short Calendar Date:_____ Oral Argument:_____

Name of Judge:_____

Decision:_____

Action Taken:_____

B. Request to Revise:_____ Obj./Compliance Due:_____

Short Calendar Date:_____ Oral Argument:_____

Judge:_____

Decision:_____

Action Taken:_____

C. Motion to Strike:_____ Obj./Compliance Due:_____

Short Calendar Date: _____ Oral Argument:_____

Judge:_____

Decision:_____

Action Taken:_____

D. Defendant's Answer: _____ Special Defenses:_____

Reply Due:_____ Counterclaim:_____

(If yes, start new check list)

E. Closed Pleadings: Certificate of Closed Pleadings:_____

Jury:_____ Fee:_____   Bench Trial:_____

V. PLAINTIFF'S DISCOVERY AND DEFENDANT'S COMPLIANCE

A. *Interrogatories and Requests to Production*

Served to:_____

Date Served:_____ Responses/Obj. Due:_____

Date Responses/Objections Received:_____

Motion to Extend Time?:_____

Discovery Conference Dates and Results:_____

Affidavit Needed?:_____ Filed:_____

Short Calendar Date:_____ Judge:_____

Decision:_____

Action Taken:_____

B. *Requests for Inspection/Examination*

Served to:_____

Date Served:_____ Responses/Obj. Due:_____

Date Responses Received:_____ Date Objections Received:_____

Motion to Extend Time Due:_____ Received:_____

Discovery Conference Results Dates and Results:_____

Affidavit Needed?_____ Date Filed:_____

Short Calendar Date:_____ Judge:_____

Decision:_____

Action Taken:_____

C. Disclosure of Defendant's Expert Witnesses

Date Disclosed:_____

Names:_____

D. Requests for Admission

Served to:_____

Date Served:_____ Responses/Obj. Due:_____

Date Responses and Objections Received:_____

Motion for Extension of Time?:_____ New Date:_____

Short Calendar Date: _____ Judge:_____

Decision:_____

Action Taken:_____

E. Request for Mental or Physical Exam

Served to:_____

Date Served:_____ Name of Doctor:_____

Objection Due:_____

Short Calendar Date:_____ Judge:_____

Decision:_____

Compliance:_____ Name of Doctor:_____

F. Depositions of Parties: Notices by Hand Delivery or Certified Mail

Name:_____ Date:_____ Notice:_____

Court Reporter:_____ Transcript Received:_____

Copy of Transcript Sent to Other Parties:_____

Name:_____ Date:_____ Notice:_____

Court Reporter:_____ Transcript Received:_____

Copy of Transcript Sent to Other Parties:_____

G. Depositions of Nonparties: Subpoenas and Notices

Name:_____ Date:_____ Subpoena: _____ Notice:_____

 Court Reporter:_____ Transcript Received:_____

Copy of Transcript Sent to Other Parties:_____

H. Other Discovery and Compliance Issues:

VI. DEFENDANT'S DISCOVERY TO PLAINTIFF AND PLAINTIFF'S COMPLIANCE

A. *Interrogatories and Requests to Production*

Served to:_____

Date Served:_____ Responses/Obj. Due:_____

Date Responses/Objections Received:_____

Motion to Extend Time?:_____

Discovery Conference Dates and Results:_____

Affidavit Needed?:_____ Filed:_____

Short Calendar Date:_____ Judge:_____

Decision:_____

Action Taken:_____

B. *Requests for Inspection/Examination*

Served on:_____

Date Served:_____ Responses/Obj. Due:_____

Date Responses Received:_____ Date Objections Received:_____

Motion to Extend Time Due:_____ Received:_____

Discovery Conference Results Dates and Results:_____

Affidavit Needed?_____ Date Filed:_____

Short Calendar Date:_____ Judge:_____

Decision:_____

Action Taken:_____

C. Disclosure of Plaintiff's Expert Witnesses

Date Disclosed:_____

Names:_____

D. Requests for Admission

Served to:_____

Date Served:_____ Responses/Obj. Due:_____

Date   Responses   and   Objections

Received:_____

Motion for Extension of Time?_____ New Date:_____

Short Calendar Date:_____ Judge:_____

Decision:_____

Action Taken:_____

E. Request for Mental or Physical Exam

Served to:_____

Date Served:_____ Name of Doctor:_____

Objection Due:_____

Short Calendar Date:_____ Judge:_____

Decision:_____

Compliance:_____ Name of Doctor:_____

F. Depositions of Parties: Notices by Hand Delivery or Certified Mail

Name:_____ Date:_____ Notice:_____

Court Reporter:_____ Transcript Received:_____

Copy of Transcript Sent to Other Parties:_____

Name:_____ Date:_____ Notice:_____

Court Reporter:_____ Transcript Received:_____

Copy of Transcript Sent to Other Parties:_____

G. Depositions of Nonparties: Subpoenas and Notices

Name:_____ Date:_____ Subpoena _____ Notice:_____

Court Reporter:_____ Transcript Received:_____

Copy of Transcript Sent to Other Parties:_____

H. Other Discovery and Compliance Issues:

VII. PRETRIAL

Date:_____ Judge:_____

VIII. TRIAL

Date:_____ Judge:_____

IX. CONCLUSION

A. Settlement:_____

B. Verdict:_____

C. Appeal:_____

APPENDIX B: ALPHABETICAL LISTING OF TOWNS/CITIES AND APPLICABLE COURTS

TOWN/ CITIES	JD	GA#	JUVENILE
Andover	Tolland	19	Willimantic
Ansonia	Ansonia-Milford	5	Waterbury
Ashford	Windham	11	Willimantic
Avon	Hartford-New Britain	16	Plainville
Barkhamsted	Litchfield	18	Torrington
Beacon Falls	Ansonia-Milford	5	Waterbury
Berlin	Hartford-New Britain	15	Plainville
*Bethany	New Haven or Ansonia-Milford	6	New Haven
Bethel	Danbury	3	Danbury
Bethlehem	Litchfield	18	Torrington
Bloomfield	Hartford-New Britain	16	Hartford
Bolton	Tolland	19	Rockville
Bozrah	New London	21	Montville
Branford	New Haven	8	New Haven
Bridgeport	Fairfield	2	Bridgeport
Bridgewater	Litchfield	18	Danbury
Bristol	Hartford-New Britain	17	Plainville
Brookfield	Danbury	3	Danbury
Brooklyn	Windham	11	Willimantic
Burlington	Hartford-New Britain	17	Plainville
Canaan	Litchfield	18	Torrington
Canterbury	Windham	11	Willimantic
Canton	Hartford-New Britain	16	Plainville
Chaplin	Windham	11	Willimantic
Cheshire	New Haven	7	Waterbury
Chester	Middlesex	9	Middletown
Clinton	Middlesex	9	Middletown
Colchester	New London	21	Montville
Colebrook	Litchfield	18	Torrington
Columbia	Tolland	19	Willimantic
Cornwall	Litchfield	18	Torrington
Coventry	Tolland	19	Willimantic

TOWN/ CITIES	JD	GA#	JUVENILE
*Cromwell	Middlesex or Hartford/New Britain	9	Middletown
Danbury	Danbury	3	Danbury
*Darien	Stamford-Norwalk or Fairfield	1	Norwalk
Deep River	Middlesex	9	Middletown
Derby	Ansonia-Milford	5	Waterbury
Durham	Middlesex	9	Middletown
Eastford	Windham	11	Willimantic
East Granby	Hartford-New Britain	13	Plainville
East Haddam	Middlesex	9	Middletown
East Hampton	Middlesex	9	Middletown
East Hartford	Hartford-New Britain	12	Hartford
East Haven	New Haven	8	New Haven
East Lyme	New London	10	Montville
Easton	Fairfield	2	Bridgeport
*East Windsor	Hartford-New Britain or Tolland	13	Rockville
Ellington	Tolland	19	Rockville
*Enfield	Hartford-New Britain or Tolland	13	Rockville
Essex	Middlesex	9	Middletown
Fairfield	Fairfield	2	Bridgeport
Farmington	Hartford-New Britain	16	Plainville
Franklin	New London	21	Montville
Glastonbury	Hartford-New Britain	12	Hartford
Goshen	Litchfield	18	Torrington
Granby	Hartford-New Britain	13	Plainville
*Greenwich	Stamford-Norwalk or Fairfield	1	Stamford
Griswold	New London	21	Montville
Groton	New London	10	Montville
Guilford	New Haven	8	New Haven
Haddam	Middlesex	9	Middletown
Hamden	New Haven	7	New Haven
Hampton	Windham	11	Willimantic
Hartford	Hartford-New Britain	14	Hartford
Heartland	Litchfield	18	Plainville

TOWN/ CITIES	JD	GA#	JUVENILE
Harwinton	Litchfield	18	Torrington
Hebron	Tolland	19	Willimantic
Kent	Litchfield	18	Torrington
Killingly	Windham	11	Willimantic
Killingworth	Middlesex	9	Middletown
Lebanon	New London	21	Montville
Ledyard	New London	10	Montville
Lisbon	New London	21	Montville
Litchfield	Litchfield	18	Torrington
Lyme	New London	10	Montville
Madison	New Haven	8	New Haven
*Manchester	Hartford-New Britain or Tolland	12	Rockville
Mansfield	Tolland	19	Willimantic
Marlborough	Hartford-New Britain	12	Willimantic
Meriden	New Haven	7	Middletown
Middlebury	Waterbury	4	Waterbury
Middlefield	Middlesex	9	Middletown
Middletown	Middlesex	9	Middletown
*Milford	Ansonia-Milford or New Haven	22	New Haven
Monroe	Fairfield	2	Bridgeport
Montville	New London	21	Montville
Morris	Litchfield	18	Torrington
Naugatuck	Waterbury	4	Waterbury
New Britain	Hartford-New Britain	15	Plainville
*New Canaan	Stamford-Norwalk or Fairfield	20	Norwalk
New Fairfield	Danbury	3	Danbury
New Hartford	Litchfield	18	Torrington
New Haven	New Haven	6	New Haven
Newington	Hartford-New Britain	15	Plainville
New London	New London	10	Montville
New Milford	Litchfield	18	Danbury
Newtown	Danbury	3	Danbury
Norfolk	Litchfield	18	Torrington
North Branford	New Haven	8	New Haven
North Canaan	Litchfield	18	Torrington

TOWN/CITIES	JD	GA#	JUVENILE
North Haven	New Haven	7	New Haven
North Stonington	New London	10	Montville
*Norwalk	Stamford-Norwalk or Fairfield	20	Norwalk
Norwich	New London	21	Montville
Old Lyme	New London	10	Montville
Old Saybrook	Middlesex	9	Middletown
Orange	Ansonia-Milford	5	New Haven
Oxford	Ansonia-Milford	5	Waterbury
Plainfield	Windham	11	Willimantic
Plainville	Hartford-New Britain	17	Plainville
*Plymouth	Hartford-New Britain or Waterbury	17	Torrington
Pomfret	Windham	11	Willimantic
Portland	Middlesex	9	Middletown
Preston	New London	21	Montville
Prospect	Waterbury	4	Waterbury
Putnam	Windham	11	Willimantic
Redding	Danbury	3	Danbury
Ridgefield	Danbury	3	Danbury
Rocky Hill	Hartford-New Britain	15	Plainville
Roxbury	Litchfield	18	Danbury
Salem	New London	21	Montville
Salisbury	Litchfield	18	Torrington
Scotland	Windham	11	Willimantic
Seymour	Ansonia-Milford	5	Waterbury
Sharon	Litchfield	18	Torrington
Sherman	Danbury	3	Danbury
Shelton	Ansonia-Milford	5	Bridgeport
Simsbury	Hartford-New Britain	13	Plainville
Somers	Tolland	19	Rockville
*Southbury	Waterbury or Ansonia-Milford	4	Waterbury
Southington	Hartford-New Britain	17	Plainville
*South Windsor	Hartford-New Britain or Tolland	12	Rockville
Sprague	New London	21	Montville
Stafford	Tolland or Fairfield	19	Rockville

TOWN/ CITIES	JD	GA#	JUVENILE
*Stamford	Stamford-Norwalk or Fairfield	1	Stamford
Sterling	Windham	11	Willimantic
Stonington	New London	10	Montville
Stratford	Fairfield	2	Bridgeport
Suffield	Hartford-New Britain	13	Rockville
Thomaston	Litchfield	18	Torrington
Thompson	Windham	11	Willimantic
Tolland	Tolland	19	Rockville
Torrington	Litchfield	18	Torrington
Trumbull	Fairfield	2	Bridgeport
Union	Tolland	19	Willimantic
Vernon	Tolland	19	Rockville
Voluntown	New London	21	Montville
Wallingford	New Haven	7	New Haven
Warren	Litchfield	18	Torrington
Washington	Litchfield	18	Torrington
Waterbury	Waterbury	4	Waterbury
Waterford	New London	10	Montville
*Watertown	Waterbury or Litchfield	4	Torrington
Westbrook	Middlesex	9	Middletown
West Hartford	Hartford-New Britain	16	Hartford
*West Haven	Ansonia-Milford or New Haven	22	New Haven
*Weston	Stamford-Norwalk or Fairfield	20	Norwalk
*Westport	Stamford-Norwalk or Fairfield	20	Norwalk
Wethersfield	Hartford-New Britain	15	Plainville
Willington	Tolland	19	Willimantic
*Wilton	Stamford-Norwalk or Fairfield	20	Norwalk
Winchester(Winsted)	Litchfield	18	Torrington
Windham	Windham	11	Willimantic
Windsor	Hartford-New Britain	13	Hartford
Windsor Locks	Hartford-New Britain	13	Rockville
Wolcott	Waterbury	4	Waterbury

TOWN/ CITIES	JD	GA#	JUVENILE
*Woodbridge	New Haven or Ansonia-Milford	6	New Haven
*Woodbury	Waterbury or Litchfield	4	Torrington
Woodstock	Windham	11	Willimantic

Notes:

1. *C.G.S. sec. 51-345(a) permits a Plaintiff to select either judicial district if either the Plaintiff or the Defendant resides in that town. See C.G.S. sec. 51-345(b) for cases involving land.

2. Judicial District of New Britain: C.G.S. sec. 51-345(a) as of 9/1/98.

As stated in the text, it is anticipated that New Britain will eventually separate from Hartford and become its own Judicial District. In addition, it may contain 2 JD courthouses: one in New Britain and the other in Bristol. Check the general statutes thereafter for cities and towns originally in the Hartford-New Britain JD.

3. Judicial District of New Haven

New Haven has two GA courts: #6 and #8. Both are held at 121 Elm Street in New Haven but have jurisdiction of different areas of New Haven County, as you can see from the list above and on the next few pages.

4. The information in this appendix can also be found in the State of Connecticut Judicial Directory which is published by the Commission on Official Legal Publications. Copies are available at Superior Court clerk's offices.

APPENDIX C: ADDRESSES AND TELEPHONE NUMBERS OF CONNECTICUT SUPERIOR COURTS*

1. Ansonia-Milford
Superior Court:	14 W. River Street, Milford, CT 06460	(203) 877-4293
GA #5:	106 Elizabeth Street, Derby, CT 06418	(203) 735-7438
GA #22:	14 W. River Street, Milford, CT 06460	(203) 874-1116

2. Danbury
Superior Court:	146 White Street, Danbury, CT 06810	(203) 797-4400
GA #3:	146 White Street, Danbury, CT 06810	(203) 797-4400
Juvenile Matters:	71 Main Street, Danbury, CT 06810	(203) 797-4407

3. Fairfield
Superior Court:	1061 Main Street, Bridgeport 06604	(203) 579-6527
GA #2:	172 Golden Hill Street, Bridgeport, CT 06604	(203) 579-6568
Housing Session:	172 Golden Hill Street, Bridgeport, CT 06604	(203) 579-6936
Juvenile Matters:	784 Fairfield Ave., Bridgeport, CT 06604	(203) 579-6588

4. Hartford-New Britain
This is the largest JD in the state. It contains two separate Superior Courts, each of which consist of two separate buildings, dividing civil matters from criminal matters. In addition, it contains six GA's, two Housing Sessions, two Juvenile Matters locations and Connecticut's only Tax Court. In September 1998, Hartford and New Britain will separate and each become a JD.

Superior Court in Hartford:
Civil:	95 Washington Street, Hartford, CT 06106	(860) 548-2700
Criminal:	101 Lafayette Street, Hartford, CT 06106	(860) 548-2700
GA #14:	101 Lafayette Street, Hartford, CT 06106	(860) 566-1630
Housing Session:	18 Trinity Street, Hartford, CT 06106	(860) 566-8550
Juvenile Matters:	920 Broad Street, Hartford, CT 06106	(860) 566-8270
Tax Court:	100 Washington Street, Hartford, CT 06106	(860) 566-7972

Superior Court in New Britain:
Civil:	177 Columbus Blvd., New Britain, CT 06051	(860) 827-7133
Criminal:	125 Columbus Blvd., New Britain, CT 06051	(860) 827-7106
GA #15:	125 Columbus Blvd., New Britain, CT 06051	(860) 827-7106
Housing Session:	177 Columbus Blvd. CT 06051	(860) 827-7111
GA# 12:	410 Center Street, Manchester, CT 06040	(860) 647-1091

GA#13:	111 Phoenix Ave., Enfield, CT 06082	(860) 741-3727
GA #16:	105 Raymond Rd., West Hartford, CT 06107	(860) 236-4551
GA#17 :	131 N. Main St., Bristol, CT 06010	(860)582-8111
Juvenile Matters:	31 Cooke Street, Plainville, CT 06062	(860) 747-5701

5. Litchfield

Superior Court:	15 West Street, Litchfield, CT 06759	(860) 567-0885
GA #18:	80 Doyle Rd., Bantam, CT 06750	(860) 567-3942
Juvenile Matters:	139 New Litchfield St., Torrington, CT 06790	(860) 489-0201

6. Middlesex

Superior Court:	1 Court Street, Middletown, CT 06457	(860) 343-6400
GA #9:	1 Court Street, Middletown, CT 06457	(860) 343-6445
Juvenile Matters:	230 Main St. Extension, Middletown, CT 06457	(860) 344-2986

7. New Haven: There are Two JD Courthouses.

Superior Court:	235 Church St., New Haven, CT 06510	(203) 789-7908
GA# 6 & GA#8:	121 Elm St., New Haven, CT 06510	(203) 789-7461
Housing Session:	121 Elm St., New Haven, CT 06510	(203) 789-7937
Juvenile Matters:	239 Whalley Ave., New Haven, CT 06511	(203) 786-0337

Superior Court:	54 W. Main St., Meriden, CT 06450	(203) 238-6666
GA #7:	54 W. Main St., Meriden, CT 06450	(203) 238-6130

8. New London: There are Two JD courthouses.

Superior Court:	70 Huntington St., New London, CT 06320	(860) 443-5363
GA #10:	112 Broad St., New London, CT 06320	(860) 443-8343
Superior Court:	1 Courthouse Square, Norwich, CT 06360	(860) 887-3515
GA #21:	1 Courthouse Square, Norwich CT 06360	(860) 889-7338
Juvenile Matters:	869 Norwich-New London Tpke., Uncasville, CT 06382	(860) 848-9213

9. Stamford-Norwalk

Superior Court:	123 Hoyt St., Stamford, CT 06905	(203) 965-5307
GA # 1:	115 Hoyt St., Stamford, CT 06905	(203) 965-5208
Juvenile Matters:	91 Prospect St., Stamford, CT 06901	(203) 348-7355
Housing Session:	17 Belden Ave., Norwalk, CT 06850	(203) 846-4332
GA #20:	17 Belden Ave., Norwalk, CT 06850	(203) 846-3237
Juvenile Matters	11 Commerce St., Norwalk, CT 06850	(203) 866-9275

10. <u>Tolland</u>
Superior Court: 69 Brooklyn Street, Rockville, CT 06066   (860) 875-6294
GA#19:   20 Park St., Rockville, CT 06066   (860) 870-3200
Juvenile Matters: 25 School St., Rockville, CT 06066   (860) 872-7143
                            mailing address: c/o GA #19, 20 Park St., Rockville, CT 06066

11. <u>Waterbury</u>
Superior Court: 300 Grand St., Waterbury, CT 06702   (203) 596-4023
GA #4:   7 Kendrick Ave., Waterbury, CT 06702   (203) 596-4050
Housing Session: 300 Grand St., Waterbury, CT 06702   (203) 596-4061
Juvenile Matters: 83 Prospect St., Waterbury, CT 06702   (203) 596-4202

12. <u>Windham</u>: There are two JD courthouses but most activity takes place in Putnam.
Superior Court: 155 Church St., Putnam, CT 06260   (860) 928-7749
GA#11:   172 Main Street, Danielson, CT 06239   (860) 774-8516
                         108 Valley St., Willimantic, CT 06226   (860) 423-6364
Juvenile Matters: 316 Pleasant St., Willimantic, CT 06226   (860) 423-7743
Superior Court: 108 Valley St., Willimantic, CT 06226   (860) 423-8491

*All of the above information may also be found in the State of Connecticut Judicial Directory which is published by the Commission on Official Legal Publications. Copies are available at Superior Court clerk's offices.

Glossary

abode service. Involves *service of process*. A *proper officer* may serve a Defendant by leaving the *Summons* and *Complaint* **inside** the Defendant's home or inside any other location where the Defendant currently lives and is most likely to receive notice of the action. See C.G.S. sec. 52-57(a).

administrative action. Legal proceedings against or involving a state agency such as Department of Motor Vehicle, Department of Income Maintenance, Department of Health, etc. Each agency has specific procedures for such legal action.

admit. When someone acknowledges that a statement is true. See *Answer*, Pbs.129, 160 et seq., *Requests for Admission*, Pbs 238 et seq.

affidavit. A written statement, sworn to or *affirmed* under oath to be true to the best of one's knowledge.

Affidavit of Debt. A written statement, sworn under oath to be true, that sets forth a sum of money claimed due. See Pbs 358.

affirm. Serves the same purpose as an oath; to verify that something is true to the best of one's knowledge

Agent for Service. An individual or entity who agrees to accept service of process on behalf of a corporation. The Agent for Service does not become liable for the corporation's actions. Instead, it merely accepts service and informs the corporation of the lawsuit. See C.G.S. sec. 33-660.

aggrieved party. Applies to appeals. A party who believes he or she has been harmed by a judge's decision which resulted in a *final judgment*. Only aggrieved parties may appeal a final judgment. See Pbs 4000 et seq.

agreement for representation. See *retainer letter*.

amended pleadings. New *pleadings*, (documents) filed in court that the author alters by adding, deleting or correcting the information set forth in the original pleadings. See Pbs 175 et seq.

Amicus Curiae. An individual or a government agency who acts as a friend of the court in a specific case pending in Superior Court or during an appeal. Usually, these types of cases involve issues of broad public interest. See Pbs 4067.

Answer. The Defendant's required response to the Plaintiff's *Complaint*. See Pbs 160 et seq. Along with an Answer, the Defendant may file *Special Defenses* to the Complaint and/or a *Counterclaim*. The Plaintiff must then file a *Reply to the Special Defenses* and an *Answer to Counterclaim*. See Pbs 112.

Answer to Counterclaim. The Plaintiff's required response to the Defendant's Counterclaim. See *Answer*, Pbs 112 and 116.

Appearance. A court-issued form, JD-CL-12, filed in court by each party in an action which identifies their legal counsel, or their pro se status. A Plaintiff's Appearance is included in the *Summons*. See 7P et seq.

Appellant. The party in a case who files an appeal to the Appellate Court or the Supreme Court. See *Appellee*, Pbs 4001A and 4064.

Appellate Court. One court which is located in Hartford, consisting of a total of nine judges who hear and decide appeals, based on the record of the trial court. See C.G.S. sec. 51-197a et seq.

Appellee. The party in a case who did not file the appeal and finds him or herself responding to the appeal by defending the trial court decision or verdict. See Pbs 4001A and 4064.

Application for Order of Notice. A pleading often filed by Plaintiffs, rather than Defendants, asking the court for permission to allow a *proper officer* in Connecticut to serve a nonappearing, out-of-state Defendant or a Defendant who can not be located. Service may be through certified mail, if an address is known, or by publication in a newspaper, etc. If the application is granted, the court will issue an *Order of Notice*. See Pbs 199 et seq.

Application for Prejudgment Remedy. See *Prejudgment Remedy*.

articulation. See *Motion for Articulation*.

bank execution. A postjudgment collection procedure: a court ordered attachment of a party's funds in a bank account that are used to pay a judgment the party owes to another. See also *property execution* and *wage execution.*

bench trial. A trial in which a judge acts as the finder of fact and decides a case, instead of a jury.

Bill of Costs. After a final judgment is entered, the party who prevailed may provide a list of his or her trial expenses to be paid by the opposing party. See Pbs 358.

borough bailiff. See *proper officer.*

brief. A document that is filed in court and addresses specific issues, by providing case law and arguments, regarding issues that have arisen in a case. Briefs may be filed in the Superior Court to address pretrial and trial issues and in the Appellate Clerk's Office to address an appeal to the Appellate Court or to the Supreme Court. See Pbs 285A, 4064 et seq. See also *Reply Brief* and *Appendix.*

burden of proof. The standard a Plaintiff must meet in order to prevail in court. In most civil cases, the Plaintiff's burden is by *preponderance of the evidence.*

capias. A document signed by a judge that authorizes a proper officer to take the party or witness into custody and bring them to court or place them in jail. A capias is usually issued after a party or witness has failed to comply with a subpoena or arrest warrant. See Pbs 245(f), 684, C.G.S. sec. 46b-231, 52-143, 54-2a, 54-64d.

case caption. Also known as a case heading. A case caption should appear at the top of the first page of every pleading filed in court. It contains the *return date* or *docket number,* the name of the parties, the Judicial District and court location, and date of the pleading. See Pbs 7KK and 7HHH.

Certificate of Closed Pleadings. A green court-issued form which either party file after the pleadings are closed, to place the case on a specific trial list. See Pbs 258 et seq.

Certification of Service. A specific statement that is required at the end of all pleadings after the Complaint is filed. Its purpose is to confirm that a copy of the pleading has been mailed or delivered to all other parties (or their counsel, if represented) of record. See Pbs 120 et seq.

challenges. Pertains to *jury selection.* Each individual party in a lawsuit is given four challenges to use to excuse potential juror from sitting on their case at trial.

charge. Also known as the j*udge's charge* or *jury instructions*. At a jury trial, after all the evidence and arguments have been presented, the judge will explain the law to the jury and instruct it regarding its role as a fact finder and in reaching a *verdict*. See Pbs 315 et seq. and *Requests to Charge*.

civil division. One of the four Superior Court divisions: civil, family, housing and criminal. See Pbs 2 et seq.

civil litigation. Proceedings and lawsuits that usually involving claims for money from Defendants for their noncriminal, but harmful acts to Plaintiffs.

claim to the jury. See *Certificate of Closed Pleadings* and *Jury Claim*.

closed pleadings. The status of the court's file on a case when the Defendant has filed an Answer and there are no other outstanding pleadings which must be filed, such as a *Reply to Special Defenses*, an *Answer to a Counterclaim*, etc. At this point, one of the parties should claim the case to the *Trial List*. See Pbs 258 et seq.

closing argument. Takes place at the end of the trial, after each party finishes introducing its evidence, it will have the opportunity to address the jury one last time and make a short statement concerning the case. The court will determine how long such argument may be. Typically, each party has approximately one hour. The Plaintiff goes first. When the Defendant is finished, the Plaintiff will have one last, brief opportunity to speak. See Pbs 297.

collateral source payments. Payments received by a claimant, (usually the Plaintiff in a lawsuit) or paid on his or her behalf, from any type of health insurance or entity for hospital, medical or any other type of heath care costs relating to a lawsuit. In essence, the Plaintiff is not permitted to recover these amounts from the Defendant because he or she was already paid by another source. This becomes relevant if a jury returns a *verdict* in favor of the Plaintiff in a personal injury case. See *Motion to Reduce Verdict*, Pbs 320, 320A, C.G.S. sec. 52-225a, and 52-225b.

commercial waiver. A clause in a promissory note that permits the holder of the note to obtain a *Prejudgment Remedy* against the signer of the note (the debtor) without court approval if the signer fails to make the payments specified in the note. See *Prejudgment Remedy* and *Ex Parte Prejudgment Remedy*.

Complaint. A written document which sets forth, in paragraph form, a Plaintiff's cause of action against a Defendant. The *Complaint* is usually the first pleading filed in court in each lawsuit. See Pbs 131 et seq.

Connecticut Appellate Reports. A series of gray, hard-bound volumes that contain Connecticut Appellate decisions. It is known as the official reporter. The *Atlantic Reporter* is known as a secondary reporter and its case citations (name, volume and page number) are known as parallel cites. See Pbs 4120 and *Connecticut Reports*.

Connecticut General Statutes. Laws that are enacted by the Connecticut legislature.

Connecticut Law Journal. A weekly publication, containing all appeals decided by the Appellate and Supreme Courts in the past few weeks. (Some Superior Court cases are occasionally included.) Eventually, each decision will be reprinted in the hard bound *Connecticut Appellate Court Reports* and *Supreme Court Reports*. This subscription also include changes in agency regulations, employment opportunities in judicial departments and notice regarding attorney reprimanded or otherwise involved with the Statewide Grievance Committee.

Connecticut Practice Book. An official publication that contains the rules for Superior Court, Appellate Court and Supreme Court procedures.

Connecticut Reports. A series of gold, hard-bound volumes that contain Connecticut Supreme Court decisions. It is known as the official reporter. The *Atlantic Reporter* is known as a secondary reporter and its case cites (name, volume and page number) are known as parallel cites. See Pbs 4120 and *Connecticut Appellate Reports*.

constable. An elected official who has the authority to perform service of process in the town or city where her or she was elected.

contingency fee. A type of legal fee. In personal injury and debt collection cases it is common for the Plaintiff's attorney and the client to agree that the attorney will receive no more than 1/3 of the gross amount that the client recovers against the Defendant. If there is no recovery, these are no legal fees. However, either way, the Plaintiff is responsible for all out of pocket costs and expenses that were necessary to prosecute the case, such as court filing fees, service fees, witness fees, etc. This agreement should be reduced to writing. See *retainer letter* and C.G.S. sec. 52-251c.

continuance. A postponement of a scheduled event or deadline. See 279 et seq.

Counterclaim. An action a Defendant brings against a Plaintiff, in the Plaintiff's lawsuit. The Counterclaim (sometimes referred to as a Counter Complaint) contains allegations that relate to the allegations in the Plaintiff's Complaint. All rules that apply to a Complaint apply to a Counterclaim; the Plaintiff must file an *Answer* to the Counterclaim. In addition, he or she may assert *Special Defenses*, which the Defendant must reply to. See Pbs 112, 116 and 168.

counts. Each cause of action against each Defendant should be stated separately. A count is the term used to designate each cause of action. For instance; Count One: Breach of Contract, Count Two; Unjust Enrichment. In addition, in those cases that involve more than one Plaintiff or Defendant, it is common to have separate counts for each of them. See Pbs 138.

court filing fees. Fees the court requires a party to pay if that party wishes to file certain documents. For instance: $185, as an *entry fee* to file a lawsuit; $60.00 to open a case that has already gone to judgment; $300 to place a case on the *Jury List* rather than the *court list* for trial; $235 when seeking a *Prejudgment Remedy* at the beginning of a case; $50 when seeking a Prejudgment Remedy in a case that is already in suit, etc. See C.G.S. sec. 52-259 et seq. Contact the courthouse to verify current fees.

Court List. Part of the *Trial List.* A list of cases that are ready for a *bench trial* and are waiting to be assigned a trial date. See Pbs 253 et seq. and *Jury List.*

court monitor. Similar to a *court reporter* in that the individual provides a transcript of deposition or trial testimony. Note, however, that a court monitor uses a recording device rather than stenograph machine or computer to record such testimony.

court reporter. An individual who is qualified to properly record entire court proceedings and, if requested, transcribe that recording into a *transcript.* See C.G.S. sec. 51-60 et seq.

Court Reporter's/Monitor's Appeal Transcript Delivery Certificate. Applies to filing an appeal. A court issued form is used by the court reporter of court monitor to inform the Appellate and Supreme Court that he or she has completed the *transcripts* that were ordered for the appeal and they have been delivered to the appropriate party. See Pbs 4019(c).

Criminal Division. A division of the Superior Court that handles prosecuting those parties who violate laws in this state. See Pbs 5.

Cross Claim. A claim brought by a Defendant against a third-person or entity who is not named in the lawsuit which alleges that third-person or entity is liable in whole or in part, for the Plaintiff's claims against the Defendant. Note that if a Defendant files a *Counterclaim* against a Plaintiff, the Plaintiff is permitted to file a Cross Claim against a third-party for the same purpose. See Pbs 116 and *Impleading,* Pbs 117. In addition, a Cross Complaint requires the same Pbs 112 pleadings procedure as a *Complaint* and Counterclaim.

cross examination. Occurs after *direct examination* of a party or witness. It is testimony of a witness (including a party) taken under oath during a *deposition*, a pretrial court argument, or during trial, pursuant to questions asked by the opposing party. Usually, these questions are close ended, requiring only a yes or no answer, and must relate to the witness' testimony that was elicited during *direct examination*. Often cross examination is used to challenge what a witness said during direct examination.

damages. A sum of money the Plaintiff claims he or she has lost or is entitled to as a result of the Defendant's wrongful actions.

default. A penalty against a Defendant has failed to comply with a court order or rule. Once a default is obtained, the Plaintiff may attempt to proceed to judgment, rather than wait for a trial.

Defendant. An individual or entity named in a lawsuit as a wrongdoer and is being sued by the Plaintiff.

Defendant's Appearance. A court issued form, filed either by Defendant as *pro se*, or by his or her attorneys, after the Defendant has been served a copy of the *Summons* and *Complaint*, or similar type of documents that require a court appearance. See Pbs 7Q et seq.

defense. Grounds relied upon to explain a Defendant's actions (or a Plaintiff's actions if there is a Counterclaim. See Pbs 112, 164 et seq., *Special Defenses, contributory negligence, comparative negligence.*

deferring an appeal. See *Notice of Intent to Appeal.*

Demand for Relief. Found at the end of the Plaintiff's Complaint under *Statement of Amount in Demand.* The Statement indicates that the Plaintiff is seeking damages under or over a specific amount stated in C.G.S. sec. 52-91. See also Pbs 131 and Pbs 182.

denied with prejudice. When a court denies a motion and will not consider changing its mind if the issue or motion is raised again at a later time in the case.

denied without prejudice. When a court denies a motion but may be willing to reconsider its decision if the motion is brought again at a later date.

deny. When a court declines to grant what a party asks for in a *motion*.

deponent. A person who testifies at his or her *deposition*.

deposition. A type of discovery in which a person appears out of court, to testify regarding what he or she knows about a case. The testimony is made under oath and is recorded by a stenographer, such as a court reporter, or may be video taped. The proceeding usually takes place in an attorney's office, with all attorneys and clients present. If requested, the court reporter will create a *transcript* of the testimony which can be used later at trial. A party who intends to take a *deposition* must notify all other parties in the action by serving them with a *Notice of Deposition.* See Pbs 243 et seq.

deputy sheriff. An individual who is appointed by the *High Sheriff* to serve legal process in the High Sheriff's county.

diarying. Using one or more calendars to record important dates, as reminders for each case.

direct examination. Questions asked to a witness from the party who called the witness to testify. For instance, during the Plaintiff's case in chief, the Plaintiff will conduct a direct examination of each witness he or she calls. Afterward, the Defendant will have the opportunity to challenge what the witness said through *cross examination.*

Disclosure of Expert Witnesses. Formal notification to an opposing party regarding the identify of any experts a party intends to call at trial to support their claims. See Pbs 220.

discovery. A formal investigation of a case, made pursuant to our Practice Book Rules. Including, *Interrogatories, Requests for Production, Request for Admissions, Request for Mental or Physical Exams, Inspection of Property, Depositions* of parties and other witnesses. Discovery takes place during the Pretrial Stage, simultaneously with filing *pleadings.* In addition, it's possible that discovery could take place during trial (during the evenings or weekends, or during a court recess) if new information or witnesses are discovered. See Pbs 216 et seq.

discovery affidavit. A written statement made under oath that the answers to discovery requests are true, to the best of the person's knowledge. See Pbs 218 et seq.

discovery conference. A required conversation between opposing parties regarding objections to discovery requests. See Pbs 218 et seq.

dismissal. A Plaintiff's case may be dismissed due to his or her failure to prosecute it with reasonable diligence. See Pbs 251.

docket number. A series of numbers assigned by the court where the action is filed which is used to identify each case. The docket number replaces the *return date* in the pleading *case caption.*

docket sheet. Applies to filing an appeal. This is a document, provided by the applicable Superior Court clerk, that contains a list of the pleadings filed in that Superior Court pertaining to a case that is being appealed. See Pbs 4013.

docketing statement. Applies to filing an appeal. This document lists the names and addresses of all parties to the appeal and their attorneys (both trial and appellate counsel), names and addresses of any person who may have a legal interest in the case that may cause a judge to disqualify him or herself, the *docket numbers* and case names of any pending appears which may "arise from substantially the same controversy the cause on appeal, and a list of trial court *exhibits*. See Pbs 4013(a)(4).

Dormancy. A court program which keeps track of all lawsuits to help prevent a case from sitting on the docket without any action for six months or more at a time, or are not yet placed on the *Trial List*. See Pbs 251.

en banc. When all the judges appointed to the Appellate Court or the Supreme Court sit at the same time to hear and decide a case.

Et Al. An abbreviation used in an case caption when there is more than one Plaintiff or Defendant.

Et Seq. An abbreviation used to indicate that more than one consecutive Connecticut General Statue or Connecticut Practice Book Section is applicable to a situation.

evidence. Testimony and exhibits: the information presented in court to support an argument or prove a case at trial. This information can be through witness testimony and through exhibits such as documents, photographs, records, etc. that are admitted into evidence through a specific witness who has a direct connection to the exhibit, unless the parties otherwise *stipulate*.

exception: pertains to disagreeing with a court's ruling on an objection. In certain circumstances, the party must inform the court that he or she takes *exception* to the court's ruling in order to preserve the right to appeal that ruling after the trial. See Pbs 315.

exhibits. At trial, exhibits are tangible items that a party introduces to the trier of fact to prove his or her case. Exhibits may include photographs, documents, records, etc.

ex parte. Communications or court orders that take place between one party and a judge, without the knowledge and/or consent of the other parties in a case. See *Notice of Ex Parte Prejudgment Remedy*.

expert witness. A witness who posses significant knowledge education and experience in a specific field which is not common knowledge to the average person. An expert witness is hired by a party to examine a situation and provide an opinion based upon his or she knowledge, education and experience. See Pbs 220.

Family Division. A division of the Superior Court that addresses issues such as divorces, custody of children, etc., etc. See Pbs 3 and 1201 et seq.

file. Two definitions: **1.** As a noun, a file is a folder which contains information about a case. **2.** As a verb, to file something means to deliver a document to court to be accepted by the clerk who date and time stamps it, then adds the title of the document to the courthouse computer system and eventually places the document in a manila folder (the court's file) that contains all the documents filed under that case's *docket number* and *case caption*. See Pbs 7MM.

final judgment. Applies to appeals. A decision by a court that may be appealed to the Appellate Court or in some cases directly to the Supreme Court. See Pbs 4000 et seq.

Geographical Area. Abbreviated GA, consists of 22 smaller Superior Courts located throughout the state of Connecticut. GAs handle *small claims*, all criminal arraignments, crimes involving some B and all C and D felonies, all misdemeanors and traffic offenses. If the *Judicial District* does not have a *housing session*, housing matters will usually take place in the GA. See C.G.S. sec. 51-348.

grant. When a court agrees to order what a party is asking for.

hearing. A mini trial in front of a judge, to resolve contested issues regarding the lawsuit. In most instances, hearings take place during the Pretrial Stage to address *Short Calendar* pleadings. See Pbs 211.

Hearing in Damages. This type of hearing takes place under the following circumstances: when the Defendant is defaulted on the issue of liability, but damages still need to be determined; when *Summary Judgment* has been granted in favor of the Plaintiff on the Defendant's liability and damages need to be determined; if the Defendant admits liability and damages still need to be determined. A Plaintiff may choose a jury and a jury to decide the damages issues. See Pbs 365 et seq.

High Sheriff. An officer, elected in each county of the state, as its High Sheriff to serve legal process and assist with court house security and prisoner transportation. This High Sheriff will in turn appoint two types of *deputy sheriffs* in his or her county: One type is authorized to serve legal process. The other type is appointed to maintain court house security and transport prisoners, but not to serve legal process.

Housing Court. This division of the Superior Court that handles landlord and tenant disputes involving residential and commercial property. Disputes include: eviction for nonpayment of rent, and other breaches of the lease, a landlord's failure to comply with his or her responsibilities such as upkeep and building maintenance; small claims for non payment of rent cases, to collect back rent, security deposits, etc.

Housing Division. One of the four divisions of the Superior Court. See *Housing Court, Housing Session*, Pbs 5A and C.G.S. sec. 47a-68.

Housing Session. The name given to courts authorized exclusively to determine housing matters. Some *Judicial Districts* have their own Housing Session (Housing Court) and judge to address landlord and tenant matters. Those Judicial Districts who do not have a Housing Session address their housing cases in the *Geographical Area* courthouses or the regular JD courthouses. See *Housing Court.*

implead. To add a third person or entity as a party to the lawsuit to address claims made by the Plaintiff or Defendant. See Pbs 117. In addition, a *Motion to Implead* requires a *memorandum of law*, Pbs 204.

Independent Medical Exam (IME). A physical or mental medical examination, performed by an independent physician, hired by the opposing party, to provide an objective opinion regarding the Plaintiff's mental or physical injuries or condition. See Pbs 229.

indifferent person. Any person, unrelated to the parties, the attorneys or the lawsuit, may serve certain documents upon an opposing party or others who are not parties in a lawsuit. Indifferent persons may serve a : *subpoena, subpoena duces tecum, Notice of Deposition, Notice of Lis Pendens, Notice to Quit, Mechanic's Lien.* He or she may also serve copies of pleadings, other than a *Complaint*, upon an opposing party under Pbs 126.

in hand service. Occurs when a proper officer actually gives a copy of a *Summons* and *Complaint*, or any other type of document or pleading, to the party or person named in the document. A *subpoena* or *subpoena duces tecum* must be served *in hand* and read to the person named in the document (52-143 et seq. and 4-104). *Mechanic's Liens* and *Notices of Lis Pendens* must be served by filing the original at the appropriate land record's office which is usually located in the town clerk's office and a copy served to the Defendant. C.G.S. sec. 49-33, 46b-80(a)(2), 52-325(c). Most other documents, including a *Summons* and *Complaint*, may be served *abode*. See C.G.S. sec. 52-57.

insufficiency of process. Occurs when there is some type of mistake pertaining to the documents that are served upon a party or other person not named in a lawsuit. For instance, if a *Complaint* was served upon a Defendant without a *Summons* attached to it. See Pbs 143 et seq.

insufficiency of service of process. Occurs when there is some type of mistake pertaining to the way a party or other person not named in the lawsuit is served a specific document. For instance, if a *proper officer* failed to properly serve a *Summons* and *Complaint* upon a Defendant. See Pbs 143 et seq.

intent to appeal. See *Notice of Intent to Appeal.*

intentional tort. Occurs when a person purposely acts or fails to act, in order to cause harm or injury to another person.

Interrogatories. Two types: **1.** *Discovery*: written questions from one party which are directed to the opposing party to be answered under oath within a specific time period. See Pbs 223 et seq. **2.** *Trial*: written questions directed to a *jury*, to be answered after it has reached a verdict in order to identify to the parties and the court the facts it relied upon to reach that verdict. See Pbs 312.

joinder. When two or more cases are consolidated and treated as one case because they arise out of the same transaction, or when two or more persons join together and become Plaintiffs in an action. See Pbs 83 et seq.

judge's charge. See *charge, jury instructions and Requests to Charge.*

judgment. A final decision in favor of one party and against the other in a case.

judgment file. In some circumstances, after a case has concluded and gone to judgment, one of the parties or the clerk will draft a document that contains the terms of a judgment.

judgment proof. When a Defendant party has little or no assets in which to pay a judgment which was entered against him or her.

Judicial District. Abbreviated *JD*, a term used to describe 12 areas (13 areas of 9/98) of the state which contain Superior Courts. See Pbs 8 and C.G.S. sec. 51-344 et seq.

jurisdiction. The authority of a court to hear, decide and enforce a judgment in a particular case.

Juris Number. A series of numbers assigned by the state of Connecticut to each attorney admitted to practice law in this state. In addition, most law firms has their own Juris Number which attorneys at that firm may use. All attorneys and law firms who file pleadings in court should include their Juris Number on those pleadings.

jury. In civil cases, six individuals selected to determine the facts of a case and reach a decision, based upon instructions provided by a judge. See C.G.S. sec. 52-215a, Pbs 303 et seq.

Jury Claim: A court-issued form used to claim the case to the *Jury List* in the event the *Certificate of Closed Pleadings* claims the case to the *Court List.* A $300 fee is required.

jury instructions. Also known as the *Charge* or *Jury Instructions.* At a jury trial, after all the evidence and arguments have been presented, the judge will explain the law to the jury and instruct it regarding its role as a fact finder and in reaching a verdict. See Pbs 315 et seq. and *Requests to Charge.*

Jury List. Part of the *Trial List.* A list of cases that are ready for trial before a jury and are waiting to be assigned a trial date. See also *Court List* and Pbs 253 et seq.

jury selection. Also known as *Voir Dire.* The process by which the parties select individuals to sit as jurors on their case. See also *challenges, for cause,* and Pbs 303 et seq.

justices. The term used for judges who are appointed to the Connecticut Supreme Court.

Juvenile Matters. Cases involving children under the age of 17 who are involved in delinquency, neglect and family with service needs proceedings.

lawsuit. A civil court proceeding initiated by a Plaintiff against a Defendant seeking damages. Also called a case, an action, a suit, etc.

Lis Pendens. A notice that a specific piece of real estate in involved with litigation. The document is filed on the land records in a town or city hall where the real estate is located and served on the owners of the property. It warns potential purchasers that they will be placed under the court's jurisdiction if they purchase the property without the court's consent. See C.G.S. sec.52-325.

litigants. The parties involved in a lawsuit; the Plaintiffs and the Defendants.

litigation. The art of persuading the trier of fact in court, pursuant to specific procedures and laws.

Major/Minor. A classification assigned to specific causes of action by the judicial department. See the back of a *Summons* for a list.

marking. A telephone call or fax to the court, indicating whether or not a party wishes a judge to decide his or her pleading that appears on a specific *Short Calendar*.

Mechanic's Lien. A type of *Prejudgment Remedy* which may be used by a party who has performed specific types of work (such as construction or repairs) or who supplied materials for work on real estate. This lien may be foreclosed on if the owner of the property does not pay for the work or materials supplied. In addition, the lien must be paid before the property can be sold or transferred to someone else. If it is not paid, the new owner will be held liable for the sum stated in the lien. See C.G.S. sec. 49-33 et seq.

memorandum of decision. A judge's written decision regarding a pleading or a trial.

memorandum of law. A pleading which is attached to a motion or objection and contain case cites and legal arguments to support the *motion* or *objection*. See Pbs 204 for a list of pleadings which must contain a memorandum of law.

military affidavit. A written statement, made under oath which state whether or not a specific Defendant is in the military or navel services in the United States. This document is needed before a court will enter a *default judgment* against a Defendant who has not appeared in an action. See Pbs 253.

mistakes in the trial court record. Applies to appeals. See *Motion for Rectification*.

monitor. See *court monitor*. Similar to *Court Reporter*.

motion. A pleading that asks the court to rule on an issue in a particular way. All motions must contain an *order*. See Pbs 196 et seq.

Motion in Limine. A pleading by either party to prevent the opposing party from introducing specific evidence during the trial, or to limit the introduction of specific evidence to within certain perimeters. In most cases, this motion is filed before trial and is decided by the judge assigned to the trial. See Pbs 284A.

Motion for Additur. A pleading which asks the court to increase the amount of a *jury verdict*. See Pbs 320 et seq.

Motion for Articulation. Applies to appeals. A pleading filed by either party, usually the Appellant, which asks the trial court to explain in writing the grounds it relied upon in reaching a decision which is now being appealed. This pleading is needed in order to present a complete record for the Appellate Court or the Supreme Court to review. It is commonly filed if the trial court did not file a *memorandum of decision* when it made its ruling, or that memorandum is unclear, or if the transcript of the proceeding at issue still makes the grounds relied upon unclear. See Pbs 4007 and 4051, *Motion for Rectification* and *Motion for Review*.

Motion for Default. A pleading filed by a Plaintiff when a Defendant has failed to appear or file a pleading according to the Practice Book Rules. See Pbs 7Q, 114, 128, 231, 351, 352 et seq, 363, 363A et seq.

Motion for Default for Failure to Appear. A pleading filed by a Plaintiff when a Defendant has failed to file an *Appearance*, within two days after the *return date*. The consequence may be judgment against the Defendant or a *Hearing in Damages* in which the Defendant has only limited rights. See Pbs 7Q and 352 et seq.

Motion for Default for Failure to Plead. A pleading filed when a party (usually the Defendant) has failed to file a pleading according to applicable *Practice Book* rules. The consequences may be judgment against the Defendant or a *Hearing in Damages* in which the Defendant has only limited rights. See 114, 128 and 363A.

Motion for Disclosure of Assets. A pleadings that asks the court to order a party to provide a list of all his or her assets and their location. It is commonly filed with a *Prejudgment Remedy*. See Pbs 230A.

Motion for Extension of Time. A pleading filed by any party which seeks additional time to comply with a Practice Book Rule, a Connecticut General Statute or a court order. See Pbs 224 et seq. Be sure to indicate on the motion whether the case has been assigned for trial.

Motion for Nonsuit. A pleading filed by the Defendant against a Plaintiff who has failed to comply with a Practice Book Rule, General Statute or court order. The consequences may result in the case being dismissed and judgment entering in favor of the Defendant. See Pbs 231, 351, 363, 377.

Motion for Nonsuit for Failure to Plead. A pleading filed by the Defendant against a Plaintiff who has filed to timely responded to a specific pleading. The consequence may result in the case being dismissed. This pleading is more commonly used when a Plaintiff fails to plead to the Defendant's *Counterclaim* pursuant to Pbs 112 and 114.

Motion for Order of Compliance. A pleading filed by either party against the other who fails to comply with discovery requests. See Pbs 231.

Motion for Order of Notice. See *Application for Order of Notice.*

Motion for Protective Order. A pleading filed by a party who believes justice requires that they not be required to disclose certain information requested through discovery by the opposing party. Reasons can include to protect the "party from annoyance, embarrassment, oppression or undue burden or expense...." As an alternative to granting the motion, the court may limit the information to be disclosed and require the Defendant to pay any costs incurred in its reproduction. See Pbs 221.

Motion for Rectification. Applies to appeals. A pleading filed by either party, usually the appellant, asking the trial court to correct an error in the trial court record. This pleading is necessary in order to prove the Appellate Court or the Supreme Court with an adequate record for review. See Pbs 4007, 4051, *Motion for Articulation* and *Motion for Review.*

Motion for Remittitur. A pleading which asks the court to reduce the jury verdict due to comply with the evidence presented or due to a mathematical error. See Pbs 320 et seq.

Motion for Review. Applies to appeals. If the trial court fails to cooperate with a party's *Motion for Articulation* and *Motion for Rectification*, the party may file a Motion for Review that asks the Appellate Court or the Supreme Court to order the trial court to comply with the party's motion. See Pbs 4054.

Motion for Stipulated Judgment. A pleading filed by either party which specifies the terms upon which the parties have settled the case.

Motion for Summary Judgment. A pleading filed by either party which states that there is no issue of material fact in the case. As a result, judgment should enter in his or her favor. A *memorandum of law* must be attached to this motion and to the opposing party's objection. See Pbs 112, 204 and 379 et seq.

Motion to Dismiss. A pleading filed by the Defendant in the Pretrial Stage under Pbs 112 seeking the dismiss the Plaintiff's *Complaint* for one or more of the following reasons: *lack of subject matter jurisdiction, lack of personal jurisdiction, insufficiency of process, insufficiency of service of process or improper venue.* See Pbs 112, 142 et seq.

Motion to Open Default. A pleading filed by a Defendant who has been defaulted for failing to appear to failing to plead, yet judgment has not yet entered. In the motion, the Defendant is seeking the court's permission to void (open) the default correct the error and allow the case to proceed as usual, rather than directly to judgment or a *Hearing in Damages*. See Pbs 7Q, 352, 363A, 374, 376.

Motion to Open Default Judgment. A pleading filed by a Defendant who has had a judgment entered against him or her as a result of a default. This motion must be filed within four months of notice sent of the judgment and asks court to void (open) the judgment, restore the case to the docket and allow it to proceed as if no judgment were entered. See Pbs 364, 377. Pbs 377 requires an affidavit to be included in the pleading. This motion requires a $60 filing fee.

Motion to Open Judgment. A pleading filed by a party within four months of notice sent of a judgment against him or her that asks the court to void (open or set aside) the judgment due to mistake, fraud, new evidence, a change of circumstances, etc. See Pbs 326. Requires *memorandum of law*, Pbs 204.

Motion to Open Nonsuit. A pleading filed by a Plaintiff who has been nonsuited. In the motion, the Plaintiff is asking the court to void (open or set aside) the nonsuit, restore the case to the docket and allow it to proceed as if no nonsuit had been entered. See Pbs 377 which requires an affidavit to be included in the pleading. This motion also requires a $60 filing fee.

Motion to Quash Subpoena. A pleading filed by any party or person who has been served a subpoena wishes to avoid appearing in court or at a deposition to testify. In the motion, the party asks the court to void the subpoena and release him or her from its authority. See Pbs 245(d) et seq.

Motion to Reargue. A pleading filed by either party asking a judge to reconsider its decision regarding a motion or objection. See Pbs 204B.

Motion to Reduce Verdict. A pleading that asks the court to reduce a jury verdict by the amount the Plaintiff previously received from a collateral source such as insurance, etc. See Pbs 320A et seq.

Motion to Set Aside Default. See also *Motion to Open Default.* A pleading filed by a Defendant who has been defaulted for failing to appear to failing to plead, yet judgment has not yet entered. In the motion, the Defendant is seeking the court's permission to void (open) the default correct the error and allow the case to proceed as usual, rather than directly to judgment or a *Hearing in Damages*. See Pbs 7Q, 352, 363A, 374, 376.

Motion to Set Aside Dismissal. A pleading filed by a Plaintiff who's case was dismissed and asks the court to remove (set aside) the dismissal and permit the case to continue. See Pbs 326. This motion must be accompanied by a $60 filing fee.

Motion to Set Aside Judgment. A pleading filed by a party within four months of notice sent of a judgment against him or her that asks the court to void (open or set aside) the judgment due to mistake, fraud, new evidence, a change of circumstances, etc. See Pbs 326. Requires *a memorandum of law*, Pbs 204, and filing fee. See *Motion to Open Judgment.*

Motion to Set Aside Verdict. A pleading filed after a jury has reached a verdict which asks the court to void (open or set aside) the *verdict* and render judgment in him or her favor, or order a new trial. See Pbs 321 et seq.

Motion to Strike. A pleading filed pursuant to Pbs 152 by a Defendant during the Pretrial stage which alleges that the Plaintiff's Complaint, or a part thereof, fails to state a "claim upon which relief can be granted" and other similar type allegations. As a result, it should be stricken. The Plaintiff may file a *Motion to Strike the Defendant's Answer, Special Defenses* or *Counterclaim*. In addition, a party to a *Cross Complaint* may file a *Motion to Strike the Cross Complaint*. A *memorandum of law* must be attached to this motion and any objection the opposing party may file. See Pbs 112, 204 and 152 et seq.

Motion to Transfer. A motion filed by either party asking the court to transfer the case to another court. this motion may be used to address a *Motion to Dismiss* based upon *improper venue* or a *Motion to Dismiss* based upon *lack of subject matter jurisdiction.* See Pbs 212 et seq.

Motion to Withdraw Appearance. A motion filed by an attorney asking the court to permit him or her to withdraw as a party's attorney. This motion is necessary if a client refuses to voluntarily hire another attorney to represent them or refuses to file a pro se Appearance, in lieu of the attorney's Appearance. See Pbs 7Y.

nonparties. Persons or entities who are not names as parties in a lawsuit but who may have information relating to the case which could require a deposition or for them to testify as witnesses at trial. Nonparties should be *subpoenaed* to attend court or their deposition, to ensure their cooperation and compliance. See Pbs 245

nonsuit. See Motion for Nonsuit. A ruling by the court dismissing the Plaintiff's case and entering judgment in favor of the Defendant due to the Plaintiff's failure to comply with a Practice Book Rule, a General Statute or a court order. See Pbs 231, 351, 363, 377.

Notice of Appeal Transcript Order. Applies to filing an appeal. A court issued form JD-ES-38 Rev. 2-89 that is required and used to order relevant portions of the trial *transcripts* that will be addressed on appeal. See *transcripts, Court Reporter's/Monitor's Appeal Transcript Delivery Certificate* and Pbs 4013 and 4019.

Notice of Application for Prejudgment Remedy. A court-issued form used when seeking a Prejudgment Remedy. See *Application for Prejudgment Remedy* and *Prejudgment Remedy*.

Notice of Deposition. A pleading that informs all parties in a case that an opposing party intends to take someone's deposition on a date and place specified in the notice. See Pbs 243 et seq.

Notice of Default. Notice sent by the court indicating that a default has entered against a party.

Notice of Ex Parte Prejudgment Remedy. A court-issued form used when seeking a Prejudgment *Remedy* from the Court without the opposing party's knowledge, or when a *Commercial Waiver* is involved. See *Application for Prejudgment Remedy, Prejudgment Remedy,* C.G.S. sec.52-278 a-n.

Notice of Intent to Argue. A pleading that notifies the court and all parties that a party intends to appear in court and orally argue a motion or objection that is marked nonarguable on the Short Calendar. See Pbs 211.

Notice of Judgment. Notice sent by the court indicating that judgment has been entered against a party. Note that Pbs 354 requires the Plaintiff to send notice of a *Default Judgment* against a nonappearing Defendant in specific contracts cases to all parties in the case.

Notice of Intent to Appeal. Applies to appeals. This pleading may be filed by a party who wishes to appeal a trial court's decision in a case that is still taking place in the trial court. This notice permits the party to preserve his or her rights to appeal after the case has conclude in the trial court. See Pbs 4002D.

Notice of Lis Pendens. See *Lis Pendens*.

Notice to Quit. A document served to a tenant informing him or her that the landlord has terminated the lease and request them to move out of the building by a specific date. A Notice to Quit may be served by a *sheriff, deputy, constable* or *indifferent person.*

objection. A pleading by a party who contests the opposing party's motion or request. The objection must be accompanied by an *order*. See Pbs 196 et seq. Keep in mind that if the initial motion required a *memorandum of law*, the objection will also require a *memorandum of law*.

Offer of Judgment. A written offer from one party to another to settle a case for a specific sum. This offer is filed in court as well as served to the opposing party and must be accepted within a certain period of time. There are different rules for Plaintiff and Defendants as well as potential consequences for rejecting an Offer of Judgment. See Pbs 342. et seq.

open default. See *Motion to Open Default:* a pleading filed by a Defendant who has been defaulted for failing to appear or failing to plead, yet the case has not gone to judgment. In the motion, the Defendant is seeking the court's permission to void (open or set aside) the default, correct the error, and allow the case to proceed as usual, rather than directly to judgment or to a *Hearing in Damages.* See Pbs 7Q, 352, 363A, 374, 376.

open default judgment. See *Motion to Open Default Judgment.*

open judgment. See *Motion to Open Judgment or Set Aside Judgment.*

oral argument. When the parties appear in court to orally argue a *motion* or *objection* before a judge.

order. A court ruling which grants or denies motions and sustains or overrules objections. See Pbs 196 et seq.

Order of Notice. *See Application for Order of Notice.* A document that requires a party to appear in court on a specific date and time. The order must be served within a specified time upon the party by a proper officer such as a *sheriff, deputy sheriff* or *constable.* See Pbs 199.

overrule. A court ruling which indicates it disagrees with a party's objection to a *motion* or *request.* The result is that the initial motion or request is granted.

parties. Plaintiffs and Defendants in a lawsuit. Also known as litigants.

penalties. See *sanctions, Nonsuit, default.*

personal jurisdiction. The authority of a court to enforce a judgment against a party. See *Motion to Dismiss* and Pbs 142 et seq.

Petition for Certification. A pleading drafted by a party who wishes to bring an appeal to the Connecticut Supreme Court. Once received, the Supreme Court will determine if it will deny the petition or grant it and permit the party to file their appeal. See Pbs 4126 et seq.

Plaintiff. The person, individual, entity, corporation, etc., that brings a lawsuit against a Defendant claiming damages.

pleadings. Documents filed in court that pertain to a specific lawsuit. See Pbs 7KK et seq and 112. In most cases, the *Complaint* is the first pleading filed in a lawsuit.

preargument conference. Applies to Appellate and Supreme Court appeals. A court scheduled meeting between the parties and a judge to assist the parties in settling their case and avoid pursuing the appeal. Note that a *Preargument Statement* should be filed along with the initial appeal. See Pbs 4013(a)(5) and Pbs 4103.

Prejudgment Remedy (PJR). An attachment (also called a lien) against a Defendant's assets, up to the amount of the Plaintiff's claims in his or her case, that is obtained prior to judgment, in order to ensure that the Defendant will not be *judgment proof.* if the Plaintiff wins the case. Note, a Defendant who files a *Counterclaim* may obtain a PJR against a Plaintiff's assets for the same purpose. See C.G.S. sec. 52-278 a-n and *commercial waiver. Mechanic's Liens and a Lis Pendens* are other types of PJRs.

Preliminary Designation of Specific Pleadings. Applies to filing an appeal. A pleading initially filed by the *Appellant* containing a list of those pleadings filed in the trial court which are relevant to the appeal. Once the Appellant files this document, the *Appellee* has 20 days to file his or her own Preliminary Designation of Specific Pleadings. See Pbs 4013.

Preliminary Statement of Issues. Applies to filing an appeal. A pleading initially filed by the *Appellant* containing specific issues the Appellant intends to present in his or her brief to be considered by the Appellate Court (or the Supreme Court if a direct appeal is permitted under C.G.S. 51-199.) Once the Appellant files this document, the *Appellee* has 20 days to file his or her own Preliminary Statement of Issues. See Pbs 4013.

pretrial conference. A court scheduled meeting between the parties and a judge (or other person authorized by the court) to assist parties settle their lawsuit rather than go to trial. These meetings are also used to narrow down contested issues and determine discovery schedules. Most courts require the attorneys to bring their clients with them to these meetings at the courthouse, or at least have them available to discuss settlement, and also a completed court-issued form entitled, *Pre-trial Memo.* See Pbs 265, 267, 268.

privileged cases. Cases which are given priority for a quick trial date due to a specific circumstance. See Pbs 259 for such circumstances.

probate. An area of law that addresses issues such as administering estates, wills and trusts, adoption and other matters relating to children, guardianships and conservatorships. Connecticut has several courts which address these matters exclusively. See Title 45a of the Connecticut General Statutes.

Pro Hac Vice. Also known as an Pro Hac Vice Appearance. This term is used to describe an out-of-state attorney who has permission to appear to appear in Connecticut court and represent a client although he or she is not licensed to practice law here. This attorney must work under the guidance of a Connecticut attorney who must also file an Appearance in the case. See Pbs 24.

proper officer. *High Sheriffs, deputy sheriffs, constables, borough bailiffs* and *indifferent person* are considered to be proper officers under C.G.S. sec. 52-50 and in certain circumstances listed therein, to serve civil process such as a Summons and Complaint, etc., within their precincts.

property execution. A postjudgment collection procedure: a court ordered attachment of a party's (usually a defendant) assets. The assets are auctioned by a *proper officer* who then gives the proceeds to the person (usually a Plaintiff) who is owed the judgment See also *bank execution* and *wage execution.*

pro se. A party who files an Appearance in court indicating he or she will represent themselves, rather than hire an attorney.

protective order. See *Motion for Protective Order*

reclaim slip. Officially called a *Short Calendar List/Claim/Reclaim*, it is a court-issued form that is used to place a pleading on the *Short Calendar* to be decided by a judge (usually) after that pleading had previously appeared on the Short Calendar and had been marked off. See Pbs 206, 122, 363.

recognizance. Found on the *Summons*, it requires a Plaintiff to designate a third person who will take financial responsibility for the Plaintiff up to $250 dollars to cover any costs that may be taxed to the Plaintiff if he or she loses at trial and cannot pay. See Pbs 52.

record. A list and contents of all documents filed and the proceeding that took place in the trial court pertaining to a case. See Pbs 4007

rectification. See *Motion for Rectification.*

Reply Brief. Applies to appeals. The *Appellants'* response to the *Appellee's brief* See Pbs 4064 et seq. In addition, any party in a trial court case may reply in writing to an opposing party's objection and brief or *memorandum of law.*

Reply to Special Defenses. The Plaintiff's response to the *Defendant's Special Defenses,* which is files as part of an *Answer* to the *Plaintiff's Complaint.* See Pbs 112 and 171.

request. A pleading which asks a party to take a specific action. If the opposing party does not object within a specified period of time the request is automatically granted an the opposing party is required to comply. A request does not require an *order.* See Pbs 196.

Request for Admission. A type of *discovery* that requires a party to admit or deny specific statements. Do not get this confused with an *Answer.* An Answer is a mandatory pleading. All discovery is optional. The responses to Requests for Admission often narrow down *contested issues* between the parties and may provide grounds to file a *Motion for Summary Judgment.* See Pbs 238 et seq.

Request for Mental Exam. A type of *discovery* that permits a Defendant to request a Plaintiff who is claiming damages for mental harm and suffering, to submit him or herself to a mental examination performed by a physician selected by the Defendant at the Defendant's expense. If a *Counterclaim* for mental injuries is filed by a Defendant in an action, the Plaintiff may make this same request of the Defendant. This exam is also known as an *IME*: an independent medical exam. See Pbs 229.

Request for Physical Exam. A type of *discovery* that permits a Defendant to request a Plaintiff who is claiming damages for physical injuries, to submit him or herself to a physical examination performed by a physician selected by the Defendant at the Defendant's expense. If a *Counterclaim* for physical injuries is filed by a Defendant in an action, the Plaintiff may make this same request of the Defendant. This exam is also known as an *IME*: an independent medical exam. See Pbs 229.

Request for Production. A type of *discovery* that permits a party to request to examine specific original documents, or to receive copies of these documents from the opposing party. This type of discovery also enables a party to request to examine tangible items that may be a subject to the suit. See Pbs 226 et seq.

Request to Inspect Property. Similar to a Request for Production, this type of *discovery* that enables a party to request to examine large tangible items, or real estate itself that is the subject of the suit and is owned or located on the opposing party's property or within his or her control. See Pbs 227.

Request to Revise. A pleading filed during the *Pretrial Stage* by a Defendant who is asking the Plaintiff to correct or clarify a portion of his or her *Complaint*. If the Plaintiff does not file a timely *objection*, the request is automatically granted and the Plaintiff must comply by filing a *Revised Complaint*. Plaintiffs may file a *Request to Revise a Defendant's Answer, Special Defenses or Counterclaim*. In addition, Pbs 147 appears to permit any party to file a Request to Revise regarding any pleading filed by the opposing party. See Pbs 112 and 147 et seq.

Request to Revise Answer. See *Request to Revise.*

Request to Revise Counterclaim. See *Request to Revise.*

Request to Revise Special Defenses. See *Request to Revise.*

retainer. Legal fees paid by the client to his or her attorney usually at the time the client agrees to hire the attorney and the attorney agrees to accept the case. The attorney's work is then billed against the amount of the retainer.

retainer letter. An agreement for representation. This letter or agreement confirms in writing the understanding between the client and the attorney regarding legal services and fees. It should be signed by both prior to the attorney beginning work on the case.

return date. A date Plaintiffs must select when they are ready to contact a *proper officer* to serve Defendants with a copy of a *Summons* and *Complaint*. This date appears on the Summons and in the case caption on the Complaint and must fall on a Tuesday in most civil cases except *Summary Process*. (C.G.S. sec. 52-48(a)). The return date is used an anchor or reference point to determine the following deadlines: The last date to serve the Defendant with a copy of the Summons and Complaint (C.G.S. sec. 52-46); the last date to file the original Summons and Complaint in court (C.G.S. sec. 52-46a); the last date is which the Defendant should file an *Appearance* (Pbs 7Q); and the last date in which the Defendant should file his or her first pleading under Pbs 112 (Pbs 114). It is recommended that the Plaintiff select no less than three Tuesdays in the future from the date of the Complaint. Pursuant to C.G.S. sec. 52-48(b), the return date should be no more than 60 days after the date of the Complaint.

Return of Service. A document, similar to an affidavit, from a *proper officer* that verifies he or she delivered (served) a specific document to a party or nonparty, as directed by the attorney or pro se. A Return of Service is needed for every document that is served by a proper officer. See also *service of process* and *service.*

return to court. To deliver by hand or by mail, documents to the court to be date and time stamped by the clerk, and placed in the clerk's file. More commonly this phrase pertains to filling the *Summons* and *Complaint* in court to begin a lawsuit. See C.G.S. sec. 52-46a.

review. Applies to appeals. See *Motion for Review.*

Revised Complaint. See *Request to Revise.*

Revised Pleadings. See *Request to Revise.*

Rules for the Superior Court. See *Connecticut Practice Book.*

Rules for the Appellate Court and Supreme Court. See *Connecticut Practice Book.*

sanctions. Penalties imposed by the court due to a party's failure to comply with court rules or orders. See Pbs 4184A et seq., C.G.S. sec. 51-84.

service. There are at least four types of service: **1.** *Service of Process*: when a Plaintiff contacts a proper officer to serve a copy of the *Summons* and *Complaint* upon the Defendant named in the documents (C.G.S. sec. 52-46); **2.** Service of a *subpoena, subpoena duces tecum* (C.G.S. sec. 52-143 et seq.), a *Notice to Quit*, a *Notice of Lis Pendens* (46b-80 (a)(2) and 52-325(c), and a *Mechanic's Lien* (C.G.S. sec. 49-33 et seq.) by a proper officer, including an indifferent person; **3.** Service of a *Notice of Deposition*, by certified mail or hand delivery (Pbs 243); **4.** Service to all parties of record by regular mail or hand delivery, of copies of all pleadings and documents filed in court by the opposing party (Pbs 120 et seq.).

service of process. This terms pertains to delivering (serving) a copy of a *Summons* and *Complaint* to the Defendants named in these documents in order to inform them that there is a lawsuit pending against them. Service must be made by a *proper officer*, either *in hand* or *abode*. If in hand or abode is not possible, service must be made according to the language of the applicable Connecticut General Statutes. See C.G.S. sec. 52-46.

set aside default. See *Motion to Open Default.*

set aside judgment. See *Motion to Open Judgment.*

Short Calendar. A computer generated calendar type document that is mailed to all parties of record who have an outstanding pleading which is scheduled to be decided by a judge. The calendar lists the name of the case, the pleadings at issue, the law firms of the parties, or pro ses, an the date, time and location of the court. See Pbs 206 et seq.

Small Claims. Civil actions in which the Plaintiff is seeking $2500 or less, not including interest. See Pbs 547 et seq.

Special Defenses. Ground relied upon to explain a Defendant's actions (or Plaintiff's actions if there is a Counterclaim.). See Pbs 112, 164 et seq., *defenses, contributory Negligence, comparative negligence.*

stenographer. Also known as a *court reporter*, a person who records testimony in court or during a *deposition.*

Statement of Amount in Demand. See *Demand for Relief.* Found at the end of the Plaintiff's *Complaint*, this document indicates that the Plaintiff is seeking damages under or over a specific amount as required by C.G.S. sec. 52-91. See also Pbs 131 and Pbs 182. It includes a case caption, the author's signature and other information that is required by all pleadings. See also Pbs 7KK and 7LL.

stipulation. An agreement by the parties. Usually, it is written and filed in court, or placed on the record. The agreement can pertain to the entire case as a settlement or to one or more contested issues in the case. See Pbs 249.

subject matter jurisdiction. A court's authority to hear, decide and enforce a particular type of case. See Pbs 142 et seq. and C.G.S. sec. 52-87.

subpoena. A document that compels the person named in the document to appear and testify in court or at a *deposition* on a specific date and time. The subpoena must be served *in hand* and read to the person by a *proper officer.* See C.G.S. sec. 52-143 et seq.

subpoena duces tecum. A document that compels the person named in the document to appear and testify in court or at a *deposition* on a specific date and time and to bring with them certain documents that are listed in the document. The subpoena duces tecum must be served *in hand* and read to the person by a *proper officer.* See C.G.S. sec. 52-143.

Substitute Complaint. A pleading that is most commonly filed after a *Motion to Strike* is granted and the Plaintiff is ordered by the court to make necessary changes to his or her original *Complaint.* See Pbs 152 et seq.

Summary Process. Connecticut's procedure used by landlords to evict tenants. Prior to serving a Summary Process action, the Defendant tenant must be served with a *Notice to Quit.* See Pbs 47a-68.

Summons. Also called a *Writ* or *Writ of Summons.* A document which is attached to a Complaint and contains the names of the parties, the address of the court where the lawsuit will be filed, the Plaintiff's *Appearance*, either pro se or by an attorney, a small amount of information regarding the *Complaint*, and instructions for the Defendant. See Pbs 49.

Superior Court. Connecticut's trial court. See *Trial Court* and Pbs 2 et seq.

Superior Court Reporter. Printed volumes of Connecticut Superior Court decisions.

Supreme Court. Connecticut's highest court, consists of seven *justices*, five of which usually sit and decide a case.

sustain. A court ruling indicating it agrees with a party's *objection* to a *motion* or *request.* The result is that the initial motion or request is denied.

taxation of costs. A party who prevails at trial is entitled to be reimbursed by the opposing party for certain costs expended to prosecute or defend the lawsuit. See Chapter 14 of the *Connecticut Practice Book:* Fees and Costs, C.G.S. sec. 52-240 et seq. and 52-257 et seq., Pbs 4118 et seq. for appeals.

testimony. Oral answers to questions posed by either party to a witness (a party or nonparty) during a trial or d*eposition.* At *trial*, testimony is part of the *evidence* each party presents to the trier of fact.

tort. An act or lack of action by an individual or entity that causes another individual or entity to suffer *damages*.

tort feaser. One who commits a tort; a wrongdoing against another.

transcript. A court argument, *testimony* or *deposition* which has been reduced to a typewritten (computer generated) document by a *court reporter*. See Pbs 4109.

trial. A legal proceeding that usually takes place in a courtroom that is located in a courthouse whereby Plaintiffs and Defendants have the opportunity to present their *evidence* (*testimony* and *exhibits*) in order to convince a *trier of fact* (either a judge or a jury) to resolve a dispute by ruling in their favor. See Pbs 283 et seq.

trial court. Two meanings: **1.** The Superior Court, which hears cases that consist of one judge, the Plaintiff, the Defendant, their attorneys, *witnesses*, *testimony* and possibly a jury. **2.** The Superior Court judges who preside over pleadings during *Short Calendar* and a trial is often referred to as the trial court.

Trial List. The waiting list a case is placed on to be assigned a trial date. The trial list is made up of two lists: the *Court List*, for cases tried to a judge instead of a jury (also known as *Bench Trials*) And the *Jury List*, for cases waiting to be tried by a jury. See *Certificate of Closed Pleadings, Closed Pleadings, Claim to Jury* and *Bench Trial.* See also Pbs 253 et seq.

trier of fact. A judge or jury who is designated to determine the facts in a case, based upon the evidence presented by the parties during a trial and reaches a *verdict* based upon those facts and the law.

venue. The proper court location where a case should be filed. See *Motion to Dismiss*, Pbs 142 et seq. and *Motion to Transfer*, 212 et seq.

verdict. The outcome of a trial which is determined by the *trier of fact*.

voir dire. Jury selection. See Pbs 303 et seq.

wage execution. A postjudgment collection procedure: a court ordered attachment of a party's employment wages that is applied to pay a judgment the party owes to another. See also *bank execution* and *property execution*.

witness. A party or nonparty who has information concerning a case and who will testify during a d*eposition* and/or at trial.

witness fees. Fees the *proper officer* will give to a nonparty witness when serving any type of *subpoena* that compels him or her to appear at a d*eposition* or at trial. The fee is based upon the mileage the witness will need to travel.

writ. Refers to the *Summons* which is attached to the Plaintiff's *Complaint*. This text uses the term "Summons" rather than Writ. See Pbs 49.

Writ of Summons. See writ: the *Summons* that is attached to the Plaintiff's *Complaint*. This text uses the term "Summons" rather than Writ. See Pbs 49.

Index